STATE AND LOCAL POLITICS

Steven A. Peterson, Ph.D.
Alfred University

Thomas H. Rasmussen, Ph.D.
Alfred University

McGraw-Hill, Inc.

New York   St. Louis   San Francisco   Auckland   Bogotá   Caracas
Lisbon   London   Madrid   Mexico City   Milan   Montreal   New Delhi
San Juan   Singapore   Sydney   Tokyo   Toronto

Steven A. Peterson is professor of political science and Chair of the Division of Social Sciences at Alfred University. He received his Ph.D. from the State University of New York at Buffalo. He has published widely in such journals as *Journal of Politics, American Journal of Political Science, Administration & Society,* and *Political Psychology.* He is also a coauthor of McGraw-Hill's College Core Book in *AMERICAN GOVERNMENT.* His areas of interest are American politics, judicial process, political behavior, and biopolitics.

Thomas H. Rasmussen is professor of political science at Alfred University. After receiving his B.A. degree from Earlham College and his Ph.D. from Syracuse University, he taught for three years in Africa at the University of Zambia. His current fields of interest are economic and environmental policy and public administration. He has contributed chapters in two books and is the author of numerous articles and papers as well as a coauthor of McGraw-Hill's College Core Book in *AMERICAN GOVERNMENT.*

Sponsoring Editor, Jeanne Flagg
Production Supervisor, Leroy Young
Editing Supervisor, Patty Andrews
Front Matter Editor, Maureen Walker

State and Local Politics

1 2 3 4 5 6 7 8 9 10 11 12 13 14 15 16 17 18 19 20 DOC DOC 9 8 7 6 5 4 3

ISBN 0-07-049671-4

Library of Congress Cataloging-in-Publication Data

Peterson, Steven A.
    State and local politics / Steven A. Peterson, Thomas H. Rasmussen.
      p. cm.
    Includes bibliographical references and indexes.
    ISBN 0-07-049671-4
    1. State governments—United States. 2. Local government—United States. I. Rasmussen, Thomas Houser, date . II. Title.
JK2408.P444   1994
320.8′0973—dc20   93-17612
                                                 CIP

This book was printed on acid-free paper.

Contents

Preface

This volume examines the institutions, processes, and policy making
of state and local governments. It provides the background necessary
for understanding how subnational governments work and how they
influence the political life of the nation. In most chapters, state and
local governments are discussed together. Linking them in this way
allows a more powerful analysis of their similarities and differences
and permits topics to be discussed together as they relate to both
states and cities. It also makes possible a more telling discussion of
the challenges facing local political leadership that are posed by the
decisions of their states.

Although clarity and conciseness are qualities that guided the
preparation of this compact, low-cost volume, the book covers the
material sufficiently, we believe, for it to serve as a primary text in
a number of courses. The volume includes contemporary examples
throughout, and what we hope are timely insights into the issues and
challenges confronting state and local governments today. We have
sought to extend the book's timeliness by incorporating the results of
some recent research on variations in the political behavior of citizens, on policy outcomes, and on the basic capabilities of the states
to act efficiently.

The book focuses on several important trends in state and local
government in the 1990s, when state and local governments are
becoming more prominent players in the American political system.
Over the last 15 years, the federal government has signalled that
states and localities must bear greater responsibility for identifying
problems, proposing solutions and raising revenues. Washington,
D.C. has reduced the flow of funds to state and local government and

the federal government attaches fewer strings to the funds it continues to provide. That state and local governments must rely more heavily upon their own resources as they deal with ever more complex problems is one important trend.

A second trend is that state and local governments are developing greater capacity to deal with perceived problems. Most notably, both legislatures and executives are becoming more professionalized, which means that elected and appointed officials have more experience, work full time at their jobs, and rely heavily upon growing staffs of technically trained experts.

A third trend is that many state governments and large cities are becoming policy laboratories, experimenting with new approaches to solve problems. We do not understand very well how to create jobs, or how to contain health care costs, or how to improve the quality of education. Therefore, it is appropriate that state and local governments be free to experiment. Successful innovations today will be noticed and implemented in other jurisdictions tomorrow.

Acknowledgments

Special thanks go to our spouses, Margaret Byrd Rasmussen and Bettina Franzese. They have very busy lives of their own as parents and working professionals, yet they still provide us with constant encouragement, support and sense of perspective. We gratefully acknowledge their contributions during the two years in which we were often preoccupied with state and local politics.

We are indebted to our colleague William Hall, an expert on police and corrections, for writing chapter 13 on the criminal justice system. Several professional readers read the manuscript, and we appreciate their generous comments as well as their care in pointing out our factual errors and inadequate explanations. The book is stronger to the extent that we have responded to their suggestions and criticisms. The stylistic and substantive good sense of Jeanne Flagg, our editor at McGraw Hill, on successive drafts has also improved the book. Her encouragement and cooperative spirit made our work easier, and we are indebted to her.

Finally, we thank our students at Alfred University for their continuing stimulation and their insight into American politics. Their penetrating questions and revealing observations challenge us daily to understand our subject better. We hope that they as participating citizens and as future employees of state and local governments will deal effectively with economic, environmental and social problems in the years ahead. This book will have succeeded if readers are better able to discuss knowledgeably how state and local governments might address the important policy issues of the day.

Steven A. Peterson
Thomas H. Rasmussen

Part I

The Framework of Analysis

CHAPTER 1

State and Local Politics: Themes and Variations

The last two decades represent one of the most dynamic periods in state and local politics since the early days of the republic. Structural changes in the economy, budget tightening at the national level, transference of responsibility to the state and local level without sufficient federal funding, the fierce competition among governments in the economic development game, the movement toward privatization of government services—all testify to a period of dramatic change in the intergovernmental system.

State and local governments have become more professional and are better able to deal with uncertainty than they were even fifteen or twenty years ago. Thus, especially at the state level, subnational governments are more capable of controlling their destinies as they steer through the shoals of change during the 1990s. State and local governments must make difficult decisions, among them the choice between equity (fairness) and efficiency (spending revenues in a cost-effective fashion). For instance, should states tax the middle class in order to provide basic medical care and better education for the poor, and risk an exodus of the middle class to other states where fewer of their tax dollars will go to those at the poverty level?

3

This introductory chapter examines in broad strokes some of the basic issues in state and local politics today. It begins with background material on federalism and intergovernmental relations, a survey of the kinds of subnational governments, and a brief discussion of state constitutions, which lay out the structure and rules governing state politics. The last part of the chapter introduces and briefly summarizes the material covered throughout this volume.

Federalism and Intergovernmental Relations

Federalism is a system of government in which power is divided between a central government and lower-level governments. The central government is sovereign and has effective decision-making power, but the subunits, especially the states, have considerable power and autonomy. In the United States, the division of power is between the national and state governments. Local governments derive their power from the states.

Although the terms ''federalism'' and ''intergovernmental relations'' are often used interchangeably, they have different implications. *Intergovernmental relations* denotes the complex interactions among the more than 80,000 governments in the United States. While the division of authority between state and national governments is an important part of intergovernmental relations, it is only one aspect of an often confusing mosaic. Among other intergovernmental relations that will be considered in Chapter 2 are state-state, state-local, local-local, and national-local relations.

Federalism is not unique to the United States; Germany and Canada have federal governments, too. Nor is federalism the only means of distributing power within a democratic government. Many other countries' governments can be classified as *unitary,* that is, the national government is the dominant center of power and lower-level units are granted rather little authority. France's national government is an example of a government with a unitary structure. At the other extreme is *confederacy,* in which the dynamism and real power lie with the smaller units and the national government's power is restricted. The American people have had two distinct experiences with confederacy: under the first constitution, called the Articles of Confederation (1781–1789), and when the southern states formed the Confederate States of America (1861–1865). Perhaps among recent or current governments there are no true confederacies, but Canada verges on being a confederacy, because of the tradition of strong and often independent-minded provinces, notably Quebec.

Kinds of Subnational Governments

The more than 80,000 subnational governments that currently operate in the United States include the fifty state governments, over 3,000 county governments, somewhat more than 19,000 municipal governments (cities and villages), almost 17,000 towns or townships, nearly 15,000 independent school districts, and, finally, some 29,000 special districts. Although the focus of this book is state and municipal governments, it is important to realize that other subnational units are at work, too.

State Governments

The impact of a state's *policy*—the decisions that government makes—on its citizens is substantial. State governments develop legal codes that govern their citizens' behavior. Laws against murder, rape, and burglary are state laws, enforceable by state and local police. Around 40 percent of the funding for elementary and secondary education comes from state governments. Since "who pays the piper calls the tune," the states therefore have much control over education policy. The states are the primary enforcement agents for protection of the environment under laws such as the Clean Air Act. A state can, through aggressive economic development policies, increase the odds of new jobs being created within its boundaries as by wooing new industry to come into the state; in this manner, the state's economy can be strengthened.

After policies are made, they have to be implemented, that is, put into operation. States must engage in *service delivery*. Obvious examples of service delivery are law enforcement and traffic control through the state police, higher education through state colleges and universities, and efficient transportation through well-maintained roads and the support of mass transit systems. State politics pervades people's everyday lives—from birth (regulation of hospitals) to death (regulation of morticians).

States serve as *policy laboratories*. When confronted with serious problems, such as unemployment or high crime rates or a proliferation of AIDS cases, certain states may try out a variety of solutions.

Other states (or even the national or local governments) can then see which policies work best and adopt those that seem most applicable. States as actors within the federal system become part of a great social experiment in deciding how best to attack the myriad problems confronting society.[1] We see, for example, the national government studying the value of state health care policy innovations in Hawaii (as discussed in Chapter 15).

Municipal Governments

Like their state counterparts, municipal governments make policy. Ordinances banning people from walking along sidewalks with open containers containing alcohol are one example of municipal policy. Local governments also deliver services, such as fire protection and garbage pickup. Many of these services, such as fresh drinking water and sewer systems that remove waste materials from the home, are taken for granted by residents, even though such services can represent significant investments and efforts by a municipality.

Municipalities may also play an important role in state politics. Increasingly, cities lobby their state governments for assistance. Municipalities may band together to amplify their voices in the halls of state government. Some large cities, like Chicago, are listened to because of the number of votes—hence, political clout—within their boundaries.

County Governments

County government is an important political venue throughout the United States. Functions of county government include keeping records (such as deeds, mortgages, births, and tax rolls), maintaining a road system, providing law enforcement through the sheriff's department, maintaining a court system and jails, and administering welfare programs. In urban counties, additional responsibilities may include planning new subdivisions that developers wish to build, administering public health programs, and maintaining recreational facilities.

Some counties are key political actors within their states. For instance, Cook County (containing Chicago) bears considerable political heft in Illinois.

Town Governments

Towns are normally among the least significant of local governments. For one thing, towns (or townships, as they are called in states like Illinois) exist as local subdivisions in only twenty northeastern and midwest states. For another, in rural townships of states like Illinois, Indiana, Kansas, and Ohio, township governments may be responsible for little more than maintaining local highways outside municipal boundaries, although other functions can be assigned to them by their respective counties. Some states, such as the New England states and New York, have much stronger town governments. These entities may have powers similar to those of municipal governments and provide like services, such as water treatment, repository of vital statistics, issuance of marriage licenses, land use regulation (zoning), building inspection, and care of local highways.

School Districts

Many school districts have been taken over by municipal governments. Nonetheless, thousands of independent school districts throughout the country have the power to raise money through taxation and the authority to decide how the revenues are to be allocated. The primary function of school districts is elementary and secondary education. Much more detail on school politics appears in Chapter 14.

Special Districts

The special district is probably the least known and least visible of the local governments. However, it performs crucial functions at the local level and can wield considerable power. Those who fly into John F. Kennedy Airport in New York City, or who pay their tolls to cross the Throgs Neck Bridge between Queens and the Bronx in New York City, or who drive into New York from New Jersey through the Holland Tunnel are in the domain of the Port Authority, one of the many special districts that exist throughout the United States. Port Authority can raise its own revenues by increasing tolls and fees (much as the state government can increase revenues by raising taxes) or by selling bonds. It decides where to construct new facilities, just as a state government decides where to place a new state highway. Most special districts are not so mammoth; they specialize commonly in such areas as mass transit, libraries, parks, water and irrigation, and sewage disposal.

State Constitutions

State constitutions specify the structure of the state government and provide many of the rules under which state politics is carried out. Briefly considered here are the structure and content of state constitutions, some problems with state constitutions, and the politics of state constitutions.

Structure and Content of State Constitutions

State constitutions are structured in a way similar to the United States Constitution, although they tend to be much longer and more specific. All define a process by which they can be amended.

Separation of Powers

Separation of powers is a central characteristic of state government as it is of the national Constitution. Thus, the odds are that no single branch of the state government—legislative, executive, or judicial—will develop overweening power and threaten the freedom of its citizens.

Bill of Rights

State constitutions include a bill of rights. Most of the freedoms mentioned are along the lines of the national Bill of Rights; however, some states have additional freedoms. For instance, Florida's fundamental law calls for the "right to work," which bars the union shop (in which, to stay on the payroll of a business that has a union, one must join the union).

Taxation and Financing

Taxation and financing powers of state government are central aspects of state constitutions. Provisions often limit the taxing power of state and local government (sometimes putting a cap on how high property taxes can go, for example). State constitutions may protect certain classes of property from being taxed, such as churches. *Earmarking* is also often a part of state constitutions. This term refers to provisions that tell where certain revenue sources must be allocated. The most common example is state gasoline taxes being dedicated to highway construction and maintenance; the revenue cannot be used for any other purpose. Ten to twenty years ago, many state constitutions earmarked over half of states' revenues. Budget experts believe that this is harmful, since it reduces the flexibility of state government to use its financial resources in the manner that it deems best for the good of the state.

Balanced Budgets

Related provisions demand that a state must balance its budget. Almost all of the states, in one way or another, limit debt; a majority of the states ban deficits outright. In addition, state constitutions commonly limit the extent to which their local governments can accumulate debt.

Limitations on Power of Local Government

State constitutions commonly comment in great detail about the power and limitations on the power of local government. Local governments are not really independent entities. To the extent that they are granted flexibility in their decision making, it is through the beneficence of the state government. State constitutions often lay out in minute terms what local governments can or cannot do. State constitutions now have relaxed somewhat their hold over their local governments by allowing *home rule.* In this instance, the states allow at least some of their cities to draw up a charter (essentially, a local constitution). Home rule can be defined as

> the power vested in a local unit of government, usually a city, to draft or change its own charter and to manage its affairs. Home rule limits [state] legislative interference in local affairs. Most states permit some degree of freedom for cities and an increasing number are granting it to counties.[2]

Problems with State Constitutions

First, state constitutions tend to be wordy, long, convoluted, and tedious in their detail, and many are outdated. As of 1990, the average length of a state constitution was 28,000 words—as compared with the spare but elegantly written 8,700 words of the U.S. Constitution. The longest state constitution is Alabama's, with 174,000 words—longer than most novels! Some states have constitutions that are cluttered with amendments. Alabama's is also the most amended, with 513 amendments to a document approved in 1901. California has made 471 amendments (to a constitution written in 1879); South Carolina, 463 (to its 1895 document); and Texas, 326 (to its 1876 document). In general, the more urban states, such as California, New York, and Texas, have the longest constitutions.

Some state constitutions date back to the Revolutionary War era. The Massachusetts fundamental law goes back to 1780; New Hampshire's constitution dates back to 1784; and Vermont's reaches back to 1793.[3]

A second problem with state constitutions is that they are the end product of a political process. Many protections for specific interest groups are written into these documents. In this manner, such interests are much better protected than if simple legislation were passed to assist them. It is, after all, harder to amend a constitution than to overturn a law. For instance, state constitutions have called for licensing boards to regulate lawyers, beauticians, and realtors—to be staffed by lawyers, beauticians, and realtors! Thus, each of these industries is given special power over itself.

However, in recent decades, significant improvements have been made in state constitutions, such as reducing the tedious detail.[4]

The Politics of State Constitutions

As noted earlier, interest groups often lobby to have protections for themselves built into state constitutions. One study shows that the stronger the interest groups in a state, the longer the constitution, the higher the proposed number of amendments per year, and the higher the number of amendments approved each year.[5] This clearly suggests the importance of interest groups in constitutional politics.

States with higher levels of partisan competition (the extent to which the two parties fight it out on fairly even terms) tend to have shorter constitutions.[6] It is conceivable that this reflects a balance, in which neither party can ''stack'' the constitution to benefit it and its constituents for political gain.

Issues in State and Local Politics

Several themes characterize state and local politics today and will continue to generate debate and shape government decisions over the coming decade.

More Responsibility for State and Local Governments

In the nineteenth century, government provided a few essential services, such as police and fire protection, road maintenance, and public schools. The greater part of these were provided by state and local governments. With the Great Depression and the election of Franklin Roosevelt as president in 1932, the focus of government action began to shift toward Washington, D.C.

Over the past century the federal government has increased its regulatory activity, protecting citizens from fraud in the banking and security industries, from unsafe products in the marketplace, and from monopoly pricing in the transportation and public utility sectors. From the time of the Great Depression, the federal government has pursued various income redistribution policies, such as social security, which effectively transferred income from some taxpayers to others. The national government has enacted a mildly progressive income tax, set up social welfare programs, built bridges and museums in favored congressional districts, and subsidized farm incomes. Federal laws have been enacted to prohibit discrimination on the basis of race, religion, gender, and age.

As the shadow of Washington, D.C., grew longer, the relative contributions of state and local governments to the provision of services declined. However, state and local governments have increased their responsibilities in absolute terms. The federal government has called upon subnational governments to administer federally funded programs. For example, states typically receive federal social welfare funds to distribute among welfare recipients in accordance with federal guidelines, and states are required to draw up air pollution control plans which will improve air quality to federally defined acceptable levels.

The states and localities, at the same time, have become more aggressive themselves in expanding their responsibilities and addressing social issues. Washington State, for example, has passed a comparable worth law, thus becoming more involved in ensuring equality in pay between the sexes.

During the 1980s, President Ronald Reagan launched a campaign to reduce the size of the federal government. Part of this effort called for returning responsibility for a variety of government services to the states, which would decide whether to collect taxes to support the programs or to cut them. State and local governments are playing a larger role than ever in providing government services and exploring new ways of dealing with long-standing problems.

However, greater responsibility has been limited by *revenue pressures*. While some states had sufficient revenues during the 1980s to handle the additional responsibilities, this ability has been unevenly distributed, with some states and many municipalities facing serious problems paying for Reagan's "New Federalism."[7] During recessions since the early 1970s, numerous states and cities have found it very difficult to meet their responsibilities. Exacerbating this situation has been an eroding tax base characteristic of many older cities of the midwest and northeast. These governments have had to assume more tasks while seeing their revenue-generating ability decline. To increase taxes would risk driving away those middle- and upper-class residents who form the heart of the remaining tax base.

State and local governments have attempted to cope with revenue shortfalls in a number of ways. One increasingly widespread tactic is to promote economic growth by offering incentives to businesses and industries willing to expand locally or even just to remain in the area. Economic growth produces more jobs and, most important, higher tax revenues—the more people working, the more the taxes paid to government. State and local governments pay more attention to providing services as efficiently as possible so as to keep down taxes and prevent taxpayers from being tempted to move elsewhere.

Innovation in States and Localities

The fifty states and their local governments are important for policy experimentation. Many major social problems resist easy solutions. Can states best promote economic development by offering tax concessions, by identifying market niches, or by retraining their workers? To improve the quality of education, should public schools be upgraded or should private schools be encouraged to compete with public schools? Do health care maintenance organizations (HMOs) hold down medical care costs more successfully than do third-party insurance plans?

When the federal government provides funding to the states to address social problems, strings are usually attached. Therefore, federal programs paid for by Washington and administered by the states tend to be homogeneous. But this "one size fits all" policy fails to recognize that states and localities vary widely in political tradition, economic resources, and social culture. Massachusetts, West Virginia, Iowa, Mississippi, and California have very different perspectives on how much the state ought to tax its citizens, to what extent the state should provide for the poor, and whether public services like highways, police protection, and schools should be excellent or merely adequate.

As some states and localities experiment with various solutions, others can observe which approaches work and which do not. For example, Oregon is currently experimenting with a method to order the costs and benefits of various medical procedures, as discussed in Chapter 15. The city of Milwaukee is trying to reduce high school drop-out rates by reducing welfare payment levels to the families of dropouts. Chicago is experimenting with local community control of its schools. Other governments will observe the results of these experiments to see if the results might be applicable to them.

More Competent State and Local Governments

One of the most welcome trends in the last two decades has been the increased professionalization and capability of governments at both the state and local levels. Whereas in the not-too-distant past these governments would have been incapable of executing their added responsibilities well, many more are now in a position to do so.

State institutions have increased their capacity to provide public services. Governors are elected for longer terms (four years per term, as opposed to the once-common two-year terms) and can normally succeed themselves at least once; this gives them more time to sponsor, implement, and modify programs. They have larger, better staffs at their disposal to provide expertise. Legislatures have become more professional. Legislators receive higher pay, enabling them to devote full attention to constituent services and policy discussion. Better-qualified people run for the legislature. Legislators and legislative bodies have larger staffs, adding to their capability to make informed decisions. Courts are called upon to decide a broad range of politically controversial issues, such as environmental damages, affirmative action, and prison conditions. Today, judges are required to have detailed knowledge of substantive issues as well as points of law. To cope with more complex decision situations and larger case loads, the judges rely increasingly on staff assistance. All in all, state officials (and, to a lesser extent, local leaders) devote more time to their work, have more experience, and are assisted by larger staffs than were their predecessors a generation ago.

Bureaucratic Experts and Democratic Government

In a democratic political system, politicians are expected to respond to the expressed wishes of the public on the important policy questions of the day. Voters breathe polluted air, worry about the rising costs of health care insurance, and question the adequacy of the school systems which teach their children. But voters generally do not have the time, energy, or expertise to be effective participants in the policy-making process.

Experts in the criminal justice, education, and health care fields tend to shape the contours of actual public policy. These experts are especially likely to dominate the policy process when the voting public, who are consumers of education and health care services, have little economic incentive to be active participants. Public school systems are virtual monopolies, because children generally attend the public school in their residential neighborhood. Attentive parents may discuss their children's progress with teachers and principal, but in most cases they cannot transfer them to a private school should they continue to be dissatisfied. Education professionals shape the public school system and work to correct what they see as its deficiencies.

Governors, legislators, and judges depend on their staffs to explain public policy issues and to assess the pros and cons of alternative choices. Educators and health care professionals are more likely than voters to have access to the staffs of political figures and, therefore, to decide policy outcomes.

Is the increasing role of experts a threat to democratic institutions? Or is it a healthy mechanism for injecting professionals' expertise into decision making? These are important questions to consider.

One traditional concern in the study of American politics has been the extent to which the people have a voice in government decisions. In a republic, one would expect some popular control. The question, though, is, How much power do the people have? To what extent can the people render government accountable to them for its actions?

Several impediments limit citizen control of their governments. For one thing, the importance of experts and the bureaucracy in the policy process may reduce the effective scope of citizen input. For another, most Americans are not deeply involved in politics. Voter turnout rates in state and local elections tend to be low. Those who have less education and income tend to get short shrift in politics because they are less likely to know how to play the game.

However, despite these significant practical problems, evidence indicates that citizens can affect their state and local governments. State government decisions tend to reflect public opinion; interest groups, presumably representing the views of many citizens, can affect government decisions; voting and other forms of political participation appear to be instruments of influence over government. Some evidence indicates that citizens and interest groups may be able to influence bureaucrats who are often thought of as being beyond democratic accountability.

Redistributive Politics

Many people have not fared well in the economic marketplace; they receive low incomes and, hence, they must do without many goods and services. Individuals with average talent and education must compete with others of similar background, and they can command only ordinary wages in the marketplace. Persons with special talents that other people value and are willing to pay for command high incomes.

Although some government spending redistributes resources from higher-income to lower-income individuals, poor people generally do not do very well politically. Low levels of education, lack of interest in politics, and modest political know-how keep the poor from voting in elections, contacting legislators, and organizing into interest groups as frequently as do middle- and upper-class citizens. This leads to less political influence for the poor and for people of modest means.

The plight of the poor has compounded since the early 1970s. In the 1960s, middle-class taxpayers were willing to fund social programs that benefited the poor. However, in the last twenty years, conflict over affirmative action and government-funded social programs has intensified, and economic conditions have worsened. Indeed, in recent years, the odds of a poor person's advancing in the socioeconomic system have decreased. One study concludes that "the poor [are] more likely to stay at the bottom of the distribution."[8] Middle-class taxpayers, seeing their real incomes fall, now resist redistributive spending programs in education, health care, and social welfare. Instead, they support higher levels of spending to promote economic growth and to lock up lawbreakers. As discussed in Chapter 9, this dynamic leads politicians at the state and local level to deemphasize redistributive programs because they fear that the taxpaying middle class will move to other jurisdictions to escape paying for those who cannot provide for themselves.

Economic Restructuring

A relatively new concern of the states is how to react to economic restructuring, which many states have experienced since the 1970s. Rapidly rising energy prices, prolonged recession, and intensifying competition from low-cost manufacturers in Asia and Latin America have forced the closing of many factories and the loss of many jobs.

High unemployment rates and sagging government tax revenues have resulted. At the same time, the federal government has cut the funds available to the states for services that the federal government demands that the states undertake. Most states are now actively involved in the process of attracting new investment to increase jobs and tax revenues needed to support essential public services. Promoting economic development thus joins the traditional government functions of educating children, providing police protection, maintaining highways, and administering social welfare programs.

One upshot of the effort to foster economic development has been increasing competition to bring in new business to an area. States and local governments compete fiercely in a game that often resembles "robbing Peter to pay Paul," as jobs relocate from one area to another—without any net increase in jobs in the country at large. Additionally, states especially have become more vigorous in pursuing foreign investment, such as new plants to manufacture Japanese or German automobiles. Once more, state and even local governments compete intensely to acquire these foreign-generated jobs. Often, government spends more to attract new investment than it receives in new taxes.

The Structure of This Volume

The chapters that follow discuss the important themes in state and local government and politics introduced here. In addition, they provide basic information on the structure of state and local governments and the politics swirling about them.

Chapter 2 defines American federalism and provides a brief history of federalism from the debate by prerevolutionary leaders on the division of power between the colonial governments and Great Britain to the New Federalism of the 1980s. Federalism has evolved from dual federalism in the nineteenth century through the post-World War II "picket-fence" federalism to the current version, New Federalism, with its emphasis on increased responsibility for both state and local governments. Various issues arise when power is divided among different levels of government. For example, state governments demand that local governments shoulder an ever larger fiscal burden. Themes include the limited ability of local governments to control their destinies and the development of more complex intergovernmental relations.

In a purportedly democratic society, citizens' views ought to be reflected in government decisions. Chapter 3 begins with a discussion of the distinct "political cultures" that characterize the different states and how they affect state politics. Next, the extent to which Americans' political activities and public opinion affect government decisions will be considered. Who participates? What difference does it make? What are possible biases built into the participatory system at the local level?

Chapter 4 examines state and local political parties as organizations, emphasizing the increasing vitality of party organizations over the past two decades, a subject often slighted in state and local government texts. Political party affiliation is an important factor in citizens' voting behavior and in the outcome of elections; just so, parties can affect public policy outputs. The structure of elections and the factors affecting election outcomes at the state and local levels are summarized. So, too, is the impact of party on policy. The chapter concludes by exploring the role of interest groups: their tactics, their political effectiveness, and the extent to which they can affect public policy.

Chapter 5 notes both similarities and differences in legislatures across the states on such matters as staffing, professionalism, and ambition. These bodies have become much more competent and are more important actors in state politics as a result. The impact of lobbying is explored. A basic theme is the increased capabilities of state legislative bodies. At the local level, legislatures are not quite so well institutionalized and have not attained the same level of capability.

Chapter 6 examines the roles of governors, mayors, and professional managers. As state and local governments have assumed greater responsibility, the powers of governors and mayors have expanded. While possible abuse of government power remains a concern, executives at the state and local levels must be strong enough to provide leadership, to monitor bureaucrats, and to coordinate service delivery. Successful governors today still enjoy shaking hands with voters, but they must also have strong administrative skills. At the local level, cities and counties today often hire professional managers to assist elected officials in providing government services efficiently.

Chapter 7 examines the structure and function of state and local bureaucracy. One focus is the extent to which bureaucracies are "modernizing"; another is the extent to which these organizations are responsive to the citizenry. The chapter also looks at how bureaucratic performance can be measured and evaluated; it discusses patronage versus civil service (personnel recruitment), affirmative action, and unionization. Some commentators assert that bureaucracy is increasingly where power lies, especially at the local level.

In Chapter 8, the structure and function of state courts are considered. Emphasis is on the historical development of court systems, the increasing professionalism of these bodies, modes of selecting judges, and the extent to which courts are "democratic." To remain efficient in a more complex society with increasing litigation pressure, courts have become more bureaucratic, making some citizens wonder whether the judges or their bureaucracies control the judiciary. Judges have made important policy decisions in recent years; thus, the judicial branch serves as a key partner in the state policy process.

Chapter 9 introduces the policy process and features a discussion of the stages in the policy-making process (agenda setting, policy making, implementation, and service delivery) and of the key actors at each stage. The relative effects of different influences on state and local policy are outlined. This chapter serves as a general framework for those to follow.

States and localities make taxing and spending decisions in contexts over which they have little control. Broader economic trends and federal government policies affect state and local finances. Chapter 10 examines the tax alternatives available to state and local governments. It considers which taxes are most and least objectionable to taxpayers and the redistributive impact of state and local taxing choices. On the spending side, the chapter describes trends in state and local spending over time and assesses some attempts to account for changing spending patterns.

Chapter 11 focuses on economic policy. State and local governments provide schools, highways, and services which are essential to economic growth. They also regulate business and industry to protect consumers from deceptive business practices and workers from being exposed to workplace hazards. Recently, state and local governments have been actively seeking to provide a positive investment climate in their jurisdictions to attract new business and generate more jobs and tax revenues.

Chapter 12 outlines the variations in state environmental and natural resource policies. Federal mandates require state governments to develop plans to improve the quality of air and water in urban areas but allow some discretion as to how states work to attain environmental quality. The problem of solid waste disposal is reaching crisis proportions. Many state and local governments are developing recycling programs as landfill space becomes scarce. Local government groups fight proposals to locate new landfills or incinerators in their neighborhoods. Since the demands of economic growth and environmental preservation compete, state and local governments must make difficult policy choices.

Chapter 13 examines the criminal justice system at both the state and local levels. Variations in structure and function across the states are described. Issues such as crime rates, prison conditions, police effort, and recidivism rates are discussed. The framework developed in Chapter 9 and themes from earlier chapters are applied to criminal justice policy, from agenda setting to actual outcomes.

One of the most significant policy areas in state and local politics is education. Chapter 14 explores the governance of schools, the mission of schools, the controversy over how well schools are performing, and the variations in educational policies across the states and across local governments. Reformers are critical of the performance of primary and secondary educational institutions. One group of reformers seeks to identify effective schools, analyze why they are effective, and persuade other schools to follow their example. A second approach seeks to create competition among schools by giving parents and students broader choice.

Chapter 15 investigates the variations across state and local governments in their approaches to social welfare policy, the factors that help to explain such variation, and the pros and cons of various approaches. One theme is the difficulty facing these governments in carrying out ''redistributive'' policies for fear of driving away the tax base. Many subnational governments have experienced increasing demand for social services while they simultaneously must cope with eroding tax bases. The cost of providing adequate health care for the poor is rising rapidly. Aid to Families with Dependent Children (AFDC) is a heavily used program that many middle-class taxpayers and conservative reformers believe discourages the able-bodied from seeking gainful employment.

State and local governments are a vital part of the American political system. With the greater responsibilities being thrust upon them by the national government and with their own increasing activism in facing the problems of the day, these subnational governments will remain central actors in our federal system. Their ability to function well helps to define the success of the American political experiment begun over two centuries ago by the Founding Fathers at the Constitutional Convention in Philadelphia.

Recommended Reading

Ann O'M. Bowman and Richard C. Kearney: *State & Local Government,* Houghton Mifflin, Boston, 1990.

Thomas C. Dye: *Politics in States and Communities,* Prentice-Hall, Englewood Cliffs, N.J., 1991.

Virginia Gray, Herbert Jacob, and Robert Albritton, eds.: *Politics in the American States,* 5th ed., Scott, Foresman, Glenview, Ill., 1990.

John G. Grumm and Russell D. Murphy: *Governing States and Communities,* Prentice-Hall, Englewood Cliffs, N.J., 1991.

Kim Quaile Hall and Kenneth R. Mladenka: *Democratic Governance in American States & Cities,* Brooks/Cole, Pacific Grove, Calif., 1992.

John J. Harrigan: *Politics and Policy in States and Communities,* HarperCollins, New York, 1991.

Charles Press and K. VerBurg: *State and Community Governments in a Dynamic Federal System,* HarperCollins, New York, 1991.

CHAPTER 2

Federalism and Intergovernmental Relations

Federalism *is a form of governmental structure in which power is divided between a central government and lower-level governments. Changes in federalism have taken place many times over the course of American history. Among the more recent changes is the movement of responsibility from the national to the state governments. Such changes help define what subnational governments can and cannot do; they have to be acknowledged in considering the decisions these governments do—or do not—make, from economic development to the environment to law enforcement and criminal justice to education. Federalism evolves as Americans reconsider how government can best address important social problems. It adapts to changing conditions of society and new challenges that arise. Under a federal system there is always the possibility of conflict among levels of government. Controversy over the relative power of national and state governments has waxed and waned over 200 years of American history. Some have argued that there should be a decided tilt toward the national government; others have contended that the states ought to be accorded more power.*

This chapter considers three main topics: the origins of American

*federalism, the evolution of federalism and intergovernmental rela-
tions, and federalism and intergovernmental relations today.*

The Origins of American Federalism

American federalism developed out of both experience and theory. Under the Articles of Confederation (1781–1789), the United
States of America was a confederacy, in which the national government had limited power and the states were dominant. State governments sometimes declined to send to the national treasury the taxes
requested by Congress, or they contributed much less than the amount
asked for. This inability to collect revenues underlined the central
government's weakness under the Articles. It is a problem endemic
to confederal forms of government, and it illustrates why they are so
unsuccessful historically. The Founding Fathers believed that the
well-being of the new country required the creation of a more vigorous central government.

Foreshadowing the Idea of Federalism

The concept of divided power had, however, been discussed earlier, even prior to the Revolution itself. During the colonial era, as
England tried to extract taxes from the colonies by such means as the
Stamp Act, debate arose about the relative authority of the colonial
governments and the central government in England. Some colonists
argued that the colonies ought to have the final word in some areas
while conceding that the mother country had authority in others—a
harbinger of the division of power between state and national government under the Constitution.

In 1767, Benjamin Franklin argued that, though the colonists owed
allegiance to the king of England and accepted his sovereignty, they
did not have to accept the rules of the English parliament. Legislation, he claimed, should issue from the colonial legislatures. Thus, he
perceived two separate sovereigns having authority over the same
people, which is one aspect of federalism.

John Dickinson's "Letters from a Pennsylvania Farmer" (1767–
1768) perhaps even more clearly foreshadowed the idea of federalism. He noted that:

The parliament unquestionably possesses a legal authority to
regulate the trade of Great Britain and her colonies. . . . We are

but parts of a whole; and therefore there must exist a power somewhere to preside, and preserve the connection in due order. This power is lodged in the parliament; and we are as much dependent on Great Britain as a perfectly free people can be on another.[1]

However, he went on to say that Great Britain had no power to impose taxes upon the colonies. He quoted one of a series of resolutions passed by the New York legislature: " 'The only representative of the people of the colonies, are the persons chosen therein by themselves; and . . . no taxes ever have been, or can be constitutionally imposed on them, but by their respective legislatures.' "[2] Thus, according to Dickinson, Parliament was supreme in matters of trade and imperial relations among the colonies, but the American colonies were superior in the enactment of taxation measures. This position represents an early argument in favor of federalism. It might be noted that the Declaration of Independence ignored Parliament and placed the onus of the colonists' problems on George III, suggesting that colonists played one power against the other, perhaps more from pragmatic than philosophical concerns.

The Constitutional Debate over Federalism

The issue of federalism was much more clearly addressed in the Constitutional Convention (1787) and in the subsequent debates between Federalists (supporters of the proposed constitution) and antifederalists (those who fought against it).

The Virginia Plan

The Virginia Plan was submitted for consideration very early in the Constitutional Convention. While this document contains little specific detail, it begins to outline a shift away from state domination. The one item that illustrates this shift most dramatically is the latter part of Section 6:

The National Legislature ought to be impowered to . . . negative [veto] all laws passed by the several States contravening in the opinion of the National Legislature the articles of Union; and to call forth the force of the Union against any member of the Union failing to fulfill its duty under the articles thereof.

This view is a marked change away from state domination under the Articles of Confederation, moving toward the eventual federalism under the U.S. Constitution.

The New Jersey Plan

The New Jersey Plan is sometimes looked at as being closer to the spirit of the Articles of Confederation. Yet it possessed a forerunner of the Constitution's *supremacy clause:* ''All Acts of the United States in Congress made by virtue and in pursuance of the powers hereby and by the articles of confederation vested in them, and all Treaties made and ratified under the authority of the United States shall be the supreme law of the respective States. . . . ''

The Federalist Papers

At the time of the ratification of the Constitution, federalism represented a unique contribution to constitutional theory by the delegates serving in Philadelphia in the steamy summer of 1787. The *Federalist Papers,* documents written by James Madison, Alexander Hamilton, and John Jay to convince New York to ratify the Constitution, present some of the most basic arguments on behalf of federalism. Madison, in *Federalist 41,* contended that a more vigorous national government was essential for the following purposes:

1. Security against foreign danger; 2. Regulation of the intercourse with foreign nations; 3. Maintenance of harmony and proper intercourse among the States; 4. Certain miscellaneous objects of general utility; 5. Restraint of the States from certain injurious acts; 6. Provisions for giving due efficacy to all these powers.

Madison argued that the states, acting individually in their respective defenses, would not be able to muster sufficient force to maintain security. Only a national government with the power to operate a military force could guarantee security (although Madison acknowledged the dangers of a powerful standing military during peace).

Madison further argued that the country as a whole would be in a better position to regulate commerce with other countries than would thirteen independent sovereign states, each conducting its own economic policy with other countries. A stronger central government could increase the economic health of the republic and of the individual states. Also, passing the power to regulate interstate commerce to the national government would end some of the abuses practiced by states against each another, such as taxes on goods entering one state from another.

The end result of the Founding Fathers' debates was, of course, the Constitution itself. This document has numerous provisions that speak in one way or another to the respective power of the state versus national governments.

Constitutional Provisions

The Constitution specifies how powers are to be both shared and divided between the national and the state governments. Briefly, some of the more significant provisions are the following:

Powers Specifically Granted to the National Government Only. The Constitution provides that Congress has the power to coin money, conduct foreign relations, regulate interstate commerce, provide for an army and a navy, declare war, establish a post office system, "make all Laws which shall be necessary and proper for carrying into Execution the foregoing Powers vested by this Constitution in the Government of the United States, or in any Department or Officer thereof." The last power is the so-called elastic clause that is the basis for the "implied powers" of the national government.

Powers Specifically Granted to the State Governments Only.
The Constitution empowers the states to determine the time, place, and manner of holding elections for the House of Representatives and the Senate (although these regulations may be altered by Congress), appoint presidential electors, and ratify amendments to the Constitution. The Tenth Amendment states that "The powers not delegated to the United States by the Constitution, nor prohibited by it to the States, are reserved to the States respectively or to the people." States traditionally have also been recognized as having "police power": the authority to regulate on behalf of public health, safety, and morals.

Powers Jointly Held by National and State Governments (Concurrent Powers).   Joint powers include the authority to tax, borrow money, establish judicial systems, make and enforce laws, and take private property for public purposes with fair compensation.

Continuation of the Debate

From the time of the Constitution's ratification, Americans have debated the powers to be exercised respectively by the state and national governments. In the 1790s, Thomas Jefferson and Alexander Hamilton, as Cabinet officers under George Washington, disagreed sharply over whether the federal government had the power to create a national banking system or whether banks were solely under the sphere of the state governments. Jefferson adopted a restrictive view of the national government's power whereas Hamilton asserted a more expansive role for the federal government.

McCulloch v. Maryland

The Supreme Court case *McCulloch v. Maryland* (1819) provided one of the first important answers to the question, What is the proper relationship between states and nation? This case involved the national bank. The state of Maryland levied a tax against the bank (McCulloch was the bank official named in the case). The United States claimed that this tax was an inappropriate use of the state taxation power; the state was attempting to tax the bank out of existence and thereby overrule the national law creating the bank. The state, in turn, said that a national bank was unconstitutional, since there was not a single word in the Constitution that empowered the United States to create a national bank. The United States argued that the bank could be authorized under the elastic clause and that the clause implied certain powers available to the national government (the *implied powers* doctrine).

Two key issues at the heart of this case are the nature of the supremacy clause of the Constitution and the scope of the elastic clause.

The Elastic Clause.   Chief Justice John Marshall's opinion on this case demonstrates the dramatic change in the national government's power in relation to that of the states that took place after the Constitution replaced the Articles of Confederation. On the issue of whether or not the Congress had the power to create a national bank, he said:

> To the [Constitution's] enumeration of powers is added that of making "all laws which shall be necessary and proper, for carrying into execution the foregoing powers, and all other powers vested by this Constitution, in the government of the United States, or in any department or officer thereof."

Since a national bank may further those powe s specifically given Congress by the Constitution, such as borrowing money, raising revenues, supporting the military, and regulating commerce, the elastic clause provides the authority to create such an institution. That is, the explicitly stated powers granted the national government by the Constitution imply the power of that government to create a national bank. Marshall concludes this segment of the case by saying:

> Let the end be legitimate, let it be within the scope of the Constitution, and all means which are appropriate, which are plainly adapted to that end, which are not prohibited, but consist with the letter and spirit of the Constitution, are constitutional. . . .

The Supremacy Clause.   In the next portion of *McCulloch v. Maryland,* Marshall focuses upon the meaning of the supremacy clause:

> This Constitution and the Laws of the United States which shall be made in Pursuance thereof; and all Treaties made, or which shall be made, under the Authority of the United States, shall be the supreme Law of the Land; and the Judge in every State shall be bound thereby, any Thing in the Constitution or Laws of any State to the Contrary notwithstanding.

He notes simply:

> The great principle is, that the Constitution and the laws made in pursuance thereof are supreme; that they control the Constitution and laws of the respective states, and cannot be controlled by them. From this, which may be termed almost an axiom, other propositions are deduced as corollaries. . . . These are, 1st. That a power to create implies a power to preserve. 2d. That a power to destroy, if wielded by a separate hand, is hostile to, and incompatible with, these powers to create and preserve. 3d. That where this repugnancy exists, that authority which is supreme must control, not yield to that over which it is supreme. . . .

Since the tax enacted by the state of Maryland on the national bank could have been used to destroy the bank, the Maryland tax was deemed unconstitutional.

John C. Calhoun

McCulloch v. Maryland is among the most basic decisions rendered by the Supreme Court; it stands as one of the definitive statements about the nature of federalism under the Constitution. It did not, however, quiet critics of national supremacy. There was tension from the beginning between those advocating states' autonomy, as had existed under the Articles of Confederation, and supporters of national supremacy. One of the most interesting of the dissenting voices was that of John C. Calhoun.

Calhoun, who served in the Congress from the War of 1812 through the Compromise of 1850 and even sat as vice president in Andrew Jackson's first term, thought that the south was increasingly threatened because the numerically superior northern states had the votes in Congress to dictate national law. Consequently, he was uncomfortable with the national government's supremacy under the Constitution. To ward off what he saw as the coming dominance of the national government by the north, he proposed a system that, in essence, returned to confederacy. Calhoun's *A Disquisition on Government* (1848) represents his effort to restructure federalism.

The Concurrent Majority. The key to understanding Calhoun is his concept of the *concurrent majority,* a measure which he proposed to prevent tyranny being exercised by a majority. He claimed that this would balance majority and minority interests. One of the minority, that is, southern, interests that he sought to defend was slavery. Calhoun proposed that each sectional majority or large interest that was not territorially based have the constitutional power to an absolute veto over any action of the federal government that, while representing the national majority, threatened the welfare of the minority. Exercise of this veto was referred to as *nullification,* the alleged right of states to nullify federal law. Calhoun felt that this plan would help to unite the country as a whole, rather than weakening it. In a passage written in the late 1840s, Calhoun claims that:

> The concurrent majority . . . tends to unite the most opposite and conflicting interests and to blend the whole in one common attachment to the country. By giving to each interest, or portion, the power of self-protection, all strife and struggle between them for ascendancy is prevented, and thereby not only every feeling calculated to weaken the attachment to the whole

is suppressed, but the individual and the social feelings are made to unite in one common devotion to country. Each sees and feels that it can best promote its own prosperity by conciliating the good will and promoting the prosperity of others.[3]

The concurrent majority, then, would protect the liberty of all interests and would prevent the national government from exercising power beyond its proper limits. In the end, according to Calhoun, the concurrent majority would even strengthen the sense of national community. He claimed that the successful experience of the Iroquois Confederacy, a league of six Indian nations, demonstrated the practicality of his proposal.

The Implications of Calhoun's Dissent.   It seems clear that enactment of this proposal, which was never a serious possibility, would have redefined the United States as a confederate form of government, since the absolute veto of regions or substantive interests would nullify the supremacy clause and make the states the final arbiter of national policy. If Calhoun had won, there would, for example, be no federal civil rights laws, no Clean Air Act, no Occupational Safety and Health Administration (OSHA) rules, and no Fourteenth Amendment protection against states' violation of individual rights. Calhoun's work demonstrates that the ratification of the Constitution and cases such as *McCulloch v. Maryland* did not end debate on the respective roles of state and national governments. Indeed, the outcry by states when the national government called for a 55-mile-per-hour speed limit on the highways in the 1970s indicates the depth of feeling still held by many about the appropriate division of power between the state and national governments.

Since the 1930s, the federal government has increasingly used various instruments of power to compel state and local governments to carry out national goals. Some of these goals have to do with *equity* (fairness). State and local governments have often historically been rather unresponsive to the needs of the poor, the disadvantaged, and the powerless, although there have been many exceptions. With a Calhoun-like system, this would doubtless remain to a large extent true today. However, an energetic national government supported social welfare programs in the 1930s, during the depths of the Great Depression, and this commitment is far different than one would expect under the concurrent majority.

The Evolution of Federalism and Intergovernmental Relations

In the early years of the republic, federalism and intergovernmental relations were, to a large extent, the same. That is, the national government and the state governments were the key figures; local governments were not deemed equal actors. With the Constitution's adoption, as one scholar put it, "American cities became creatures of their respective states."[4] The Constitution, in effect, recognized the national government and state governments, not localities. This marked a dramatic change for cities, which had possessed considerable autonomy in the colonial era. County governments, too, were seen as mere agents of the state's authority. For all practical purposes, the key intergovernmental relations were between the national government and the various state governments, with the remainder of the republic's governments having rather little independence.

Four major stages in the evolution of intergovernmental relations are dual federalism, cooperative federalism, "picket-fence" federalism, and New Federalism.

Dual Federalism

The earliest phase of intergovernmental relations is often referred to as *dual* federalism, which means that the national sphere of influence was seen as being largely separate from the state sphere of influence. The metaphor of a *layer cake* is sometimes used to describe this situation.

Separate Powers

Under the starkest interpretation of dual federalism, each level of government was assumed to possess certain powers that it alone would exercise; the other level had a separate sphere. While the two levels of government sometimes worked together, the simpler scale of life made this the exception rather than the norm. The metaphor of the layer cake, suggesting that like two layers of a cake the national and state governmental realms were separate, is simplistic.[5] Nonetheless, it does serve to illustrate the essence of dual federalism.

People clearly understood that the national government was responsible for national defense and that the states would take care of enforcing basic criminal laws. In a day when the nation was less complex, this understanding had a certain plausibility. The Tenth Amendment provided a further rationale for this division, as proponents of states' rights claimed that the amendment acted to prevent the national government from usurping states' power. The Tenth Amendment reads: "The powers not delegated to the United States by the Constitution, nor prohibited by it to the States, are reserved to the States respectively, or to the people."

Hammer v. Dagenhart

The Supreme Court case of *Hammer v. Dagenhart* illustrates the use of the Tenth Amendment to challenge a national law affecting states. In 1916, the Congress passed a law, the Keating-Owen Act, prohibiting child labor in factories. The law was based on the power of Congress to regulate interstate commerce; under it, any goods produced in factories using underage children could not be shipped in interstate commerce.

Justice William Day, writing for the Supreme Court majority, used the Tenth Amendment as a basis for striking down the Keating-Owen Act as unconstitutional. He began by noting that "the grant of authority over purely Federal matters was not intended to destroy the local power always existing and carefully reserved to the states in the 10th Amendment of the Constitution." He went on to argue, after misquoting the Tenth Amendment:

> In interpreting the Constitution, it must never be forgotten that the nation is made up of states, to which are intrusted the powers of local government. And to them and to the people the powers not expressly delegated to the national government are reserved. . . . To sustain this statute would not be, in our judgment, a recognition of the lawful exertion of congressional authority over interstate commerce, but would sanction an invasion by the federal power of a matter purely local in character, and over which no authority has been delegated to Congress in conferring the power to regulate commerce among the states.

In those phrases is the idea that it is possible to discern fairly clearly the dividing lines between state and national power; those clear lines are the indicators of dual or layer-cake federalism.

Restrictions on Federal Power

Before the early twentieth-century Progressive era (with its antitrust legislation) and the Great Depression of the 1930s (with the advent of federal grant-in-aid programs in unprecedented numbers), the federal government had a rather restricted sphere of activity. In this earlier era, city hall, the county courthouse, and the corridors of the state legislature were, in the eyes of many people, the vital centers of American politics, not far-off Washington, D.C. The governments that most touched Americans in their everyday lives were those at the state and local level.

Cooperation in the Layer Cake

The preceding discussion, though, does simplify greatly a more complex reality. While the layer cake is a useful metaphor, there was a degree of intergovernmental cooperation within its historical sweep. For instance, the national government helped to finance state militias in the early 1800s; the national government built some state canals and roads in the nineteenth century; and the Homestead Act of 1862 made federal lands available to settlers in the midwest and west.

The Morrill Act of 1862 provided land to the states to support colleges teaching agriculture (the so-called ''land grant'' colleges). Indeed, even under the Articles of Confederation, the Congress provided that land be made available for educational purposes under terms of the various Northwest Ordinances.

The national government developed extremely significant programs providing funds to the states in the early decades of the twentieth century. For example, the Federal Aid Highway Act of 1916 granted federal monies to the states for highway construction. Federal assistance for each state was based on a statistical formula taking into account the state's size, population, and rural mail route mileage. Other major grant programs followed.[6]

Still, it was not until the 1930s that the major impetus toward federalism began, even though the boundaries between the layers of the layer cake had already been blurred.

Cooperative Federalism

With the Great Depression, the nature of intergovernmental relations became much more complex. The responsibilities of local governments became more substantial as the tradition of Dillon's Rule—that local governments are just the creatures of state government—began to be undermined and dual or layer-cake federalism came to be less descriptive of the actual relations between levels of government. The second stage is sometimes referred to as *cooperative federalism;*

it began in the 1930s (although some have claimed that its origins might be traced to Theodore Roosevelt's presidency[7]) and was dominant up to the 1960s. The metaphor used to describe this phase is the *marble cake,* symbolizing the intermeshing of different governments working together to attack a problem. Indeed, some aspects of this model continue today in certain policy arenas,[8] such as the Community Development Block Grant (CDBG) program in which the federal government makes funds available to the localities to meet certain federal goals.

Grants-in-Aid

State and local governments were unable to cope with the almost unimaginable dislocation and hardship of the Great Depression. The federal government under Franklin Roosevelt responded in several ways to the crisis. This response was the basis of cooperative federalism. A number of programs were created under which the state, national, and local governments would work together on serious problems. One tool was the *grant-in-aid,* by which a national government makes funding available to lower-level governments to address issues of mutual concern. Although national grant programs to lower-level governments had existed before (for example, the Morrill Act of 1862), they took on a new importance as the number of such programs increased. One of the best illustrations of cooperative federalism is an example used by Morton Grodzins: the "sanitarian," a representative although fictional public health official. Grodzins says:

> The sanitarian is appointed by the state under merit standards established by the federal government. His base salary comes jointly from state and federal funds, the county provides him with an office and office amenities and pays a portion of his expenses, and the largest city in the county also contributes to his salary and office by virtue of his appointment as a city plumbing inspector. It is impossible from moment to moment to tell under which governmental hat the sanitarian operates. His work of inspecting the purity of food is carried out under federal standards; but he is enforcing state laws when inspecting commodities that have not been in interstate commerce; . . . [he is] a local officer when insisting that the city butchers adopt more hygienic methods of handling their garbage. But he cannot and does not think of himself as acting in these separate

capacities. All business in the county that concerns public health and sanitation he considers his business. Paid largely from federal funds, he does not find it strange to attend meetings of the city council to give expert advice on matters ranging from rotten apples to rabies control. He is even deputized as a member of both the city and county police force.[9]

One can see that the intermixing of responsibilities by different levels of government is consistent with the marble-cake idea. The notion that the functions and responsibilities of different levels of government can be separated easily is confounded in the example of the sanitarian.

Over time, more and more grant-in-aid programs were developed by the national government, and states developed increasing numbers of grant programs for their subsidiary governments, as well. Many of the grant programs are "categorical," that is, narrowly drawn, technical, and directed at specific activities. Medicaid is one such program. A good portion of the funds for such grants are distributed on the basis of formulas built into national legislation, as noted earlier with the Highway Act of 1916. One type of categorical grant, the *project grant,* is competitive, meaning that a limited number of grants of a particular type are available, and, ideally, the governments that submit the best grant proposals receive funding.

Of course, politics plays a role in the grant process, as some states seem to play the grant game better than others. States with governors who have served in Congress are more successful at getting federal grant funds, as are states that hire lobbyists to go to Washington, D.C., to advocate the states' programs and positions.[10]

Expansion of Bureaucracy

Once grant monies became available and began to be obtained, state and local bureaucracies expanded. Why?

The expertise needed to apply for project grants helped spawn the "grantsmanship game." Since the competition might be fierce for project grants, a city, for instance, might wish to hire a professional grant writer to try to obtain funding. The grant writer might well require staff support to help in researching proposals; clerical staff might also be necessary. When federal assistance money comes in (whether obtained via project grants or formula grants), additional help is needed. Once the money is received, say, for constructing a new mass transit system, experts must be hired to plan and actually construct the system. When the system is in working order, other experts in transportation must administer and run the program. Hence, the local government will hire engineers and administrators who have expertise in mass transit. And, of course, clerical help and administrative assistants and others are needed as well. As this process is repeated over many different policy areas, including welfare, education, mental health, health care, housing, and parks, the local bureaucracy expands. Indeed, over the past several decades, the growth of government bureaucracy in terms of number of employees has been occurring most rapidly at state and local levels. (See Chapter 7 for further discussion of these trends.)

Increase in Government Spending

State government has become much bigger over the course of the twentieth century, and marble-cake federalism appears to be a major cause of this growth. One study has investigated forces that have impelled an increase in the amount of state government spending as a proportion of the state's total economic output. Bureaucracy and the intergovernmental grant system seem best to explain the growth of state government spending relative to state economic output.[11]

Size of Bureaucracy. The size of the states' bureaucracy (the percentage of government employees in the states' total population) is related to increased government size: the more bureaucrats, the greater the growth of government. In part, this reflects the propensity of government employees to turn out and vote (for government growth) and their consequent political clout. Also, the jobs of bureaucrats depend upon a vigorous public sector, and bureaucrats tend to want to expand their domains.

The Intergovernmental Grant System. The second factor increasing government size is the intergovernmental grant system. The more federal grant dollars that states bring in as a percentage of total state government spending, the greater the increase in government size. Since many of these grant programs require matching by the states, state spending increases. For instance, the Boating Safety Financial Assistance Program calls for the U.S. Department of Transportation to provide 50 percent of the funding for states participating in the program; the states choosing to accept the federal money must then put up 50 percent themselves. Thus, receipt of grant-in-aid funds from the federal government spurs the growth of state governments. Both of these effects obviously spring from the cooperative federalism era and its aftermath, when grants facilitated bureaucratic growth, which in turn spurred even further growth of state government.

"Picket-Fence" Federalism

The increasing bureaucratization at the state and local levels led to a third stage in the evolution of intergovernmental relations: *picket-fence federalism*, in which competition and even conflict becomes more pervasive. This stage may be said to begin in the 1960s with lingering relevance today. Figure 2.1 illustrates.

Policy Generalists

The horizontal "slats" in the picket fence represent national, state, and local levels of government and the "policy generalists" in each. Mayors, governors, the U.S. president, Congress, state legislatures, city councils, and so on develop public policy and make basic government decisions. Since these officials are responsible for their policy decisions and may be held accountable by voters if things go awry, they wish to maintain ongoing supervision and control of programs.

Policy Generalists

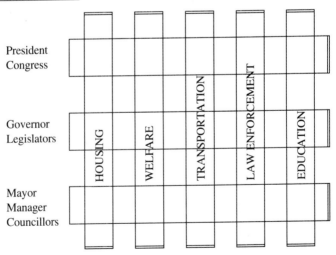

Functional Area Experts
(Bureaucracy)

Fig. 2.1   The Picket-Fence Model of Intergovernmental Relations

Bureaucratic Experts

However, policy generalists must compete with the vertical slats of the fence, that is, the experts in the bureaucracy at all levels of government. These bureaucrats believe that they ought to be allowed to run their programs in terms of what their expertise and professional judgment tell them. They do not appreciate what they see as "meddling" by policy generalists, who normally have little grasp of the technical details of the bureaucrats' responsibilities. Furthermore, bureaucrats within a particular area, for instance, transportation, meet together at professional conferences, read the same professional journals, and accept the same general assumptions about how to go about doing their jobs. Thus, federal, state, and local bureaucrats within transportation work together; in the process, they can be a powerful political force.

Competition for Funds

At the same time, bureaucrats in different areas, say law enforcement and education, compete with one another for government funding. It was not surprising in the 1970s, for example, to see police unions at the local level complaining about substantial raises granted to teachers. They argued that because their work was more dangerous and more important, they ought to get preference in the struggle for scarce economic resources. And, of course, the educators disagreed. Thus, competition between bureaucrats in the various specialized areas emerged as a problem in coordinating policy. This added yet one more source of conflict to the system.

Former Senator Edmund Muskie once said, "The picture, then, is one of too much tension and conflict rather than coordination and cooperation all along the line of administration—from top Federal policymakers and administrators to the state and local professional administrators and elected officials."[12]

New Federalism

Intergovernmental relations have moved into a fourth phase, referred to as *New Federalism*. This phase developed in the late 1960s and early 1970s under the administration of President Richard Nixon. The hallmark of New Federalism is a turning back of responsibility from the national to the state and local governments and the provision of greater flexibility to those governments. For instance, the national government would pull out of certain policy areas, leaving it up to the state and local governments to take over. Some aspects of dual federalism are revived here, as the national government and state governments work together less and as states take over certain types of policies once shared with the national government. Advocates of this brand of federalism assume that the national government has taken too much power unto itself and has usurped some of the functions of state governments. They decry the abundant use of categorical grant programs, which tell the recipient government exactly how the money must be spent without consideration of either the priorities of the state or local government or its unique context that might not be taken into account by the strings attached to the grant.

President Nixon's proposals for *block grants* and *general revenue sharing* illustrate some of these points.

Block Grants

Block grants provide more flexibility to grant recipients. For instance, the Community Development Block Grant (CDBG) program, which originated when older categorical grant programs, such as Urban Renewal and Model Cities, were folded into CDBG, has fewer "strings" attached to the money by the federal government than did the original programs. CDBG enabled cities to craft programs that would directly meet their unique needs without worrying as much about having to meet certain requirements that might not be applicable to a specific locality's situation. Thus, local governments gained somewhat greater responsibility, while still being in a position to receive federal funding.

General Revenue Sharing

General revenue sharing was another of Nixon's innovations. The State and Local Assistance Act, passed in 1972, called for the federal government to use a formula, based on factors such as population and need, to calculate how large a check ought to be written to each state and local government. The recipient government could then spend the money more or less as desired (one important restriction was that the money could not be used in such a fashion as to discriminate on grounds of race). General revenue sharing allowed state and local governments to receive funding with even fewer strings attached than with block grants and was therefore an extremely popular program among local governments and the states.

With Ronald Reagan's presidency, however, general revenue sharing was finally terminated in 1986. Reagan believed that state and local governments should decide what services to provide and should convince the voters to pay for them. In his view, legislators and bureaucrats in Washington, D.C. should not collect taxpayers' money from each state only to turn around and send that same money back to the states—this seemed to the president to be both inefficient and overly bureaucratic.

Federalism and Intergovernmental Relations Today

President George Bush's policies continued trends started under his Republican predecessors. He urged a continuing shift of responsibility to the states to provide services. States resisted many of these initiatives since they were being asked to accept greater responsibility without receiving commensurate federal funds.

Among elements of the New Federalism in place today are (1) a reduction in categorical grants, with their many detailed stipulations, made available by the national government; (2) a pulling back from domestic policies generally, as a consequence leaving greater responsibility in this policy arena to state and local governments. (Despite this trend, as of 1987, according to the Advisory Commission on Intergovernmental Relations, a total of 422 grant programs were operated by the national government, with categorical grants accounting for about 86 percent of total grant funds available.[13])

One commentator goes so far as to claim that New Federalism has undergone a metamorphosis into "go-it-alone federalism," which is a partial return to pre-Civil War perspectives on national-state relations. (In that earlier era, the term "United States" was used as a plural noun, literally meaning a collection of states; later the term "United States" came into use as a singular noun, reflecting one unified country rather than a collection of independent states.) The sluggish national economy during the Bush years led to serious budget pressures for many American states. One result was that many cut back on programs for the poor and middle class. Henry Raimondo concludes:

As the United States approaches the end of the twentieth century, the federal system is not well positioned to expand economic opportunity. The federal government has no coherent domestic agenda to enhance economic competitiveness.

The states meanwhile are disinvesting in people and public infrastructure. . . .

Go-it-alone federalism has changed the nature of intergovernmental relations in the United States. The federal government and some income classes are neglecting their financial responsibilities to the society as a whole. Pre-Civil War thinking will not allow states to educate their people, rebuild their infrastructure, provide for their homeless, tend to their elderly and infirm, and still balance their budgets.[14]

While this dismal picture is overstated, it does indicate one implication of the trends discussed above. However, it is equally clear that federal partnership with the states is changing substantially with the Clinton administration.

National-State Relations

New Federalism increasingly describes the national-state linkage, although, as noted earlier, elements of both marble-cake and picket-fence federalism persist. The national government has devolved greater responsibility to the state governments for programs in welfare, health, housing, and transportation—but without providing additional resources.

In addition, the national government *mandates* certain programs or actions by the states. Mandates force state governments to undertake certain actions or programs, with the states picking up some or all of the tab. Environmental legislation is a prime example. The Clean Air Act Amendments of 1970, for instance, call for state governments to establish a body to enforce the act. The process works as follows: The Environmental Protection Agency issues regulations on the ''safe'' amount of pollutants that can be in the air. States are then to design plans that will lead toward attainment of these standards (where air is dirtier than called for) or maintain clean air in areas that already meet the standards. The state picks up much of the cost for enforcement of a law passed by the federal government. Thus, the states' action is mandated—and this serves as an irritant to the states.[15]

How have the states responded to the devolution of responsibility downward from the national government? No single answer adequately addresses this question. However, one study suggests that different states are apt to respond differently. Part of Reagan's New

Federalism was a cutting back on contributions by the national government to state governments for enforcing and carrying out environmental programs. A study of state responses to these cutbacks shows that many states simply did not replace the federal funds thus lost; in the end, there may have been "an adverse impact upon protection of the environment in the early 1980s."[16]

State-State Relations

Extradition of fugitives from justice from one state to another and the right to freely travel from state to state are two familiar aspects of interstate relations. The Constitution defines the nature of the relationship among the states in several clauses, discussed below.

The Full Faith and Credit Clause

The *full faith and credit clause,* in Article IV, Section 1, says that "Full faith and Credit shall be given in each state to the public acts, records, and judicial proceedings of every other state." This means that the states must respect one another's laws and judicial decisions. For instance, a landlord who loses a suit against a tenant in Kentucky cannot move to Tennessee to escape paying the resulting fine. Tennessee would recognize the liability of the landlord.

Privileges and Immunities Clause

Article IV, Section 2, the *privileges and immunities clause,* states that "The citizens of each state shall be entitled to the privileges and immunities of citizens in the several states." Generally, this clause means that states cannot discriminate against nonresidents in terms of fundamental rights, such as access to the courts and making a living. The clause does not apply to other discriminations, such as nonresident students paying higher tuition at a state school.

Interstate Compacts

Article I, Section 10 provides that "No state shall, without the consent of Congress . . . enter into any agreement or compact with another state. . . . " Thus, states may enter into binding agreements with one another, but they need the consent of Congress. Some compacts are made between two states (such bilateral compacts are the most common); other compacts may involve all fifty states. Subjects of compacts include interstate boundaries, navigation on interstate waterways, and conservation. The popularity of interstate compacts has increased dramatically in recent decades. Before 1920, there were only about three dozen such agreements; over 100 have been entered into since World War II.

Interstate Communication Networks

A most important contribution of contemporary federalism to American government is the role of the states as great experimental laboratories. Advocates of federalism assume that the various states can experiment with different policy initiatives to see what works. If one state happens upon a policy that seems to do well, other states may decide to follow suit. In this way, new ideas will spread ("diffuse") across the country. Innovations (new policies) diffuse via several different mechanisms. One of the more obvious is through contacts among public officials (both elected and appointed officials and career civil servants): as officials of the several states meet, they can discuss their common problems and how they go about solving them. As arenas for this sort of communication have increased over time (for example, professional organizations, newsletters, professional publications, and formal conferences), the rapidity with which innovations spread has increased apace. In addition, job mobility, with bureaucrats moving from one state to another for career advancement, helps spread innovations as they carry ideas from one state to another.[17] Thus, interstate communication networks facilitate the dispersion of policy initiatives that might solve recurrent problems across the states.

State-Local Relations

Dillon's Rule

Historically, as noted before, state-local relations have been best described by "Dillon's Rule." Judge John Dillon, an expert in municipal law, put it thus in the 1911 edition of his famous work:

> It is a general and undisputed proposition of law that a municipal corporation possesses and can exercise the following powers, and no others: First, those granted in express words; second, those necessarily or fairly implied in or incident to the powers expressly granted; third, those essential to the accomplishment of the declared objects and purposes of the corporation—not simply convenient, but indispensable. Any fair, reasonable, substantial doubt concerning the existence of power

is resolved by the courts against the corporation, and the power is denied.[18]

Supreme Court Justice Pierce Butler put it even more bluntly in *Trenton v. New Jersey* (1923): "In the absence of state constitutional provisions safeguarding it to them, municipalities have no inherent right of self-government which is beyond the legislative control of the state." In short, local governments under this doctrine can be referred to as "creatures of the state."

However, in recent decades, local governments have gained somewhat more autonomy through the passage of home rule legislation or the adoption of home rule through state constitutions, as noted in Chapter 1. Home rule undermines to some extent the full force of Dillon's Rule.

Grants-in-Aid

An important mechanism in state-local linkages is the grant-in-aid. Just as the national government has created a series of grant-in-aid programs that provide funding sources for state and local governments, so, too, do states develop grants for their local governments. Just as with national grant programs, state programs come with strings attached, indicating how the money may be used by local governments and what restrictions are imposed on the expenditure of the funds. In addition, some states have revenue sharing programs, by which money is allocated by formula to local governments. These revenue sharing programs dispense funds that have very few strings attached and can be used more or less as local governments wish.

The Mandate

Currently, one of the most important issues in state-local relations is the mandate. Here, as with national-state mandates, the state compels the local government to carry out certain programs; that is, the state mandates local government action with local government having to pay some or all of the cost of carrying out the mandate. A study published in the early 1980s indicates that the average state has thirty-five different mandates requiring spending by local governments.[19] For example, a 1971 New Hampshire law mandated that each city and town provide a disposal site for materials pumped from septic tanks, without any state funding.[20] Of course, that is the rub—the states tell the local governments that they must carry out certain activities or adopt certain programs, often without providing financial assistance.

A 1981 survey of state and local officials identified state mandating as the biggest problem in subnational politics. A 1976 survey showed that local political officials see mandating as unfair. Fifty-four percent of the policy functions carried out by localities that year had been mandated by state government. The most common mandates focused on special education, solid waste disposal, and eligibility for police and firefighter pensions. Local leaders often come to feel that the states are intruding into their domain and that, because the state government often provides no funds to carry out such mandates, they are squeezing cities financially dry.[21] To illustrate the impact of state mandates on local governments, consider Niagara County, a county in New York State. Of the 1993 $50.7 million tax levy against its citizens, 71 percent goes toward state-mandated programs such as Medicaid, public assistance, and Education to Handicapped Children.[22]

Mandates do help create uniformity in policy within a state and can increase the coordination of policies within a state. However, these mandates increase the burden on localities. Given the fiscal pressures at the national level, states are unlikely in the near future to reduce mandating. As unhappy as local governments might be, Dillon's Rule leaves them little option but to comply. The question then becomes, How can these governments meet current needs and still fulfill the mandates?

Local-Local Relations

Local governments interact to deal with problems facing them in a variety of ways.

The Lakewood Plan

One approach is the *Lakewood Plan* (or intergovernmental contract plan), by which several cities will contract with the county government, for instance, to provide law enforcement. Lakewood is a suburb of Los Angeles and lies within Los Angeles County. The county contracted with the community to provide an agreed-upon number of cars and deputy sheriffs to serve in place of a local constabulary. This solution may provide cost-effective services for communities, although it may also compromise their ability to control their destinies.[23]

Councils of Government

A second mechanism for interaction among local governments, of considerable importance in recent years, is the *Council of Govern-*

ments (COG). Representatives of several local governments will meet regularly to discuss matters of common concern and, perhaps, even adopt united action. The COG's governing board, the representatives from each government, may receive funds from members and even hire a staff to develop and coordinate planning actions. COGs address such functions as transportation, parks and recreation, sewers, and land-use planning. One example is the Twin Cities COG (Minneapolis and St. Paul, Minnesota), which has its own tax base, the power to review all federal aid projects for the area, and control over metropolitan-wide concerns such as the airport, mass transit, and sewage. The form of COGs is normally a confederation with a great deal of member autonomy.

As state mandates continue to put pressure on local governments, it is likely that this species of cooperative venture will become even more prominent. Localities will have to work together to deal with common problems and stretch their scarce resources as far as possible. As noted in Chapter 1, national and state mandates serve to put greater and greater fiscal pressure on local governments while simultaneously demanding that those governments assume even greater policy responsibilities.

Intergovernmental Consolidation

The most extreme form of interlocal coordination is *intergovernmental consolidation*. One example is *metropolitan government* (''metro''), in which an areawide government is established. One form of metro is for the county government to become the central government for an area, with the different municipalities therein surrendering many or most of their original powers. Some metro governments retain a federal structure in which the local jurisdictions retain some independence; others move to a more unitary structure. Metro has been unpopular in the United States, with just a small number of areas instituting it (such as Nashville-Davidson County and Miami-Dade County).

In the future, it may well be that consolidation and a reduction in number will be the only option left open for local governments. By merging, several local governments can increase the pool of resources available to them for the services that they must deliver and most likely realize cost savings in the process. At a minimum, several neighboring communities might share certain functions, such as law enforcement. For example, operation of ten separate police departments in ten adjoining municipalities requires ten separate dispatchers. However, if the ten communities were to share this function, some of the dispatchers' positions might be eliminated, thus saving funds.

National-Local Relations

Creative Federalism

President Lyndon Johnson's *creative federalism* expanded direct linkages between the national and local governments. One notable precedent, the Housing and Urban Renewal Act of 1949, called for federal assistance to localities to help acquire and clear land that would subsequently be sold to private developers. The federal grant money would go to the local government. Under Johnson, programs such as Model Cities (a program under which cities could apply for federal funds to support the development of a demonstration project designed to attack poverty and urban problems in a coordinated fashion) and the War on Poverty (under which local Community Action Organizations could develop programs to combat poverty) solidified and extended the example set by the 1949 act. Another program that benefited local government was the Urban Mass Transit Act (UMTA), which facilitated highway and mass transit construction and operation. Under Richard Nixon's proposals to produce a new federalism, general revenue sharing was added as one more tie between the national and local governments.

New Federalism

However, in the 1980s, President Reagan's New Federalism served to erode these linkages. One index of this is the dollar value (adjusted for inflation) of federal assistance to local governments. Table 2.1 shows the dramatic reduction resulting from the federal government's cutting back on assistance.

In program after program, federal funding has either dropped sharply or, as with Urban Development Action Grants and general revenue sharing, has been eliminated altogether. The 1991 federal budget showed an overall decline of 68 percent in dollars targeted to urban programs over a ten-year period. Given the importance of intergovernmental transfer of funds for state and local governments, this is a very substantial cutback. This reduction in revenue came about as states also saw fewer federal dollars coming their way and, as one response, imposed more mandates upon local governments. Local governments were confronted with the problem of shrinking

Table 2.1   National Funding of Primarily Urban Programs

	Fiscal 1981*	Fiscal 1991 (Proposed)	Real % Change
Community Development Block Grants	5.7	2.7	-53%
Urban Development Action Grants	0.6	0.0	-100
General Revenue Sharing	7.3	0.0	-100
Mass Transit	5.4	2.5	-54
Employment and Training	8.4	3.5	-59
Economic Development Administration	0.6	0.0	-100
Justice Assistance	0.4	0.6	+40
Clean Water Construction	5.4	1.6	-70
Total	33.8	10.9	-68%

* Adjusted for inflation; in billions of dollars

Source: Ellen Perlman, "Spending Plan Will Force More Local Belt Tightening," *City & State* 7 (February 12, 1990), 1.

resources as federal and state assistance was cut and, at the same time, the need to deliver basic services and take on additional responsibilities due to New Federalism and state mandating.

We may anticipate many changes in the intergovernmental system over the next decade. While the national government is pressing the state and local governments to take on more responsibility, it is also providing less financial assistance for the states and raising money from traditional state and local sources, thus making it more difficult for those governments to make up the difference. However, the national government has not become a minor actor in the current system. It still makes laws that affect every state and local government in the country; its reach remains long.

Nonetheless, the state and local governments are being challenged to do more. And, as the national government has pushed responsibility downward without commensurate financial assistance, so, too, are many states demanding that their local governments assume more responsibility without concomitant financial assistance from the state capitol. Thus, a downward spiral in programmatic responsibility is apparent.

One important factor mitigating the potentially devastating effects of this process is the increased capability of both state and local governments. Already noted is the enlarged bureaucracy at both levels, which enhances capability. In later chapters, we will see that other institutions at the state and local level have also become more able to exercise the increased responsibilities being thrust upon them. And, at both the state and local level, new sources of revenue have been tapped to enlarge the potential revenue base available to them.

Recommended Reading

R. J. Dilger, ed.: *American Intergovernmental Relations Today: Perspectives and Controversies,* Prentice-Hall, Englewood Cliffs, N.J., 1986.

Daniel Elazar: *American Federalism: A View from the States,* 3d ed., Harper & Row, New York, 1984.

Russell L. Hanson: ''Intergovernmental Relations,'' in Virginia Gray, Herbert Jacob, and Robert Albritton, eds., *Politics in the American States,* 5th ed., Scott, Foresman, Glenview, Ill., 1990.

David C. Nice: *Federalism: The Politics of Intergovernmental Relations,* St. Martin's Press, New York, 1987.

Laurence J. O'Toole, Jr., ed.: *American Intergovernmental Relations,* Congressional Quarterly Press, Washington, D.C., 1993.

Paul Peterson: *City Limits,* University of Chicago Press, Chicago, 1981.

Deil S. Wright: *Understanding Intergovernmental Relations,* 3d ed., Brooks/Cole, Pacific Grove, Calif., 1988.

Part II

Subnational Political Institutions and Processes

CHAPTER 3

Political Culture, Public Opinion, and Political Participation

The ideal of democratic theory is for the people to have significant input into government decisions. Few analysts call for pure democracy, with mass 'town meetings'' to make basic decisions at the state and local levels. More commonly, representative democracy is viewed as the practical means for citizens to have a voice in policy matters. That is, people elect representatives to act on their behalf. After electing public officials, segments of the public engage in many different actions—such as making phone calls, sending telegrams, and joining local groups—designed to make their representatives listen and act on specific issues (for example, putting in a new stoplight on a dangerous street). This chapter explores the extent to which the public has influence on its elected representatives. Does the unique political culture of a city or state affect policy outputs? What do citizens of state and local governments think, and what difference do their opinions make in terms of what government actually does? What is political participation and how might it affect government decisions?

One common argument is that state and local governments are closer to the people than is the national government and that gov-

ernment close to the people ought to be responsive to them. This chapter focuses very directly upon one of the themes of this volume: the extent to which state and local governments are accountable to their citizenry.

Political Culture

Political culture refers to a system of beliefs or values that define political situations and structure people's understanding of politics itself. Such values are widely shared within the given polity (whether at the state or local level) and are enduring. Daniel Elazar has defined political culture as "the historical source of such differences in habit, concerns, and attitudes that exist to influence political life in the various states."[1]

State Political Culture

The political culture of any particular state comes about as a result of geography, economics, religion, and historical events. The states differ across these factors and these variations produce disparate political cultures. For example, the dominance of Mormonism in Utah lends a unique cast to politics in that state; the legacy of the Civil War created quite different political cultures in the southern as opposed to northern and western states.

Types of Cultures

Elazar has hypothesized that there are three very general political cultures manifest across the American states: individualistic, moralistic, and traditionalistic.

Individualistic Political Culture.   This culture posits a limited role for government. That is, states dominated by this ethos are likely to have less government involvement in the various sectors of life within that state. Citizens who are part of this culture have great faith in the marketplace as a means of responding to citizens' demands and a consequent belief that state government should nurture economic development and encourage private initiatives. New programs should not be started up by the state unless public opinion demands it, and change in general should only come about if a majority wish it to. People in this culture tend to think that politics normally ought to be left to the professionals; politics is often viewed as "dirty business," best practiced by those who revel in it. States with individualistic cultures, such as Pennsylvania, Ohio, and Illinois, tend to have heavy Roman Catholic populations in cities and a large ethnic stock of Southern and Eastern Europeans and Irish.

Moralistic Culture.   In contrast to individualistic cultures, moralistic cultures favor "positive government," the view that the state ought to intervene in the economy to help disadvantaged people and to ensure the public welfare. Bureaucracy is seen positively, as a force that can implement programs and bring about desired changes. According to this culture, all citizens ought to participate in politics as part of their civic duty. The goal of politics is to use the tools of government to advance the common interest, the public good. States with moralistic cultures, such as Wisconsin, Minnesota, and Vermont, tend to have larger percentages of liberal Protestant denominations and more people with Northern European, English, and German ethnic heritages. More affluent states tend to be moralistic.[2]

Traditionalistic Culture.   Such cultures focus upon maintaining the existing order. They hold that the masses should play only a minimal role in politics; the better sort, the elite, ought to dominate. Traditionalistic state cultures exhibit great antipathy toward change, considerable personalism in politics, and the understanding that the sons and daughters of the elite are groomed to inherit their parents' place in power. Political competition is between factions of the elite striving for control. Fundamentalist Protestants dominate. Examples of states with traditionalistic cultures are Georgia, Alabama, and Mississippi.

Effects of State Political Culture

Much research has explored the impact of political culture on cooperation among states, policy liberalism, policy innovativeness, party competition, tax policy, and tolerance. In later chapters, the role of political cultures surfaces over and over as a factor in state politics.

Cooperation among States.   The level of cooperation on such things as compacts varies among states. For example, a study that focused on six interstate compacts, such as the Vehicle Equipment Safety Compact, found that twenty-six states approved all six compacts, while ten states refused to approve more than one.[3] What distinguishes more cooperative states from less cooperative states? Research findings indicate that states dominated by Republicans are less cooperative, as are southern states. Most relevant here, though, is the finding that moralistic states are far and away the most cooperative, while traditionalistic states are the least so.

Policy Liberalism.   Liberalism here is defined in terms of support for antidiscrimination laws, more generous social welfare benefits, increased consumer protection, and the Equal Rights Amendment (ERA). A number of studies show that moralistic cultures are most apt to generate liberal state policies—even when taking into account other factors such as the wealth of the state, the educational level of its citizens, urbanism, and the like.[4]

Policy Innovativeness.   Some states are more innovative than others in their public policy choices. They are more likely to develop new programs not in existence in any other states and quicker to adopt innovations developed in other states. Consistently, research findings show that moralistic states are the most innovative and traditionalistic ones are the least so.[5]

Party Competition.   The extent to which the two major parties fight it out on fairly even terms is affected by political culture. Moralistic and individualistic states produce greater degrees of party competition, whereas in traditionalistic cultures, interparty competition is less keen.[6]

Tax Policy.   Given that the moralistic culture accepts the positive state and accepts the burden of a commitment to public welfare, it is unsurprising that states with this type of culture have heavier tax burdens. Since "there is no such thing as a free lunch," greater policy liberalism must be paid for with higher taxes. Citizens in moralistic states appear to be willing to accept higher taxes. Traditionalistic states have lower tax burdens.[7]

Political Tolerance.   To explore this quality among the states, one study examined factors affecting levels of repression against members of the American Communist party in the 1950s. Findings suggest that traditionalistic states generated much more repressive laws—for instance, banning communists from public employment and political office.[8]

Local Political Culture

Scholars have also applied the idea of political culture to the local level.

The Yankee Ethos versus the Immigrant Ethos

One effort to relate political culture to the community distinguishes two orientations toward government and the public interest. Banfield and Wilson claim that:

These patterns reflect two conceptions of the public interest. . . . The first, which derives from the middle-class ethos, favors what the municipal reform movement has always defined as "good government"—namely efficiency, impartiality, honesty, planning, strong executives, no favoritism, model legal codes, and strict enforcement of laws against gambling and vice. The other conception of the public interest . . . derives from the "immigrant ethos." This is the conception of those people who identify with the ward or neighborhood rather than the city "as a whole," who look to politicians for "help" and "favors," who regard gambling and vice as, at worst, a necessary evil, and who are less interested in the efficiency, impartiality, and honesty of local government than in its readiness to confer material benefits of one sort or another upon them.[9]

If this view is correct, a clash of values began in the nineteenth century between immigrants and "Yankees." The residues of that dispute continue today in cities with large and diverse ethnic populations. Historian Richard Hofstadter notes the sharp cleavage between the immigrant ethos and the Yankee ethos:

The Yankee's idea of political action assumed a popular democracy with widespread participation and eager civic interest. To him, politics was the business, the responsibility, the duty of all men. . . . The immigrant, by contrast, coming from autocratic societies with strong feudal traditions, was totally unaccustomed to the active citizen's role. He expected to be acted upon by government, but not to be the political agent himself.[10]

Effects of Local Political Culture

Banfield and Wilson contend that some groups (following from the "Yankee ethos") are more *"public-regarding,"* basing choices about government decisions on some view of the larger public interest or on the welfare of the community at large, whereas others are more *"private-regarding,"* that is, more likely to base their political views on a "what's in it for me and my neighborhood and my family" view. In their study of the Chicago and Cleveland metropolitan areas, they report that wards or communities with higher incomes tend to be more public-regarding and will vote to use their taxes for new hospitals, zoos, and welfare programs from which they themselves will not necessarily benefit. Banfield and Wilson note some specific findings with respect to ethnic groups: In the Cleveland metropolitan area, for example, Poles and Czechs were least likely to be public-regarding. Across the two areas studied, white Anglo-Saxon Protestants, Jews, and, to a lesser extent, blacks were labeled as public-regarding. The authors conclude that different ethnic groups develop a sense of how much a citizen ought to sacrifice for the good of the larger community. The makeup of a community in terms of these groups with distinct cultural views toward public versus private responsibility will have a measurable impact on debate and decisions within that community. There have been many criticisms of this approach;[11] nonetheless, ethos theory illustrates one mechanism by which political culture can affect local politics.

Parallels between Local and State Political Culture

One of the most important points to note here is the clear parallel between local ethos and state political culture. The public-regarding orientation of the Yankee ethos is analogous to the moralistic state culture. They share the imperative to participate and the desire to act on behalf of a larger public interest. And the private-regarding views of those following the immigrant ethos have some similarities to elements of both the individualistic and traditionalistic cultures at the state level. For instance, Catholics are both individualistic and private-regarding. Both individualistic cultures and private-regarding individuals/areas within communities accept private deals, and they devalue political participation and defer to professionals in making political decisions. It is clear that political culture, whether at the state or local level, affects policy.[12]

Effects of Public Opinion

State Level

A variety of studies have explored the public opinion–public policy linkage in the American states. These studies reveal that, in fact, public opinion does affect what state governments do.

Findings of Polls

Gallup polls from the 1930s provide data on three issues: capital punishment, a child labor amendment to the United States Constitution, and allowing female jurors to serve on state trial courts.[13] In each case, even when socioeconomic conditions in the states were accounted for, such as per capita income, public opinion was associated with what states actually decided. As public opinion increasingly favored capital punishment or a child labor amendment or women being allowed on juries, states seemingly listened to the *vox populi*.

Computer Simulations

An estimation of public opinion generated by computer simulation was used to explore the opinion-policy linkages in the following policy areas: right-to-work laws, state aid to parochial schools, teacher unionization, police unionization, the death penalty, civil rights laws, and requirements of permits to purchase firearms.[14] Actual state laws were compared with the simulated public opinion; there was reasonable correspondence. Interestingly, different levels of public support affected different policies. For instance, for states to require gun permits, about 70 percent of the public would have to support that bill; on the other hand, if 36 to 38 percent of a state's citizenry supported a death penalty, that state was apt to enact one. Why the difference? The gun lobby, the National Rifle Association, is strong enough to thwart firearms bills unless public support is overwhelming. On the contrary, few people overtly and forcefully defend the rights of those convicted of capital crimes.

The New York Times *Survey*

The New York Times gathered survey data on all fifty states some years ago. The results can be used to explore whether the degree of liberalism in public opinion is reflected in the extent to which state governments pass liberal social welfare policies.[15] The survey data from all fifty states include questions on self-identified liberal or conservative views.

Next, extent of policy liberalism in each state was ascertained (based on such decisions as educational spending per pupil, Medicaid spending per recipient, Aid to Families with Dependent Children [AFDC] payments, extent of consumer protection laws, liberal criminal justice laws [such as legalization of marijuana, no death penalty, and victim compensation], legalized gambling, approval of the Equal Rights Amendment, and progressivity of the tax structure). Results graphically show that as public opinion becomes more liberal, states pass more liberal legislation. This continues to be so even when one statistically takes into account differences in state residents' incomes and education levels and the state's level of urbanization. The conclusion seems inescapable that public opinion is reflected in states' policy outputs.

Change in Public Opinion

One last study to be mentioned here addresses the question of linkage between citizens and their state governments differently. Page and Shapiro used poll results from 1935 to 1979 and identified questions regarding issues of the day on which public opinion changed greatly.[16] They found 357 such issues. They also gathered data on policy changes enacted by the states over time and then checked the extent to which shifts in people's views corresponded with altered state policies. They found that as public opinion changed, so, too, did states' decisions. Other studies suggest that hot issues of the day generate a stronger role of public opinion in terms of actual state decisions.[17] Also, when nonincremental major changes occur in states' public policies, these changes tend to bring that policy into greater harmony with public opinion.[18]

Local Level

We have seen that public opinion can make a difference in state policymaking. What about at the local level? Here, too, some evidence suggests that government responds to the people. Perhaps the single best example remains Verba and Nie's study of political participation.[19] When people were asked what serious problems faced them, three areas emerged—welfare, income, and education. About a third of the 1967 national sample indicated that they had a welfare problem (i.e., making ends meet), such as poor housing, employment difficulties, or hardships in paying medical bills. If only those who participated in politics most were considered (that is, those who voted, took part in political campaigns, worked with others to try to solve community problems, and so on), only a fifth of the respondents thought that they had a welfare problem. If leaders pay close attention only to those who participate (the *participation strategy*), they tend to underplay the dimensions of problems faced by ordinary people, since they hear from those with the fewest such problems. Similarly, leaders attentive only to those people who are politically active would hear from those people more concerned with education than they would from the public at large. Thus, a distortion can occur. Verba and Nie comment:

It would seem that the leader who used the participation strategy [listening to the desires of those who participate as a guide to what public opinion is on a matter] would be less sensitive to the existence of severe personal economic problems in the society than would the leader who used [public opinion polls]. And the more narrowly he limited the population he observed—if he were attuned only to the most active 5% of the population, for instance—the more such personal economic problems would be obscured. Participation makes some problems more visible and others less so.[20]

Do leaders follow this participation strategy? Overall, the views of leaders are similar to those of the most participant citizens, even taking into account individual officials' social and economic backgrounds (the authors refer to this as "concurrence"). Participation does make a difference; however, it matters who participates. As Verba and Nie conclude: "The fact that the participation input comes from a small and unrepresentative sample makes a difference in how leaders respond. Participation is a powerful mechanism for citizen control, but how that mechanism works depends on who participates."[21] Thus, the better-off end up having the most influence since they are the ones who are most active politically.

However, some cities have instituted explicit schemes to build citizen participation into the local decision-making process. An exploration of the impact of such systems in five cities—Birmingham, Alabama; Dayton, Ohio; Portland, Oregon; San Antonio, Texas; and Saint Paul, Minnesota—suggests that creation of direct channels of communication between citizens and their local leaders (elected officials plus top bureaucrats) can reduce the bias discovered by Verba and Nie.[22]

For instance, Saint Paul, Minnesota, has a system of seventeen district councils, each with specific responsibilities in zoning, housing, and economic development. Each council has a budget to hire staff to develop plans and programs for the area; the council can also fire these employees. District councils have important input into basic decisions. Citizens communicate regularly with their councils and the councils carry out vigorous outreach efforts to communicate with citizens (through, for instance, district newspapers which publicize issues being discussed by the local councils).

Surveys of residents, elected officials, and bureaucrats in cities with participative structures suggest that "concurrence" is higher than in cities without such structures. Thus, conscious efforts to link citizens and their governments appear to produce more responsive local governments.

Political Participation and Behavior

State Political Participation and Behavior

At the state level, two types of participation have drawn great attention: (1) voting and (2) direct democratic mechanisms (initiative, referendum, and recall).

Voting

When Americans think about how they can control their elected representatives, the vote is probably the first thing that comes to mind. Historically, however, the extension of the right to vote to a large portion of the populace has been slow. After the Constitution of the United States went into effect in 1789, the states were allowed great power in defining the electorate for elections to Congress. In the beginning, property restrictions for suffrage were common across the states; so, too, was exclusion of women and blacks (most of whom were slaves). Over time the American voting universe expanded, yet even 100 years ago only about 5 percent of the total population had been granted suffrage.[23]

Constitutional Amendments.   Before the Civil War, freed blacks had suffrage in some states. In 1870, the Fifteenth Amendment provided the right to vote to former slaves, although the southern states used great ingenuity to thwart this right. More recent constitutional amendments have expanded the franchise. The Nineteenth Amendment, approved in 1920, gave women the right to vote. The Twenty-third Amendment (1961) granted residents of the District of Columbia the right to vote for presidential electors. The Twenty-fourth Amendment (1964) outlawed the poll tax (a common means to discourage blacks and poor Americans in general from voting). Finally, the Twenty-sixth Amendment (1971) made eighteen rather than twenty-one the voting age for federal, state, and local elections. In a number of cases, it must be noted, individual states had already previously taken the action later mandated by constitutional amendment.

The Voting Rights Act.   The Voting Rights Act was the most recent major piece of national legislation designed to expand the electorate. The original law was passed in 1965 and has since been amended. The broad contours of this law are outlined below:

1. *Phase I: The triggering mechanism.* The law applies most acutely to those states and counties in which less than half of the potential voters have actually registered to vote or those in which less than half of the voters turned out in the last presidential election.

2. *Phase II: Preclearance.* For those areas thus identified as trouble spots, any change in election laws must be approved by the United States Justice Department. There is, in that sense, a presumption of guilt against the state or local government in which there are ''suspicious'' voter turnout figures; the suspicion is that these low figures are due to discrimination against blacks or others.

3. *Phase III: Evidence.* When evidence of voting discrimination is presented, United States registrars can go into the affected area and register voters themselves, thus bypassing the state or local government's normal registration procedures.

The end result of the Voting Rights Act of 1965 has been a dramatic increase in the number and proportion of black voters turning out in elections, especially in the south. For instance, from 1960 to 1971, the proportion of blacks who had registered to vote in southern states went up from about 29 percent to 58 percent. In terms of results, the Voting Rights Act has been one of the most profoundly effective federal laws passed in recent history.

Factors Shaping Voter Turnout. What factors shape the actual turnout levels in state elections? Voters are more apt to be strong party identifiers, to have higher-prestige occupations, to be more educated, to be older, and to be more informed about and more interested in politics.

Turnout is higher in those states where it is easier to register to vote. For instance, some states have evening registration hours; some states allow mail registration; and some states have voter registration offices that are open at times that vary from day to day during the week. Everything else being equal, turnout will be higher in states with regular daytime plus evening hours for registration.

Turnout is higher for state contests held during a presidential election, when more voters take part in the electoral process, although even at these times people still turn out less often in the southern states.[24] Close elections and greater competition between the two major parties (that is, where the parties fight it out on fairly even terms) serve to increase turnout in state elections.[25]

Direct Democracy

Some states have experimented with facets of direct democracy, such as initiative, referendum, and recall.

Initiative.   Initiative gives a state's citizens the authority to put forward a legislative proposal or constitutional amendment outside the normal route through the state legislature. Citizens, then, are able to propose possible legislation. The specific mechanism is via petition; once a certain number of signatures are obtained, then the proposal must be considered.

Referendum.   This is the process by which citizens vote on a legislative proposal or constitutional amendment, advanced either through initiative or the decision of the state's legislature. In this case the citizens act in a legislative capacity, actually enacting laws.

Recall.   Using this mechanism of direct democracy, citizens are able to remove an elected official from office during the representative's term in office. Normally, a specified number of signatures must appear on a petition; then, once the requisite number is gathered, a special election is held with the question normally in the form: "Should X remain in office?" If a majority of those voting say "nay," the official is removed from office.

Use of Direct Democracy.   Not all states offer these mechanisms of direct democracy to their populace; some states allow none, while other states allow one, two, or all three. New York allows only referendum, for example, and has continually rejected efforts to establish initiative or recall. California allows all three, while Maine provides for initiative and referendum—but not recall.

Criticisms of Direct Democracy.   Some critics maintain that ordinary people are simply too ill-informed to be entrusted with initiative, referendum, and recall. Such skeptics cite findings that signatories of initiative petitions often do not even read the petition or, if they read it, do not understand the nature of the issue(s) involved. A related argument is that voters are unaware of the issues involved in a referendum and cast their ballot without knowledge of the facts. Others claim that "drop-off," or voter fatigue, leads to rather few of the voters who turn out in an election actually bothering to vote for a referendum item. Drop-off refers to the tendency of people to vote for candidates and issues placed at the beginning of the ballot but not to vote through to the end of the ballot. As a result, those voting for referenda may not be typical of the voting universe in a particular election.

A third contention is that minorities may suffer at the hand of a majority of those who vote in a referendum. Indeed, this has sometimes been the case. For instance, in 1910, Oklahomans approved a "grandfather clause." This clause was normally coupled with literacy tests or poll taxes, requirements to vote designed to prevent many blacks from voting. The grandfather clause allowed a person to vote if his grandfather had voted. Since former slaves' grandfathers had not had the franchise, they could not vote if they failed some other requirement. However, many poor whites would still be able to vote—even if they failed the literacy test—because their grandfathers had had the franchise and had voted. Thus, the Oklahoma referendum was part of a process that helped to disenfranchise blacks.

Conclusion.   In the final analysis, data suggest that people do not do that badly when directly involved in decision making. One study concluded, in fact, that "over the long period, the electorate is not likely to do anything more foolish than the legislature is likely to do."[26]

Local Political Participation and Behavior

Types of Local Political Participation

Several types of participation can take place at the local level. Among these are voting, involvement in partisan or campaign-related political activity (attending a local political rally, contributing money to a campaign or candidate or party), communal participation (working with others in one's neighborhood to try to get government to respond to a community problem), and particularistic contacting (contacting local government officials to ask them to take care of an individual problem).

Factors in Participation

Several factors influence extent of political participation within a community: (1) individuals' personal characteristics, (2) political factors, (3) electoral structures, (4) type of community.

Personal Characteristics.   Those who are more apt to take part in elections and a range of other political activities have more education and higher incomes. They may have a sense of group consciousness; for instance, blacks who possess "black consciousness" are much more likely to vote and be politically involved than those without such consciousness. The politically active tend to have more group memberships, have lived in a community for a longer period of time, be Republicans and conservatives, and be older.[27]

Political Factors.   More people turn out to vote in municipal elections when races are tighter. Tighter races generate more interest, and, in turn, greater interest leads people to be more apt to vote. Those who identify with a political party, those who feel that they can influence government, and those with a belief in civic duty (including the obligation to vote) turn out more at the local level.[28]

Electoral Structures.   The very structure of elections can affect turnout rates. If local elections, such as for school board and city council members, feature representatives elected from the entire city ("at-large" elections) rather than from a geographic segment of the community, turnout declines. If elections are nonpartisan (that is, the candidates' party affiliations do not appear on the ballot) or if a city manager, rather than the mayor, serves as day-to-day executive of a city, voter turnout tends to be lower.[29]

Type of Community.   Finally, the type of community in which a person lives affects the probability of his or her being politically active. What might happen to political participation if a person moves from a small country town into a large central city? The *mobilization model* predicts that the person's overall participation is going to increase. Life in a big city, where so many things are happening and where many media compete for people's attention, is bound to be more stimulating than life "in the sticks." The result of the increased stimulation would be greater political activism.

The second model, *decline of community*, predicts the opposite. As people move from rural areas and small towns to the big city, they move from a small society where interactions are face-to-face and where ordinary citizens know their political representatives personally. The large city is an impersonal place. People can become overwhelmed, losing track of whom to contact about problems and feeling distant from the corridors of power. If this view is correct, there would be *less* political activity in large cities than in smaller ones. Which model is right?

The decline of community model appears to best describe political reality. Levels of political participation are highest in isolated villages (that is, those located some distance away from a large city), rural areas, and isolated towns and cities, after taking statistically into account the fact that rural dwellers are poorer and less educated than city dwellers. The least activity occurs in suburbs and cities near a core city. Participation in central cities tends to be lower than in small, isolated communities. Over the past several decades, those communities traditionally fostering participation are becoming less populated, and suburbs are becoming more so.[30]

Negative Trends.   Two key trends depress rates of participation: first, greater adoption of "reformed" political structures and, second, the growth of populations in suburban areas. The likelihood of the citizenry influencing political officials' agendas decreases as political activity is diminished. Thus, decline of community and the continuing move toward reform both reduce participation and, hence, the impact of public opinion on decision makers at the local level. One scholar concludes, "Trends toward nonpartisan elections, atrophied political parties, and lack of electoral competition at the local level suggest that conditions for effective citizen participation in American communities may no longer obtain."[31]

Government Contacts by Citizens

Many citizens believe that bureaucracy is increasingly the most important part of government, because bureaucrats make the decisions that affect people's lives.[32] It is not surprising, then, that much political activity is directed toward bureaucracy. Several different factors affect whether or not citizens make such contacts.

Need.   Evidence suggests that those with greater needs are somewhat more likely to contact agencies.[33]

Awareness.   People must be aware of available programs before they are motivated to contact appropriate agencies and bureaucrats.[34]

Socioeconomic Status.   Since bureaucratic contact is a kind of political behavior, one would expect that higher socioeconomic status might be related to greater contacting behavior. Some evidence supports this expectation, but the picture is not totally clear. Indeed, if need leads to greater contacting, one would not also expect higher income to have the same effect.[35]

Social Involvement.   Those who are more socially involved, probably because they can more easily learn from their involvement about whom to contact if problems arise, seem to contact bureaucrats more often.[36]

It is important to understand who contacts bureaucracies, because these agencies can respond to people's demands. Verba and Nie discovered a high degree of concurrence between participating citizens and the agendas of bureaucrats, suggesting that they respond to the politically active populace.[37] However, as the next chapter shows, not all citizens are equal in generating bureaucratic responsiveness. Nonetheless, it is important to know that bureaucracies, often thought of as beyond citizen influence, do respond at least somewhat to the people.

Protest in the Cities

Protest behavior is exemplified by demonstrations, mass marches, civil disobedience, rent strikes, and violence. The riots in Los Angeles and lesser protests in other cities in 1992 after the Rodney King verdict rendered in Simi Valley indicate that this issue is not merely of historical interest. A local jury, after reviewing a videotape of police officers beating King found the officers not guilty. Outraged blacks in Los Angeles began rioting thereafter.

The Kerner Commission Report testified to the widespread nature of racial protest in the cities in the 1960s. Between 1964 and 1968, there were 329 major hostile outbreaks; 53,000 persons were arrested for riot-related offenses; 8,400 people were injured; at least 220 persons were killed. Unrest continued into the early 1970s in substantial amounts. And, as evidenced by rioting in Miami's Liberty City and other regions in the 1980s and the Los Angeles disturbances in 1992, urban unrest is not just of historical interest.[38] The urban disturbances of the 1960s and early 1970s generated much research on the causes and consequences of protest behavior. Next, the chapter considers: (1) the causes of protest, (2) the types of people who take part in protests, and (3) the political effects of protest.

Causes of Protest.   President Lyndon Johnson established the Advisory Commission on Civil Disorders to explore the causes of the violence in America's cities. According to the commission's report, popularly referred to as the Kerner Commission Report (1968), evidence indicated that very specific racially related grievances were associated with outbreaks of protest. At the highest level of intensity were three grievances in particular: discriminatory police practices, unemployment, and inadequate housing.

1. Discriminatory Police Practices.   The Kerner Report noted that claims of excessive use of force by the police were often implicated in the outbreak of violence. For example, say someone living in a black section of the city was picked up or questioned by the police. Words might be exchanged and the police officers might push the person up against a wall vigorously. Neighbors who saw this scene might spill out into the streets, and rioting could ensue. Often, the immediate predisposing actions seem relatively minor. But the Report pointed out that citizens in black neighborhoods harbored anger against police over long periods of time, and this would boil over after seemingly trivial incidents. The Rodney King incident in Los Angeles indicates that similar underlying hostility over police practices by minority communities continues.

2. Unemployment.   A second primary grievance was unemployment or underemployment (that is, people would want to work but could not get full-time employment or had to accept jobs at a lower level than they were qualified for). Many blacks felt that they were discriminated against in the labor market because of race. This discontent festered and was manifested in some cities by explosive violence.

3. Inadequate Housing.   Blacks complained that their housing was bad, that city governments did not require landlords to live up to housing codes, and that urban renewal programs destroyed serviceable housing for blacks in order to make room for shopping plazas, restaurants, convention centers, domed stadiums, and condominiums.

The Protestors.   Some claimed that protestors were ''riff-raff.'' The evidence, though, is that within communities people who took part in protests were somewhat higher in socioeconomic status than nonprotestors. Both black and white protestors tended to be of higher status than average, belonged to more social groups, and had more education. Those who took part in protests were interested in politics, had high information levels about politics, and were cynical about the political system.[39]

Even those who did not protest in black neighborhoods tended to be supportive of such action. When asked if it was wrong to join in public demonstrations, 62 percent of whites interviewed in Buffalo, New York, in the late 1960s agreed, whereas only 21 percent of black respondents agreed. Is attending protest meetings wrong? Twenty-nine percent of whites said yes, while only 8 percent of blacks said yes. What about joining in a protest march? Fifty-two percent of whites interviewed thought this was wrong, and only 14 percent of the blacks interviewed agreed.[40]

Explanations of protest varied markedly by race. Thirty-eight percent of whites interviewed in Milwaukee said that protest came about because of trouble-making or imitation by some blacks of what they saw on television taking place elsewhere; only 8 percent of the black respondents saw it this way. Fifty-six percent of black respondents said that protest came about because of instrumental reasons (to gain attention for grievances, to win demands, and so on); only 36 percent of whites accepted this explanation. Blacks were much more positive toward protest as a form of political behavior. For instance, 24 percent of the blacks interviewed agreed that ''Demonstrations are better than voting . . . because [they] are about the only way to get your point across.'' Four percent of whites agreed. Another statement on the questionnaire was: ''Demonstrations and mass marches are one good way to get the city government to listen to you.'' Sixty-nine percent of blacks approved of this argument, as compared with only 23 percent of the whites.[41]

Thus, whites and blacks observed the same phenomena, but through almost completely different lenses. Whites tended to deny the legitimacy of black grievances.

The Political Effects of Protest.   According to Feagin and Hahn, three main results of the urban protest of the 1960s and early 1970s were the formation of study commissions, government law enforcement actions, and social and economic reform.[42] Formation of the Kerner Commission was a standard way of trying to ''cool out'' a situation. By setting up commissions, government can delay addressing underlying causes of protest; by the time reports are issued, the impetus behind the protest may have evaporated.

Another consequence of the urban riots was the strengthening of local police forces by the purchase of antiriot equipment and the provision of antiriot police training. Hence, the single most important grievance noted by the Kerner Commission—abusive police practices—was largely ignored.

What of social and economic reform, some of the goals expressed by protestors? At the local level, cities had too few resources to address adequately social and economic problems. Hence, Feagin and Hahn[43] conclude that protests led to better-equipped and better-trained police, consulting fees for social scientists from the Kerner Commission, and not much else.

Another study looked more directly at the effects of protest in generating government responsiveness. Paul Schumaker reports sending questionnaires to forty-six American cities, asking government officials whether or not protests had taken place in their cities, what the behavior of protestors and dissident groups had been, and the extent to which city government had responded to the demands of the protestors.[44] Results indicated that protestors were more likely to be successful if they enlisted the support of certain groups within the city, such as agency officials, the media, the middle class, and elected officials. More militant rhetoric, radical demands, and violent behavior are associated with *reduced* political responsiveness at the local level.

Implications for the Future.   Many of the conditions that sparked urban unrest in the 1960s and early 1970s quite obviously still exist: black males are much more likely to be unemployed than their white counterparts, the black community continues to be critical of police behavior, and quality of life (for instance, in terms of life expectancy or likelihood of imprisonment) is much lower for blacks than whites. Cities are less able to deal with the problems facing them as state and national governments have devolved more responsibility—with less financial aid—downward. People more generally accept protest now as a strategy of political influence.[45] What does all of this portend? Will there be a new wave of protest in the cities? The violence in Los Angeles and elsewhere in 1992 certainly suggests that there is the potential for considerable urban unrest. However, the questions posed above can only be answered with the passage of time.

Americans want their governments to represent them and be accountable to them. They feel that citizens are too often manipulated by their leaders and have little real input into government decisions. The evidence presented in this chapter gives reason for more hope than despair. At both the state and local levels, it appears that elected leaders and even local bureaucrats respond in some manner to the desires of the citizenry. This surely should give comfort to those who see government that is closer to the people as being more responsive to the people.[46]

However, some potential problems were highlighted in this chap-

ter. For one thing, the problems facing poor minorities and the poor in general are not really being addressed squarely by state and local government. And given limited resources and increasing demands upon them (see Chapters 2 and 9 for greater detail), these entities are not likely to come up with any new initiatives. Certainly, the federal government, under conservative administrations, is unlikely to launch any large-scale efforts to address these problems. Even under a Democratic Clinton administration, the constraints on helping state and local governments due to the massive federal budget deficit are considerable. The festering conditions continuing to haunt blacks and other minorities might lead to a recurrence of the urban conflagrations which people thought ended in the 1960s, a possibility underscored by outbreaks of violence in the early 1990s.

A second problem is the continuing existence of traditionalistic cultures, in the sense that these work against democratic involvement of the mass of citizens. Recall that traditionalistic cultures emphasize deference to elites and a limited role for the people, a troubling view for those of other political cultures who believe that "government by the people" should be more than oratory. Finally, demographics may be undercutting responsiveness, as the decline of community model and the expansion of suburban development continue.

Recommended Reading

M. Margaret Conway: *Political Participation in the United States*, 2d ed., Washington, D.C., Congressional Quarterly Press 1991.

Robert S. Erikson, Norman R. Luttbeg, and Kent L. Tedin: *American Public Opinion*, 4th ed., MacMillan, New York, 1991.

Malcolm E. Jewell and David M. Olson: *Political Parties and Elections in American States*, The Dorsey Press, Homewood, Ill., 1989.

Benjamin I. Page and Robert Y. Shapiro: *The Rational Public*, University of Chicago Press, Chicago, 1992.

Sidney Verba and Norman H. Nie: *Participation in America*, Harper & Row, New York, 1972.

CHAPTER 4

Political Parties and
Interest Groups

This chapter examines the role of political parties and interest groups at the state and local levels of government. Both are important means for citizens to have some input into the decision-making process. The chapter begins by considering what parties are, what their three distinct facets are, how they function at the state and local levels, and how they might evolve. Next, it looks at interest groups: how their political activity varies across the states, the tactics they use, and the effect that they have on decision making at the state and local level.

The previous chapter discussed the role of public opinion and political participation in subnational politics. Parties and interest groups are designed to provide additional mechanisms for citizen influence on government. This chapter considers the extent to which that goal is met.

Several themes emerge from this consideration: the demise of party organizations after the heyday of the political machine and the recent revitalization of these organizations; the continuing role of old-fashioned politics even in a media-dominated era; the role of party identification; party competition and its effects on what gov-

ernments do at the state and local level; the impact of interest groups on policy; and the bias built into the interest group system.

Political Parties

Definition of Party

Parties differ from other political organizations, such as interest groups, in that they sponsor candidates and provide recognizable labels that enable citizens to identify candidates as representing some broad policy (or ideological) perspective.

A political party has three distinct facets: party organization, party-in-government, and party-in-the-electorate. The *party organization* refers simply to the actual structure of the party itself, from the local precinct to the state party chair. This is the concrete face of party, its most tangible aspect. *Party-in-government* is the candidates for office under the banner of a party and, much more critically, those who actually serve in government. *Party-in-the-electorate* is the citizenry—and the role of party in their voting behavior.[1]

The Party Organization

Basic Structure

The basic party organizational chart is fairly standard at the state and local level, although the specifics vary widely from state to state.[2] Figure 4.1 illustrates this structure.

The Precinct.   At the base is the precinct, the local voting unit in elections. Each precinct has a designated polling place at which people cast their ballots during elections. Theoretically, each party has a precinct captain (or committeeperson) within each precinct—although moribund party organizations tend to have many precincts with no one staffing them. The precinct committeeperson is responsible for getting out the vote for the party within the precinct and keeping track of what is going on at this level. Precinct committee persons are selected in a variety of ways, one of the more common being by election.

Local Committee.   Next, there is a town or village or district or ward committee (depending upon the locale and the state). Its functions are more diffuse, varying considerably from place to place, but may include recruitment of candidates.

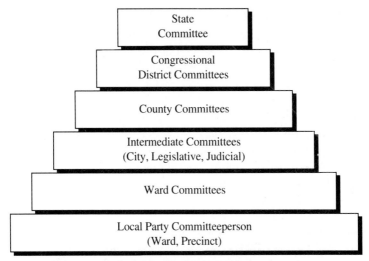

Fig. 4.1   Typical State Party Organizational structure

County Committee.   The apex of the local party organization is the county central committee, headed by the county party chair. Here lies the local party's decision-making center, if the county party is at all well-organized (and, of course, many county parties fail to meet this description). The county organization raises money, sponsors candidates for office, may recruit people to stand for elections, and organizes campaign strategy. Some county committees are very powerful. In the days of the Chicago Democratic machine, the Cook County Democratic Committee was, for all intents and purposes, the Illinois Democratic Party.

State Central Committee.   Sitting atop the various county central committees is the state central committee. Different states select members differently. Normally, the central committee is little more than an honorific post for its members. The most active role is played by the state party chair and his or her staff. This office coordinates the activities of the state party.

Although an organizational chart creates an illusion of a clear hierarchy, from precinct to city to county to state organization, the reality is much messier. The different levels of the party organization often do not mesh together well; there is much room for autonomy at lower levels of the organization. Evidence indicates that officials in various levels of the party organization have only a fuzzy idea of what lower levels are supposed to do.[3]

The Political Machine

The zenith in the party organization's power came with the hey-day of the political "machine."[4] A machine is simply a party organization—but one that has very specific characteristics. Attracting votes was critical for the machine, since if it did not control government it lost the tools needed to maintain people's support, such as money from the public treasury and patronage jobs.

Favors.   The machine operates on the "politics of favoritism," by which it attempts to get votes in return for favors distributed to voters. The machine, in turn, expects recipients of these benefits to vote for the machine's candidates and, in many cases, to proselytize others to support the machine as well. Patronage, a major tool of the machine, refers to public jobs provided to party loyalists as a reward for past party support and an incentive to work for the party and, minimally, to vote for its candidates in the future.

The machine also curried favor, especially with the poor, by providing help when times got tough. If a family were burned out of its home, the party organization might provide temporary housing, supply blankets, and otherwise help the family (albeit minimally) to survive the crisis. Coal might be given to poor families in the winter. Once more, those who received help from the machine were expected to reciprocate and support the machine.

Corruption.   Of course, fraud as a method of getting out the vote was not unknown. The machine would garner extra votes at election time through such tactics as "repeat voting" (the same person would vote several times for the machine's candidates), threats (goons would stand in the polling place and intimidate people to "vote right"—and beat them if they did not), providing derelicts with cheap wine in return for their vote, ghost voting (in which the votes of dead people were counted toward the party), and stuffing the ballot box.

In addition, corruption commonly accompanied machine domination of local politics (and even state politics). The machine's leaders would often engage in practices such as taking kickbacks in return for granting monopolies to electric companies or awarding contracts to construction companies building new roads. Leaders of the machine might dip into the public treasury to bolster their own incomes or to buy the support of voters (a couple of dollars to many citizens was inducement enough) or to purchase goods that could gain the support of the poor (coal, food, blankets, and other necessities, as noted before).

Demands for Reform. The machine was normally simply the county party organization—but an organization that was powerful and that played the politics of favoritism to the hilt. Since the machine could bring in the votes, candidates for office were beholden to the organization. The party organization, through caucuses or conventions, had nearly complete control of the nomination process; hence, the party-in-government in machine areas was subservient to the organization itself.

The middle class was appalled at the excesses of the machine and spearheaded reform efforts to diminish its strength. This, in fact, was one of the centerpieces of the Progressive movement, which began to gain prominence around the turn of the century. Reformers targeted some of the central features of the machine's operation. To attack patronage and, hence, reduce loyalty to the party of citizens who would no longer directly benefit from its largesse in handing out jobs, reformers called for civil service. To get a job, then, an applicant would have to demonstrate merit by "objective" and "scientific" standards—not just support the right party organization. To reduce officeholders' dependence on the machine and to remove the power over nominations from the bosses, reformers demanded the direct primary. To attack the party base of the machine, many reformers urged the development of nonpartisan elections at the local level.

Party Organizational Strength

After the machine's demise as a dominant actor in the early decades of the twentieth century, the party organization lost considerable strength. The direct primary took much of the control over nominations out of the hands of the organizations, thereby increasing the independence of the party-in-government. People began regarding the party organization as irrelevant. Books with titles like *The Party's Over* appeared. Candidates, even at the local level, have increasingly adopted media-oriented campaigns, sought professional consultants rather than the party organization to run their campaigns, and so on. However, recently it has become clear that the story of the party organization's death has been greatly exaggerated. Indeed, it seems that there has been a considerable renaissance in the party organization.

State Trends. At the state level, the following trends are evident, starting in the 1960s: development of a permanent party headquarters (earlier, it was not unusual to find the state party headquarters in the party leader's own home or business office); increasingly professional leadership (a full-time chief executive of the party, with a staff); greater division of labor in the state organization (for instance, hiring fund-raisers, public relations experts, comptrollers, researchers, and so on); expanded budgets; the development of new party programs (from organization-building programs to strengthen the party structure to campaign-oriented programs that provide services to the party's candidates). Overall, Republican party organizations have strengthened more than have their Democratic counterparts. From 1960 to 1970, both parties developed at about the same rate; thereafter, Republicans outpaced Democrats in organizational development.[5]

Local Trends.   At the local level, the trend has also been toward greater organization building. In the late 1970s, as compared with 1964, county parties became much more active in raising money, distributing campaign literature, arranging political events, and organizing registration drives. Data similar to those gathered on state organizations were obtained for local parties. Although the county parties are not as professional or well-organized as their state counterparts, they have become much stronger organizationally over time. At the local level, both major parties have strengthened at about the same pace; there is no gap between Republicans and Democrats as there is with the state parties, although the Republicans are gaining strength organizationally in the south, while local Democratic parties remain rather weak.[6] Generally, as one party increases its local organizational strength, the other also beefs up its organization.

Party Effort

Party effort refers to the work that the party organization puts into elections. The basic question to be answered is, Does party effort make a difference?

The "New Style."   The "new style in campaigning" (or "rent-a-party" as it is sometimes referred to) is a threat to the vitality of state and local party organization, although not so much so as it is at the national level. The use of consultants hired directly by the candidate bypasses the machinery of party. Media-oriented campaigns are very costly and place great pressure on candidates to emphasize fund-raising and to depend upon their consultants. In the process, the candidates are no longer beholden to the party organization (in this sense, the party-in-government becomes more independent of the party organization). The office for which a candidate is running makes a great deal of difference in his or her selected campaign style. The "new style" is more likely to be used in gubernatorial contests than in contests for city council, because it is simply not worth the expense or effort for many candidates for local offices. Instead, party effort is normally expended in the old-fashioned way, through labor-intensive activity designed to make personal contact with the electorate and, in the process, generate more support for the party's candidates.

The "Old Style."   The classical political machine exemplified the old style of campaigning. Here, the precinct captains and other patronage employees would talk with people in their neighborhoods about the "right way" to vote. The precinct captains would try to do favors for residents and take care of problems as well as they could (including providing turkeys for the poor at Thanksgiving, finding patronage jobs for party loyalists who had become unemployed, and so on). George Washington Plunkitt, a ward leader in New York City's Tammany Hall machine around the turn of the century, said that the way to win elections is to "study human nature and act accordin'." The machine would sponsor glee clubs, baseball teams, and boxing clubs, thereby giving neighborhood residents a chance to have fun and show off their skills to the residents of the election district—courtesy of the party organization. In return, the participants would reward the party with a vote for its candidates on election day. Or, to quote Plunkitt:

> If there's a family in my district in want I know it before the charitable societies do, and me and my men are first on the ground. I have a special corps to look up such cases. The consequence is that the poor look up to George W. Plunkitt as a father, come to him in trouble—and don't forget him on election day.[7]

The same process can be discerned in recent political machines, such as the one that existed in Chicago in the 1950s and 1960s under Mayor Richard J. Daley.[8]

Effects of Party Effort.   The preceding observations are largely anecdotal. Fortunately, serious research on party effort has been carried out. Generally, it seems that the party organization can increase its support among voters by between 4 and 10 percent—a sufficient number to make a difference in a close election. One study explored the impact of precinct committeepersons' efforts at getting out the vote in Gary, Indiana. The researchers began by calculating what proportion of the vote in each precinct the Democratic party's candidates should have received based upon the residents' social and economic characteristics. Then they studied the extent to which voter turnout in those precincts in which party workers were most active (in terms of such behavior as hours spent per week on party duties and number of people known to them personally within the precinct) differed from the expected turnout. Good precinct captains were able to generate 4 to 5 percent more support for their party's candidates than were less involved precinct leaders.[9]

As discussed earlier, party organizations at the state and local levels have strengthened in recent decades. Drawing upon data from 626 counties across the United States, one study examines the impact of party organizational strength upon the vote received by the two parties. Overall, the stronger the Democratic party organizations, the greater the proportion of the vote for Democratic candidates. Republican organizations did not demonstrate the same pattern, however. It appears that the major impact of Republican organizational strength is in the more populous areas of the country; in less populated counties, the strength of the organization is unrelated to the vote for Republican candidates. Overall, though, greater party organizational strength in either party can increase a party's share of the vote by about 7 percent.[10]

Thus, although the "new style of campaigning" receives a great deal of attention from the media and is the strategy adopted in many campaigns, at all levels of government, politics the old-fashioned way, by dint of labor expended by members of the party organization on behalf of its slate of candidates, still makes a difference.

Party-in-Government

Party has a considerable impact on the behavior of decision makers at the state and local levels. One reason is that once a party organization has helped an official get elected, he or she feels obliged to work with that organization. In addition, however, there are ideological differences between Democrats and Republicans who hold office. Generally, Republicans are somewhat (or much) more conservative and Democrats more liberal. Their ideological distinctions alone would, then, move party members to vote in opposition to the contending opposition party. Finally, the party's legislative leadership often has great power to discipline rank-and-file members of that party. This, too, can lead to the party's having an effect on decision making.

Legislative

Leadership Structures.   The leadership structure of state legislatures is similar to that of Congress. There are majority leaders and minority leaders; also there is, normally, a speaker of the lower house. In some states, these and other leaders (senior committee chairs, for instance) wield great power over other legislators within their party. In such states, if a member of the legislature crosses the party leadership, that member puts his or her legislative career in some jeopardy. For example, as "punishment," committee assignments may not be what the member would prefer; bills that the member wishes to have passed may be killed; or the member may find that the state party does not help at the next election. In other states, members are much freer to act on their own. Nonetheless, the party leadership is one important factor in the legislative party-in-government.

Voting Behavior.   Once more, there is great variation from state to state, but ordinarily there is a pattern quite like that in the national Congress: a majority of the members of one party voting against a majority of the members of the other party (this is defined as a *party vote*). There is more cohesion among members of each party when the level of competition between the parties is high and when the leaders of both parties are strong. Party voting is also more likely to occur in industrial, urban states.[11]

Executive

Campaigns.   Candidates for governor are likely to engage in the "new style of campaigning." The office is visible and the stakes are high. If candidates can raise enough money to carry it out, the new style makes sense. Candidates have more control over their campaigns and are not dependent on the party organization to get out the vote and carry out various campaign activities. This means that, in many cases, victorious candidates for governor will be less beholden to the party organization, thus reducing the party organization's role in state government.

Governor as Head of Party.   The governor can become the effective head of the state party. First, the governor serves as the elected leader of the entire state, a claim no legislative official can make. This position provides a symbolic mantle to the governor's claim as head of the state's party. If a governor's election has provided a "coattails effect" (that is, when candidates for lower offices pick up support because the "top of the ticket" draws many votes), other elected officials of the governor's party are more likely to accept his or her leadership role. Their jobs are, to some extent, dependent upon the governor's role as leader of the party's electoral ticket. It is also common for governors to have a significant role in selecting state party chairpersons, providing another important tool of party leadership. Of course, party leadership can be undermined by a governor's disinterest in the party machinery or by rampant party factionalism. If the party organization is split, it is difficult for a governor to exercise effective control.

Judicial

For judges, party can be quite relevant. One well-known study demonstrated that Democratic state supreme court judges were more liberal in their decisions on a host of issues as compared to Republican jurists. Thus, their actual votes in cases before them demonstrate a considerable role for party. For instance, Democratic judges were more likely to support claims on behalf of defendants' or criminals' rights than were their Republican colleagues.[12] This tendency is not simply "toeing the party line" as laid down by state party leaders, but results from the fact that Democrats and Republicans differ in their orientation toward many issues.

Party-in-the-Electorate

Party identification is still an important factor shaping citizens' voting decisions. The effect is more pronounced at the state level. One phenomenon much noted is that often Republican candidates for president do very well even while states remain largely controlled by Democratic governors and legislators. "Dual identification" is a part of the answer to this seeming paradox. Apparently, a fairly substantial number of voters identify with the Republican party for national elections (especially for president) and with the Democratic party for state and local elections.[13] Also, increased split-ticket voting has taken place over time—between state and local offices and between national and state offices.[14] Finally, the number of voters who call themselves independent has risen in the electorate at large.[15]

Ideological polarization between the two parties at the state level has a demonstrable effect on citizens' voting behavior. Some states, like California, are highly polarized—the Democrats are very liberal and the Republicans are quite conservative. Other states, such as Alabama, are not very polarized at all, because the Republicans and Democrats do not differ much from one another ideologically. The greater the polarization, the less the split-ticket voting within the state; the less likely voters are to defect from their party identification in order to vote for a candidate of the other party; and the less likely citizens are to switch their votes from one party to the other over the course of two consecutive elections (that is, there is less "volatility" in voting behavior).[16] A study of Ohio's statewide races in 1990 shows that split-ticket voting declines as an individual's party identification strengthens. However, if a candidate of the other party is extremely visible and well known, party identifiers may well split their tickets to vote for the known quantity.[17]

The variables that influence people's voting behavior for legislative, judicial, and executive elections at the state and local level are summarized below.

Gubernatorial Elections

By far the most research has been carried out on gubernatorial elections. Among the factors affecting how people vote in gubernatorial elections are party identification, condition of the state's economy, presidential popularity, and incumbency.

Party Identification. Party identification is clearly important. One study reports that between 1972 and 1982, about 80 percent of those who identified with a party voted for that party's candidate for governor.[18]

Economic Conditions. A state's economy also has an impact. A Louisiana study found that if people thought that the economy was in good shape, they were more positive toward the incumbent governor; if they felt negatively about the economy, they judged the incumbent harshly.[19] Presumably, evaluations of the state economy would translate into votes on election day, although the condition of the national economy has little direct effect on a person's vote for governor.[20] Also, state tax increases during a governor's tenure do not normally strongly predict the incumbent's defeat; in fact, tax increases seem to have rather little effect on governors' chances for reelection.[21]

Presidential Popularity.   The popularity of the president seems to have at least a modest effect on gubernatorial elections. Some evidence suggests that Independent voters are likely to use their votes for governor as a referendum on the president's performance, voting against the candidate of the president's party if they rate the president negatively and for the gubernatorial candidate if they approve of the president's performance. There is, however, not much effect of presidential approval among party identifiers.[22]

Incumbency.   Incumbent governors are returned to office 70 to 80 percent of the time when they seek reelection—not as high a figure as for members of the United States House of Representatives, for instance, but still clearly significant. As more and more state constitutions have been changed to allow governors to seek reelection, the incumbency effect becomes more important across the American states.[23]

State Legislative Elections

Central forces affecting electoral outcomes for legislative races include party identification, incumbency, presidential approval, "coattails," and economic conditions.

Party Identification.   Party identification strongly affects people's votes; as their ties to party wane, so, too, does the effect of party identification on legislative elections at the state and local levels.

Incumbency.   Incumbency is powerful, too; roughly 90 percent of those who seek reelection are successful.[24]

Presidential Approval.   Approval of the president is especially significant among independent voters. If they happen to disapprove of the job the president is doing, they will vote against state and local legislators of his party (and vice versa).[25] For party identifiers, presidential approval is not as potent a force.

"Coattails."   Sometimes there are "coattails effects." Candidates for the presidency, the governorship, and the U.S. Senate all can affect state legislative races—and all three are roughly equal in their effect on such campaigns.[26] Campbell finds that from 1944 to 1984, presidents tended to pick up 3.2 percent more seats in state legislatures in presidential election years. However, effects of coattails may disappear in those nonpresidential years in which state elections take place. The president's party tends to lose 7.3 percent of seats representing their party in midterm state legislative elections.[27]

Economic Conditions.   More generally, it appears that if the president is thought to be responsible for negative changes in the national economy, his party will lose seats in state legislative contests; just so, if voters see the president as being responsible for gains in the national economy, his party picks up additional state legislative seats.[28] However, changes in a person's actual personal income have little impact on his or her voting for state legislatures.[29]

State Judicial Elections

One common method of selecting state judges is through elections (more detail is provided on methods of judicial selection in Chapter 8). In some states their campaigns are partisan; in other states, non-partisan elections are mandated for state judgeships. Key variables influencing citizens' support for judicial candidates include party identification and incumbency.

Party Identification.   Citizens tend to vote for judicial candidates of their own party, just as they do with other state and local elective offices.

Incumbency.   Incumbent judicial candidates do very well; when voters stray from their partisan identification, they usually shift to support incumbents of the other party. Rarely are state judges voted out of office.

Local Elections

Party can be very important in local elections. Without party as a cue, voters, who are often not very knowledgeable about individual candidates for office, use every shred of information off the ballot that they can in order to cast a vote, including such nonrelevant factors as ethnicity of surname, gender of candidate, whether or not the candidate uses a nickname, and the position of the candidate's name on the ballot.[30] Where party is on the ballot, it serves as a key cue for voters in deciding whom to support in the polling place.

One study focused on Cincinnati, Ohio, to assess factors in vote choice for city council elections in a nonpartisan city in which ballots do not provide information about candidates' party. The study found that the strongest correlates of voting for a candidate for city council include having a political following, receiving the leading newspaper's support through an official endorsement, and obtaining party endorsements. Central to having a political following are being an incumbent, spending a lot of money on the campaign, and having considerable prior campaign experience. It is worth noting, though, that even in a nonpartisan city, party can still play a role.[31] A second study of nonpartisan elections in Lexington, Kentucky, concluded that the most important factors affecting voters' choices in local elections included agreement with candidates' ideologies, personal qualities of the candidate, extent to which voters thought that a candidate cared about the election district, and simple name recognition of the candidate.[32]

Party Competition

What is the relevance of political party competition for policy making within states? A series of studies points to the impact that party can have on state politics.

The Basic Argument: V. O. Key

V. O. Key long ago noted that when two parties competed, the "outs" would promise benefits to the people as a way of enticing their support, and the "ins" would pass legislation to help voters in order to generate support from those same voters. Thus, two competing state parties would tend to lead to greater government activism, more government services, and so on. However, in states where only one party had a reasonable chance of winning, that party had much less incentive to promise anything, since the voters had no real alternative.[33]

Effects of Party Competition

Currently, the evidence is somewhat mixed on the effects of party competition. However, competition does affect some policies, as discussed below.

State Expenditures. The first major research effort testing Key's observation studied the extent to which party competition in the states affected welfare expenditures.[34] Party competition was measured by acquiring information across the states about the percentage of seats held by each party within the state legislature, the percentage of time that each party controlled the governorship and legislatures, and the percentage of time with divided control of state offices (e.g., a Democratic governor and Republican legislature). The evidence suggested that the greater the extent of party competition (that is, the more evenly the two parties fight it out), the more liberal the social welfare policies (expenditures on education, Aid to Families with Dependent Children, etc.). However, the effects of the states' wealth on expenditures was found to be greater than the impact of party competition. That is, wealthier states can afford a more liberal social welfare program; party has little to do with it. The extraordinary interpretation given this study by some political scientists was that politics played no role at all in determining the level of welfare expenditures.

Such a shaky conclusion could not last long. And, indeed, more recent studies have made clear that both party competition *and* the wealth of a state have real effects on what state governments do. For instance, the most significant setup for a party's success in getting legislation passed seems to be when one party controls both legislative branches (or the one branch in Nebraska's unicameral legislature) and the governorship—and the other party is a vigorous, active, competitive minority. When the control of a state legislature changes from Republican to Democratic, there is a greater-than-average increase in education and welfare spending and less-than-average increases in other areas. Democratic control of the state legislature is also related to increases in civil rights legislation and proenvironment policies. Republican control is related to greater spending on highways and heavier financial burdens on local government.[35]

Taxes.   Party competition has implications for certain aspects of taxation policy. For instance, as party competition increases within a state, the odds increase that the system will be progressive (taxes will hit the richest hardest).[36] There is also a somewhat greater likelihood that states will provide some relief from property taxes when party competition is greater.[37]

Welfare Programs.   It appears that the impact of party competition has changed over time, becoming greater in recent years. In the period 1914 to 1929, social and economic characteristics of states were the dominant factors shaping how liberal a state's policies were. Party competition was a rather weak factor. However, from the period spanning 1930 to 1945, to the period spanning 1946 to 1963, party competition became an increasingly strong force in predicting how liberal a state's policies would be. Of course, socioeconomic conditions of the states remained significant factors shaping welfare policy.[38] More recent evidence suggests that increased party competition still produces an increase in annual benefit levels in welfare programs.[39]

Corruption.   In a somewhat different vein, it is interesting to observe that states with high levels of party competition tend to have fewer successful charges of corruption pursued against public officials. It appears that the possibility of a corruption-related scandal's sending votes and support to the other party reduces the temptation for public officials to engage in improper actions.[40]

AIDS Policy.   States have adopted many different AIDS policies. Among these are laws forbidding discrimination against people with AIDS and mandatory AIDS education in the schools. One study shows that greater party competition is related to antidiscrimination laws and mandatory AIDS education in public schools.[41]

Education Policy.   Party competition has an effect on education policy, too. Increasing party competition is related to how much states pay for education in terms of dollars spent per citizen.[42]

Civil Rights Legislation.   Among laws passed to advance civil rights in the American states are open housing acts, laws to revoke old laws against mixed marriage, and public accommodation laws. One of the factors associated with more liberal civil rights policies is greater party competition.[43]

Measurement of Party Competition

How is party competition measured? The most common approach is probably the Ranney Index, composed of three different measures: percentage of votes won by each party for the governorship and both houses of the state legislature, duration of success (the length of time each party has controlled the governorship and state legislature), and frequency of divided control (percentage of the time that control of the governorship and state legislature is divided between the parties). A score of 1.00 means total Democratic control of state politics and a score of .00 signifies Republican hegemony. A score of .50 reflects "perfect" two-party competition, where the parties fight it out on even grounds. Examples of states where Republicans tend to dominate include Wyoming, New Hampshire, Colorado, Idaho, South Dakota, and Utah. Democrats are more dominant in states such as Mississippi, Hawaii, Georgia, Maryland, Massachusetts, Maine, and California. More or less balanced two-party competition occurs in states such as Illinois, New York, Oregon, Connecticut, Pennsylvania, and Indiana, among others.[44]

Trends in Party Competition

Several observations are worth noting. First, party competition has increased in recent years. The overall index of party competition was .64 (indicating a Democratic advantage) from 1974 to 1980; it declined to .60 from 1981 to 1988, indicating a modest increase in competitiveness across the states. One factor affecting the index is the greater vitality of the Republican party in the south, where, formerly, only the Democratic party had any reasonable expectation of winning elections. However, if we look further back into the past, the Democrats still look strong. From 1946 to 1962, the Ranney Index was .54; it moved up to .59 from 1962 to 1973. Thus, the Democratic party continues to do well at the state level when compared with earlier historical periods. Will Republicans continue the recent trend toward greater representation in state legislatures? That is an issue to watch in the coming years.

Factors in Party Competition

What factors shape the extent of party competition within a state? Higher educational level seems to be the single most important predictor of increased party competition, followed by strength of party organizations (if both parties' state organizations are strong, party competition will increase), larger population size, and greater proportions of citizens who own their own homes. Reduced competition within a state due to Democratic dominance is most evident where black populations are large, in more populous states, and in states that are poorer and have a less-educated citizenry.[45]

Unfortunately, there has been little analogous research at the local level. However, one would expect the same general features to appear in that context as well as at the state level. This is an area that calls for more research activity.

Interest Groups

Interest groups are organizations of people who share a common interest or interests and engage in political activities to advance those interests by influencing government policy. In this section, we explore variations in interest group politics across the states, tactics used by these groups at the state and local levels, and the effects of interest groups on state and local decision making.

Variations in Interest Group Politics

Level of Activity

First, certain groups are active across many of the American states as well as in local governments. A massive effort to catalog which groups were active how often in which states shows that some groups are nearly ubiquitous (present in over forty states) and continually active. Among these are individual business corporations, local government units (such as the mayors of a state's larger cities), business trade associations, banks, insurance companies, public employee unions, farmers' organizations, labor unions, and environmentalists.[46] At the local level, the more generally active types of interest groups include business groups, labor unions, public employees, neighborhood groups, and public officials.[47]

Amount of Power

Some groups are more powerful than others. At the state level, the top five in reputed influence are school teachers' organizations (especially NEA, the National Education Association), general business organizations (such as the state chamber of commerce), bankers' associations, manufacturers, and traditional labor organizations (such as the AFL-CIO).[48] At the local level, the most powerful groups appear to be civic groups (like the League of Women Voters), business groups (such as the chamber of commerce), professional organizations (such as the local bar association), political organizations, and public employees.[49]

Influence within States

Interest groups are more powerful actors in some areas than in others. Thomas and Hrebenar classify the fifty states in terms of the overall impact of interest groups in each.[50] States in the *dominant* category feature interest groups as a major influence in state politics. States in which interest groups are dominant include Alabama, Florida, New Mexico, and West Virginia. States termed *complementary* are those in which interest groups are important but must share the political stage with other actors, especially political parties; examples are Colorado, Illinois, Michigan, and New York. Finally, a state deemed *subordinate* is one in which interest groups are clearly subordinate to other political actors. To illustrate, Connecticut, Minnesota, and Vermont tend to lean toward the subordinate column (however, very few states feature interest groups that are actually weak). In most of the states, interest groups are major partners in the political process; that is, most states are considered dominant or dominant-complementary states, in which groups are important but other actors have some significant role.

Tactics of Interest Groups

Two key weapons used by interest groups are lobbying and election activities.

Lobbying

The best-known tactic of interest groups is probably lobbying, that is, communication with government officials to try to influence their decisions. Research suggests that lobbyists adopt a series of roles to advance their groups' interests,[51] as outlined below.

Contact Person.   This type of lobbyist defines his or her proper role as establishing face-to-face relationships with legislators or their aides. Then, when issues important to the group come before the legislative body, the contact person presents the group's case directly to the legislator. Since persuasive communication and information can be important influences on a legislator's behavior, this can be a potent form of lobbying. In fact, lobbyists rate it as the preferred method of influencing legislators. However, most do not adopt the role of intensive cultivation of contacts because time constraints make it impractical.

Campaign Organizer.   The person taking on this role sees as his or her primary task the organization of grass-roots pressure to try to muscle legislators. This task could include generating letter-writing campaigns. For instance, the National Rifle Association has been very successful in lobbying state legislatures when gun control legislation is introduced. Massive letter-writing campaigns against the bill ensue, and usually legislators back off.

Informant.   The informant believes that the best way to affect policy is to provide testimony at committee hearings, sometimes without even taking a specific position on the issue at hand. The idea is to let the "facts speak for themselves." If the information is strong enough, that may itself sway some legislators.

Watchdog.   Here, the lobbyist acts as a distant early warning system for the interest group. He or she keeps a close eye on the legislative calendar, follows the pending legislation, and, when a bill associated with the interest group appears, informs the group so that the organization itself can mobilize and develop a strategy to advance its interests. The lobbyist's task is done when the word is passed along to the group.

Strategist.   This person is sometimes referred to as the "lobbyists' lobbyist.'' It takes great skill to play this role. This person essentially tries to knit together a coalition of interest groups in support of or opposition to some proposed legislation. In essence, the strategist acts as a field marshall, orchestrating a complex web of groups to maximize their influence in the decision-making process, amplifying their voices more than would be possible if they acted on their own in an uncoordinated fashion. The strategist is a rather rare type of lobbyist at the state or local level.

Degree of Effectiveness of Different Tactics. Lobbyists rank contacting and informing (for example, personal presentation of ideas to legislators, presenting research results, and testifying at hearings) as the most effective tactics. Next most effective is communicating through intermediaries, for example, by organizing letter-writing campaigns from constituents. Lobbyists rate as least effective such activities as entertaining legislators, making campaign contributions (discussed below), and outright bribery.[52]

Election Activities and Campaign Contributions

Interest groups often become involved in the electoral process. One of the most obvious methods is via campaign contributions to candidates or to parties. Political action committees (PACs) are major vehicles for this activity. An organization, for instance, a labor union or an industry, will set up a PAC to gather funds from individuals and spend these on behalf of candidates or parties to advance the interests of the sponsoring group. In the states, most PAC contributions go to incumbent state legislators. PACs are also generous to legislative leaders in the states, since they are often the pivotal figures in decision making within legislative bodies.[53]

Alternatively, groups can provide volunteers to candidates for office to help in the myriad activities associated with elections, from stuffing envelopes with campaign literature to phoning people on election day to remind them to vote. PACs will sometimes develop and air or print their own campaign advertising for candidates.

Policy Impact of Interest Groups

Hrebenar and Thomas's research, mentioned in earlier paragraphs, provides part of the answer to the question about the extent to which interest groups affect state policy. They find that interest groups are extremely potent actors in quite a few of the American states, with the strongest groups usually representing business, professions, and organized labor.

State Level

Other evidence also points to the potential power of interest groups. The stronger the business-related interest groups in a state, the greater the likelihood of state government developing policies that benefit business interests (such as state-sponsored industrial development agencies, state loans to business for equipment purchases, the opening of university research and development facilities to business, tax exemptions for corporations, and so on).[54]

Evidence that interest groups are able to advance their interests has some important implications. If the economist Mancur Olson is correct, strong interest group systems work to the long-range detriment of the American states. He claims that over time, as groups press government to adopt laws that will protect their interests, the effects of these laws will produce a drag on the state economy, since these protections insulate industries from market forces. This renders them less efficient and, in the long run, produces a more stagnant state economy.[55] However, the evidence is mixed on the extent to which Olson's theory holds true.[56]

Our own statistical analysis of information from the fifty states suggests that interest groups are stronger in states with lower income levels, nonmoralistic political cultures, and less liberal political ideology. Those states characterized as having stronger overall interest groups seem to exert a lower tax effort (that is, the tax load is relatively low) and to play a lesser role in developing industrial policy.

Local Level

At the local level, there is evidence that interest groups can affect bureaucratic decision making. The groups that are most effective in this undertaking include professional, civic, and business groups. Groups that make moderate demands rather than those urging radical action tend to be more influential. Poor people and racial groups tend to be the least likely to get bureaucracy to respond to their demands.[57]

Finally, there is an interesting relationship between interest group strength and the vitality of political parties at the local level. In those cities with ''reformed'' political structures (such as nonpartisan elections, council manager form of government, and the like), parties tend to be less influential and interest groups tend to be more powerful. Parties are powerful in 83 percent of unreformed cities, but only in 41 percent of those that can be classified as reformed.[58]

Political parties and interest groups are two actors in state and local politics that serve United States citizens as intermediaries to government. Parties and interest groups give voice to the views of state and local residents and can affect government policies. While the voices of some citizens are rendered louder than others (for instance, business and professional interests seem to carry more weight in interest group politics), parties and groups help magnify the voices of ordinary citizens. Thus, they are two important institutions affecting what subnational governments actually do.

Recommended Reading

John F. Bibby: *Politics, Parties, and Elections in America,* Nelson-Hall, Chicago, 1987.

Ronald J. Hrebenar and Ruth K. Scott: *Interest Group Politics in America,* Prentice-Hall, Englewood Cliffs, N.J., 1990.

Malcolm, E. Jewell and David M.Olson: *Political Parties and Elections in American States,* 3rd ed., Dorsey Press, Chicago, 1988.

Frank Sorauf and Paul Allen Beck: *Party Politics in America,* 7th ed., HarperCollins, New York, 1992.

Clive S. Thomas and Ronald J. Hrebenar: "Interest Groups in the States," in Virginia Gray, Herbert Jacob, and Robert Albritton, eds., *Politics in the American States*, 5th ed., Scott, Foresman, Glenview, Ill., 1990.

CHAPTER 5

State and Local Legislatures

The legislature has been called the people's branch of government. Historically, citizens have seen the legislature as the most representative and most responsive branch of government—whether at the state, national, or local level. However, a great deal of variation exists in how legislative bodies work across both the states and their local governments. The principal differences are in degree of power, level of professionalism, extent of staffing, and dependence on other political actors for information.

Several key points are highlighted in this chapter. The increasing professionalization of legislatures, especially in the states, is one of the most significant, for it has made these bodies more effective and more responsive. A clearly related issue is the extent to which legislatures are truly representative. The chapter also evaluates the structure and the functions of legislatures at the state and local levels and portrays the kinds of real people who work as legislators.

First, though, some historical perspective is useful. In prerevolutionary America, representative assemblies were often in conflict with colonial governors appointed by the king of England. The royal governors had great powers on paper, such as the veto, the power to dissolve assemblies at will, power over the judiciary, and the ability to make church appointments. The colonists saw the governors' legal powers as both threatening their freedoms and violating the (unwritten) English constitution. The representative assemblies were their bulwarks against executive tyranny.

Now, while the governors had great paper powers, their authority was much less in actual practice. For example, they did not have the power of the purse. The elected legislatures normally exercised this power. Hence, governors had to work with the colonists' representatives. Moreover, it was difficult for the governors to exercise power by getting their cronies elected to the legislature because of the practice of "instructing" representatives. Constituents in many places would literally tell their representatives how to vote, thus reducing the ability of the governor to control affairs within the assemblies.

The result was frequent confrontation between colonial governors and legislatures. Mutual distrust grew.[1] After the Revolution, Americans feared reestablishing strong executives. They had come to view elected legislatures as the best defenders of their freedom. From the beginning, then, Americans have looked to their legislatures as the most naturally representative bodies in government.

In addition, the colonists were steeped in the Lockean liberal tradition, with a belief in limited government (government constrained in the extent of power granted it), separation of powers (legislative, executive, and judicial powers in different hands), and government by consent of the governed. These different values, as read through the lenses of English radical Whig thinkers whose ideas were embraced by the colonies, also supported the notion of a strong and independent legislature.[2] When the colonists feared that their independent legislatures were being assaulted by royal governors, the distrust increased even further.

Structure of Legislatures

The Structure of State Legislatures

State legislatures are bicameral; that is, they have two houses, just as Congress does. (There is one exception: Nebraska has a unicameral body.) One house is usually designated as an "upper" house (often, but not always, called a Senate), which has fewer members, and the other as a "lower" house, often referred to as a House of Representatives, although other terms are used as well (such as "State Assembly" in New York).

Leadership

Normally, each house in a bicameral legislature has a clearly defined presiding officer. In the lower body, the person is most often dubbed the Speaker. The Speaker comes from the party controlling the House of Representatives (or whatever term is used for the lower house) and in many states has great powers. He or she refers bills to committee, recognizes speakers, and presides during deliberations. The Speaker can be a dominant figure and extremely powerful. There may be other important majority party figures as well, such as a majority leader. The minority party also normally has a member in a formal leadership position (usually referred to as the minority leader).

In the upper house, the presiding officer is often technically the lieutenant governor (in over half of the states). However, the day-to-day leader is the majority party's leader (commonly called the majority leader). In some states, the leaders of the two houses are the key players in the whole state legislature. In New York State, for instance, the Speaker of the Assembly (the lower house) and the Senate's majority leader are central actors in budget making. If they disagree, it is very difficult to get things done. The work of the legislature comes to a standstill until the two legislative leaders and other top officials within the two bodies can come to an agreement. The pattern varies, of course, from state to state. Nonetheless, the state legislative leaders can wield much more power than can their counterparts in the U.S. House of Representatives and Senate.

Committees

The nature of committee systems is quite different from state to state and across localities. Overall, such committees are not usually as powerful as are their counterparts in the national Congress. For one thing, legislative leaders tend to have a great deal of power, and the committees are disadvantaged as a result. Also, there is more turnover in the states than in Congress so that committee membership is unstable. This reduces the ability of these committees to generate many members who become experts on the subjects addressed by the committee and whose expertise then becomes a source of power within the legislature. More detail on the work of committees appears below, in the discussion of how bills become laws in the American states.

Professionalization

Professionalization of legislatures has several components: salary, staffing, and support services. Not surprisingly, the higher the salary, the more staff assistance, and the more ancillary services available to an office, the more attractive that office is. Hence, so the argument goes, better-qualified candidates are likely to run for office, thereby raising the ''quality'' of the people who serve as elected representatives. Over time, there has been a movement from part-time legislators who are political amateurs to those who wish to make a career of legislative politics.

Salaries.   Salaries of state legislators have steadily increased over time. Data from 1990 show that salaries range from no pay (in Kentucky and Montana, for example) to $57,500 per year (in New York). In many states, legislators used to see their jobs as part-time—and received part-time pay. The result was government by amateurs; those seriously interested in political careers would not find the legislature a particularly attractive starting point. Now, state legislators appear to be, on the average, more ''ambitious.'' (Those desiring to stay in a specific office exhibit *static* ambition; those wishing to move on to higher office have *progressive* ambition.) Increasing salaries undoubtedly make the positions more desirable.

Staffing.   Level of staffing varies widely across the states. In 1979, Delaware, North Dakota, Vermont, and Wyoming had only between 1 and 25 professional staff members for the entire legislative branch; on the other hand, New York and California had between 701 and 800.[3] But the trend has been toward employment of more professional staffers. Twenty to thirty years ago, state legislators received relatively little staff assistance. Now, more and more states have provided for increased staff help. These employees may be assigned to individual legislators, to committees, to the party leaders in the legislative body, and to the body as a whole. For example, some state legislatures have special staff whose task is to draft bills at the request of members of the legislature; others have staff available to carry out research for individual members.

Staffers of members of legislatures include administrative aides (who help organize the legislator's office), legislative aides (who help to develop legislation), clerical staff (to keep records and control the flow of paper), and caseworkers (to deal with constituents' problems). The change over time has been dramatic and has led to an increasing number of state legislatures becoming more proficient. Evidence indicates that more professional legislatures are less dependent on the governor during the budgetary process, more able to oversee bureaucracy, less dependent on the governor and interest groups for information, and less dependent on the governor and interest groups for initiating new policies.[4] In short, legislatures are more capable bodies now than they were thirty years ago.

There is another side to the story, though. The question has arisen as to whether these unelected officials are gaining too much power. The more staff help available, evidence suggests, the more elected officials come to depend upon staffers in their day-to-day work and the more they rely on staff for ideas about new legislation.[5] As noted in Chapter 4, interest groups can be dominant figures in state politics; however, the more professional legislatures are less likely to be influenced by these interest groups because they have their own sources of information and expertise—their staffs. But while staff members are usually responsible to their employees in the legislature, they are not accountable to the electorate, leading to the growing fear that staff is becoming a more powerful influence on politics than is the public.

Effects of Professionalism. The more professional legislatures tend to have more bills introduced each session, suggesting greater activism as one result of longer sessions and higher salaries.[6]

Professionalism has an impact on actual decisions, too. One early study discovered considerable variation across the states in terms of legislators' pay, money allocated for staff help, and services (such as research or bill drafting) made available to members. Further examination demonstrated that those states with more professional legislatures tend to spend more on assistance to the elderly, Aid to Families with Dependent Children, aid to the blind and handicapped, teachers' salaries, and unemployment compensation.[7] More recent evidence, from our own analysis of the relationship between professionalism and welfare liberalism, shows that the same pattern continues. On the other hand, the more professional legislatures are somewhat less apt to spend large sums of money on highways.[8]

Professionalism has other effects on policy. Chapter 4 showed that party competition can sometimes affect policy choices made by states. Legislative professionalism appears to mediate this relationship. In those states with more professional legislatures, the linkage between party competition and policy is fairly robust: greater competition leads to more liberal policies (in terms of amount of money spent on social programs). However, in states with less professional legislatures, party competition has only a modest impact on state policies.[9]

A comparative politics data base we developed showed the following effects of legislative professionalism on actual policy outputs:

1. Greater activism in developing a state industrial policy. The more professional state legislatures appear to pass legislation to create a better business environment to produce more jobs. Among policies thus adopted include state grants and loans to businesses and customized training of employees for businesses.

2. Greater tax effort. The more professional legislatures tend to make a greater effort to raise revenues through taxes. Doubtless, this is related to their greater policy activism and liberalism.

Process of Legislation

The common process by which a bill becomes a law is quite similar to that at the national level. Figure 5.1 illustrates, using a kind of "average" representation of the processes employed throughout the American states.

A bill is drafted and then submitted to one or the other house by a legislator. The actual drafter of the bill might be legislative staff, executive agencies, lobbyists, individual members, or even a special bill-drafting service. However, the bill—whatever its source—is introduced by a member of the legislature. The draft may go to the clerk of the house into which it is to be introduced or to the presiding officer of the body. It is then referred to a committee. Legislative leaders who are unsympathetic to a bill might refer it to a committee that they are sure would be hostile to the legislative proposal. In this manner, the proposal might die a quiet death and never get to the floor of the legislature.

Much of the legislative work actually takes place in committee, although the extent to which this is the case varies from state to state. Committee members go over proposals to refine them; compromises may be hammered out. To get input from experts and other interested parties, hearings are held so that a variety of views will be heard on the proposed legislation. Committees may handle a bill in several ways: they can ignore it, they can "kill" it by explicitly deciding not to send it to the larger legislature, they can report it to the larger chamber unchanged (a rare occurrence), or they can revise the bill (by "marking up" or rewriting it) to send it to the floor. If the bill is written up in a form that is acceptable to the committee, it then goes to the floor of the body.

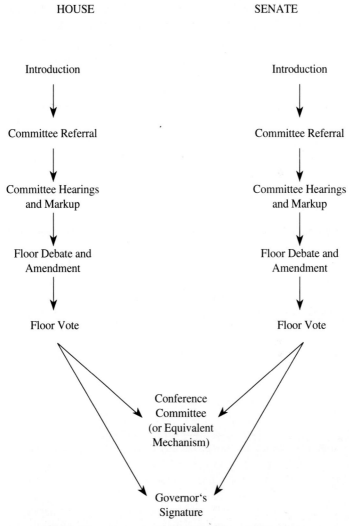

Figure 5.1 How a Bill Becomes a Law in the States

Debate then takes place. Amendments from the floor may be considered and either accepted or rejected. Finally, the actual vote on the bill by the members of the whole body ensues. If the bill is passed in a different form in the two houses, then a conference committee (consisting of members from each body) usually meets to try to iron out the differences, or the house of origin (where the bill was first introduced) approves the changes in the bill suggested by the other body. When approved by both houses, the bill moves to the governor for signature (or veto). Governors' vetoes are rather rare and, when wielded, are seldom overridden. For instance, in the 1986–1987 sessions of the state legislatures, only 1 percent of the bills were vetoed, and of these only about 4 percent were overridden.[10]

As at the national level, the process is conservative, in that it is normally easier to kill a bill than to move it through the variety of hurdles existing at each stage. The legislative process is an obstacle course that renders change difficult.

The Structure of Local Legislatures

Types of Local Government

Local municipal legislative bodies, normally called city councils (although the term varies; for instance, in Chicago it is called the Board of Aldermen), are almost always unicameral. Three different organizational schemes are mayor-council, commission, and council-manager. There are, of course, other local legislatures as well, from school boards, to town (or township) boards, to county legislatures,[11] but these are not considered here.

Mayor-Council Systems.   The structure of mayor-council systems is analogous to the structure of state government, with the mayor serving as the executive branch and the city council as the legislative branch. Two types exist. The *weak mayor* variety features a mayor and a city council; however, the heads of agencies do not report directly to the mayor. They may be directly elected by citizens or appointed jointly by the mayor and council or even by the council alone. This supposedly weakens the mayor's ability to administer programs on a day-to-day basis, since agency heads do not have to look solely to the mayor for leadership. The *strong mayor* system has both a mayor and a council; in this case, however, department heads are appointed by and report directly to the mayor. Theoretically, this makes accountability easier to determine, since it is clear exactly who reports to whom. The mayor, in addition, normally has a veto, which enhances his or her power (weak mayors tend not to have veto power). The legislature has a louder voice in cities with weak mayors than in those with strong mayors.

Commission System.   In the commission form, there is no independently elected mayor. Members of the commission select one of their number to serve as mayor, but the main role is simply to preside over council meetings. In addition, the mayor would normally administer one of the departments, just as do the other commissioners. Each elected councillor is assigned a specific department to head—that is, one member of the commission will supervise public works on a day-to-day basis, another will be responsible for parks and recreation, a third will oversee public safety, and so on. Over the past fifty years or so, the number of municipalities with the commission form of government has declined.

Council-Manager System.   In council-manager government, the voters elect a council which, in turn, hires a professional manager to "run" city government on a day-to-day basis. Department heads report to the manager, who acts as top administrator. The theory upon which this approach is based is that government is most efficiently run when elected officials make basic policy decisions and then turn over administering the city to a professional administrator, the "manager." Managers can be hired and fired at the whim of a council, although that does not usually happen. Managers are most likely to be at risk when city politics is characterized by different factions fighting for power. More detail on the city manager appears in Chapter 6.

Correlates of Type of Structure

Cities of more than a million people tend to adopt the mayor-council system, as do cities of 500,000 to 1 million people; communities ranging from 250,000 to 500,000 people are likely to select either a mayor-council or a council-manager framework; and populations of 25,000 to 250,000 seem to generate a greater likelihood of council-manager governments. For all communities over 2,500 in population, the mayor-council system is the most prevalent, with the council-manager system not too far behind. Other forms (including town meetings) are far less numerous. Chapter 6 discusses this in more detail. Whatever the format selected, the city council is, on paper, a primary policy-making body, although, as noted below, many councils have little independent power.

Leadership in Local Legislatures

City councils tend to be small. The average size is perhaps five to seven persons, although councils can run up to fifty or more members (as in Chicago). Most of the time, councillors have four-year terms, although two-year terms are not uncommon. Many councils elect a majority leader to structure the business of the council. However, city councils are often junior partners to the mayor (or city manager) and may be relatively weak bodies. Because most councils are small, there is little likelihood of their having a meaningful committee structure.

Professionalism in Local Legislatures

Local legislative bodies are much less professional than are those at the state level. Most councils have no staff help at all; councillors tend to be poorly paid (if they are paid at all). Hence, turnover is fairly high compared to turnover in the state legislatures. Lack of staffing makes local councils less able to challenge the executive branch or interest groups for real power. Simply put, part-time amateur city councillors do not have the expertise of the executive branch and its bureaucracy, and without their own independent staff they cannot compete. Thus, they come to depend upon the mayor and his or her bureaucracy for basic information. In fact, city councils are often little more than rubber stamps.[12]

As one source puts it:

> It is the chief executive who controls the organizational resources that make general policy leadership possible. The chief executive's office prepares the budget, manages finances, and arranges credit. The typical city council has little staff even to oversee these activities. . . .
>
> With most sustained policy efforts growing out of dealings among the heads of large organizations, mayors are able to take their place in these activities. . . . Local legislators, on the other hand, have few bargaining chips for participation in such negotiations.[13]

Functions of Legislatures

The two basic legislative functions are lawmaking and representation. Narrower, more specific functions are budget making, impeachment, casework, and oversight.

Lawmaking

The primary manifest function of a legislature is, of course, to make laws. Legislators themselves define this as their single most important task and report spending more time on it than on any other aspect of their job.[14] Although at the local level, councillors are often dependent on the mayor, they still have the legal responsibility for making laws.

State legislators have been found to adopt one of several roles relating to legislation, two of the more important of which are lawmaker and broker. Some legislators define themselves as *lawmakers*; they focus on policy issues and have clearcut policy goals. Their major motivation is to enact legislation. Such representatives tend to be responsible for a significant proportion of legislation passed at the state level.[15] Other legislators see themselves as *brokers*, trying to work out compromises and make deals with other legislators and with various interest groups in order to advance legislative goals. Many state legislators think of themselves as brokers.[16]

Representation

Legislative bodies are normally seen as the most representative bodies in government. That is, because of the number of their elected representatives, they are in a better position to speak for and on behalf of people throughout a state or a locality. Representatives may adopt one of three roles to define their behavior with respect to their constituencies. The role of *delegate* may be adopted by a representative who believes that he or she has been selected to serve as a mouthpiece for the electorate; as far as practicable, the representative attempts to carry out the wishes of those who voted him or her into office. On the other hand, some representatives view themselves as *trustees*, chosen to serve in order to carry out their own independent, mature judgment—even if that puts them in opposition with a majority of their constituents. Finally, there is the *politico*, who may on occasion behave as a delegate and at other times as a trustee. In four state legislatures studied over thirty years ago, most of the officials defined themselves as trustees. The electoral situation affects which role legislators choose. In more competitive districts (that is, where the winner has to work hard to gain a rather close victory), winners are more likely to select the delegate orientation. This disposition suggests that they wish to please the voters and respond to them in order to remain in office.[17]

Among city councils, trustees seem to predominate, according to a study of the San Francisco Bay area city councils of the late 1960s. About 60 percent of the councillors interviewed for the study defined themselves as trustees; only 18 percent considered themselves to be delegates.[18] This is also the case with state legislators, where the majority seem to define themselves as trustees.[19] Interestingly enough, the general American public seems to prefer delegates, representatives who will do their bidding.[20]

Some evidence at the local council level from the Buffalo, New York, area indicates that two factors enhance "policy responsiveness," that is, the extent to which local legislators will vote on matters before the council in a manner consistent with public desires. The two factors are value of housing and extent of competition in elections. That is, wealthier communities seemed to put greater pressure on councillors to follow their will, and tighter races appear to render local legislators more responsive to public opinion on policy matters.[21]

Budget Making

The legislature shares budget-making responsibilities with the governor and with state agencies. Though much in this process has changed over time, there are some important continuities in the role of legislative bodies. The standard pattern appears to be that agencies request budget increases from the previous year, governors trim requests (ranging from 4 percent cuts to 28 percent cuts, on average), and legislatures tend to go along with governors. When comparisons are made, legislatures seem to have a greater role in the budgetary process in the 1980s and 1990s than they did in the 1960s,[22] exactly as one would expect given their increasing professionalism.

Impeachment

Almost all the states provide for removal of public officials by impeachment. The standard process has proceedings begin in the state House of Representatives with trial in the Senate. A two-thirds vote is the usual margin needed to remove a governor. Only a few governors have ever been impeached and successfully removed from office. The most recent example is Governor Evan Mecham of Arizona. In 1988, the Arizona House voted to try him and the state Senate convicted him, whereupon he was forced from office. Most states also provide for removal of judges by impeachment. Grounds for impeachment would normally be serious crimes or malfeasance in office.

Casework

Casework refers to taking care of constituents' problems. It is sometimes referred to as "errand running" behavior, or constituency service. Over the past several decades, errand running has become an increasingly salient part of a legislator's job. Evidence collected on four state legislatures, including Ohio's, in the 1950s indicates that only about 27 percent of those interviewed spontaneously said that errand running or casework was an important part of their job.[23] Another study published twenty-five years later, based on interviews with Ohio state legislators, found that almost half consider casework an important part of what they should do as representatives. About 90 percent of those interviewed claimed that casework was important— even if it was not part of their definition of a representative's responsibility.[24] Why the change? Perhaps the greater professionalism of legislatures plays an important role here. As legislative seats have become more attractive to seek and hold, tactics designed to keep an office, such as errand running, become more widespread. When legislators were less career-oriented, the extraordinary effort needed for successful errand running as a means of reelection would not have seemed worthwhile.

Casework is even important at the local level. Local legislators in the Buffalo, New York, metropolitan area report that this is a high priority for them. Greater electoral competition seems to be one driving force leading these elected officials to carry out casework.[25] In local councils where elected officials do not care so much about getting reelected or advancing to higher office, casework is much less of a priority.[26] Thus, a supply of ambitious legislators may be important in rendering elected officials more responsive to the citizenry's needs.[27]

Oversight

Oversight refers to legislative review of the executive branch's performance, with special emphasis on keeping an eye on how agencies function. Legislative bodies are deemed the appropriate functionaries to oversee the activities of the executive bureaucracy in order to ensure that laws are being faithfully carried out in a manner consistent with legislative intent. Legislators themselves, though, normally put rather little effort into oversight,[28] although this appears to be changing somewhat. One reason for legislators' lack of zeal is that oversight has little electoral payoff; that is, voters do not primarily reward legislators for keeping a close eye on agencies. Another is that oversight can take a great deal of time and effort. Of course, agencies are usually delighted if the legislature exercises little oversight; bureaucrats often see oversight as "meddling" in their domain.

Tools of oversight include committee review of agency actions and sunset laws. For instance, an agriculture committee would hold hearings where Agriculture Department officials would speak to how their agency is administering agricultural legislation. Sunset laws involve legislation calling for a specific life span, such as seven years, for an agency and its programs. At the end of that time, the agency will expire unless it can provide convincing evidence that it ought to continue.

The Legislators: Who Are They?

Characteristics

State legislators are not typical of the general population of a state. Legislators are predominantly white, male, professional, relatively well off financially, and from politically active families. Lawyers appear to be the single most prevalent occupational group appearing in state legislatures.[29] However, as state legislatures have become more professional, the hegemony of lawyers has declined. In fact, the full-time occupation of many state legislatures is now "state legislator"![30]

Over the past several years, increasing percentages of women and blacks have appeared among the ranks of state legislators, but there are far fewer female and nonwhite legislators serving than one would expect, given their representation in the general population. The same is true of Hispanics and Asian-Americans. As of 1990, the percentage of women serving in state legislatures ranged from a low of 2.1 percent in Louisiana to a high of 33.3 percent in Vermont.[31] What factors affect the number of women elected to a state legislature? Over a period of time, those states having the highest numbers of female legislators are more liberal and have moralistic political cultures. The states least likely to be conducive for increasing female representation are the traditionalistic southern states.[32]

State legislators tend to mirror the religious and ethnic structure of their election districts (for example, Catholic districts will elect Catholic legislators), have deep roots in their constituencies, and are more educated than the general public.[33]

State legislators tend to be ambitious. Most had demonstrated considerable political interest before getting involved in electoral politics. Many were active in their political parties and had served in various offices at the local level.[34] Studies of legislators in Iowa and South Carolina suggest that state legislators exhibit a characteristic psychological profile: self-confident, gregarious (extroverted), and tolerant of others.[35]

At the local legislative level, councillors are not typical of the citizenry either, although the bias is much less dramatic than at the state level.[36] The study of the San Francisco Bay area mentioned earlier in this chapter was carried out in 1966 and 1967 and included interviews with 435 councillors. The study showed that incumbents tended to be male, white, and white-collar and were more educated and more affluent than the population in general. People entering city councils have long been politically interested.[37] A more recent International City Management Association survey reports that about 87 percent of local legislators are male, around 4 percent are black, and about 1 percent are Hispanic. Dominant occupations included business executives (31 percent), business employees (24 percent), retired people (12 percent), teachers (8 percent), and other professionals (8 percent).[38]

Effectiveness

One key concern for the public is how "effective" their representatives are, that is, how well do they perform within their respective legislative chambers? Can they get laws passed? Are they able to influence others? One definition of effectiveness is the reputation that legislators develop in the eyes of their peers, lobbyists, and journalists. A study of North Carolina state legislators finds the following to be the most consistent predictors of effectiveness: greater number of terms served, number of bills introduced into the legislature, serving in a formal leadership position, being a committee chair, and being in the majority party. In turn, reputation for effectiveness increases the odds that a legislator will win by large margins, attain leadership positions, and successfully shepherd bills through the legislative maze to be enacted into law. In short, effective legislators produce.[39] An alternative means of measuring effectiveness is in terms of legislative success—actually getting bills passed by the legislative body. A study of Missouri state legislators finds that being a member of the majority party, holding a leadership position, and having greater seniority in the chamber are the three most important factors shaping effectiveness.[40]

This finding becomes especially significant in light of the movement in several states to limit the number of terms that a state legislator can serve. Many feel that legislators who serve many terms ''lose touch'' with their constitutents and cease being responsive to them. Thus, voters in a number of states have moved to put limits on how many consecutive terms a legislator might serve. To illustrate: limits enacted vary from six consecutive years in the lower house (in California) up to twelve years (Oklahoma).[41]

What are the consequences? One often alleged result is the apparent tradeoff between greater accountability and effectiveness. Since serving longer makes a representative more effective, term limits will likely reduce the pool of effective legislators, perhaps rendering legislatures less able to compete with governors and the bureaucracy.[42] The irony is that limiting terms may not necessarily render legislators any more responsive to the desires of constituents. Some evidence suggests that those who decide to serve for rather short periods of time before leaving service may be less apt to be responsive to the voters' desires. Since they cannot serve long careers, fewer ambitious persons run for office and make a commitment to public service. One correlate of the desire to stay in office, as noted before, is greater casework and attention to the desires of the electorate—a tactic used by ambitious legislators to curry favor with the voters. By weeding out those would-be candidates who have greater ambition, it is conceivable that term limits may cause legislators, as a group, to actually become less responsive.[43] However, such speculation must await the test of time before the true consequences can be known.

How They Get There

Legislative elections were discussed in Chapter 4. However, other processes related to elections are important for understanding how people come to sit in the legislative body, at both the state and local level. Among these are reapportionment, gerrymandering, and at-large versus ward elections.

Reapportionment

The U.S. Constitution requires that the national government carry out a census every ten years. Because of landmark Supreme Court decisions, the census sets into motion redrawing legislative district lines in the states if population patterns have changed significantly. Before 1962, the number of people in state legislative districts varied enormously. Thus, for instance, one district with 20,000 people might elect one member to the state House and another district with 100,000 persons might also elect just one legislator. The end result is that people in the first district are "overrepresented": each vote in their district is equal to about five votes in the more populous district. *Baker v. Carr*, a 1962 U.S. Supreme Court decision, suggested that citizens who felt deprived could challenge such districting in the federal courts as a violation of the equal protection clause of the Constitution. Shortly thereafter, in *Reynolds v. Sims* (1964), the Supreme Court actually declared such *malapportionment* to be unconstitutional, violating people's Fourteenth Amendment right to equal protection of the laws. The opinion stated that as nearly as possible, the standard should be that "one man's vote should be equal to another's." That is, each election district for a particular legislative body ought to have very close to the same number of people in it as every other district.

Population shifts may occur within the states. What in 1980 was a well-apportioned legislature might, in 1990, no longer fit the "one person-one vote" standard. Hence, the Supreme Court requires reapportionment if the decennial census shows that significant population shifts have taken place. Then, the state legislature must draw up a new set of district lines comporting with constitutional guidelines. This can lead to gerrymandering, discussed next. Recasting lines can be quite painful. Often, legislatures have no recourse but to redraw lines in such a way that two incumbents have to face off against one another to determine which one will represent a consolidated district; and, if a legislator has created problems for party leaders, he or she may be punished by finding district lines redrawn so that that the incumbent will almost surely be defeated in the next election.

Gerrymandering

Gerrymandering means drawing election district lines in such a way as to benefit candidates of one party over those of another. At the state level, when one political party controls both houses of the legislature as well as the governorship, that party is in a good position to draw district lines to maximize its odds of doing very well at the next election. For instance, Indiana's drawing of House district lines in 1981 was crafted to help Republicans. Democratic votes were concentrated in a few Indianapolis districts and scattered among Republican votes in Fort Wayne. The end result: Democrats won only 43 percent of the House seats in the following election—even though they won 52 percent of the popular vote for the House.[44]

At-Large versus District (Ward) Elections

In cities, elections for the local legislature usually take place in one of two ways. In *at-large elections*, voters from throughout the city vote for the members of the council. In *district elections*, the city is divided into a series of geographically distinct election districts, each selecting one representative. The type of approach adopted makes a difference; for example, at-large elections tend to reduce the number of representatives who are black if blacks are in a minority within the city. In such a situation, nonblacks can simply vote for a set of nonblack candidates and swamp the vote of those who support blacks for office. One study suggests that in at-large elections blacks receive only 46 percent of the representation that one would expect given their proportion in the population. In cities which have district elections, that figure increases to 77 percent.[45] However, it appears that at-large elections more recently have come to have a less disproportionate impact on black candidates' odds of success.[46]

One additional option, which has been adopted rather infrequently, is *cumulative voting*. In this system each voter is given a number of votes equal to the number of persons who can be elected to office. For instance, if a local city council has seven seats to fill, each voter may cast seven votes. These can be allocated among candidates as the voter wishes—including seven votes for one candidate or one vote for each of seven candidates. The largest city in the recent past to experiment with such a system is Peoria, Illinois.

Data from Alamogordo, New Mexico, suggest that citizens can learn how to use the system, seem to understand it well, and even come to like the process. One significant side effect is that racial minorities, such as Hispanics and blacks, can gain representation on councils by concentrating their cumulative votes on candidates representing their ethnic or racial group. In this manner, representation of minorities is actually enhanced.[47]

Why They Leave

The trend in state legislatures has been toward less turnover, as representatives decide to make careers there. As mentioned previously, people serve more terms than they used to because the positions are much more attractive as professionalization has increased across the states.[48] But, then, what accounts for voluntary departure from state legislatures?

One study of voluntary departure focused on Arkansas. Between 1968 and 1980, 157 legislators departed; most of those who left did so of their own volition. Of the 157 who left, 64 were either defeated in elections or died; 93 chose to quit. Of these, 37 ran for higher office and their departure from the state legislature allowed them to pursue progressive ambitions. The most common reasons advanced by the others were personal situations, including divorce proceedings, age, health problems, frustration over accomplishing little during their careers, and financial problems. Most important were family problems: unhappy marriages, threatened divorces, guilt about long absences from younger children, and concern over teenagers.[49]

At the local level, fewer representatives choose to make a career of politics. "Volunteerism," serving out of a sense of civic duty, is fairly common. A "volunteer" is often appointed to fill out the term of a legislator who has resigned. Such volunteers may serve for a term or two or three, and then, when they believe that they have met their civic duty, they resign (or choose not to run for reelection). In the former instance, the volunteer is replaced by someone appointed to serve out the term.[50] This situation is doubtless common to many local legislatures throughout the country, although it is also clear that many who serve at the local level are not purely volunteers but serve out of a complex mix of policy incentives and personal motives. Furthermore, many who serve are enthusiastic about becoming involved in the hurly-burly of local politics.[51]

Factors in Decision Making

How do state and local legislators make up their minds about how they will vote? A number of distinct factors play a role. One means of discerning how legislators make their decisions is to ask with whom they consult. According to one study, in order of descending importance, the sources of information, guidance, and cues include friends in the legislature, legislative specialists (that is, legislators who are experts in a particular area, such as pending legislation on agricultural education services for farmers), interest groups, committee chairs or the ranking minority member, a legislator of the same party from the same or a nearby district, a party leader in the legislature, a bureaucrat who is a specialist in the issue area under consideration, legislators of both parties from the same or neighboring districts, party leaders from outside the legislature, the governor, and—dead last—constituents.[52] When asked which sources of written information are most important, state legislators ranked the following as most important: fellow legislators, executive agencies, interest groups, and other governments (for example, written communications from local governments). Once more, public input seems to be rather unimportant.[53] Nonetheless, recall the discussion in Chapter 3 of the importance of public opinion on state and local policy. Although representatives may not consult their constituents, they do appear to take their views quite seriously.

Several factors affecting decision making call for more detailed treatment here. Among them are representational role, the governor, interest groups, norms, and the constituency.

Representational Role

Those state legislators who define themselves as delegates are more likely to focus their attention on their district than on the state at large in making decisions, indicating that they are responsive to what they see as the desires of their constituency.[54] Furthermore, delegate-type legislators are more likely to try to reflect constituency opinions in their voting.[55] However, representatives who try to vote as their constituents want may have inaccurate perceptions of the voters' opinions. One study even found that self-defined delegates were less accurate in their perceptions of public opinion than were trustees.[56]

At the local level, councilors with static ambitions (those who want to stay in the office) seem responsive to the public's policy preferences.[57] Volunteers, on the other hand, are much less likely to claim to follow constituency opinion when making decisions.[58]

The Governor

The governor of a state has several bases of influence over the legislature. As noted in Chapter 4, he or she may have had a powerful coattails effect during elections, in which case representatives may feel that they owe the governor their loyalty and support. After all, without the coattails vote, they would not be in office.

Most governors can threaten to veto legislation that they do not like. As of 1991, forty-three states provided the chief executive with the *item veto*, which allows the governor to veto a specific part of a law rather than the whole law itself.[59] The threat of a veto is a potent weapon, since few vetoes are overridden by the legislature.[60]

Much of a governor's ability to influence decisions is based on the ability to persuade (see Chapter 6). Of course, there are tools available to make the persuasion more effective. Governors can do favors for members of the legislature; they can campaign on their behalf (or choose not to do so). They might appoint to office people recommended by a legislator—or they might ignore that suggestion. The more professional the legislature, the better able members will be to resist the demands of a governor.

Lobbyists

The more professional legislatures are more independent of lobbyists, as noted earlier. In that sense, interest groups may have less direct power in state legislative corridors than they had previously. Professionalism has reduced the dependence of state legislators on lobbyists for information and legislative initiatives. Nonetheless, interest groups remain important voices, as noted in Chapter 4. Furthermore, their ability to contribute to legislators' reelection bids gives them considerable leverage. The irony is that as legislatures have become more professional, individual representatives are more desirous of staying in office. To stay in office, they must campaign continuously (doing errand running and campaign fund-raising). With respect to campaign financing, interest groups can be very useful; hence, lobbyists representing interest groups continue to have power, although the nature of their relationship with legislators has changed.[61]

Interest groups may be even more influential at the local level, since local legislators have less staff assistance to provide information and since local lobbyists are often civic leaders. Indeed, some observers have pointed out that many councillors may feel that they represent specific interests, such as realtors, builders and contractors, or labor unions.[62]

Norms

Norms are standards of what a person ought to do in a particular role. In the legislature, norms are the informal, unwritten rules of the game that a representative is expected to follow. One study suggests several basic norms undergirding the operation of state legislatures: performance of obligations (be honest, keep your word, do what you are supposed to do), reciprocity (if someone does a favor for you, you are obliged to return that favor later), and interpersonal courtesy. Persistent violation of norms has an effect on the decision-making process. State legislators who consistently defy norms may find that their proposed legislation is obstructed—whether by the party leadership or by others.[63]

The Constituency

Chapter 3 summarized evidence that the public's opinions seem to affect decision making in state and local government. There was also evidence given that political participation could make a difference.

Legislatures are the most representative branches of government at the state and local levels. Over time, state legislatures have become more capable and more professional, but in the process they may have become somewhat less responsive to the people. As state legislatures have become more bureaucratized, they have lost some of their flavor as the voice of the people. Will efforts to limit the number of terms change this? That is one current issue that should be closely observed.

Local legislatures still manifest some of the atmosphere of amateur politics. However, as a result, they are unable to compete effectively for power with the mayor (or city manager) who, through the executive bureaucracy, has access to much more information than a council usually does. Thus, because they are less bureaucratized, city councils are also less able to function effectively on their own.

Recommended Reading

Heinz Eulau and Kenneth Prewitt: *Labyrinths of Democracy*, Bobbs-Merrill, Indianapolis, 1973.

Heinz Eulau and John C. Wahlke, eds.: *The Politics of Representation*, Sage, Beverly Hills, Calif., 1978.

Malcolm E. Jewell and Samuel C. Patterson: *The Legislative Process in the United States*, 4th ed., Random House, New York, 1986.

Samuel C. Patterson: "State Legislators and the Legislatures," in Virginia Gray, Herbert Jacob, and Robert Albritton, eds., *Politics in the American States*, 5th ed., Scott, Foresman, Glenview, Ill., 1990.

Alan Rosenthal: *Legislative Life*, Harper & Row, New York, 1981.

John C. Wahlke, Heinz Eulau, William Buchanan, and LeRoy C. Ferguson: *The Legislative System*, John Wiley, New York, 1962.

CHAPTER 6

Governors, Mayors, and Professional Managers

This chapter examines the changing roles of state governors, city mayors and city managers, and county executives and county managers. State and local governments employ more workers, spend more money, and provide more services today than ever before. Two hundred years ago, the United States was a lightly populated, primarily rural society whose self-sufficient people required minimal government services, valued close control of their elected officials, and feared strong executive authority. With rapid industrialization in the late nineteenth century, Americans became increasingly urban, interdependent, and in need of more government services. Although the center of governmental power in the United States has shifted to Washington, D.C., in the last sixty years, state and local governments play a large role in implementing programs mandated and financed by the federal government.

As state and local governments are called upon to assume greater responsibility, they have given governors and mayors more power. States and localities require executives strong enough to provide leadership, to monitor bureaucratic performance, and to coordinate service delivery. Also, in order to provide services more efficiently, state and local governments are building a work force of politically neutral, technically expert civil servants.

The Dimensions of State and Local Government

The federal government relies heavily upon state and local governments to implement programs. Some of the taxes it collects are transferred to state and local governments to support highway construction, health care delivery, and many other services. Per capita state and local government expenditures (in constant 1982 dollars) have more than doubled since 1959. Federal employment has increased by 35 percent, state and local employment by over 200 percent.[1] State and local government expenditures have grown more rapidly than direct federal government spending over the last thirty years.

The largest state and local governments amass resources and provide services that are comparable to those provided by the largest American industrial corporations, as Table 6.1 shows. In 1989, twenty-eight states had budgets larger than the annual sales of the 100 top-ranked corporations on the *Fortune 500* list. New York City, where city and county functions are combined, dwarfs all other city budgets at $26.3 billion in 1989. More representative are Los Angeles, Chicago, Philadelphia and Washington DC, where annual budgets average $2.65 billion—larger than one half of the *Fortune* 500 companies. State and local government is big business.

The responsibilities of a state governor are comparable to those of

Table 6.1   Annual Sales of Large Industrial Corporations and Budgets of Largest States, 1990 ($ Billions)

Corporation	*Fortune 500* Rank	Annual Sales	State	Rank	Annual Budget
General Motors	1	$126.9	California	1	$39.1
General Electric	5	$ 55.3	New York	2	$29.4
Texaco	10	$ 32.4	Texas	3	$13.2
Boeing	15	$ 20.3	Illinois	4	$12.3
Dow Chemical	20	$ 17.7	New Jersey	5	$11.8
McDonnell Douglas	25	$ 15.0	Pennsylvania	6	$11.7
Phillips Petroleum	30	$ 12.5	Ohio	7	$11.4

Sources: *Fortune*, April 23, 1990; *Statistical Abstract of the United States, 1990*, p. 285.

the chief executive officer (CEO) of a larger industrial corporation. Both set basic priorities for the state or corporation. Both supervise and coordinate the efforts of many thousands of employees. Both oversee provision of services worth billions of dollars.

Yet governors and mayors are not paid salaries commensurate with their responsibilities. In 1990, the average governor and large city mayor earned about $75,000 per year.[2] Individuals in the private sector who manage similar numbers of people and administer similar budgets typically earn much more. The chairman of IBM received a salary of $841,000 in 1987, ten times the $85,000 George Deukmejian earned as governor of California. Many people with successful business or professional careers would have to take a pay cut in order to serve as a governor or mayor, and for this reason many capable people choose not to run for office.[3]

Factors in State and Local Government Growth

Several factors help to explain the dramatic growth of state and local government activity.

Population Increase

Americans have increased in number, from 151 million in 1950 to 250 million in 1991. Contributing to this increase are high birth rates that occurred in the 1950s; increases in average life expectancy from sixty-eight years in 1950 to seventy-five years in 1990; and higher rates of immigration to over 600,000 per year in recent years, primarily from Latin America and Asia. More people require the services, for example, of more teachers, more police officers, and more social workers.

Migration to Cities

Americans have continued to move from farms and small towns to the cities. In 1840, 90 percent of Americans lived on the farm; by 1990, 77 percent lived in cities and towns. America's largest metropolis in 1840, New York, had 369,000 persons; by 1860 its population had reached the million mark, and after the wave of European immigration from 1890 to 1920, New York's population was 5.6 million. Chicago, a frontier town in 1840 with 4,000 inhabitants, swelled to 112,000 in just twenty years. By 1920, Chicago was a major railroad and agricultural marketing center with a population of 2.5 million.[4]

City populations require levels of government service that self-sufficient farm populations do not. Police and courts supplement family and church in regulating social relations among crowded, culturally diverse people. Bridges, roads, and mass transit systems must be built to move workers between home and job. Large quantities of garbage must be collected and disposed of in the city. In times of economic depression, the self-sufficient farmer could still feed and clothe his family and heat the family home, but the urban worker who lost his job needed help from the community.

Rise of Public Expectations

As incomes increased over the past forty years, Americans came to expect more and better state and local government services. Local residents began to take it for granted that their state and local governments would provide a better education for their children, maintain an adequate system of highways and bridges, collect the garbage regularly, supply clean drinking water to each household and carry sewage away from it, provide police and fire protection, and make health care available to needy citizens.

Citizens have also come to value amenities such as zoos and museums, parks and recreation areas, and well-maintained and clearly sign-posted highways, which improve the quality of life.

Federal and State Mandates

Federal Mandates

The federal government in Washington, D.C., has pressured states and localities to provide higher levels of service than these governments would do if left to their own devices. The federal government tells states, for example, that public facilities must be accessible to the handicapped, that a plan to reduce air pollution must be put in place, that school buses must conform to federal safety standards. As mentioned in previous chapters, states have no choice but to conform to these mandates, which often are costly and politically controversial. Moreover, states often complain that federal funds provided to pay for the mandate are inadequate.

Federal Funding

Often the federal government dangles a carrot before the states and localities, offering to pay a percentage of the cost of a program to encourage a high service level. For example, the U.S. Department of Health and Human Services will pay a percentage of health care costs, and the Environmental Protection Agency will pay most of a city's sewage treatment plant construction costs. The federal grant system make federal dollars virtually free in the eyes of state officials and state voters.

Federal aid to state and local governments peaked in 1978 at $78 billion, which constituted 28 percent of the total revenues of those governments. By 1988, federal funds had slipped to 17 percent of state and local budgets as President Ronald Reagan fought to reduce federal involvement in state and local affairs (see Chapter 2).

President Reagan thought that if states had to choose between providing more government services and raising taxes or reducing government services and lowering taxes, states would choose the latter course. He was wrong. During the 1980s, state spending nearly doubled, from $258 billion in 1980 to $525 billion in 1989. This increase amounted to 3.5 percent per year after inflation. The number of state employees reached an all-time high.[5]

State Mandates

Just as the federal government imposes mandates on the states, so too do the states impose mandates on city and county governments to spend money on particular programs. For example, the state gives financial assistance to local school districts and requires that they hire reading specialists, provide bus transportation, and teach a foreign language. The state sets standards for drinking water purity and for landfill design and construction to which local communities must conform, often at considerable expense. A common complaint of city and county officials is that state officials impose costly mandates without providing adequate funding.

The Evolution of Executive Power

Popular control of executive power is a strong American political tradition. In the seventeenth and early eighteenth centuries, many colonists fled England to escape from royal religious and political persecution. Their descendants suffered under colonial governors who were appointed by and served the king rather than the people he ruled. The American colonists who cried "No taxation without representation" in 1776 felt they were being denied the fundamental rights of Englishmen. The U.S. Constitution was crafted in 1787 to minimize the possibility that president or governor might suspend the rights and privileges of free citizens.[6] During much of the nineteenth century, the American states were largely governed by popularly elected legislatures, and the powers of governors were closely checked.

The City Mayor

In 1860, about 20 percent of Americans lived in cities, the largest cities being the commercial centers of New York, Philadelphia, and Boston. Weak mayors shared power with other independently elected officials and council members. By the turn of the century, 18 million European immigrants had settled in the growing cities to work in the mills and factories. In 1900, 40 percent of Americans lived in urban areas, and Chicago, Cleveland, and Pittsburgh were now major industrial cities. City government was called upon to build more roads and bridges, provide water and sewer facilities, and make rudimentary social services available. In the process, the structure of urban government was transformed.

Political Machines

The first generations of city mayors were generally economically successful Protestant males with close ties to the business community. The dominant ethic was that government should provide only those services necessary to support a free enterprise economy. For example, investment in physical infrastructure was more highly regarded than investment in social services during the early industrial era. The priorities of these mayors were to build up the infrastructure which industry required and to maintain law and order.[7]

As the new immigrants made the transition from their lives as farmers in Europe to being urban factory workers, the background and priorities of mayors changed. By the end of the nineteenth century, political entrepreneurs, primarily Irish Catholics, had taken control of city politics. They built effective political machines, largely within the Democratic party.[8]

Urban machine politicians would find jobs for loyal supporters or give them a $20 bill. They might help a son in trouble with the law, arrange a doctor's appointment for a sick child, or take care of a traffic ticket. A machine politician might invite the faithful to a Labor Day party, provide the prize at the church raffle, and buy a round of drinks at the local tavern. By sending Christmas cards, giving gifts to newly married sons or daughters, or attending family funerals, the machine politician accorded recognition and respect to immigrant workers. In exchange, recipients were expected to vote for the machine candidates in local elections.

These "bosses," such as Boss William Tweed in New York City, James Curley in Boston, and James Pendergast in Kansas City, were adept at the art of investing their political resources so that every dollar expended and every appointment made increased their political power. At the base of the political machine was the neighborhood ward, where the alderman bestowed material resources and recognition in exchange for the votes of his neighborhood constitutents. A ward leader's success depended on being able to reward one's friends and punish one's enemies.

A potential boss needed to forge coalitions among various ward leaders. In exchange for a ward leader's support, a potential boss would promise the right to distribute patronage jobs or a lucrative appointment to a board or a judgeship. Once loyal supporters were placed in prominent offices, their decisions further enhanced the power of the boss. The successful boss could control the behavior of key decision makers, even if they were independently elected. Immigrant voters benefited from the machine, but so did business interests who needed favorable rulings from judges beholden to the machine or city contracts to build bridges or water systems.[9]

Inefficiency of Political Machines

The political machines did help ease the burdens of the new immigrants, and the bosses did begin the job of coordinating urban resources to build roads, bridges, and water systems. But, in doing so, they exacted a considerable price in corruption and inefficiency. For the entrepreneurial immigrant, politics was a route to upward mobility. Ward leaders went into politics to gain wealth and prestige, and they were quite willing to accept kickbacks from city contractors, take bribes from gambling dens in exchange for immunity from police harassment, and appoint an inexperienced brother or son as fire chief or building inspector.

In general, machines were inefficient providers of low-quality services. Roads and bridges were designed poorly and constructed with poor-quality materials and workmanship. The machine tolerated monopolistic pricing of public utilities and transportation in exchange for payoffs. City residents who voted for machine candidates ultimately paid the bill. Reformers also documented that social services did not meet the needs of working-class populations and were generally available only to machine supporters.

The Progressive Reform Movement

In the early 1900s, the Protestant middle-class sensibilities of progressive reformers were deeply offended by the corruption, inefficiency, and Catholic immigrant orientation of the urban machines. Politically, reformers aimed to return power to the voter and to weaken the party machine. They sought to remove party designations from the election ballot, so that voters would vote for candidates on the basis of their individual qualifications, not their party endorsement. Successful reformers lengthened the election ballot, requiring that voters choose judges and police commissioners formerly appointed by the mayor.

Civil Service Systems

Administratively, the reformers wanted city government to be run like a business. They believed that tax dollars should be spent only on projects valued by taxpayers, not on projects which lined the pockets of political entrepreneurs. Reformers advocated creation of civil service systems to ensure that city jobs would go to applicants who were trained and experienced rather than to those who were politically well-connected. Today, all fifty states and most large cities hire according to civil service rules requiring that employees have certain educational and experiential qualifications and that the recruitment process be open.

The City Manager

Critics of the corrupt, inefficient urban political machines also supported the city manager concept. City managers are appointed, usually by the city council, to draft a budget, set up a personnel system, and supervise the work of city employees. Between 1910 and 1920, about 150 cities hired city managers.[10]

Advantages of Professional Managers.   As budgets and work forces grow in response to larger, service-demanding populations

124   Part II: Subnational Political Institutions and Processes

and state and federal mandates, the efficiency advantages of hiring a professional manager to oversee the day-to-day operations of a city or county become apparent. The professional manager can plan, monitor, and coordinate the activities of city or county employees more effectively than can elected officials preoccupied with resolving major policy questions, attentive to the concerns of their constituents, and untrained in the arts of administration. Today, one-third of U.S. cities are run by city managers.

Which Cities Hire Professional Managers?   As touched upon in Chapter 5, the likelihood of a city's adopting a city manager form of government depends upon city size, as shown in Table 6.2.

Medium-sized cities are most likely to use the council-manager form of government. Their predominantly middle-class populations are likely to value efficient use of the taxpayers' dollars highly, and therefore to support hiring a professional city manager.

However, the largest American cities do not make extensive use of city managers, as Table 6.2 indicates. Presumably, strong mayors in large cities build their power bases on providing services to large, low-income minority populations. Efficient service delivery is of less importance.

Smaller cities also tend to prefer the mayor-council system. Since small cities hire fewer employees and operate fewer programs, governing is less complex and a professional manager's skills are not usually required. Cities with primarily white populations tend to elect white mayors and often employ city managers, 89 percent of whom are white males. Their predominantly white middle-class constituents generally have secure positions in the private economy and are

Table 6.2   Size of City Population and Form of Government

Form of Government	Over 500,000		25,000–500,000		Under 25,000	
	N	%	N	%	N	%
Mayor-Council	25	78%	400	35%	3376	57%
Council-Manager	7	22%	657	58%	1994	33%
Town Meeting, Other	0	0%	75	7%	594	10%
Total	32	100%	1132	100%	5964	100%

Size of City Population

Source: *Municipal Yearbook 1990*, p. xiv.

primarily interested in seeing that their hard-earned tax dollars are used well. They favor efficiency-oriented city administration.

Some 300 black mayors govern American municipalities. The typical black mayor heads a small southern town with a black majority population. Large cities including Atlanta, Birmingham, Chicago, Cleveland, Detroit, Gary, and Washington, D.C., elected black mayors in recent decades after the black population increased as whites moved to the suburbs. Much as did the nineteenth-century urban machine politicians, black mayors emphasize delivering services rather than efficient, low-cost government.[11] Since blacks find it more difficult to move out of the city, they call upon their elected leaders to provide generous social services and employment opportunities within the city.[12]

Large urban counties, often combining city and surburban towns, tend to employ professional county managers. In 61 percent of large counties with over 100,000 residents, the elected county council hires a professional chief administrative officer.

Management of Small Governments

Most county governments are predominantly rural. About 54 percent of America's counties contain fewer than 25,000 residents, and 10 percent of all Americans live in these counties. America's small towns and rural counties are governed today much as they were 200 years ago, and the traditional *commission* form of government predominates. Voters elect commissioners who pass laws, work up the budget, and supervise appointed officials. Typically, these counties elect no central executive like a mayor or governor, nor do they hire a professional administrator. The commissioners are typically local business owners, lawyers, or real estate agents who work part-time as county commissioners, receive very limited compensation for this office, and have little political background or management training. They get by because their counties are lightly populated, their budgets are small, and their functions are limited. A small city or county cannot afford a professional manager, whose salary must be paid by relatively few taxpayers.

Similarly, America's small towns tend to be governed by untrained, part-time elected commissioners, who carry out legislative and executive responsibilities. Of America's 19,200 municipal governments, 80 percent are small towns with populations under 5,000. About 12 percent of Americans live in these small towns.

Why Run for Governor or Mayor?

Men and women seek to become governor or mayor for various reasons. Some office seekers, motivated by the desire for personal gain, may view a governorship as a financially lucrative opportunity. Serving as mayor or governor can also be a stepping-stone to higher public office. Mayors may run for statewide office or a Senate seat, and governors are often touted as possible presidential candidates. Recently, Jimmy Carter, Ronald Reagan, Michael Dukakis, and Bill Clinton won their political party's presidential nomination after serving as governor. Governors have become candidates for either president or vice president in forty-four of fifty-one presidential elections, and sixteen former governors have become president.

Political and administrative experience as chief executive of a large state is excellent training for national office. About 15 percent of state governors are appointed to high-level federal posts, and about 10 percent convert their name recognition into a successful run for the U.S. Senate. In 1986, sixteen former governors served in the Senate. However, about 60 percent of departing governors leave public life, returning to law practice, moving into private sector business, or retiring.[13]

Governors and mayors also enjoy the visibility, status, and power that accompany high public office. They control substantial budgets and staff and their decisions affect many people. Mayors and governors feel important when they make regular appearances on local television, receive invitations to speak before large groups, and know that others want to be in their company. These psychic rewards are important to many officeholders.

Finally, mayors and governors run for office because they want to contribute to the community. The challenge of reducing crime rates, improving education, bringing in new jobs, and reducing taxes appeals to them.

The Functions of Governors and Mayors

In an increasingly interdependent society, citizens call upon governments to provide a broader range of goods and services. As state and local governments employ more people and spend more money, strong executives must provide leadership, monitor the performance of government workers, and coordinate agency activities. Therefore, governors, mayors, and city managers have become important power figures in American states and cities.

To deliver billions of dollars worth of such services as building parks, maintaining wastewater treatment plants, and providing women with prenatal care requires planning and coordination. The governors of the states and the mayors of our cities are positioned to define a package of services that respond to the needs of the electorate and to deliver those services efficiently. Legislators are not up to the task. They are many in number and are better able to discuss and deliberate than to supervise the detailed implementation of new laws. Even their lawmaking authority is shared with the governor or mayor, who is elected by all of the people and therefore more inclined to craft legislation that is widely supported. Legislators, by contrast, are primarily interested in representing their own narrow constituencies.

Providing Leadership

An important element of leadership is setting government priorities. Is it more important to deliver a check to a needy person quickly or to spend additional time and money to ensure that the applicant is truly eligible? Should road maintenance crews fill all of the potholes in the streets with cheap material or fill some with long-lasting material? Should the police crack down on speeding or target only flagrant violators of the posted speed limit? Should state aid to school districts be distributed according to school-age population size or according to need? The answers to these questions are not self-evident. Governors and mayors decide priorities in light of political considerations, personal inclination, and their sense of the public interest.

When disaster strikes, decisive, prompt, coordinated action is needed and the chief executive normally takes the lead. Governors organized the response to the Three Mile Island nuclear plant disaster in Pennsylvania in 1979, the Mediterranean fruit fly infestation in California in 1981, and Hurricane Hugo in South Carolina in 1990. Mayors coordinated the response to the San Francisco earthquake in 1990 and to paralyzing snowstorms in Chicago and Buffalo in the 1980s.[14]

In time of social crisis, people look to governors and mayors to provide leadership. Over the years, such crises have included the rise of unchecked monopolistic industrial corporations in the 1890s, economic depression in 1893 and 1929, the desegregation controversy in southern states and cities during the 1950s and 1960s, and urban riots in northern cities in the 1960s. In the 1980s and 1990s, key issues have included declining economic competitiveness, increasing crime rates and drug addiction, and taxpayer unrest.

Monitoring Bureaucratic Performance

A second function of chief executives is to monitor state and local agencies to ensure that employees are doing what they are paid to do. Diligent governors and mayors expect regular reports from agency heads on agency activities, assuming that employees who are held accountable will work harder and more effectively than those who are not. Chief executives also set up positive incentive systems, rewarding hardworking and productive employees with recognition, pay raises, and promotion. (The dynamics of the monitoring process are considered in more detail in Chapter 7.)

Coordinating Agency Activities

A third function of chief executives is to coordinate the activities of state and local agencies. Complex policy needs, such as attending to homeless people, discouraging drug addiction, and promoting economic development, require the cooperative attention of many government agencies. A serious campaign against drug addiction will involve police effort to cut the drug distribution network, appropriate sentencing procedures in the courts, antidrug education programs in the schools, and expanded drug detoxification programs in communities. The success of an antidrug campaign requires coordinated effort among government agencies, and an attentive governor or mayor can pressure agencies to assign priority to interagency cooperation. Governors spend about one-half of their time monitoring performance and coordinating agency activity.[15]

Serving as Intermediary

Governors and mayors also serve as intermediaries with other levels of government on behalf of their state or city. Governors estimate that 15 percent of their time is spent lobbying the federal government or negotiating with local governments within their state.

The growth of the National Governors Association (NGA) indicates the importance of this activity. With a staff of eighty, the NGA lobbies the federal government, conducts research on important issues, and publicizes issues of common concern.[16] States have received as much as 28 percent of their revenues from the federal government, and states provide grants-in-aid to local governments. In New York State, for example, about two-thirds of state revenues are channeled to school districts and other local governments.

Strengthening Executive Leadership

Increasing authority of the chief executive is a characteristic of twentieth-century American government. The governors of the fifty states, the mayors and city managers of our cities, and county-level chief executives supervise more government employees, spend more money, and provide more services with each passing year. Chief executives have gained greater power as state and local governments have provided more services for their citizens.

The Expanding Powers of the Governors

In the last three decades, reforms have expanded gubernatorial power, and the governors of the fifty states cast an ever-lengthening shadow across state political landscapes. The most heavily urbanized states in the northeast and midwest led the way in expanding the powers of their governors. Recently, gubernatorial power has increased in those southern and western states that are urbanizing most rapidly.[17] Governors are weakest in smaller, rural states where demands on government are limited. The power of governors is enhanced as length of service increases, staff size increases, and administrative efficiency is improved.[18]

Longer Terms

An important source of the enhanced power of governors is that they can expect to serve as chief executive for longer periods of time. A governor who may expect to serve for four or eight years can exercise more control than can a two-year governor. In 1956, governors in nineteen states were limited by state constitutions to a single two-year term; in 1986, only New Hampshire, Rhode Island, and Vermont retained the two-year term.

Once constitutional barriers are removed, reelection prospects are good. In the 163 gubernatorial elections held from 1977 to 1981, 78 percent of those governors eligible sought reelection and 74 percent of them were successful.[19]

Governors spend about one-third of their time dealing with the public. They attend social club luncheons and participate in ribbon-cutting ceremonies. They communicate with individual citizens on the telephone, through the mail, and in their offices. In an age of television, governors use their high visibility to sell their policies and achievements to the public.[20]

Larger Staffs

Today's governors have much larger staffs (compared with those of previous governors) to advance the governor's political priorities and to oversee the day-to-day operations of state government. In 1960, average staff size was under seven persons; in 1990, average staff size had expanded to fifty. A pivotal member of a contemporary governor's staff is the chief of staff, a trusted political confidant who frames policy issues for the governor. The chief of staff typically determines who sees the governor, what issues are brought to the governor's attention, and how the governor spends his or her time. Governors also rely upon a legislative liaison to build support for the governor's policies in the legislature, a legal counsel to provide legal advice, and a press secretary to coordinate communications with the press.

Improvement of Administrative Efficiency

Finally, many states have implemented administrative reorganization programs to streamline service delivery and to improve coordination. The 1949 Hoover Commission report had recommended that authority and responsibility for administering programs be concentrated in the governor's office, that dozens of independent state agencies be consolidated into a much smaller number, and that a cabinet system be created to improve coordination.

For more than a decade, rural legislatures resisted giving greater powers to governors. Vested interests in the existing system opposed change, and existing structures were often written into state constitutions and protected by difficult amendment procedures.

However, by the 1960s, the political logic of administrative reorganization prevailed, as political power shifted toward the cities and state government continued its inexorable growth. Many states implemented the Hoover recommendations. Legislatures gave their governors authority to reorganize, subject to legislative veto.[21] In a typical state, 100 independent boards, commissions, and agencies were consolidated into 10 superagencies, with the governor having the power to appoint and to remove the new agency heads.

Although intended to improve administration efficiency, reorganization served mostly to strengthen gubernatorial power. Cost savings were few, as eliminated agencies had small budgets and staff and most personnel were reassigned to higher-priority tasks. While reorganization reduced the number of organizations to manage, the larger, consolidated agency had more layers. The total number of managers remained about the same.[22]

Do States with Strong Governors Provide More Benefits?

Some evidence suggests that states with strong governors pay their teachers more, spend more per pupil for public education, provide greater welfare benefits, and spend more per capita for health care than do states with weak governors. But these differences in policy are largely explained by differences in state per capita incomes. Rich states can afford to spend more on education and health care. When two states are about equally wealthy, they tend to have similar policies even if one has a strong governor and the other a weak governor.[23]

Limits on Executive Power

Although the formal powers of governors and mayors have increased since the mid-1960s, limits on gubernatorial and mayoral power are very real. First, power is shared with the independently elected legislators, whose reelection chances depend more upon pleasing their constituents than pleasing the governor or mayor. Second, governors and mayors share power with other independently elected officials who have their own priorities and power bases. Third, state and local employees, protected by civil service and union rules and subscribing to their own professional norms of behavior, may resist gubernatorial or mayoral direction.

Fourth, the average term of office for a governor or mayor is about four years, which means that civil servants have a good chance of outlasting the chief executive. Fifth, governors and mayors have little control over their environment. Economic conditions affect spending needs and tax revenues, and important political decisions affecting states and localities are made in Washington, D.C.

Informal Executive Power

Governors and Mayors

Whether a governor or mayor is successful depends upon more than having strong formal powers. In any public organization, a CEO quickly learns that his or her formal powers are limited and that the power to persuade is the essence of political power.[24] A successful governor or mayor must rely heavily upon the cooperative behavior of others in dealing with the most challenging public problems, such as reducing racial tensions, providing better law enforcement or education, and encouraging new economic development. A successful CEO must persuade the reluctant, mediate among conflicting interests, and build popular support through artful use of the media.

Successful political entrepreneurs like Huey ''Kingfish'' Long in Louisiana and Chicago's former mayor Richard C. Daley relied heavily upon their informal political skills to build political dynasties. Although their formal powers were few, they filled government jobs with supporters, received financial contributions from recipients of contracts, and ensured election of political allies to elected offices.[25]

Individual governors and mayors vary in their personal approaches to the job of being chief executive. Some are rather passive custodians in office, fulfilling their essential responsibilities, deferring to legislators and other elected officials, and avoiding controversy. Conversely, activist governors and mayors define policy priorities aggressively and fight for the legislation, appropriations, and popular support needed to achieve their goals.

City Managers

Despite their limited formal responsibilities, artful city managers can influence how policy issues are resolved. The city manager usually determines the agenda for city council meetings, deciding what subjects will discussed, how to frame the issues, and even the order in which topics are considered—all of which can affect outcomes. The city manager prepares supporting evidence and interprets its meaning. The city manager drafts the budget, which outlines city spending priorities. The policy impact of a politically skilled city manager is considerable.[26]

Most city managers see themselves as policy managers sensitive to political circumstance, not as narrow administrators. However, because they are hired by city council members to oversee the day-to-day workings of government, city managers must be cautious in advocating particular policy initiatives. Managers without professional training in city administration or those with engineering degrees who work in their home communities are more likely to accept a narrowly administrative definition of the job as city manager.[27]

Managers who provoke open disputes with council members on policy matters tend to have short tenures. A city manager, as any successful politician, is well advised to avoid taking public stands on the most controversial issues facing the community. One survey of city managers indicates that one in ten city managers had been fired at least once, and that 75 percent of these firings had their origin in political conflicts with the council.[28]

Over the last 200 years, as Americans have increased in number, moved to cities, and earned higher incomes, they have come to expect state and local governments to provide schools, highways, police protection, and many other services.

As state and local governments spend more money and hire more employees, legislators have called upon governors and mayors to provide leadership, monitor government employees, coordinate agency activities, and negotiate with the federal government. To assist them, today's governors have greater powers and larger staffs, and many larger cities and counties have hired professional managers.

Recommend Reading

Thad L. Beyle: "From Governor to Governors," in Carl Van Horn, ed., *The State of the States*, CQ Press, Washington, D.C., 1989.

Ann O'M. Bowman and Richard C. Kearney: *The Resurgence of the States*, Prentice-Hall, Englewood Cliffs, N.J., 1986.

Dennis R. Judd: *The Politics of American Cities*, Little, Brown, Boston, 1984.

Herbert Kaufman: *Politics and Policies in State and Local Governments*, Prentice-Hall, Englewood Cliffs, N.J., 1963.

Municipal Yearbook (annual editions), International City Management Association, Washington, D.C.

Alan Rosenthal: *Governors and Legislators: Contending Powers*, CQ Press, Washington, D.C., 1990.

Larry Sabato: *Goodbye to Good-time Charlie: The American Governorship Transformed*, CQ Press, Washington, D.C., 1983.

CHAPTER 7

Bureaucracy

Our elected governors, mayors, and state and local legislators pass laws and allocate funds to operate schools and hospitals, to hire police officers and judges, to maintain highways and recreation areas, and to provide clean water and collect garbage. In our complex interdependent society, the quality of our lives depends upon how well 14 million state and local employees carry out these basic services. These employees, called bureaucrats, have considerable discretion in implementing policy directives and spending money. Bureaucratic rules and regulations define the law as citizens experience it; therefore, bureaucrats have real power over our lives.

This chapter discusses basic principles of bureaucratic organization, how well state and local bureaucracies work, and to what extent bureaucrats are representative of and responsive to the broader population. In a highly industrialized society, bureaucracy is the dominant organizational form because people organized in hierarchies who develop specialized skills and follow standard operating procedures can accomplish tasks more efficiently than if each person works alone or with very few others.

Real-world bureaucrats in both public and private organizations sometimes work together well in pursuit of the organization's goals, and sometimes do not. Individual bureaucrats have personal goals which may or may not be consistent with the organization's goals. By monitoring behavior, evaluating performance, creating incentives, and encouraging employees to identify with the organization, managers increase the odds that employees will work for the organization and its goals.

Finally, citizens are supposed to have control over state and local bureaucrats through their elected governors, mayors, and legislators. At issue is to what extent bureaucrats are representative (have demographic characteristics similar to the broader society) and responsive (implement policies that reflect accurately the preferences of the citizenry). The adoption of the civil service system for hiring bureaucrats increased efficiency, but it also increased civil servant autonomy and created a predominantly white male bureaucracy. Recently, affirmative action and comparable worth policies have increased the representativeness of the bureaucracy, but such policies have generated considerable controversy over fairness and efficiency issues.

Complex Organizations in American Life

When the American republic was founded in 1789, most Americans lived on small farms and provided for many of their own needs. A farmer was, for better or worse, his own carpenter, furniture maker, weather forecaster, veterinarian, and soil analyst. A farm woman was candle maker, food preserver, tailor, pharmacist, and nurse. Whatever services the farm family needed or could afford (general store, community church, one-room schoolhouse, blacksmith) were available in the local town.

Two hundred years later, 75 percent of Americans live in urban areas and depend heavily upon others to provide for their needs. People work as plumbers, accountants, or data processors and pay others to grow food, repair their cars, or provide television entertainment. Americans rely heavily upon state and local governments to provide a wide variety of essential services from the cradle (providing prenatal care for low-income pregnant women) to the grave (licensing morticians).

Some 12 million employees work for state and local governments, about 8 percent of the American labor force, and the number is increasing. The number of state and local employees grew by 37 percent between 1970 and 1990. Education is by far the largest state and local government function, with cities and local school districts providing primary and secondary education and states concentrating on higher education. About half of all state and local government employees work in the schools.[1]

Characteristics of Bureaucratic Organizations

The sociologist Max Weber, writing in the early twentieth century, first noted the extent to which goods and services are provided through the cooperative effort of individuals working together in complex organizations.[2] About three-quarters of American employees work in complex organizations employing more than twenty workers, such as automobile manufacturers, television stations, hospitals, supermarkets, schools, and police departments.[3]

Weber argued that several important characteristics of bureaucracies enable them to produce more goods and services using fewer resources than if each person works alone or with very few others, as they had in frontier America. Among the important characteristics are hierarchy, specialization, and procedural formality.

Hierarchy

Hierarchy is the division of authority between a superior or boss, who coordinates activities and monitors performance, and subordinates, who are the direct providers of goods and services. An organization chart expresses these hierarchical relationships. The constellation of units, often called offices, divisions, or bureaus, resembles a pyramid; a superior, often called a secretary or director, is responsible for each unit. Typically, from five to eight units report to the next higher level in the hierarchy.

Figure 7.1 is a simplified version of the organization chart of the Massachusetts State Police. At the base of the organization are the state troopers, organized crime and narcotics specialists, fingerprint and firearms experts, and staff specialists who recruit personnel, manage the budget, and do public relations.

The Massachusetts State Police is organized into five bureaus, with a bureau commander presiding over each. The Commissioner of Public Safety sets basic policy priorities. Should the agency concentrate on apprehending intoxicated drivers on the highway or cutting the flow of drugs into the state? The same commissioner also coordinates activity of the various bureaus. Is the personnel department recruiting the right type of employees? Are the fingerprinting and

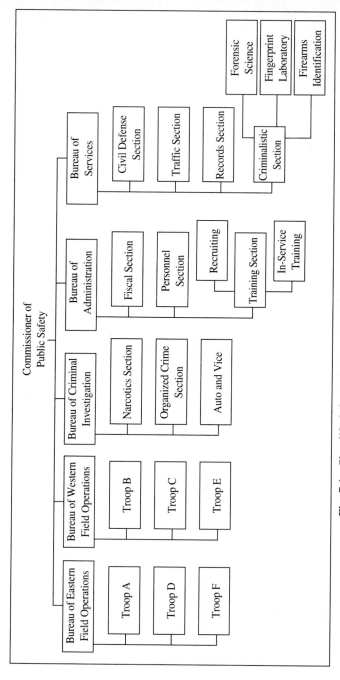

Fig. 7.1 Simplified Organization Chart, Massachusetts State Police

Source: Massachusetts Department of Public Safety.

ballistics units getting reports out to investigating officers quickly? Finally, the commissioner monitors the performance of his or her bureau commanders, expecting that each will support policy priorities, foster cooperation with other departments, and monitor subordinates effectively.

Specialization

People who work in organizations usually have thorough and expert training in narrow specializations. Managing a budget, doing fingerprinting, and keeping files are activities that require special training and experience. Bureaucracies are efficient providers of goods and services precisely because bureaucrats are expert at their jobs. Within the Massachusetts State Police organization, for example, employees who acquire expertise in investigations or data processing are likely to make a career of it. Today's thirty-year-old ballistics expert, accountant, or state trooper will often work at the same type of job at age fifty. New specializations are constantly being created. For example, state and local governments now rely heavily upon purchasing offices to buy automobiles and computers and to hire consulting firms and expert witnesses.[4]

Many occupational fields that require higher education, foster adherence to standards of work and behavior, and create a sense of identity among practitioners are called *professions*. The Bureau of Labor Statistics estimates that the professions grew from 4 percent of the work force in the 1920s to 15 percent in the 1970s. Because state and local governments hire so many teachers, fully one-third of their employees are professionals.[5] Nurses, social workers, sanitation employees, and other occupational categories become more professionalized each year and seek appropriate recognition.

City and county managers, who are hired to supervise the day-to-day running of local government, illustrate the trend toward professionalization. The first city and county managers were not professionals. Many were local department heads with little training or experience to handle broader responsibilities. However, by 1989, two-thirds of professional managers had a master's degree in a managerial field, and many had been promoted from the rank of assistant manager. Being a professional manager is now a career.[6]

Procedural Formality

In bureaucratic organizations, employees are recruited and perform their jobs according to well-defined procedures. They are hired on the basis of appropriate education and experience qualifications. All states and most large cities have civil service systems that conduct examinations to determine eligibility for a position, maintain a list of candidates eligible for jobs, and protect employees from arbitrary dismissal. However, state and local governments vary in how carefully they adhere to civil service rules, and knowing a bureau commander may still help a candidate land a job.[7]

Once hired, bureaucrats are expected to follow standard operating procedures or established routines. The job of receptionist or criminal investigator is carefully defined, and the organization expects that whoever fills that job will do the job in about the same way, regardless of personal characteristics. Employees keep the same hours, dress appropriately, and follow the same rules.

Ideally, bureaucrats apply organizational rules impersonally to their clients. The Massachusetts State Police organization expects that all drivers stopped for speeding, all criminal suspects, and all citizens who are victims of a crime will be treated in a standard way. Following established procedures helps assure equal treatment for all. Although incidents of discriminatory treatment happen, they are the exception and not the rule. Indeed, citizens often complain that bureaucrats ignore their special circumstances and wrap their cases in procedural red tape.

Bureaucrats have incentives to conform to organization rules and procedures. Their superiors monitor their conformity more than their outcomes because the latter are so hard to measure. Also, going by the book insulates the bureaucrat from public criticism, even if flexible decision making might serve some clients better.[8]

Motivation of Bureaucrats

Two schools of thought contend about what motivates bureaucrats: one believes that an ideal of public service motivates them, the other that they are primarily motivated by self-interest.

Public Service

According to proponents of the first view, government employees are public servants responding to a public interest; they report to an executive elected by the people in democratic elections, and they spend money raised from the general taxpaying public. Therefore, the argument goes, the ethically responsible bureaucrat must take a broad view of the public interest. Indeed, we commonly call someone who works for a state or local government a public servant. The government bureaucrat serves the people and must subordinate self-interest to the public good. As compared with bureaucrats in private organizations, public administrators must be responsive to a broader range of people and organizations: for example, interest groups, legislators who provide funding and oversight, and bureaucrats in other government agencies.

Resistance to Elected Officials

Elected politicians often instruct state and local bureaucrats to allocate resources in a politically responsive way. A small, inefficient branch office may be kept open, a museum to commemorate a local industry established, or a highway built through empty countryside at the behest of prominent local legislators. In fact, bureaucrats resist efforts of political leaders to politicize service delivery. In Chicago, even during the era of the strong Daley political machine, basic service delivery decisions were made according to bureaucratic procedures and technical criteria, not political criteria.[9] Along these lines, bureaucrats interviewed see themselves as protecting the public from the special interests that influence elected officials. Politicians seek to maximize their reelection chances, while bureaucrats are more inclined to pursue productive efficiency or the public interest.[10]

Restriction of Political Activity

One consequence of the view that bureaucrats serve all of the people is that the right of state and local employees to participate in political party activity may be restricted. The intention is to protect civil servants from political pressure. In the nineteenth century, state and local politicians appointed most government employees. These political appointees were expected to work in reelection campaigns, make campaign contributions, and respond to their requests.

Later, national forces attacked this entrenched spoils system in state and local government. In the 1930s, the federal government pressured states and local governments to adopt civil service reforms by threatening to withhold federal grants if they did not. In 1940, the Hatch Act, which prohibited federal employees from participating in partisan political campaigns and contributing to political candidates, was extended to state and local employees whose salaries were partially paid by federal grants. The Hatch Act protected skilled bureaucrats from governors and mayors who would tie continued employment to active political support.

Prohibited Labor Activity

Government employees historically were denied the right to join trade unions in pursuit of higher wages or better working conditions. Since government employees theoretically served all of society, the reasoning went, they should not organize as a special interest group against society. Not until the 1960s did government employees receive the right to form unions and bargain collectively. Today over half of all state and local government employees belong to unions. Most heavily unionized are schoolteachers, police and firefighters, and public works employees. Unionization varies from state to state. Nineteen states, mostly in the south and west, do not recognize employee unions or bargain with them about wages and working conditions. In the industrialized northeast and midwest states, more than two-thirds of state employees are covered by union-negotiated contracts.[11]

Even when public employee unions can bargain with governments on wages and working conditions, employees are generally prohibited from striking against the society which they serve. Many public services, such as police protection and garbage collection, are regarded as essential, whereas private sector manufacturing is not. Leaders of public employee unions are subject to arrest and the union subject to fine if workers strike illegally. Public sector work stoppages sometimes take place in disguised form, as when workers call in sick in large numbers.

Several states permit public unions to strike if public welfare is not at risk and if all efforts to reach a settlement have failed.[12] From 1969 to 1977, the number of strikes against state and local governments was about 350 annually, and the number rose to about 500 per year through 1980.[13] Strikes declined sharply in the 1980s as unions were weakened by successful strikebreaking activities and lack of public support for higher wage demands in a period of economic stagnation, budget deficits, and antitax sentiment.

Self-interest

In contrast to the view that bureaucrats are motivated to serve the public, another theory is that bureaucrats are motivated primarily by self-interest. In a classic study, William Niskanen argued that government grows because bureaucrats are continuously seeking to expand the size of agency budgets, in order to maximize some combination of salary, reputation, power, and service output.[14] Bureaucrats get their way, according to Niskanen, because they have a monopoly of information about the true cost of producing goods or services. Legislative committees, under pressure from special interest groups, are inclined to accept agency requests for more funds. In the 1970s and 1980s, bureaucrats proposed endless ways to spend money and propelled state and local government growth.[15]

Niskanen has probably overstated the extent to which government is enlarged by budget-maximizing bureaucrats. Certainly in the 1990s, bureaucrats struggle to avoid layoffs and cutbacks as elected state and local officials resist spending proposals requiring tax increases. Whether bureaucrats succeed in increasing their budgets depends upon the support of clientele groups, the governor and mayor, and key legislators. Some agencies always do better than others. Whether social priorities are building highways, attacking urban blight, fighting drug use, or preventing crime depends upon what voters, interest groups, and other political actors see as the pressing issues of the day.[16]

The Temptation to Shirk

An example of self-interested behavior in bureaucracies is the temptation to get away with working less hard than one's fellow bureaucrats. Terry Moe argues that most people consent to work in large organizations where their activity is closely monitored by bosses because they are paid more than they could earn working alone. Effective hierarchical coordination, specialization, and procedural formality really are in everyone's interest because closely monitored employees produce more and are paid more. In principle, subordinates have an incentive to cooperate with their bosses because the rewards to be shared in a more productive organization are greater.[17]

In practice, employees do not always cooperate fully. In bureaucratic organizations, it is not possible to judge precisely the value of an individual worker's contribution. That is why all employees who do similar work are paid at the same rate. Most state and local governments classify jobs into twenty or thirty categories according to training required, level of difficulty, and level of responsibility. A teacher, a nurse, and a librarian with the same job rating are generally paid at the same rate, regardless of how well they work.

In effect, the employee is paid the average salary for employees in that work classification. An employee who is above average in effort, skill, and ambition is likely to move to another employer, quite possibly in the private sector, who will pay a higher wage. Thus, the organization will tend to be heavily populated with employees who are average or below average in effort, skill, and ambition.[18] Why should an employee work exceptionally hard when a less diligent coworker will be equally well rewarded?

A shirking worker who does the job poorly, reads the newspaper on the job, and goes home early hurts the organization's productivity, and these losses are borne by everyone. Meanwhile, the shirker gains 100 percent of the value of a more relaxed approach to the job. Why should a state trooper sacrifice a longer coffee break in order to stop more speeders? Shirkers benefit themselves but hurt the organization. If everyone were to shirk, the organization would be unproductive and everyone would lose. So employees must be discouraged from shirking.

Niskanen and Moe remind us that bureaucrats are not selfless public servants, implementing the letter of policies articulated by elected legislators and chief executives. They believe that bureaucrats are ordinary people with a strong desire to pursue self-interest within the limits imposed by their organization. But Niskanen and Moe probably understate the motives of bureaucrats who work hard and productively on behalf of the taxpayers who pay their salaries. Professional norms of performance reinforce the cultural norm of a fair day's work for a fair day's pay.

How Organizations Combat Shirking

Organizations seek to minimize shirking by close monitoring and by performance evaluations and incentives.

Close Monitoring.   Organizations monitor how employees spend their time. Employees can be required to punch a time clock on arrival and departure and instructed to limit their coffee breaks to ten minutes. Detailed rules and regulations specify how employees' work is to be done. Work-load measures keep track of how many letters they type, speeding tickets they write, potholes they fill, licenses they issue, and so on. Close monitoring is common practice in state and local bureaucracies.

One problem with this approach is that monitoring is costly. If a department head spends time and energy monitoring workers, less time is available for making policy decisions and coordinating the work effort and communicating with legislators, the chief executive, and related agencies. A supervisor may well conclude that close monitoring takes too much time and energy or has too little effect on employee behavior.

In principle, a supervisor will increase monitoring activity only so long as the value of preventing employee shirking exceeds the value of the supervisor's time and energy.[19] The supervisor who is paid a salary of $45,000 regardless of how well the organization works has little incentive to spend time on the thankless task of monitoring workers closely. In fast food or automobile repair franchises, local managers whose diligent monitoring pays off in extra profits are often rewarded with a share in those profits. However, few state and local governments have offered managers pay raises or bonuses for efficient monitoring that increases organizational productivity. The movement to decentralize schools and other government services is rooted in the thought that decentralized service providers will be held more responsible by their clients than will a central bureaucracy in city hall or the state capital.

In a state park, highway department, or social service office, the supervisor has little reason to exact more than the minimum effort from workers. Close monitoring is most feasible in simple and routine decision situations. For example, collecting garbage involves a simple, repetitive process, and close monitoring is feasible to ensure that sanitation workers do not skip houses or generate complaints. But in complex, nonroutine situations, subordinates need to exercise discretion and cannot be controlled closely.[20] Close monitoring would exact a price in employee productivity.

Individual service delivery typically requires that caseworkers exercise considerable flexibility and discretion.[21] For example, in determining eligibility for subsidized municipal housing, bureaucrats need to interpret rules and evaluate individual situations flexibly to protect client and taxpayer interests. For example, a caseworker may need to judge whether a particular family voluntarily become homeless in order to move higher on a housing eligibility list, in the process displacing a family seeking refuge from an abusive husband and father.

Sometimes, organizational goals are unclear or in conflict. If some balance between two desirable goals must be struck, then subordinates have to use their discretion in deciding individual cases. For example, in enforcing housing codes, it is important to protect the health and comfort of tenants yet still allow landlords to make a reasonable profit.

Finally, close monitoring is difficult when bureaucrats must work closely with bureaucrats in other agencies.[22] For example, whether state and local police agencies and courts combat drug use by providing treatment for addicts or by sentencing them to jail terms depends upon the willingness of the health service delivery and corrections systems to cooperate.

Performance Evaluations and Incentives.   Organizations also rely upon performance evaluations and incentives to combat shirking. Performance evaluations attempt to grade employees on how well they do their jobs, with salary increases and promotion prospects being tied to the quality of performance. Top performers within an agency are rewarded for their effort and skill. Knowing that monetary incentives and recognition are available for good performance, employees are motivated to work hard in order to get pay bonuses and special recognition. One detailed survey revealed that about half of the local governments linked monetary rewards to performance ratings.[23]

Poorly performing employees are rarely dismissed, because bureaucrats enjoy civil service protections. While critics complain that firing government employees is impossibly difficult, it appears that dismissal rates are no lower for public jurisdictions than for those in the private sector. In both cases, workers have an interest in doing minimally acceptable work, and managers seek to avoid the costs of training replacements.[24]

Several obstacles make effective performance evaluation difficult. First, it is possible that rewarding a few top performers will discourage the remaining employees, who will slacken their work effort rather than working harder.[25] Second, public sector employees do not have a simple bottom-line summary that allows an observer to compare an organization's output with the value of resources used to produce that output. In a recent survey of administrators in ten states, the difficulties of rewarding outstanding employees and of disciplining underperforming employees were mentioned as the most serious impediments to effective agency management.[26]

State and local employees resist efforts by supervisors to evaluate their performance. Professionals believe that only other professionals, not general administrators, can evaluate their performance as accountants, engineers, and teachers. Even street-level social workers resist supervisors' attempts to second-guess their judgments in individual cases.[27]

Unions protect workers who fear that granting supervisors the right to evaluate performance will open the door to arbitrary treatment and abuse. Employees also prefer to bargain collectively for higher wage contracts than to compete individually for higher performance ratings and higher pay.

Eliciting Cooperation

The difficulties of monitoring have convinced many managers that they must elicit the willing cooperation of their workers. To minimize the need for monitoring, supervisors encourage workers to have a sense of professional pride in doing their job well, a strategy that works better for accountants, teachers, and nurses than for sanitation workers and file clerks. Supervisors seek to instill a sense of loyalty to the organization and identification with its goals. The purpose of installing suggestion boxes, designating ''employees of the month,'' and holding agency picnics is to encourage employees to work diligently without being monitored closely.

Chester Barnard, a successful executive and leading proponent of the human relations school of management, believed that subordinates ultimately decide whether or not they will follow the lead of their bosses. Authority in an organization ultimately rests with the workers, not their superiors. The successful manager is sensitive to which orders are not acceptable to the employees and will refrain from issuing them.[28]

Measuring Productivity

Productivity refers to output per worker. Most state and local governments attempt to measure productivity, but with mixed success. One problem is that few state and local governments have invested major resources in measuring productivity. Another problem is the difficulty of measuring typical government outputs such as quality of education, highway maintenance, or police protection. In the private sector, comparing the value of inputs (wages, capital equipment, office supplies) and outputs (cars, haircuts, pizzas) is relatively easy. Since firms in the private sector sell their output in the marketplace, the value of their goods and services to society is what people are willing to pay.

Several techniques to evaluate the effectiveness of government activity are available to state and local governments.

Management by Objectives.   Aware of criticisms that government agencies continue to follow well-established routines even as their environment changes, agencies are now seeking to define their goals. Agencies will perform better and can more readily be held accountable if they state what they are trying to accomplish. Stating goals clearly also focuses attention on the next step, measuring to what extent those goals have been achieved.

Program Budgeting.   Traditional line-item budgeting sought to keep track of how the agency used its resources rather than of the output that the agency produced. How much did the agency spend on salaries, office supplies, telephone, capital equipment, and other categories? Budget monitors were principally concerned that the funds be expended in a timely manner throughout the budget year, and that the funds were not spent for unauthorized purposes.

In program budgeting, the focus is less on the inputs and more on the outputs. What did the agency accomplish with those resources? What were the agency's outputs? Did better highway signage speed traffic flow and reduce traffic accidents? How many nights of shelter were provided for homeless persons? To prevent crime in a community, should the police department allocate funds to an employee incentive program or a new piece of diagnostic equipment?

Program Evaluation.   The purpose of a government agency is to provide valuable services to the public, not simply to spend the taxpayer's money. Increasingly, bureaucrats are asked to document what a given program achieves. Does providing education for four-year-olds improve their subsequent performance in school? Should police officers spend their time in highly visible patrol work or devote resources to raising the percentage of crimes solved? (One famous study cast doubt on the efficacy of patrol activity as a deterrent to crime.[29])

States and municipalities vary widely in how accurately and thoroughly they measure productivity. About three-quarters of the states now use performance measures in evaluating public programs and believe that the measures are effective.[30]

Table 7.1 shows that cities use management tools extensively. Large cities use them more than do smaller ones, presumably because their monitoring needs are greater in their more complex policy environments. Also, larger cities can afford to hire specialists in these techniques.

Only 42 percent of cities responded to the survey, and it seems likely that those using management tools extensively were more likely to respond. Therefore, the numbers in the table may overstate the use of these management tools in American cities.

The Value of Measuring Productivity.   Skeptics doubt that measuring productivity is a very useful exercise. The first argument is

Table 7.1 Use of Management Tools by American Cities

Tool	% of Cities Using
Program Budgeting	66%
Revenue and Expense Forecasting	68%
Performance Monitoring	67%
Program Evaluation	77%
Employee Incentive Programs	64%
Quality Circles	32%

Source: Gregory Streib and Theodore H. Poister, ''Established and Emerging Management Tools: A 12-Year Perspective,'' *The Municipal Yearbook 1990–91,* Chapter 5.

that since some decisions are made in response to political pressures, efficiency measures are simply irrelevant. If a powerful legislator intends to have a sewage treatment plant located in his or her small town, it really doesn't matter if the need is greater in a large city.

The second argument focuses on the fact that the technical difficulties of developing reliable performance measures in many social service settings are considerable. It is intrinsically difficult to gauge the impact of raising teachers' salaries or reducing class size on learning outcomes. And harried bureaucrats often feel that they can barely keep up with everyday service delivery, much less take time to conduct performance evaluation exercises. When an eager agency head insists that they make time, bureaucrats can select and interpret data to support their preferred conclusion.

In one state, a study found that state budgeting decisions did not correlate with performance data. Agencies with high performance ratings did not receive more funding than agencies with low performance ratings.[31] Despite these difficulties, it is clear that with each passing year, state and local bureaucrats are being held more accountable for how efficiently they spend their resources.

Bureaucracy and Democratic Government

Writing in 1887, Woodrow Wilson described an important difference between politics and administration. Politics, thought Wilson, involves making basic policy choices. Elected politicians make policy decisions about taxing and spending levels, about the broad content of the high school curriculum, about the relative importance of highway maintenance and social services. The electorate holds politicians accountable for their decisions.

Administration, according to Wilson, involves putting those policy decisions into effect. Bureaucrats are expected to follow closely the policy directives of elected officials and to use their specialized skills and experience to implement the policies in an efficient, businesslike way.[32] While politicians should be responsive to the people, bureaucrats should be politically neutral experts.

Influence of Bureaucrats on Policy

Close students of state and local government today believe that Wilson's distinction between politics and administration is too simple. First, the expertise of bureaucrats gives them influence over the governors and legislators who formally make policy. About half of state agency heads are licensed professionals, which means that their technical advice usually carries great weight with the governor.[33]

Second, most state agencies actively lobby the legislature. In one survey, 40 percent of agency heads report that they initiate at least half of the legislation affecting their units.[34] Third, in implementing the law, bureaucrats shape the broad policy directives of the legislature or the chief executive. Some people win and some people lose as bureaucrats implement the law, and that is the essence of politics. Bureaucrats often devise the formulas for determining how aid will be distributed to school districts, or decide how strictly to apply the criteria for determining eligibility for social welfare programs.

The Civil Service System

In the early years of the republic, when government had few responsibilities, any competent person could perform simple bureaucratic tasks adequately. Commonly, a newly elected governor or mayor would appoint his or her own supporters and fire the incumbents. This *spoils system* ensured that bureaucrats were closely responsive to the official who appointed them and were representative of the geographic, occupational, and ethnic background of the political majority.

The dilemma of reconciling political responsiveness and technically neutral expertise is clearly seen in the evolution of the civil service system, which is responsible for personnel policy in many state and local jurisdictions. As the functions of government expanded in number and complexity, reformers demanded that in order for government to operate more efficiently, bureaucrats should be chosen for their technical competence and protected from arbitrary dismissal. The Pendleton Act of 1883 established a federal Civil Service Commission, empowered to build a technically competent, politically neutral federal work force. The commission developed examinations to determine competency and rules to protect employees from arbitrary dismissal.

In the decades following 1883, many state and local governments formed similar civil service commissions to recruit and protect qualified employees. School districts were among the earliest to adopt civil service protections because teachers, who were professionalized by the 1890s, sought protection from political interference. In general lightly populated county and township governments and small cities were the slowest to install civil service systems.

A Tradition of Discrimination

The civil service system upgraded the quality of state and local government, building a core of well-trained, experienced bureaucrats capable of implementing public programs efficiently. But these bureaucrats were largely white male professional technocrats, neither representative of the public nor responsive to it. State and local governments, like private firms, systematically excluded women and minorities from many jobs. Employers assumed that women and blacks would not fit in, would make clients or other workers uncomfortable, and were not capable of doing many kinds of work. They also carelessly believed that women and blacks did not need jobs that paid well. In many city fire stations, for example, virtually all of the firefighters were white males, even though many blacks and Spanish-speaking citizens lived in the city and could undoubtedly do fire-fighting work competently. And women were restricted to traditionally female and generally semiskilled jobs.

Discrimination violates the democratic belief in equal opportunity for all, regardless of race, religion, or gender. Everyone pays taxes for state and local services, everyone uses them, and therefore everyone should have equal access to jobs providing them. Furthermore, state and local governments have a legitimate interest in increasing minority employment. Women, blacks, and Hispanics may be better served by teachers, nurses, and social workers who share the same background. A California state medical school, for example, enrolled a disproportionate number of blacks and Spanish-speaking students in the belief that having more minority doctors would improve doctor-patient relationships and raise the quality of medical care in black and Latino communities.[35]

Equal Employment Opportunity

The federal Civil Rights Act of 1964 declared that ''it shall be the policy of the United States to ensure equal employment opportunities for all federal employees'' and created the Equal Employment Opportunity Commission to enforce this policy. The act guaranteed equal consideration for employment and promotion regardless of gender, race, age, religion, or physical handicap.

Affirmative Action

Beginning in the late 1960s, affirmative action programs sought to change the composition of a technically competent, politically neutral bureaucracy dominated by white males. Affirmative action means that a state or local government will make a positive effort to find well-qualified minority applicants to fill positions. While a minority person need not be hired for a job for which he or she is not qualified, in cases where a minority candidate and a white male were equally qualified, the minority applicant would receive preference. For example, if a local police force has virtually no black employees, and if about one in every six subsequent hirees is black, the police force will continue to have relatively few blacks for many years to come. To speed the integration process, states and cities gave preferential treatment to minority applicants, hiring one minority person for every one or two white males hired.

Supporters of affirmative action argue that today's minorities should enjoy the same privileges that an earlier generation of disadvantaged white males did. In the nineteenth-century spoils system, government jobs were a major channel of upward mobility for Italian, Irish, and Jewish immigrants who were subject to discriminatory treatment in the private sector. Immigrants were the beneficiaries of an unstated affirmative action program. So, too, were their sons, who did not have to compete for jobs with ethnic minorities and women. Men were also given special preference for serving their country in the armed forces.

Have affirmative action programs improved the fortunes of females and minorities? Table 7.2 indicates that state and local governments have hired more minorities and women since 1973. The salary gap between white males and minorities has narrowed by a very slight margin. Minority salary gains are much smaller than their employment gains because a disproportionate number of minorities and women have relatively few years in service and start at entry-level jobs. Their

Table 7.2   State and Local Government Full-Time Employment and Salary, by Gender and Race

	Employment (%)				Median Annual Salary*			
Year	Male	Female	White	Mi-nority†	Male	Female	White	Mi-nority†
1973	65%	35%	82%	18%	$ 9600	$ 7000	$ 8800	$ 7500
1978	61%	39%	78%	22%	$13300	$ 9700	$12000	$10400
1983	59%	41%	76%	24%	$20100	$15300	$18500	$15900
1987	58%	42%	74%	26%	$24100	$18900	$22400	$20900

† Minority includes blacks and Hispanics only.
* Salaries are in current dollars, not adjusted for inflation.
Source: Adapted from *Statistical Abstract of the United States 1990*, p. 300.

pay raises and promotions lie in the future. Among city managers, for example, 5 percent were female in 1989, up from 1 percent in 1974. But one-third of assistant city and county managers are female, and many of them will become tomorrow's city managers.[36]

For 25 years, the courts generally have ruled that it is not necessary to find that a particular individual was personally victimized to establish that discrimination exists. One need only compare the percentage of qualified minority individuals in the work force with the number of qualified minorities employed. If 6 percent of a city's police officers are black compared to 14 percent of the city's work force, discrimination exists by definition. To redress gender or racial imbalance, state and local governments could use preferential hiring methods.[37] As stated earlier, though, no employer need hire someone who is not fully qualified for the job.

A 1971 court decision held that employers may not use educational qualifications or test scores to screen out applicants unless they can demonstrate the relevance of those criteria to the job.[38] For example, a county government or school district cannot require a high school education for unskilled work if such a requirement does not relate to performance on the job (and might possibly screen out some minority applicants). A city cannot require its firefighters to scale an eight foot wall if such a test has little relevance to fire-fighting practice and potentially screens out women.

Reverse Discrimination?

Affirmative action has generated considerable controversy. White males who were passed over for admission to training programs claimed that affirmative action programs denied them the equal protection of the laws guaranteed under the Fourteenth Amendment. They claimed to be victims of reverse discrimination.

In 1986, the Supreme Court supported preferential hiring of minorities in the case of Cleveland firefighters and New York sheet metal workers.[39] These decisions left government agencies free to adopt voluntary programs to hire and promote qualified minorities and women. But more recently, the Court has stressed that white males are protected under the equal protection of the laws clause of the Fourteenth Amendment. Affirmative action must not turn into reverse discrimination. In cases involving firefighters in Memphis, Tennessee and schoolteachers in Jackson, Michigan, the court has limited the ability of local governments to protect affirmative action gains by laying off whites before women and blacks with less seniority.[40]

Comparable Worth

Women have made more rapid gains in the workplace than have minorities, particularly at the professional and managerial levels. Middle-class women have had more access to higher education and have developed valuable organizational skills in the course of household management and volunteer work experiences. However, women continue to earn about two-thirds of what men earn. Part of the reason is that women typically have less education and less work experience than their male counterparts. Women tend to delay their careers while raising children and maintaining the household, while their husbands work and continue their educations.

However, in a comparison of matched groups of men and women who have the same education and work experience, women still earn about 15 percent less than do men.[41] Why? The principal reason is that 50 percent of women are now in the labor force and women tend to seek employment in traditional "women's occupations." The resulting intense competition for jobs as nurses, clerical workers, secretaries, elementary school teachers, and other female-dominated occupations drives down the average wage.[42]

This discrepancy in the wages paid in traditional male and female occupations has generated interest in the concept of comparable worth. Advocates of comparable worth amend the well-accepted notion of equal pay for equal work to equal pay for equally valuable work. If two employees are doing the same job, they surely should be paid at the same rate. Comparable worth advocates argue that jobs requiring equal knowledge, skill, effort, and responsibility should be paid equally. For example, in a job analysis, the jobs of highway maintenance worker and clerk/stenographer earn the same score. But the salary of the predominantly male highway worker category is 15 percent higher than that of the female-dominated clerk/stenographer category.[43]

Minnesota introduced a thorough revision of its job classification system in the 1980s. The state added $22 million, about 3.7 percent of the state salary base, to underpaid, female-dominated job categories. By 1987, twenty states had made some pay equity adjustments based on comparable worth principles. About 10 percent of American cities and counties have comparable worth policies.[44]

Some state and local governments are reluctant to endorse the comparable worth concept, since salary revisions would probably cost some money. Also, critics of comparable worth note that labor markets will reduce these disparities without policy intervention. As more high-paying jobs open up to women, the critics say, women will leave nursing and secretarial work, and wages in these occupations will rise. The eventual higher wages for such socially valuable, currently underpaid jobs will then begin to attract white males.[45] However, despite its critics, the policy innovation of comparable worth is likely to spread, if only because it is a useful bargaining tool for unions representing female-dominated occupations.

Complex bureaucratic organizations educate our children, maintain our roads, and protect our communities. Americans have ambivalent attitudes toward the state and local bureaucrats who provide these and other services. Citizens expect bureaucrats to treat all clients in the same manner, yet they complain of red tape when their individual cases are not given special treatment. They know that self-interest motivates behavior in the workplace, yet they are disappointed when bureaucrats do not act as selfless servants of the public interest. Most Americans believe that government creates more problems than it solves, yet most Americans also believe that government should do more to protect the environment, educate children, fight crime, and improve health care. Americans want a technically competent bureaucracy chosen without regard to gender, race, or creed, but they also want to increase minority representation in the civil service.

The fifty state and 83,000 local government bureaucracies exper-

iment in an effort to find efficient and equitable ways to monitor performance, measure productivity, and implement antidiscrimination programs.

Recommended Reading

Anthony Downs: *Inside Bureaucracy,* Little, Brown, Boston, 1967.

Hans Gerth and C. Wright Mills, eds.: *From Max Weber,* Oxford University Press, New York, 1946.

Judith Gruber: *Controlling Bureaucracy: Dilemmas in Democratic Governance,* University of California Press, Berkeley, Calif., 1987.

Michael Lipsky: *Street Level Bureaucrats: Dilemmas of the Individual in Public Services,* Russell Sage Foundation, New York, 1980.

Terry M. Moe: "The New Economics of Organization," *American Journal of Political Science,* 28:4, 1984.

William Niskanen: *Bureaucracy and Representative Government,* Aldine Atherton, Chicago, 1971.

CHAPTER 8

State Court Systems

Each state has its own unique judicial system, and court structures vary widely from state to state. This chapter explores similarities and differences across the American states. It begins with some historical background, then outlines the structure and functions of the state court systems. Local courts are part of the state system and therefore are not discussed separately. This chapter also considers the kinds of people who are likely to serve as judges and examines various methods of selection.

In any state, civil and criminal procedures are clearly drawn. These procedures are summarized as background for discussion of the factors that shape the courts' decision making.

Historical Background

Before the American Revolution, there was no tradition of an independent judiciary. Royal governors had considerable influence over the colonial judicial system in many of the colonies.[1] This situation led to a general wariness about the possible misuse of judicial power.

After the Revolutionary War, the role of the state courts was quite different from that of the colonial courts. The most important difference was that state courts asserted the power of *judicial review,* the ability of a court or judge to strike down a law (or executive action or administrative rule) as unconstitutional. Under the Articles of Confederation, some state courts asserted that they had the power to strike down state laws which the judges saw as inconsistent with state constitutions. For instance, in *Bayard v. Singleton,* a 1787 North Carolina case, the state's supreme court invalidated a state law requiring trial courts to dismiss any suits for the recovery of property arising under an earlier Tory confiscation law. The court held that any party trying to establish property rights had a right to a jury trial. Some state legislatures became outraged over the assertion of judicial review and would ask the judges to appear before the legislature to explain themselves. However, judicial review quickly became established at the state level. Between 1787 and 1803, state courts voided more than twenty state laws.[2] The acceptance of judicial review is one measure of the extent to which state courts had become viewed as legitimately independent branches of government.

Structure of the State Courts

Although court structure varies from state to state, there are three basic levels: trial courts, intermediate courts of appeal, and appeals courts of last resort.

Trial Courts

States commonly have *trial courts of general jurisdiction,* where major criminal and civil cases—for example, murder and grand theft auto—take place. Also tried in these courts are negligence suits: for example, an action against a local company that stored dangerous materials which then exploded, resulting in injuries. *Trial courts of limited jurisdiction* deal with more mundane cases: for example, small claims court (of the type made famous in Judge Wapner's televised show ''The People's Court'') or courts designed for specialized cases, such as traffic court or family court. Cases, then, begin in those courts designed to process specific types of grievances, complaints, and crimes.

Intermediate Appellate Courts

Three-quarters of the fifty states have intermediate appellate courts. Parties who lose in trial courts and who believe that errors of law have been made there (for example, a judge giving an improper charge to a jury in a criminal case, or a judge showing obvious favoritism in ruling on motions for one side in a case) may be able to appeal the decision to a higher court. Appeals courts do not hear evidence or determine guilt or innocence, as trial courts do.

State Courts of Last Resort

Finally, sitting astride the state's judicial system is its highest appeals court, normally called the Supreme Court (although, in New York State, the court called the Supreme Court is a trial court of general jurisdiction and the highest court in the state is called the Court of Appeals—the term that most states reserve for their intermediate appeals courts!). If questions arising under the national Constitution or federal law are at issue in a case being decided by a state supreme court, the losing party has the option of petitioning the U.S. Supreme Court to hear the case.

Functions of State Courts

State courts serve several functions. Among these are norm enforcement, policy making, and administration.[3]

Norm Enforcement

Much of what state courts do is routine. From day to day, most decisions that are rendered by judges, from the justice of the peace to the state supreme court, simply apply existing laws, doctrines, and precedents (previous cases dealing with similar issues) to the case at hand. The principle of *stare decisis* (the directive to follow precedent, literally "to let the decision stand") is respected. In that sense, the function of norm enforcement is to make sure that the existing rules are enforced. This is the basic business of trial courts. The judge who fines a careless driver fifty dollars is carrying out norm enforcement.

Policy Making

Some decisions do not just apply the rules as they currently exist; they set new precedents, establishing new guidelines for future decisions. This action is called *policy making*. It is most often carried out by appellate courts, especially state supreme courts.

State supreme courts have often produced innovative decisions, sometimes paving the way for new approaches to long-standing problems. It was in some of the state courts that property taxes were struck down as a violation of citizens' right to equal protection of the laws under state constitutions. The California Supreme Court in *Serrano v. Priest* (1971) used provisions in both the national Constitution and the California state constitution as grounds for attacking the property tax that helped fund public education. The court explained that poorer communities would have a much more difficult time raising funds for education and, hence, citizens of those communities were being disadvantaged in access to a good education. While the United States Supreme Court later interpreted the U.S. Constitution as not prohibiting the property tax as a means of funding education, in *San Antonio v. Rodriguez* (1973), since the California tribunal also relied on independent state constitutional grounds, its decision stood. Hence, California had to devise a new mechanism for funding its schools, using general state revenues. Some other state supreme courts followed suit (as in New Jersey's in *Robinson v. Cahill,* 1972). Thus, this change in school financing arose from state supreme court decisions. This is an example of policy making.

Administration

The state court system is a bureaucracy that employs many people, from clerks to bailiffs to administrative assistants. As such, it must be administered on a day-to-day basis to ensure that the organization operates smoothly. The administrative function includes organizing courts, making sure that records are properly kept, hiring court personnel, maintaining schedules, and so on. In fact, the growing administrative bureaucracy of courts has raised some concern that judges may be losing control over their courts as ''creeping bureaucratization'' sets in, a subject discussed at greater length on pages 174 and 175.

Judges

Methods of Selection

There are three major types of selection systems. Judges can be appointed to office; they can be elected; or they can be chosen by a combination of appointment and election.

Selection by Appointment

There are two means of getting appointed to office: gubernatorial appointment and legislative appointment.

Gubernatorial Appointment. The governor appoints at least some state judges by this method, although the exact mechanism varies from state to state. Normally, governors' nominees must be confirmed (approved); the body usually responsible for confirmation is the state senate.

Governors use several criteria for selecting judges. One is the ideology of the potential nominee. Governors often wish to leave an imprint on the type of decisions that state courts make. Thus, a governor who is a conservative Republican may well use his or her appointment power to fill available judgeships with conservatives. Similarly, Democratic governors will most often appoint members of their own party. After all, plenty of capable individuals within either party would make fine judges, so why would a governor select a judge representing the other party?

Governors may nominate individuals for judgeships for political reasons. If, for instance, Italian-Americans are a major group in the state, the governor might well appoint several Italian-Americans to the state courts to demonstrate that he or she is aware of the group and is responding to its needs—and, in the process, perhaps garner some additional votes from Italian-Americans at the next election. Powerful political figures within the state may be placated by the governor's giving judgeships to individuals suggested by them. In some states, governors take into account very seriously the desires of powerful county party chairs. Finally, governors may weigh well-known judicial competence into their selection calculus; some potential judges may be so respected that it makes good political sense to nominate them.

Legislative Appointment. Legislative appointment is a remnant of the early republic, with only Rhode Island, South Carolina, and Virginia still practicing the method. In Rhode Island, for example, the state legislature selects the state's supreme court members (although trial judges are appointed by the governor). Criteria for selection are similar to those in gubernatorial appointments; however, former state legislators appear to be disproportionately selected as state judges![4]

Selection by Election

Various states select judges by either nonpartisan elections or partisan elections.

Nonpartisan Elections.   In some states, judges are elected by the citizens, but party labels do not appear on the ballots. (Only the merit plan—discussed in later paragraphs—is more popular as a way of choosing state judges.) Many states, including California, Kentucky, Michigan, and Wisconsin, use nonpartisan elections as at least one mechanism for selecting judges for state courts. In some states which are officially nonpartisan, the party organizations may nonetheless sponsor and publicize their respective choices standing for election.

Partisan Elections.   In partisan elections, a party label is attached to the various candidates for judgeships. This can be a significant cue to the voters, since party identification is a powerful factor affecting vote choice throughout the political system (see Chapter 4). There is even a coattails effect in some states. In Texas, for instance, Republican candidates for trial court judgeships run better and receive more votes when the top of the state Republican ticket does well.[5]

Incumbency and Judicial Elections

When states use elections to select judges, incumbency is a significant factor in the outcome.

Incumbency Advantage.   Those who already hold judgeships are rarely defeated when they run for reelection. One reason for this is that the general public has little information about most judges and judicial candidates, although those most likely to vote tend to be reasonably well-informed.[6] Hence, in the absence of information, citizens tend to vote for the incumbent.[7] Since incumbents win regularly and by large margins, many incumbents for judicial office run unopposed.

When Incumbents Can Lose.   Incumbents are not invincible. Although they normally win by large margins, they can be beaten. When a sitting judge represents a party whose supporters comprise what is obviously a minority of the state's electorate, the incumbent may be in trouble. Sometimes, judges who render unpopular decisions may find themselves in peril. A trial judge in Wisconsin, for example, was defeated in a recall election after he made a decision releasing an accused rapist because the judge believed that the woman involved encouraged the rapist by her dress and demeanor. In a more dramatic instance, three members of the California Supreme Court were defeated upon their run for reelection because voters felt that all three, Chief Justice Rose Bird and Associate Justices Joseph Grodin and Cruz Reynoso, were too soft on crime.[8] Over time, it appears that elections for state supreme courts are becoming more hotly contested. Perhaps citizens and partisan leaders are increasingly realizing that the makeup of the state judiciary can influence the kinds of decisions that courts make.[9]

The Merit Plan

Merit selection takes place in several different ways. A generic example is as follows: The governor selects three laypersons and the state bar association chooses three attorneys to be members of a judicial nominating commission; a state judge is also selected (the method of selection varies) to serve on the commission. The seven-person commission is activated when a vacancy in the state courts occurs. Members peruse the credentials of potential judges; they will, after deliberations, send three names to the governor. The governor nominates one of these to the state judgeship. The nominee serves one year and then faces the voters in a "selection retention" election. The ballot asks, "Should Judge X be retained on the state court?" and if a majority of the voters vote "yes," then the incumbent will serve a fourteen-year term before facing the voters in another selection retention election (if the judge wishes reelection). This is one of several ways that the merit plan is implemented. It is presumed that the procedures developed for a merit plan selection system will increase the odds of truly meritorious individuals being nominated (a dubious proposition, as we shall see). The merit plan is often called the Missouri Plan, in honor of the "Show Me" state's being the first to adopt such a mechanism for judicial selection.

The underlying motivation for this system, long championed by the American Bar Association, is to make the judiciary less responsive to political influence and to make selection more likely to be on the basis of a candidate's merits rather than on the basis of crass political considerations. Does the merit plan meet these goals? Studies show that governors have considerable influence on who the commission nominates; after all, three members are his handpicked selections, and they are likely to advocate nominees who fit the governor's agenda. Members of the commission also tend to respect the judge's views. One classic analysis of the Missouri Plan concludes that "governors have used their appointments to reward friends or past political supporters."[10] In other words, the merit plan often functions as a "disguised" version of gubernatorial appointment.

Trends in Selection Methods

Over time, Glick and Vines have contended, the states have behaved as if judicial selection methods were "fads."[11]

Legislative and Gubernatorial Appointment

From 1776 to 1831, when a state instituted a new method for selection of judges, two techniques predominated: legislative selection (instituted 49 percent of the time when a state adopted a new method) and gubernatorial appointment (instituted 42 percent of the time). That legislatures were primary actors should not be surprising. Before the Revolution, royal governors had great power over the colonial judiciary. Citizens saw their elected representatives in the legislatures as their guardians of liberty. Hence, it is hardly surprising that the people turned to their legislatures during the revolutionary and postrevolutionary periods to select judges.

Partisan Elections

From 1832 to 1885, those states that came into the union or that altered their existing mode of judicial selection stampeded to adopt partisan elections (73 percent of the changes were to partisan elections). This trend is normally interpreted as an embracing of the ideals of "Jacksonian democracy," which extolled the virtues of ordinary men and held that they were capable of serving in office or selecting those who would serve.

Nonpartisan Elections

From 1886 to 1933, there was yet another fad. The excesses of the spoils system and the political machine manipulating who won elections led reformers to seek a new way of selecting judges. Nonpartisan elections emerged as the mechanism of choice. During this period, states entering the union or states changing their selection method overwhelmingly turned to nonpartisan elections; 64 percent of the systems chosen over this time period were nonpartisan elections. This way of choosing judges was thought to reduce the power of the political machine and increase the odds that judges elected to office would not be beholden to political bosses.

Merit Selection

From 1934 to the present, merit plans have been clearly the trend, with the strong endorsement of the American Bar Association. From 1934 to 1968, 72 percent of the time that a new system of choosing judges was implemented, that system was the merit plan. From 1968 to the present, the percentage is higher still.[12]

Impact of Selection Methods

Type of Judge Selected

Do the five different selection techniques—partisan elections, nonpartisan elections, legislative appointment, gubernatorial appointment, and merit plan—result in different kinds of people being selected as judges? Most evidence suggests that differences are modest. To illustrate, until the 1960s, merit plan judges tended to be somewhat more localistic in their backgrounds (that is, born and educated in the state of their judgeship),[13] but that no longer seems to be the case.[14] The one difference is that those selected by the merit plan may be less diverse in their backgrounds, and, in that sense, less representative. Merit plans are more likely to select high-status Protestants and fewer Catholics and Jews. Thus, there may be some subtle biases at work on the basis of religious background of possible judicial nominees. Since religious background has a mild relationship to how judges make decisions (Catholics and Jews are somewhat more liberal in their decisions than Protestants), this discovery has some policy implications.[15]

Decision Making

Does method of selection affect how judges make up their minds on cases before them? One study explored the impact of selection method on decisions rendered by state supreme courts, such as support for the state when the state government is bringing a case to the court, support for a criminal defendant when that person is bringing the case to the court of last resort, support for the corporation as an appellant (the one asking the supreme court to hear a case), support for "upperdogs" (the economically advantaged, such as corporations), and support for "underdogs" (those who are poor or who have relatively few economic resources). Statistical analysis indicates that method of selection is not directly related to how judges rule on a wide array of issues.[16] To understand how judges make decisions, we must look beyond method of selection (see the discussion later in the chapter).

Removing Judges

Occasionally, state judges may be incompetent or corrupt, may become senile, or may otherwise cease to be able to carry out their responsibilities. States have developed a number of mechanisms for removing such judges.

Impeachment

The most familiar method for removing judges is impeachment. In impeachment proceedings, one body of the state legislature finds enough evidence to consider removing a state judge from office; then the other body (often the state senate) sits as a jury to decide whether or not the evidence warrants removing the judge from office.

Recall

Some states provide for recall elections of judges. If a judge were to make extraordinarily unpopular decisions or demonstrate incapacity, the people could remove the judge by recall.

Commissions

Other states have formed judicial commissions, in which members of the commission investigate claims of wrongdoing or incompetence by judges. If the claims are substantiated, sanctions may be brought to bear, from mild criticism to removal from office.

Rejection on Election Day

In states where judges are elected to office, the voters can remove those deemed no longer fit for office at the next regularly scheduled election, as the aforementioned purge of California Chief Justice Rose Bird and her two liberal colleagues exemplifies.

Characteristics of Judges

Judges, like incumbents of other state offices, tend to be white males from upper-middle-class (or even more privileged) backgrounds. They are often active politically. State supreme court judges studied in 1969 had held an average of 2.3 offices before gaining a judgeship. State judges are recruited and trained locally, that is, within the state. Party affiliation is an important factor. Not surprisingly, Democrat-dominated states tend to produce state supreme court judges who are solidly Democratic; Republican-dominated states tend to produce state supreme court judges who are Republican, and states with balanced two-party competition have fairly even numbers of both. Overall, state supreme court judges are largely Protestant (about 60 percent). Most have had prior experience as judges and had practiced law for about fifteen years before joining the court.[17]

Women are underrepresented in state courts, but the proportion of female jurists is increasing. Blacks are also relatively few, although their number has been growing in recent decades. Black judges are more likely to sit as judges on courts of limited jurisdiction. As of 1989, thirty state supreme courts had no black judges, and seventeen states with an intermediate appeals court had no sitting black jurists. Indeed, in five states (for example, Rhode Island and Arkansas), there were no black judges on trial courts of general jurisdiction.[18]

In the United States, there is no school where one learns to become a judge. Newly elected or appointed judges must learn on the job, although some states provide limited training for judges, such as workshops, short courses, and the like.

Criminal and Civil Procedure

Courts handle two distinct types of actions: criminal and civil cases. Although the precise series of steps in the civil and criminal process varies from state to state, a reasonable approximation of the process in each category can be made, as set forth in this section.

Criminal Procedure

Criminal cases are often among the most dramatic events in the judicial process, riveting national attention. Jeffrey Dahmer, Mike Tyson, and William Kennedy Smith are among the names that generated much public attention and debate in state court trials in the early 1990s. This section outlines the criminal process and some of the issues raised by its operation. More detail is provided in Chapter 13, which examines criminal justice policy.

Criminal law is that portion of the state laws which defines what actions constitute violations of the public order. Examples of criminal offenses include larceny, burglary, auto theft, rape, and murder. Criminal actions may be defined as either *felonies*—serious offenses like those noted above, in which the penalty is significant time in prison (one year or more)—or *misdemeanors,* which are petty offenses like disorderly conduct or driving an automobile without a valid inspection sticker.

The Process

1. A person is arrested for violation of the criminal code.

2. A preliminary hearing is held, in which the prosecution (nor-

mally represented by the local District Attorney's office) must show probable cause that a criminal act has been committed and that the suspect is the perpetrator. If the prosecution can demonstrate probable cause, the person will be held for further proceedings. Many people will then be released on bail or on their own recognizance if it appears that they are unlikely to try to leave the area to escape prosecution.

3. A grand jury indictment, rendered by a body of citizens who examine the evidence and decide whether or not there is sufficient justification for the suspect to stand trial, moves the process forward to the next stage. Alternatively, an *information,* a document filed by the District Attorney in which he or she argues that there is sufficient evidence to warrant prosecution, is delivered in some states.

4. At arraignment, the suspect is read the charges as established by the grand jury indictment or prosecutor's information and pleads guilty, not guilty, or *nolo contendere* (that is, the person does not contest the charge but does not admit guilt, either).

5. There are pretrial proceedings, in which motions may be made or plea bargaining carried out.

6. A trial is held. The trial may be either in front of a jury or in front of a judge alone (a *bench trial*), as the suspect wishes.

7. The verdict is reached at the end of the trial. If it is a jury trial and the case is a major one, a unanimous verdict is normally called for (in lesser offenses, something less than unanimity may suffice).

8. The sentence, which represents the court's punishment of the guilty party, is pronounced.

9. There may be an appeal (if the suspect loses and wishes to pursue the case in appellate court).

10. The sentence is enforced if appeals fail.

The process is long and cumbersome, and few suspects take advantage of "their day in court." One study reports that only about 4 out of 100 persons arrested actually go to trial; 47 percent of cases end with guilty pleas, normally the result of plea bargaining.[19]

Issues in the Criminal Process

Several noteworthy issues regarding the criminal process are discussed below in detail: U.S. Supreme Court decisions that impose limitations on actions of state criminal justice organizations; plea bargaining; the competence of juries; and the adequacy of representation for the poor.

U.S. Supreme Court Decisions.   Decisions by the U.S. Supreme Court are external forces that structure the day-to-day workings of the criminal process. At the moment a suspect becomes the focus of an investigation, he or she must be read the ''Miranda rights,'' which arose from the case *Miranda v. Arizona* (1966). In this case, the Supreme Court ordered that all of those taken into custody must be informed of their right to remain silent, of their right to an attorney, of the option of the court's appointing an attorney if the person cannot afford to retain one, and of the police's ability to use any statements made by the suspect to prosecute the suspect in a court of law. Another key case is *Mapp v. Ohio* (1961), which applied the *exclusionary rule*—any evidence of a crime seized without a proper search warrant will not be admitted as evidence—to the state law enforcement system. *Chimel v. California* (1969) limits the power of police to search widely when arresting a person; search incident to arrest is limited to the suspect's immediate vicinity (unless, of course, the arresting officers also have a proper search warrant). Since some suspects who are guilty may go free if crucial evidence is contaminated by faulty police procedure, controversy has erupted over these decisions. However, although the more conservative U.S. Supreme Courts under Chief Justices Burger and Rehnquist have allowed somewhat more flexibility to the police, the broad outlines of these (and other unpopular decisions) remain in operation.[20]

After the U.S. Supreme Court in *Furman v. Georgia* (1972) temporarily halted state execution of those convicted of capital crimes because of the arbitrary way in which death sentences were rendered, the U.S. Supreme Court allowed routes to be available for states to produce acceptable death penalty statutes. First, states could remove discretion from the judge or jury in deciding when to administer the death penalty by making death the mandatory—not discretionary—punishment for certain types of heinous crimes. Second, states could develop a two-tier system in capital cases. A first trial would determine guilt or innocence of the accused. A subsequent trial would be held for those found guilty at the first; the issue at the second trial would be whether or not to impose a death penalty. Within a few years, thirty-five states had enacted death penalties adopting one or the other mechanism. In *Gregg v. Georgia* (1976), the U.S. Supreme Court concluded that such approaches did not violate the Eighth Amendment; thus the death penalty, if properly arrived at, is not currently deemed cruel and unusual punishment.

Plea Bargaining.   This is the practice whereby a prosecuting attorney, usually referred to as a district attorney (DA), will reduce charges against a suspect if he or she pleads guilty to a lesser charge. For instance, if a suspect is accused of first degree murder, the penalty could be death if the murder was committed in a state with the death penalty. The prosecutor might have reasonable evidence to prosecute for first degree murder, but perhaps the evidence is not airtight. Hence, the DA may make a deal with the suspect and counsel: for example, if the suspect pleads guilty to manslaughter (which garners a much lighter penalty), the DA will not go forward to trial on the original first degree murder charge. Such plea bargaining helps the won-lost record of the DA, who has a conviction without taking the chance of a trial in which the suspect might be found not guilty, and the suspect does not have to risk the potential death penalty if found guilty. In addition, the court, usually nearly overwhelmed by a large caseload, does not have to tie up resources in a possibly lengthy trial. The debate arises over whether or not this system of plea bargaining best serves justice. Innocent suspects have been known to "cop a plea" to avoid the possibility of a heavier punishment; they will not have their "day in court" to prove themselves innocent. On the other hand, people guilty of serious crimes may receive relatively mild penalties through plea bargaining.[21]

The Jury.   Defendants have the right to a trial by jury, although they may choose a bench trial, in which there is no jury and the judge makes the determination of guilt or innocence. One center of controversy about the use of juries is how well ordinary citizens do in rendering verdicts. The famous Chicago Jury Study examined how often juries and presiding judges agreed with one another and discovered that judge and jury reached the same conclusion 81 percent of the time in criminal cases. In the other cases, juries were more likely to acquit defendants than were judges.[22]

Adequacy of Representation for the Poor.   Many believe that poor defendants get inferior representation through either the public defender's office or through appointed counsel systems. Public defenders are often young lawyers right out of law school, with little prior criminal law experience, and they carry heavy caseloads. Indeed, articles with titles like "Did You Have a Lawyer When You Went to Court? No, I had a Public Defender"[23] make the point. However, some evidence indicates that public defenders can do a good job representing their clients. One study of the public defender program in New York City shows that when they go to trial, public defenders are about as likely to win a case and are as disposed to make motions and raise challenges to prospective jurors as are their more experienced counterparts in the DA's office.[24] The heavy caseloads borne by counsel for indigents facing criminal charges create problems; nonetheless, representation in such cases is much better than it is for the poor in civil cases, as noted below.

Civil Procedure

Civil law focuses on disputes between citizens, such as whether or not one has violated a contract, whether or not one person has wronged another (for instance, through negligence), divorce proceedings, and the like. In reality, of course, some violations can be treated as either civil or criminal in nature. For example, manufacturers who endanger the lives of their workers through unsafe practices can be charged under either criminal or civil law.

The Process

1. The civil process begins when one party, believing himself or herself aggrieved by a second party, files a complaint, in which the person alleges wrongdoing committed by the second party.

2. The complaint is then served on the second party, informing them that a complaint has been filed.

3. The second party draws up a response, in which the charges outlined in the complaint are addressed.

4. At this point, called the pleadings, the issue is joined, when a complaint and its response are filed with the court.

5. Discovery comes next, during which time information regarding the case is gathered and shared between the parties.

6. A pretrial conference is often held, at which point possible pretrial settlements are discussed. If a settlement is reached, there is no trial.

7. Trial is held, with or without a jury.

8. The jury or the judge decides which side in the case has the preponderance of evidence (that is, the jury or judge reaches a verdict).

9. The judge issues the judgment, in which he or she indicates the penalties to be imposed upon the losing side.

10. The loser may appeal.

11. After appeals are exhausted, assuming that the original verdict and judgment are left in place by appeals court judges, the loser in the case complies with the judgment.

Issues in the Civil Process

One key issue in civil proceedings is the disadvantages accruing to the poor. Another is tort reform (torts are ''wrongs,'' exemplified by negligence cases), and a third is growing caseload pressure.

Disadvantages for the Poor. Civil courts are sometimes referred to as the courts of the ''haves,'' based upon the view that poor people receive short shrift. This happens for several reasons: (1) the poor find it harder to receive competent counsel in civil than in criminal cases; (2) the poor may not understand that they have a cause of action against a powerful party and, hence, may not pursue a valid claim; on the other hand, powerful individuals or organizations are much more likely to understand that they have recourse to the courts; (3) the poor are more likely to feel that pursuing a civil claim is hopeless; (4) the poor do not have the same level of access to counsel in civil cases as they do in criminal cases. The end result is that the poor tend to be disadvantaged in civil courts.[25]

Tort Reform. Earlier in American legal history, it was difficult for people to sue for damages that they had suffered. Immunity was provided by the courts to government agencies and nonprofit organizations. It was possible to sue manufacturers for defective products (product liability) only if one could demonstrate a very plain and clear negligence on the manufacturers' part. Manufacturers were normally held not to be responsible for injuries suffered by employees on the job. In recent years, though, state courts have made it easier for citizens to recover damages from product liability, negligence, and so on. One result has been skyrocketing damage awards to victims of negligence.[26] Indeed, the innovation by state courts in making it easier for people to get monetary damages has led to a countermovement to cap awards. However, evidence that, for instance, medical malpractice awards by juries are excessive is very unclear.[27]

Caseload Pressure.   Civil cases represent the greatest source of increased caseload pressure in recent years. Evidence indicates a steady climb in the number of civil filings in both courts of general jurisdiction and courts of limited jurisdiction (such as small claims court). Over a ten-year period ending in 1986, civil cases nearly doubled.[28]

Factors Shaping Judicial Decision Making

Among factors that influence how state judges arrive at their decisions are social background, ideology, judicial role, and public opinion. This is not to say that judges' decisions—whether at trial or on appellate review—are idiosyncratic and arbitrary. The state law and state constitution and extant precedent often render decisions very easy and obvious. However, when issues are not as clearcut there is considerable room for other elements to come into play.

Social Background, Party, and Ideology

Religion of a jurist has a modest effect on judges' decisions. High-status Protestant judges tend to be more conservative in their decisions (that is, less likely to support economic underdogs, less apt to rule in favor of criminal defendants' claims, and so on), whereas Catholic state supreme court judges are modestly more liberal. Ethnic background has a minor impact, with state supreme court judges of British background being somewhat more conservative than judges from other ethnic groups.[29] However, the statistical link between background and judges' decisions is rather weak. Somewhat more robust findings demonstrate that, as one would expect, Democratic state supreme court judges are more liberal than their Republican counterparts.[30]

Judicial Role

Role refers to the expectations that attach to holding a certain position. Role definition helps to shape actual behavior. One study of supreme court judges in four states identified three roles: *law interpreter* (such judges follow precedent and are loath to second-guess the state legislature and governor by striking down laws that have been enacted), *law maker* (these judges are more innovative in decisions that they make, more apt to try to set new precedents), and *eclectic* or *pragmatist* (these judges combine the styles of law interpreters and law makers).[31] Law interpreters are likely to define themselves as conservative, while law makers define themselves as liberal. Judges from urban areas who are either Catholic or Jewish are more inclined to call themselves law makers.[32]

Role appears to affect decision making. State supreme court judges who adopt a law-making, activist role appear to be more liberal in criminal cases, that is, less likely to support the prosecution.[33]

Public Opinion

Public opinion, too, has an effect on decision-making behavior. For example, California voters expressed preference for or against decriminalization of marijuana in an initiative in 1972. Judges' sentencing behavior before and after the vote tallies became known suggests that judges altered their sentencing behavior to comport more closely with their counties' views on marijuana.[34] As another example, judges on the Louisiana Supreme Court must face the voters to stay in office, and those judges who have views inconsistent with the majority of their colleagues *and* the majority of their constituents were found to disagree less with majority opinions than would normally be expected. They ''go along'' in order not to rouse public opinion against them.[35]

Bureaucratization of State Courts

One problem facing state courts, as noted earlier, is heavy caseload pressure. Judges have to organize their dockets and record-keeping and offices more carefully than ever. There have been a variety of reform efforts to make state courts more manageable. One common approach has been some degree of bureaucratization.

The federal courts have increased their staffs (including more law clerks who carry out research and may even draft opinions for judges) and gone so far as to develop a new class of ''subjudges'' (such as federal magistrates) who now assume many of the responsibilities that the United States District Judges once did. The problem is that growing staff size could undermine the independence of the judges, since they come to rely more and more on their increasingly large bureaucratic organizations. Furthermore, the judges themselves may come to lose track of their caseloads and the concerns of those who use the federal courts.[36]

The problem of heavy caseloads is also relevant at the state level. One response to the higher case burden has been increasing staff, including law clerks and staff attorneys.[37] Recent evidence suggests (although it does not prove) that adding a research staff to state appellate courts may lead overworked judges to depend more and more upon their staffs. There is a very high level of agreement between centralized research staff recommendations and judges' actual decisions.[38] Thus, the desire to make courts more efficient may be making judges more dependent upon a newly developing bureaucracy.

Courts are political institutions as well as legal organizations. Politics intrudes from the selection of judges to the courts' decision making. State courts face very heavy caseloads. One response to the pressure has been bureaucratization, including hiring research staff. Critics of this approach fear that the judiciary may thereby lose its independence and possibly its legitimacy as well.

State courts have often been innovators and, in that sense, have illustrated the proposition that state and local governments serve as great laboratories for experimentation. In this, state courts perform a similar function as other state political institutions.

While some people worry that the poor and otherwise disadvantaged are shut out of the judicial system, they appear to be adequately represented in criminal cases; in civil affairs, however, the situation is not so equitable.

Recommended Reading

Henry Abraham: *The Judicial Process,* 5th ed., Oxford University Press, New York, 1986.

Lawrence Baum: *American Courts,* 2d ed., Houghton Mifflin, Boston, 1990.

Henry Robert Glick and Kenneth N. Vines: *State Court Systems,* Prentice-Hall, Englewood Cliffs, N.J., 1973.

Herbert Jacob: "Courts: The Least Visible Branch," in Virginia Gray, Herbert Jacob, and Robert Albritton, eds.: *Politics in the American States,* 5th ed., Scott, Foresman, Glenview, Ill., 1990.

Herbert Jacob: *Justice in America,* 4th ed., Little, Brown, Boston, 1984.

Lloyd L. Weinreb: *Leading Constitutional Cases on Criminal Justice,* Foundation Press, Westbury, N.Y., 1991.

Part III

State and Local Policy Making

CHAPTER 9

The Policy Process in State and Local Politics

How do decisions get made by state and local governments? What actors are involved? Who wins and who loses? What forces help to shape the actual choices made by governments at the subnational level? These are the questions addressed in this chapter.

The policy process itself is often divided into several stages: problem recognition, agenda setting, decision making (or policy making), implementation, service delivery, evaluation, and feedback. Different dynamics govern each stage, and different actors are dominant at each stage. Policy itself has been defined as "whatever governments choose to do or not to do."[1] In short, in the context of state and local governments, policy is what these governments do and the decisions that they make (or choose not to make). This chapter examines five stages of the policy process, from problem recognition through service delivery.

The chapter concludes by looking at some of the factors that affect decisions actually made by state governments. Prior chapters have noted the importance of intergovernmental relations, public opinion, political culture, interest group activities, party competition, the executive, the legislature, the courts, bureaucracy, and socioeconomic factors. In the following six chapters, these various influences will be reexamined in light of several major policy areas to see the extent to which they help to shape the contours of state policy.

Actors in the Policy Process

Many people and organizations are involved in making policy. This simple fact thereby leads to complex political interactions since so many distinct actors with disparate goals and motivations are involved. Sometimes various actors cooperate with one another; at other times, they will be in competition. The cast of policy makers in state and local government, with a brief description of their respective roles, is outlined below.

Bureaucracy is a key actor; the experts have a role at each stage of decision making, with that role perhaps being greatest during problem recognition, implementation, and service delivery.

Elected officials in the executive and legislative branches are central at the agenda-setting and policy-making stages; their influence often drops off later in the process, although this is not necessarily the case.

Interest groups are active throughout, from problem recognition to agenda setting to policy making to implementation, although their role at the back end of the process is less important than at the front end.

The public (through public opinion, voting, and the like) can be a significant actor at the problem recognition, agenda-setting, and policy-making stages, although its attention to a particular issue or problem waxes and wanes in such a manner as to make its impact somewhat unpredictable.

The judicial branch can be central. Decisions of state courts can reshape the agenda. For instance, New Jersey's supreme court struck down the property tax as a device for financing public education; this necessitated adoption by the state legislature of an alternative formula for paying for the state's education system. In essence, the court set the agenda.

Political parties may have influence during the earlier stages of the process and in policy making. Their participation in policy drops off in the latter stages.

The media can be influential, but their involvement in policy making is sporadic and idiosyncratic.

While all these actors can influence the process, other forces must be taken into account, as well. The state or local government's economic position, for instance, shapes the possibilities of policy making. A poor state is much less likely to attempt to enact certain policies than is a wealthier state. Decisions by the national government play a role, too. Washington, D.C., can mandate that states carry out certain actions, just as states can issue mandates to local governments. Federal funds may flow more readily to some states than to others.

Stages of the Policy Process

Problem Recognition

The first stage in the policy process is problem recognition—coming to realize that there is a specific problem ''out there.'' Before government can take any action, it must determine that a problem exists. This is hardly an automatic process, since there are myriad potential problems in a society at any single point in time. For example, if there are many homeless people within a city and residents are not aware of this, the situation represents no problem to them. If, however, local citizens become aware of the extent of homelessness, then they may come to believe that something is wrong and action is needed.

Routes to Problem Identification

Problems can be identified in a number of ways, some of which are discussed below.

Social Indicators.   Social indicators (statistical data) can spotlight the existence of serious problems. Social indicators are measures of how well a particular state or locality is functioning. For instance, if the numbers of arrests for DWI (drinking while intoxicated), people undergoing alcohol treatment in hospitals, and alcohol-related accidents have been increasing within a community, then these indices can show a local government that alcohol is becoming a problem. This recognition may eventually lead to some kind of action by that government, such as more aggressive police action and education programs. At the state level, if the number of new jobs being created each year has been declining over several years, economic stagnation may be perceived as a problem, and the state may consider an economic development policy to redress it.

Events.   Events can lead to problem recognition. If a major earthquake were to strike the northeastern United States, there would be much devastation, since buildings are not constructed to sustain the effects of a major quake. In the aftermath, both state and local governments would be likely to recognize a problem and move to upgrade construction standards. On occasion, gunmen have used assault weapons to attack innocent people in fast-food restaurants or students in schools; governments have defined this as a problem and subsequently have taken some action, such as legislation making access to assault weapons more difficult.

Feedback.   A third route to problem recognition is feedback, the process by which public officials hear about how well or poorly programs are working. For example, if elected city council members routinely hear from their constituents that garbage pickups are missed, they will get the idea that something is wrong with the trash collection service and may look at the situation to try to improve it.

Participants in Problem Recognition

Who is important at the problem recognition stage? Many agencies are involved in monitoring social indicators, to pick up trends in society. In this manner, bureaucrats can play a role in recognizing a problem. The public can also play a role: If the general public becomes aroused about a certain problem, substantial attention may be given to the issue by public officials. Interest groups are surely important actors. The NAACP (National Association for the Advancement of Colored People) engaged in many different activities to make state governments more aware of problems with civil rights in the 1950s and 1960s. As already indicated above in the example of feedback, elected officials are part of the process as well. Also, if the media begin focusing on certain issues, such as homelessness or rape, this may spark recognition that a problem exists.

Agenda Setting

Thomas Dye has stated that ''the power to decide what will be a policy issue is crucial to the policy-making process. Deciding what will be the problem is even more important than deciding what will be the solutions.''[2] Agenda setting is deciding what to decide about. Many potential problems never get recognized, but even if problems are recognized, there is no guarantee that government will seriously attack them. Of the uncountable potential issues or problems that government might choose to deal with, few get to the agenda-setting stage. However, over time, governments at all levels have increased the scope of government action by considering more and different types of issues as worthy of discussion. Thus, the agenda has expanded greatly over time. For example, at one point, state governments did not feel the need to license accountants. However, states then came to believe that licensing of such specialists has a legitimate place on the agenda.

What gets an item placed on the agenda? Besides problem recognition, several other factors come into play.

Political Circumstances

Political conditions must be right. Significant political actors must support agenda placement. On political elements, John Kingdon has said of national agenda setting (and the comments are equally applicable to state and local circumstances):

> Political events flow along according to their own dynamics and their own rules. Participants perceive swings in national mood, elections bring new administrations to power and new partisan or ideological distributions to Congress, and interest groups of various descriptions press (or fail to press) their demands on government.[3]

Consensus may emerge that certain conditions call for government consideration. This can be a product of a bargaining and negotiating process among a host of participants.

Participants in Agenda Setting

In agenda setting, the visible political actors—such as the governor or mayor, the legislature, top appointees of a governor or mayor, media, political parties, and interest groups—are most important. Ambition can be one factor impelling an elected official to take a leadership position. New ideas and the image of being able to tackle new problems can be vehicles for electoral success. Of course, those officials who are wed to the status quo would be less likely to promote new agenda items. If few or none of the political actors listed above advocate agenda placement for a problem, it is unlikely that that problem will move along in the policy process. Occasionally, though, one person can make a difference by becoming a *policy entrepreneur.* This person devotes himself or herself to getting a certain issue placed on the agenda. Examples include Ralph Nader as a crusader for consumer safety, Jack Kemp as the apostle of supply-side economics, and Mitch Snider as an advocate for the homeless. In each case, one person cajoled, pleaded, and argued a case to a larger audience to gather support.

Less visible participants have a role, too. Academics, "think tank" specialists, policy analysts, planners, and staff aides to mayors or governors or legislators may not normally have a grand overt impact on issues being placed on the agenda, but they can be critical in developing alternative proposals that "bubble up" through policy communities—that is, groups of people who focus on specific problems and push specific policies that are adopted by the more visible political actors.

Biases

Biases are built into the agenda-setting system. E. E. Schattschneider, for instance, has pointed out that "All forms of political organization have a bias in favor of some kinds of conflict and the suppression of others because *organization is the mobilization of bias.* Some issues are organized into politics, while others are organized out."[4] Any political unit's basic values will narrow the range of issues considered appropriate for agenda placement. For instance, in the states of the Deep South before the 1960s, white supremacy values made it literally impossible for the governor of one of those states to place on the agenda the issue of integration of racially segregated schools. This issue would have been "mobilized out" of consideration for agenda placement, since it went against basic values accepted by whites and their elected representatives. Biases, then, can reduce the scope of debate in the agenda-setting process radically and prevent certain policy alternatives from ever being examined, no matter what their objective merits.

Economic Conditions

The economic conditions facing a state or local government also affect its agenda setting. If a state government is facing a serious financial shortfall, putting new items on the agenda may be an option foreclosed from the start. It makes little sense to debate whether something ought to be done about homelessness when the state's treasury is bare and revenues are inadequate for normal business.

Policy Making

There comes a point at which a government decides exactly what it will or will not do in response to a problem that has been placed on the agenda. Laws are passed, ordinances approved. This is the stage in which ideas on the agenda are either acted upon or are postponed or rejected. Since many potential issues have been screened out at the problem-recognition and agenda-setting phases, those issues actually decided upon comprise only a very narrow slice of all decisions that could conceivably be made.

Models are simplified perspectives on how things work. Many models attempt to explain how decisions get made. Since decision making is so complex, models can help clarify important parts of the process. Two models, the rational-comprehensive model and incrementalism, deal with *how* decisions are actually made, or at least how some people think they ought to be made. Three other models focus on *who* influences decisions: in elitism, the few and the powerful; in pluralism, numerous groups and individuals through a negotiation process; in bureaucratic politics, bureaucrats in competition with other bureaucrats or even with elected officials (recall the picket-fence model discussed in Chapter 2 in this context).

How Decisions Are Made

Rational-Comprehensive Decision Making.   This model assumes that rationality best describes how decisions are (or should be) made. The process involves six steps:

1. Officials carefully define the problems facing their state or locality.
2. Specific goals are formulated, so that a policy meeting those goals will answer the original problem. Example: If the problem is unemployment, setting a goal of reducing unemployment to 4 percent would help to structure solutions to the problem.
3. Existing programs dealing with the problems are enumerated and an array of reasonable alternatives is adduced to see what a complete set of policy options might look like.
4. The single best alternative (or combination of them) from this set is selected. This would normally be chosen on the basis of which option gives the most benefits for the least cost, that is, which is the most cost-effective solution. In terms of the

unemployment example, the state might decide that a manpower training program is the preferred choice.

5. After the program is selected, it must be implemented, or put into actual operation. In the case of training the unemployed, sites must be developed or rented for training, personnel must be hired to carry out training, and skills training and available openings must be matched.

6. After the program has operated for a reasonable period of time, evaluation is carried out. Investigators examine whether or not the program is meeting its goal. Is unemployment being reduced? Is the program operating in a cost-effective manner? If the program is not achieving the various goals set for it, program managers will use the results of evaluation to try to recalibrate the program so that its chances of goal attainment increase.

In reality, this model describes rather few decisions that are ever made. Nonetheless, it serves as an ideal for many who believe that policy making ought to be conceived and carried out as a rational process.

Incrementalism. This model posits that a policy continues what has been done before, with some modest tinkering. Decision makers cannot each year comprehensively review every decision beforehand to see whether or not changes are called for, as the rational-comprehensive model suggests ought to be done. Practically, decision makers begin by assuming that previous decisions will stand; they will suggest minor modifications to improve the functioning of existing programs.[5]

This approach to decision making makes a great deal of sense, too. First, decision makers have neither the time nor the information to closely examine every program, develop alternatives, and select the single best alternative. Rational-comprehensive decision-making is not practical, so the argument goes. Second, it is easier to continue existing programs because groups benefiting from in-place policies will support them. Efforts at great change yield political controversy because affected groups will fight for the perceived benefits they receive under existing policies. Politicians would not want to engage in such battles routinely. Finally, it seems unnatural for humans, including political leaders, to think along rational-comprehensive lines. People tend to look for solutions that are quick and satisfactory—not optimal. They stop searching for alternatives when they find one that seems workable.[6]

Who Makes Decisions

The rational-comprehensive and incremental models of decision making focus on the *process* of policy making—how decisions get made. The next three models concentrate on *who* makes decisions: the elite, competing interests, or bureaucracy. Each is important to consider, since those represent some of the most common answers to the question of why policies get made.

The Elite.   Elitism contends that the few rule and the multitude are ruled; only the few with real power are significant in deciding what gets done. Basic assumptions of elitism include the following:

1. Society is divided into the few with power and the many without it.
2. The few who have power are not typical of the many who do not possess it.
3. The elite share basic values that work to support the system which, in turn, maintains their power.
4. Policy does not reflect the wishes of the mass of people but, instead, is made by the elite to advance their own interests.

An elite theorist would look at state and local policies from this perspective. For instance, if a state government provides tax breaks to keep a major manufacturing plant from leaving the state by reducing its costs of doing business, the elite theorist would point to this action as an example of the rich and powerful using government to give themselves a real, tangible benefit. Or, an elite theorist would look at the decision of a large city's mayor to bulldoze a neighborhood over the objections of its residents in order to locate a Cadillac plant there as ample evidence that the people's will is secondary to that of a powerful corporation, as happened in Detroit's Poletown.

Competing Interests.   Pluralism is the view that competition and the subsequent negotiation and bargaining among multiple centers of power is the key to understanding how decisions are made. This framework starts from the assumption that a society is composed of many different groups and that the interactions of some of these groups in the political process shape actual decisions by state and local governments. Simply, government responds to the demands of interest groups. In Chapter 15, we note how medical groups influence health care policy in the American states. Often, though, groups are in direct competition with one another—for example, the automakers and auto unions in Michigan. This competition necessitates bargaining and negotiation among groups in order to build a coalition strong enough to triumph in the group struggle. Thus, a number of groups working together will all benefit if the coalition wins, as will citizens who are members of these groups.

For instance, say a battle rages over whether state governments ought to put money into highways or into rail transportation in central cities. Predictable coalitions form on either side of the issue. Groups favoring the highway/automobile policy might include oil companies, the auto companies, auto dealers, asphalt or cement companies, bus interests, and the like. Arrayed against this alliance would be advocates of the rail option: rail companies, rail users, environmentalists, and so on. These groups would lobby the state legislature and, possibly, the governor's office to press their claims. The legislators would examine the arguments of the groups and also consider public opinion on the issue (after all, these officials often desire reelection or even advancement to higher office).

Bureaucracy.   Bureaucracy as an institution has already been thoroughly discussed in Chapter 7. Many analysts believe that this is where power has come to lie, especially at the local level. Indeed, some have argued that bureaucracies represent "the New Machine" in urban life.[7]

The classical political machine (or "old machine") was a corrupt, hierarchical party organization that maintained power by dispensing favors and patronage to its supporters, as discussed in Chapter 4. The old machine was based on fraternal loyalty by its members, trust for fellow machine officials, a sense of discipline due to years of service within the organization, slow promotion through the ranks, and centralized control. Its power was based on the services that it delivered to people. According to Theodore Lowi, modern bureaucracy has many elements that make it similar to the old machine:

> Sociologically, the New Machine is almost exactly the same sort of organization. The definition of the Old Machine needs no alteration to serve as the definition of the New Machine. . . .
>
> The New Machines are machines because they are relatively irresponsible structures of power. That is, each agency shapes important public policies, yet the leadership of each is rela-

tively self-perpetuating and not readily subject to the controls of any higher authority.[8]

In answer to the question of who governs in urban America, some claim that "Nobody governs."[9] As bureaucracy has increasingly become the center of authority, the cities' agencies operate within their own separate domains with no single overall source of community power. The buck stops nowhere, since power is diffused and dispersed throughout the multitudinous bureaucracies.

Bureaucracy as a source of power calls for somewhat more discussion. Recall several points made in Chapter 2: (1) The multiplicity of federal grant-in-aid programs led to increasing bureaucratization at the state and local levels; (2) the expertise located in bureaucracy in part helped to trigger greater professionalization within state and local governments (state legislatures, for instance, need to hire their own experts to serve as a check on the experts in the governor's office and in the bureaucracy); (3) the confluence of these two trends increased dramatically the capability of state and local governments to assume additional responsibilities thrust upon them by the proliferation of grant programs and, later, through the devolution of responsibility under New Federalism. Increased capability for state action, in some sense, may have been acquired at the cost of greater power being located within the diverse bureaucracies of state and local governments.

Decision Makers in How Models

The two *how* models of decision making suggest somewhat different answers to the question of *who* the key actors are in the policy process at each stage.

Rational-Comprehensive Model. The rational-comprehensive model emphasizes the importance of bureaucracy as a source of power. In the bureaucracy, in think tanks, and in legislative committees, among others, are experts in a certain subject area who can fully deal with a list of proposed alternatives and, using appropriate methods, determine which option is the optimal solution.

Incrementalism. Incrementalism identifies a number of distinct actors as being central. Interest groups, defending programs that serve their needs or advocating others that would meet their needs, can make it politically unrewarding to oppose their proposals. Political officials (at the state level, governors and state legislatures; at the local municipal level, mayors and city councillors) faced with myriad decisions tend to tinker with the status quo rather than engaging in rational-comprehensive tactics. Bureaucracies, interested in defending their turf, maintaining control of the programs assigned to them, holding onto their budgets, resisting major tampering. The combination of such dynamics produces incrementalism. One classic example of incrementalism is budgetary politics, as discussed in greater detail in Chapter 10.

Decision Makers in Who Models

The *who* models are more explicit still.

Elitism.   In elitism, the major actor is the cadre of powerful figures comprising the elite. Elected officials serve as mere ''tools'' of this group. Public opinion is manipulated by the elite through their control of media and other institutions (such as the church). So, the focus must be on the elite to understand why decisions are made as they are.

Pluralism.   Pluralism identifies interest groups as the most central actors, along with elected government officials (who serve to mediate competing groups' demands). Because elected officials wish to stay in office, the general public also becomes important, as officials try to discern what course of action would be met with the greatest approbation by the electorate.

Bureaucracy.   The bureaucratic (or ''New Machine'') view locates power within the bureaucracy, so divided up among the numerous agencies that no center of power can be identified. To understand why policies are made, one must understand the attitudes and behavior of those agencies involved in the policy area (for instance, if one is studying welfare policy, one would examine all those agencies having something to do with welfare programs).

The Element of Randomness

The process of selecting specific alternatives involves much randomness. John Kingdon claims that generating policy alternatives is

analogous to biological natural selection. In what we have called the policy primeval soup, many ideas float around, bumping into one another, encountering new ideas, and forming combinations and recombinations. . . . Through the imposition of criteria by which some ideas are selected out for survival while others are discarded, order is developed from chaos, pattern from randomness. These criteria include technical feasibility, congruence with the values of community members, and the anticipation of culture constraints, including a budget constraint, public acceptability, and politicians' receptivity.[10]

The process is dependent to some extent on chance events, on political currents, and on the desires of visible political actors. Various policy communities, groups of people from government, think tanks, higher education, and so on who are interested in a particular issue have specific proposals that they think would work if adopted and carried out by government. For instance, the environmental policy community within a state might advocate enlarging state parks or encouraging speedier efforts to implement clean air standards under the Clean Air Act. These ideas are then publicized by the policy community. They may be ignored or taken seriously, depending upon decision makers' priorities and events taking place at the time. At some point, though, policy proposals floating around in the "primeval soup" and pushed by policy communities may be coupled with the pressure to "do something" about a problem that has made the agenda. This increases the odds that a specific proposal will be enacted into law.

Will the policy be incremental? Or will the policy innovation be a more dramatic departure from the status quo, as suggested by the rational-comprehensive model? Either avenue is possible, depending upon the political currents and chance events. Kingdon's analysis seems to fit comfortably into a pluralist perspective, since he emphasizes the role of many actors.

Types of Policy

Different types of policy lead to very distinct political dynamics and outcomes. That is, policy shapes politics, just as politics shapes policy. One important argument posits that there are, in essence, three substantive types of policy: developmental, redistributive, and allocational.[11] Each of these carries with it a unique dynamic with its own political implications.

Developmental Policy.   Developmental policy aims to enhance a state's or city's competitive economic position. Such policies are designed to strengthen the economy and enlarge the tax base. A key to defining a policy as developmental is a cost-benefit calculus: does the cost-benefit ratio lean in the direction of the average and above-average taxpayer? Cities and states like to develop policies that benefit taxpayers so as to provide an incentive for those who provide revenues to government to stay and to induce taxpayers from other areas with a lower cost-benefit ratio to relocate. Examples of developmental policy are incubators, industrial parks, shopping centers, and wildlife preserves. Chapter 11 explores some of these issues.

Redistributive Policy.   Redistributive policies take money from the better off and shift it into the hands of the less well off. Welfare programs (explored in Chapter 15), for example, redistribute funds from those who can pay taxes to those who pay very little or no taxes. This type of policy will hurt the local economy, since those who can afford to pay average and above-average taxes may not perceive that they are receiving any benefits from the redistribution. They may then commence a search to find a new residence in a jurisdiction where the cost-benefit ratio is more favorable to them.

Allocational Policy.   The third category of policy is allocational. In this case, there is neither a direct positive nor a direct negative impact on average taxpayers. In a sense, they ''break even.'' Allocational policies include many essential services that governments provide, such as police and fire protection and garbage pickup. Everyone benefits from these services roughly equally. Criminal justice policies are included in this category; they are further considered in Chapter 13. Education, another important allocational policy, is discussed in much more detail in Chapter 14.

Political Implications of Policy Type.   Political implications differ for each of the three types of policy. Since city and state governments do not wish to see their tax bases evaporate, they have a very large incentive to minimize welfare programs and maximize developmental policy. If this entire perspective is correct, the relevance of devolution of responsibility for social welfare programs from the national level downward is obvious. State and local governments will simply not pick up the tab; they will tend to reduce services to the poor and disadvantaged to reduce the risk of having the average and above-average taxpayer leave for other locales. The incentive is to emphasize those policies—developmental and even allocational—that benefit the taxpayer. In this sense, equity as a goal is likely to take a backseat to efficiency.[12]

Implementation

Once decisions are made, they have to be put into operation. Paper decisions must become concrete. When a governor decides that a new highway must be built and the state legislature agrees, this is only the beginning of the story. Once this policy has been arrived at, the state must (1) have engineers determine the construction plan and routing of the highway, (2) organize actual construction of the stretch of highway, and (3) maintain the highway once it has been built. Policy becomes reality during the implementation stage.

Participants in Implementation

The central figures in this often invisible stage of the policy process are administrators of programs and bureaucrats in agencies charged with putting policy into operation. However, officials in the state legislature or city council or executives can have an effect by serving as "fixers," prodding, if necessary, the bureaucracies in charge of implementation.[13] Other actors can get involved as well. Interest groups with a stake in a new program can pressure agencies at this stage; they may also use the courts to challenge a program before it can be fully implemented.

Problems in Implementing Policy

What happens during the implementation stage is often unpredictable. Some commentators even claim that it is surprising that any programs are successfully implemented.

Vaguely Worded Laws. Laws that are passed may be vaguely worded as a result of the bargaining and compromise needed to garner legislator support in the first place. The result can be an unclear document that provides vague guidelines to the bureaucracy. Vaguely worded laws or decisions can lead to implementation that moves in directions not anticipated by policy makers.

Insufficient Resources. Resources may be inadequate for programs. For example, say a program is designed by the state to provide in-home care for the poor elderly so that they do not have to be moved to nursing homes. If the state allocates only enough money to give assistance to three or four needy elderly persons in a county, the program's implementation is strangled by lack of resources.

Interagency Conflict. At times, several agencies will be given a role in implementing a single program, often leading to conflict among the different agencies. For example, if a state were to try to stabilize its financial institutions, such as insurance agencies and banks, it might create a program run jointly by two agencies—one designed to oversee the insurance industry and the other to keep tabs on banking. The two agencies may have very different views of how to regulate their respective industries, and this could lead to conflict rather than cooperation in carrying out the program.

Conflict of Interest.   Another problem in implementation may occur when an agency is entrusted with implementing a policy that it opposes. Given the frequency of vaguely worded laws, this can lead to botched implementation as the agency undermines the original intent. Often, for example, agencies designed to regulate the insurance industry actually make decisions designed to help that industry. If the state government passes laws that the agency deems harmful to insurance companies, the agency may undercut legislative intent by regulating the industry much more loosely than provided for by the new law.

Flaws in Programs.   Finally, some programs are flawed in their conception, that is, their logic is simply erroneous. When this happens, problems in implementation crop up. For example, the Economic Development Administration (EDA) tried to attack unemployment in Oakland, California, in the middle 1960s. The agency asked several employers in the area to draw up plans indicating how they would use EDA funds in projects (such as construction of an airline hangar) to increase the number of jobs for the hard-core unemployed. In fact, tens of millions of dollars were spent on several projects, yet there was no significant job creation for the target group. The logic of the policy was flawed. Those receiving federal funds were required only to *promise* to hire the minority unemployed; there was no provision for paying the employers upon performance, that is, when they actually hired the jobless. And, it is clear in retrospect, the promises were seldom kept.[14]

The "New Machine" and Service Delivery

Earlier, the "new machine" of bureaucracy was discussed, and it is a critical concept for understanding that part of program implementation leading to actual delivery of services to citizens. Bureaucracy, as noted earlier in this chapter, is a key actor in delivering services. Its importance emerges dramatically in a study of decision making in such areas as education, parks, and fire protection in

Chicago under Richard J. Daley's administration as mayor, when Chicago had one of the last big-city political machines in the country. One study reports that the new machine of bureaucracy was more potent in structuring delivery of services than the "old" machine of Richard Daley.[15] It turns out that service delivery, across many different jurisdictions, seems more influenced by routinized decision-making procedures based in bureaucracy.

Are these bureaucracies responsive at all to those whom they serve? It depends. Interest groups can lobby bureaucracy; some do fairly well in generating responsiveness. One study of sixty-one American cities concludes that interest groups representing advantaged sectors of society (such as civic groups, chambers of commerce, professional organizations, and political parties) were more likely to get a response from service-delivering bureaucracies. Groups can also enhance their odds of success by adopting "public-regarding" rhetoric and by using conventional bargaining tactics, while radical demands and rhetoric seem to be counterproductive.[16] Bureaucracies respond to complaints that people are not receiving services due them; they are less enthusiastic about challenges to existing service delivery routines.[17] Finally, it is appropriate to note that appointed officials seem to respond to those who participate in local-level politics.[18]

Influences on Policies

State Policies

A complex interplay of influences shapes the structure of state policy making, from the number of dollars spent in programs to the nature of the programs themselves.[19] Many of the factors that affect state policy also move local policies, as noted later. Some influences are more immediate to the actual policy choices rendered; others are more removed. More distant for state decision making are national government policies, the level of state socioeconomic development, and the state's political culture. More immediate influences include public opinion, party politics, interest group demands, and the structure of state governmental institutions (for example, the governor's power, the level of state legislative professionalism, and the like). The end product, of course, is the actual decision made by state government.

Distant Influences on Policy

National Government Policy.   The national government can pass laws affecting the states, such as the mandates under the Clean Air Act or grant-in-aid programs that reward states for carrying out the federal government's desires (the strings attached to grant programs specify the national government's goals). Or, the national government can reduce funding available to the states, thus limiting the policy options open to their governments.

State Socioeconomic Development.   Level of industrialization, per capital income, average education level of the citizenry, urbanization, ethnicity, and religion all can influence states' policy choices. To take but the most obvious example, wealthier states are simply able to do more than are poorer ones. Evidence makes it abundantly clear that wealthier states are apt to spend more on education[20] and highways,[21] for example.

Political Culture.   Bountiful evidence indicating the role of political culture in state policy was presented in Chapter 3. It seems clear, then, that political culture can affect policy choices in the American states. For instance, states with moralistic cultures tend to be more liberal, more apt to invest in infrastructure, and more willing to invest in education.

None of these distant influences normally affects policy directly. Their influence is indirect, through their effects on public opinion and decision-making institutions. Below is a quick summary of actors making direct demands on state government.

Direct Influences on Policy

Public Opinion.   This can be a critical factor in the policy process. Government officials in the executive, legislative, and even judicial branches appear to pay some attention to public opinion, as noted in detail in Chapter 3.

Demand Making.   The desire for state government to enact a policy becomes a demand when that wish is formally made known in the political system. This is most commonly done through interest groups and political parties. Demand making is also shaped by public opinion, national forces, political culture, and the socioeconomic development of a state. Of course, state governments do not have to respond to these demands, but these forces do place pressure on those governments. (Supporters of the theory of elitism would add that the power elite within the state would have a substantial role to play at this point.)

After demands are made, they must be processed by the basic decision-making institutions following the rules of the game laid out in state constitutions, laws, and practice. Decision-making institutions respond by ignoring demands, considering and dropping them, providing only symbolic attention, or acting upon them in some concrete manner.

Demands chosen to be acted upon are converted into explicit policy proposals. A wide array of actors and processes are involved in whether or not—and, if so, how—government responds to demands. Many of these factors have been discussed elsewhere, such as party competition, interest group strength within a state, legislative professionalism, the power of a governor, bureaucratic professionalism, and so on. National policy, level of a state's socioeconomic development, and political culture can all have an impact, too, at this stage—as could perhaps, the state's power elite.

The end result of this lengthy sequence of events and array of actors is the formation of state public policy.[22]

Local Policies

A similar process is at work at the local level.[23] Clearly, federal and state mandates and the availability of federal and state grant assistance are major influences on exactly what local government can accomplish. Socioeconomic development is perhaps more significant an influence here than at the state level. Data indicate that local policy options are strongly shaped by their revenue base.[24] For instance, redistributive policies are much more likely to occur in wealthy communities—where there is little need for such policies.[25] Local culture can play a part in the policy process at the local level as well, as noted in Chapter 3.

Public opinion can be an important intermediary at the local level, as discussed in Chapter 3. Demographic and exogenous factors are probably more significant at the local than at the state level. Demands made by national and state governments are major elements determining what local governments must attend to;[26] the states are not nearly as constrained as are their "creatures" (local governments). Demographic indices are powerful shapers of demands made on local governments. Larger, more densely populated, more heterogeneous environments generate far more demands on local governments than do other types of communities. To the extent that there is a local elite, this acts also as a substantial factor in affecting demands.[27]

The conversion process is affected by institutional factors, such as the strength of a mayor, the professionalization of local legislatures, the ambitions of those serving on councils, and the like. Interest groups clearly have the ability to affect policy making.

Local governments are more constrained in the policy process than are the states. As time passes, this constraint on their freedom of action is forcing local governments to contemplate new initiatives to deal with their increased responsibilities and continuing fiscal pressures. We noted some of these in Chapter 2 (metro government, councils of government, consolidation). Chapter 11 discusses yet another means of addressing these problems: privatization, the effort either to use private sector approaches to handling problems or to involve the private sector more directly in actual provision of services.

The Future of State and Local Governments

One particularly gloomy scenario portrayed for the future of Buffalo, New York, suggests how desperate the plight of the cities might eventually become. Although this scenario doubtless paints too pessimistic a picture, the simple fact that such arguments exist in the literature is itself noteworthy. The scenario:

It's 1995, the end of Buffalo as we know it.

Community agencies ran out of money and now turn away many of the hungry and homeless.

The libraries shut down. So did municipal parks, swimming pools, skating rinks, senior citizen centers, and youth programs throughout Western New York.

Finally, the Buffalo Philharmonic Orchestra's music died.

The Buffalo Zoo, denied government funding, closed.

Towns, villages, and cities provide only basic services— police protection, garbage collection, snowplowing, and sewer maintenance—at a reduced level. Most everything else is gone. Hundreds of government workers lost their jobs.

Still, property taxes increase as much as 12 percent a year. The people are angry and confused. . . .[28]

The decline in national and state aid to the cities and the concomitant heavy load of mandates from higher governments combine to send local government to its knees. Of course, this doomsday scenario for Buffalo, New York, is almost certainly too negative a picture of localities' futures. Nonetheless, its extremism is a distressing reminder of the squeeze that faces municipalities. And while states are not in the same situation, they, too, must face the challenges created by federal mandating and the inherent difficulties of meeting social and economic problems.

In the final analysis, politics is about policy. The decisions that government makes are the end result of a complex process. Many potential issues never get discussed seriously by political leaders; and policy is not necessarily determined even for those issues on which serious debate takes place. Even after policies have been announced, the politics of the policy process continues, as efforts may be made to shape implementation of programs.

Different models of the policy process spotlight different actors as being central to the process. There is room for democratic input; bureaucrats can have a substantial effect on the policy process; elected officials are important figures. Although the process is a complex one, the student of state and local politics must develop an understanding of the policy maze.

Recommended Reading

Thomas Dye: *Understanding Public Policy,* 6th ed., Prentice-Hall, Englewood Cliffs, N.J., 1987.

Virginia Gray, Herbert Jacob, and Robert B. Albritton, eds.: *Politics in the American States,* 5th ed., Scott, Foresman, Glenview, Ill. 1990.

Bryan D. Jones: *Governing Urban America: A Policy Focus,* Little, Brown, Boston, 1983.

Paul E. Peterson: *City Limits,* University of Chicago Press, Chicago, 1981.

William Schultze: *State and Local Politics: A Political Economy Approach,* West Publishing Company, St. Paul, Minn., 1988.

Jack Treadway: *Public Policy-Making in the American States,* Praeger, New York, 1985.

Robert J. Waste: *The Ecology of City Policymaking,* Oxford University Press, New York, 1989.

CHAPTER 10

Taxing and Spending

States and localities make taxing and spending decisions in economic, political, and demographic contexts over which they have little control. National economic trends, for example, affect taxing and spending decisions. Federal government policies also affect state and local taxing and spending decisions. The federal government mandates that states and localities make public facilities accessible to handicapped persons, devise plans to reduce air pollution, and provide health care for the medically indigent. Politicians in Washington may change the level of funding available to carry out these mandates.

The politician's dilemma is that voters and interest groups favor most government spending programs but dislike paying the taxes to support them. That is why the federal government has consistently run budget deficits over the last thirty years. Since most state constitutions prohibit state and local governments from running deficits, governors and legislators must put together balanced budgets of taxing and spending that will be tolerable to the electorate. This chapter examines the tax alternatives available to state and local governments, discusses which taxes are most objectionable to taxpayers, and assesses the redistributive impact of state and local taxing choices.

On the spending side, the chapter describes trends in state and local spending over time and assesses some attempts to account for changing spending patterns. More detailed discussion of spending in particular policy areas, including education and health care, will be reserved for subsequent chapters. Social welfare, the fastest-growing portion of state and local government spending, has had a substantial redistributive impact and is the most controversial policy area.

In years of fiscal crisis, governors and legislators who make up the budget are caught between declining revenues and the rising cost of providing services. During hard economic times, personal incomes stagnate and unemployment rises. Government revenues fall and taxpayer resistance to higher taxes intensifies. At the same time, the cost of providing police protection and meeting social welfare obligations rises rapidly.

The Context of Taxing and Spending Policy

State and local governments have limited control over their taxing and spending environment. National and international economic trends, changes in federal government mandates to state and local governments, changes in federal funding levels, and demographic patterns affect state and local taxing and spending decisions.

National Economic Trends

The strength of the national economy affects state and local taxing and spending. When the economy is strong, employment is high and taxpayer incomes grow. Tax revenues automatically increase and taxpayers grumble less about the size of their tax bills. When the economy is weak, unemployment is high, taxpayer incomes are stable at best, and taxpayers resist any tax increases that will further erode their standard of living. Tax revenues stabilize just as demand for social welfare services increases.

Decline of Heavy Industry

Unfortunately, state and local government budget makers have had to do their work during recession years in 1973–1975, 1979–1982, and 1990–1992. In the last two decades, much traditional heavy industry in steel, automobiles, heavy equipment, and textiles has been less able to compete with lower-cost foreign producers. Many plants have closed down. The painful restructuring of the economy hit the middle west particularly hard, while the coastal states were more successful at developing high-technology replacements in telecommunications, financial services, and computers. How state governments promoted economic growth in the 1980s is discussed in Chapter 11.

Declining Employment and Productivity

Although some 10 million new jobs were created during the 1980s, they generally paid lower wages than the industrial blue-collar jobs that were lost over the same period. Steelworkers retired early, and their children took jobs delivering pizzas. Real wages of production workers were lower in 1990 than they were in 1972.[1] To forestall declines in their standards of living during a time of real decline in average wages, many American families have put second or third wage earners to work and have taken out second mortgages on their homes. Over the last two decades, the incomes of middle-class families has held constant at about $26,000.

Also, productivity growth (measured as output per worker) sank to less than 1 percent per year from 1974 through 1983. Among the reasons were rapid obsolescence of energy-intensive capital equipment, lower labor force experience as young baby boomers and older women entered the labor force, and greater investment in a safer workplace and a cleaner environment.[2]

Because the national savings rate, which supports investment in new processes and technology, is abysmally low, a return to high rates of economic growth is unlikely. Public and private debt soared in the 1980s, as people have found ways to spend more than they earn. Americans save less than 5 percent of their national product, while Japanese save about 20 percent. That means that Americans are spending their money on consumer products while the Japanese are investing in research and development of tomorrow's technological processes and products.

International Economic Trends

International economic trends also hurt the economies of states and localities and complicated the governmental budget-making process.

Rise in Energy Prices

Escalating energy prices have buffeted the American economy since 1973. The Arab oil embargo in 1973 drove the price of a barrel of oil from $1.25 to $16.00 within a year, sharply driving up prices and shrinking the consumer's purchasing power. After stabilizing until 1979, oil prices rose to $32.00 per barrel for two years when the Iran-Iraq war interrupted supplies. Rising energy prices contributed heavily to the onset of recession in 1973 and 1979.

Foreign Competition

A second international trend affecting the U.S. economy is intensifying economic competition from foreign producers of manufactured goods. Since 1980, the United States has been importing about $150 billion more in goods and services than it exports to other countries. In 1970, about 9 percent of all goods faced significant competition from foreign producers; by 1980, about 70 percent did.[3]

Intensified foreign competition is partially caused by lower wages and higher productivity abroad. But two-thirds of the deterioration in the terms of trade is due to the federal government's high-interest-rate policy during the 1980s, which strengthened the dollar in international trading.[4] A strong dollar abroad had a negative impact on local economies. The following example illustrates why.

If the cost of manufacturing a shirt in India is 240 rupees, and $1 equals 24 rupees at the official exchange rate, an American wholesaler must pay the bank $10 to get the 240 rupees to pay the Indian manufacturer for a shirt. Now if the dollar strengthens and $1 equals 32 rupees, the wholesaler needs only $7.50 to buy the rupees needed to pay the manufacturer for the shirt.

The strong dollar brought prices down, which benefited buyers of shirts and other consumer goods, but at the cost of workers in textile factories in North Carolina and Georgia, in automobile plants in Michigan and Ohio, and on farms in Minnesota and Iowa who endured wage cuts or lost their jobs. American employment in high-wage manufacturing declined from 27 percent of the work force in 1970 to 20 percent in 1983. From 1979 to 1984, about 5 million workers (about 5 percent of the labor force) lost their jobs due to plant closings or employment cutbacks. In 1986, 40 percent of these workers were unemployed or had dropped out of the labor force and 30 percent had found jobs at lower wages.[5]

Federal Government Policies

Federal government policies affect state and local taxing and spending. The federal government itself generates one-quarter of the total value of goods and services in the economy. This economic activity is not distributed equally per capita among the states. Wealthier states like Connecticut and California receive more money per capita than do poorer states like West Virginia and Maine.[6]

The federal government mandates that state and local governments spend money in specific ways. For example, states are required to pay for the medical expenses of the poor and the disabled. And states must devise plans to ensure that their cities meet air pollution standards. Complying with federal mandates costs state and local governments about $100 billion per year.[7]

States complain bitterly that the federal government mandates increased state and local spending while cutting back on federal assistance to help pay the bills. Federal aid to state and local governments increased from 11 percent of state and local budgets in 1958 to 26 percent in 1978; it then declined to about 17 percent in 1988. The downward trend is expected to continue.[8]

Particularly hard hit are federal programs targeted to cities. These include community development block grants, sewage treatment construction, mass transit, and employment and training. Urban programs received $33.8 billion (after adjusting for inflation) in fiscal year 1981 but only $10.9 billion in 1991.[9]

Demographic Trends

Demographic trends also shape state and local government taxing and spending. A very high fertility rate in the 1950s created the baby boom generation—people who needed schools in the 1960s and colleges in the 1970s and who will require retirement benefits and health care in the 2020s.

Birthrates have been much lower since the late 1960s, which means that tomorrow's population will contain more dependents and fewer workers and taxpayers. This demographic trend will challenge state and local governments in coming decades. Twelve percent of the population was over age sixty-five in 1990, and this percentage is certain to increase over the next thirty years. Taxing and spending patterns in states like Arizona and Florida will be particularly affected by the aging of the population.

Population is generally moving toward the warmer states. Population in California, Florida, and Texas has increased by over 40 percent since 1970, while New York, Illinois, and Michigan have grown by less than 5 percent. Detroit, St. Louis, and Cleveland lost a third of their population from 1970 to 1988, while the population of many medium-sized cities in Texas and California increased by 50 percent.[10] Because of these demographic trends, states and localities will differ in their capacity to tax and in their service delivery priorities.

The Politics of Taxation

Raising revenue is politically difficult. State and local government officials try to put together tax programs that will support their spending in the most painless way possible.

State Revenue Sources

States receive about 20 percent of their income in the form of transfers from the federal government. About 18 percent of the revenue that states raise themselves is derived from sale of services and user fees, including public higher education tuition, highways tolls, liquor store sales, and hospital charges. Their remaining revenues are raised through taxes.

Sales Tax

Table 10.1 indicates that state governments rely upon the sales tax for about half of their revenue. Virtually all states rely upon the sales tax. Many exempt food from the tax, but all tax, gasoline, alcohol, and tobacco heavily. The gasoline tax is advertised as a user fee, by which those who are using the highways pay for highway maintenance. Most consumers know how much it costs to fill up the tank, but not how much of the cost is tax. Therefore, gasoline tax hikes are

Table 10.1   State Tax Revenues, 1980 and 1988 Compared ($ Billions)

	1980		1988	
	$	%	$	%
Total Tax Revenue	150	100.0%	264	100.0%
Individual Income Tax	37	24.7	80	30.3
Corporate Income Tax	13	8.7	22	8.2
Sales	68	45.3	130	49.3
Other	32	21.3	32	12.2

Source: *Statistical Abstract of the United States 1991,* p. 279.

more politically acceptable when gasoline prices are falling than when they are rising.[11]

Heavy alcohol and tobacco taxes are justified in many states as deterrents to undesirable behavior. Public opinion polls indicate that, if taxes must go up, taxpayers prefer to see increases in these ''sin taxes.'' However, large tobacco-producing states like North Carolina have very low taxes on tobacco products.

The advantages of the sales tax are that taxpayers perceive that everyone pays it and exempting food makes the sales tax less burdensome on low-income families. The tax is not very visible because consumers pay it in small, relatively painless installments with their weekly purchases, and no record keeping is required. Also, when additional revenue is needed, legislators raise the tax rate by 1 percent or less, inflicting minimum pain on the taxpayer. Or they extend the sales taxes to previously exempt goods and services (for example, in 1991 sales taxes were extended to newspapers and candy in California, used cars in Arkansas, and restaurant meals in North Carolina).

Attempts to apply the sales tax to services that originate outside the state can create a fire storm of opposition, as legislators in Florida discovered. In 1987 the government decided that if a service was used in the state, such as national advertising appearing on Miami television or the work of a New York accounting firm for a Tampa company, the value of that service would be taxes at the state's 5 percent rate. In protest, various national industry and professional organizations canceled business meetings in Florida. Ultimately, these well-organized special interests persuaded the legislature to repeal the law, discouraging other states from attempting to tax such services.[12]

Income Tax

About forty states have introduced income taxes, which are the fastest-growing source of state revenue. About 38 percent of state revenue is collected through individual and corporate income taxes, up from 16 percent forty years ago. Income tax laws tend to be passed during time of economic crisis when sales tax revenue falls and the need for new tax revenue is widely apparent. Also, an income tax is more easily passed when one party controls both the legislature and the executive mansion, because the political risk to the incumbents is lower.[13]

Gambling

Many states have established lotteries and casino gambling to raise new revenue. In 1989, twenty-eight states had adopted lotteries, in which ticket holders buy a chance to win large cash prizes. About 50 percent of cash from lottery ticket purchases is returned as winnings to the players, 10 percent covers overhead and administration costs, and the remaining 40 percent goes to the state's general tax fund. A majority of the public approve of lotteries, and 49 percent of those polled indicate that they have purchased a lottery ticket in the preceding twelve months.[14]

States vary in their willingness to sponsor lotteries. States with high per capita incomes are more likely to adopt lotteries than are poorer states. Lottery players apparently regard participation as entertainment, and in wealthier states more people have money which they can afford to bet on a regular basis. Most fundamentalist Christians oppose gambling as a matter of religious principle, and most states with large fundamentalist church membership (primarily in the south) do not operate lotteries.[15]

The penchant of Americans for gambling has prompted a dozen states to license riverboat gambling casinos, with the state skimming off 20 percent of the proceeds.[16] Like lotteries, riverboat gambling appeals to states because the contributors are happily spending their money on entertainment, not surrendering it grudgingly in the form of taxes.

Local Revenue Sources

Local governments received $139 billion from their states in 1987. About two-thirds of this aid goes to local school districts, which depend on the state for more than half of their revenue.

Property Tax

Table 10.2 shows that local governments rely heavily upon the property tax. However, the property tax is highly visible and is difficult to administer. Rising property taxes have irritated taxpayers, especially during the 1970s and 1980s when assessed valuations, and therefore tax liability, rose much more rapidly than did incomes. Assessing market value fairly is technically difficult, and the process invites political favoritism. Consequently, local governments have reduced their reliance on the property tax. Property tax revenues for counties declined from 30 percent in 1976 to 26 percent in 1986.[17]

Table 10.2   Local Tax Revenues, 1980 and 1988 Compared (billions)

| | 1980 | | 1988 | |
	$	%	$	%
Total Tax Revenue	86	100.0%	171.6	100.0%
Property Tax	66	76.7	127.2	74.1
Sales Tax	12	14.0	26.1	15.2
Income Tax	5	5.8	10.3	6.0
Other Taxes	3	3.5	8.0	4.7

Source: *Statistical Abstract of the United States 1991,* p. 271.

User Fees

A growing source of local government revenue is user fees, that is, charges imposed upon citizens who use services provided by government. Since the mid-1970s, revenues from local government user fees have more than tripled, rising from 17 percent of total revenue in 1976 to 21 percent in 1987. Citizens have always paid for their water and sewer use and for golf course play. Now they often pay for garbage collection, tennis court and swimming pool use, and for police, fire, and city ambulance calls.

User fees meet with less opposition than do tax increases because payers are receiving a valued service for their money. User fees also serve to ration scarce resources like beaches and parks; casual users will choose another activity to avoid paying the entrance fee. However, user fees are burdensome for poor people. Paying five dollars to use the city park on Sunday is more difficult for a minimum-wage worker than for a high-income professional.[18]

Income Tax

Several dozen cities have enacted income taxes in recent years. In Ohio, the five largest cities collect over 75 percent of their revenue from an income tax.[19] The appeal of the income tax is that workers who live in the suburbs and commute to jobs in the city pay their fair share for police protection, road maintenance, and other government services. Since impoverished inner cities and wealthy suburbs are integrated parts of the same metropolitan area, it is neither feasible nor just to expect the city to pay the entire cost of dealing with urban problems.

In order to introduce a new tax, local governments must receive permission from their states. Most states are reluctant to share their sales or income tax potential with local governments. States prefer to collect revenue themselves and then return funds to localities along with close instructions about how those funds must be used. For example, state governments will mandate drinking water purity standards, road maintenance requirements, social service eligibility, and employee training rules. States theoretically provide the funding to attain these levels, but local government officials commonly complain that the funds are inadequate to support mandated levels of service.

Minimizing Opposition to Taxes

Citizens are not pleased to pay higher taxes. Therefore, elected politicians who feel they must raise taxes tend to keep several important guidelines in mind:

1. Make any tax increase as invisible as possible. For example, although the sales tax is broadly based and generates large revenues, the tax is buried in the purchase price of goods and services that consumers purchase daily.

2. Tie the tax payment to a specific benefit received. For example, lotteries are popular because a dollar buys a dream of winning a big payoff, and user fees charge for valued services received.

3. Raise existing taxes rather than enact new taxes. Initial opposition to the income tax is stronger than is subsequent opposition to marginal increases in tax rates. A state may initially levy a sales tax on goods and then gradually extend it to include restaurant meals, haircuts, and other services.[20]

4. Keep taxes in line with the tax rates in neighboring jurisdictions. High sales tax may drive consumers to shop in the next town or county where the sales tax is lower. If your state income tax is too high, people may choose to commute to work from a neighboring state. Ultimately, business itself may leave to escape corporate income taxes or high personal income tax rates for their employees.

5. Raise taxes when your party controls the governorship and the legislature and your political opponents are weakened.

6. Raise taxes in the year after an election, not the year before an election.[21]

Sustained economic growth facilitated expansion of the welfare state in the 1960s. Workers brought home larger weekly paychecks and governments received more tax revenues. In the 1970s, when real incomes stabilized but real government spending continued to increase, a middle-class tax revolt swept across the nation. More workers participated in the underground economy, taking unreported payment in cash. Voters supported tax revolts in California and thirty-seven other states supported Reagan conservatism strongly in the 1980 national elections.[22]

Who Pays the Taxes?

Different taxes impose varying burdens on the rich and the poor. A tax is *proportional* if the percentage of income paid in tax is constant regardless of income. A tax is *progressive* if the percentage of income paid in tax increases as income increases. A tax is *regressive* if the percentage of tax decreases as income increases.

Whether a tax is regressive or progressive matters because the distribution of family income in the United States is quite unequal. Over the fifty-year post-World War II period, the poorest 20 percent of households consistently has earned about 5 percent of the income, while the richest 20 percent of households has earned about 41 percent of the income.[23] During the 1980s, only the richest 20 percent have enjoyed income growth after taxes, while post-tax incomes of the poorest 20 percent have declined.[24]

To illustrate tax burden, consider a gasoline tax. This tax is regressive because paying it takes a larger percentage of a poor person's income. Two similar families, one earning $15,000 per year and the other $80,000 per year, drive about the same number of miles per year and pay about $100 in gasoline taxes. That $100 is a more burdensome sum to the poorer family because it represents a much higher percentage of the yearly income. A sales tax is regressive because everyone must pay the same 5 or 7 percent rate on taxable items. To make the sales tax less regressive, about half of the states exempt food, but nearly all tax alcohol, tobacco, and gasoline heavily.

A few states (Massachusetts, Minnesota, Oregon, and New York) have income taxes that are progressive. For example, a family earning $15,000 will pay 2 percent of its income in taxes, while the family earning $80,000 pays 4 percent. Most states have income taxes that are proportional, which means that all families pay about the same percentage of their income.

The urban American family earning $25,000 pays about 8.1 percent of its income in state and local taxes; the urban family earning

$100,000 pays about 8.9 percent of its income for these taxes. Of U.S. cities, Memphis, Tennessee, has the lowest and also most regressive taxes. In Memphis, the tax rate for a family earning $25,000 per year is 7.6 percent; for a family earning $100,000 per year it is 5.7 percent. High-tax cities are Milwaukee, Wisconsin (14.6 percent), and Portland, Oregon (14.1 percent). New York City has the most progressive tax structure: a $25,000-per-year family pays taxes at a 9.9 percent rate, while a $100,000-per-year family pays at a 13.8 percent rate.[25]

Most local governments rely heavily upon taxes on property. Whether the property tax is regressive depends upon whether or not property owners can shift their tax burden to their renters. Since renters usually pay a substantial portion of the property tax, in their monthly rent, property taxes are regressive or proportional.[26]

Since federal aid to states and localities is heavily funded through the progressive income tax, cutbacks in federal aid mean that state and local services are largely funded through regressive property taxes, sales taxes, and user fees. Thus, the poor bear much of the burden of fiscal decentralization.[27]

Why do state and local governments not use the tax system to reduce the great disparity in rich and poor incomes? Continuing reliance upon regressive sales and property taxes reflects the historic political weakness of the poor, who are not well represented by interest groups and whose voting turnout rate is low. Politicians, who are themselves not poor, have every reason to respond to the tax preferences of the corporations and professional associations of the wealthy. Some middle-class taxpayers think the system is more progressive than it is, and public opinion polls indicate little support for a more progressive tax system. As Benjamin Page concludes, ''The overall shape of social welfare policy is broadly consistent with the expressed preferences of the public for social insurance and some assistance to the needy but not much redistribution of income.''[28]

The Redistributive Impact of Taxes and Social Welfare Spending

For federal, state, and local taxes combined, the redistributive impact of taxes is also very limited. Table 10.3 divides households into 10 equal groups (deciles) according to size of household income. The table shows that most Americans pay about 26 percent of their incomes in taxes, but the poorest 10 percent pay more in taxes than

Table 10.3   Taxes and Transfers as a Percentage of Income (1980)

		% of Income	
Decile	Taxes	Transfers	Net Difference
0–10	33%	98%	+65%
11–20	23	58	+35
21–30	24	35	+11
31–40	25	24	−1
41–50	26	15	−11
51–60	26	11	−15
61–70	26	8	−18
71–80	27	6	−21
81–90	28	4	−24
91–100	29	3	−26

Source: Joseph A. Pechman, *The Rich, the Poor and the Taxes They Pay,* Boulder, Westview Press, 1986, p. 26.

do the richest 10 percent. Many social welfare programs are means tested and do redistribute income from rich people to poor people. Families earning under $30,000 receive more in transfer payments than they pay in taxes; families earning over $40,000 pay more in taxes than they receive in transfer payments, as Table 10.3 shows.

The Politics of Spending

State and local government spending has increased dramatically during the twentieth century. A growing economy requires more government investment in infrastructure like roads and bridges. When markets fail to allocate resources efficiently and fairly, government is called upon to regulate activity and redistribute income. In this section, we examine trends in state and local spending, alternative explanations for spending levels, and the dynamics of the budgetary process.

Trends in State and Local Spending

In 1929, state and local spending dwarfed federal government spending. During the next twenty-five years, federal spending increased rapidly because of New Deal measures to combat the Great Depression, followed by World War II and the Korean War. Table 10.4 uses data from selected years to illustrate this point (but note that the figures in Table 10.4 understate local government spending

Table 10.4   Government Expenditures, Selected Years, 1929–1988

	Year			
	1929	1954	1974	1988
Federal spending per capita (constant 1982 dollars)	$152	$1640	$2645	$3841
Percentage of GNP	2.6%	18.9%	20.7%	23.0%
State spending per capita (constant 1982 dollars)	$118	$315	$787	$1061
Percentage of GNP	2.0%	5.4%	6.2%	6.4%
Local spending per capita (constant 1982 dollars)	$299	$338	$616	$795
Percentage of GNP	3.4%	3.9%	4.8%	4.8%

Source: Adapted from James J. Gosling, *Budgetary Politics in American Governments,* Longman, New York, 1992, pp. 50–52.

because federal and state transfers to local governments are counted as federal and state spending).

In the late 1980s, state and local spending per capita continued to increase even as federal dollars shrank, recession reduced tax revenues, and taxpayers resisted further tax increases. Even in economic hard times, citizens do not want to see local school aid cut, or roads unplowed by 7:30 A.M. in January, or even longer lines at the Motor Vehicle License Bureau. Also, federally mandated spending for programs like Medicaid and Aid to Families with Dependent Children (AFDC) accounts for 60 percent of many state budgets. Local demand for education and corrections spending is strong. Annual health care costs are expected to increase by 25 percent, corrections by 12 percent, and education by 8 percent in the early 1990s.[29]

According to public opinion polls, people believe that state and local governments should spend more on health care, environment, and education. However, nearly half of those polled thought government currently spends too much on social welfare programs. Tax revolt sentiment has been in large measure a symbolic expression of dissatisfaction with redistributive policies, affirmative action, and school busing.[30]

Explanations for Spending levels

Why do states and cities spend at the levels they do? Differences in taxing and spending patterns are attributable mainly to economic differences; states and cities with high per capita incomes tax and spend more than do states with low per capita incomes. Differences in political structure do not matter much. Cities with city managers and nonpartisan elections tax and spend no differently than do ethnic cities with partisan bosses and ward leaders, when size of city, region, and economic characteristics are taken into account.[31] For the fifty states, political variables like degree of political party competition, whether Republicans or Democrats are dominant, and levels of interest group activity are not related to size of government.[32]

One study of spending decisions in fifty states over thirty-four years found that spending patterns in education, health and hospitals, and highways best supported an *incremental* model. That is, expenditures in a given year are a stable percentage of last year's expenditures. Budget participants use this year's appropriation as the base for next year, add an increment for inflation, and, finally, add or subtract a small policy increment.[33]

The study found little support for three other plausible hypotheses. First, spending does not follow the ups and downs of the economy, growing in good economic times and declining in recession years. Second, annual spending is not driven by perceived program needs as expressed by interest groups and public opinion. Third, states do not follow the initiatives of leader states in their region.

One reason for the prevalence of incrementalism is that much state budgeting is uncontrollable. Spending levels are locked in by federal rules and earlier, multiyear legislative commitments. In California, for example, over 90 percent of the budget is beyond control of the ordinary budget process; therefore, it is certain that next year's budget will resemble this year's.[34]

The Budgetary Process

The politics of taxing and spending come together in the budgetary process.

Predicting Revenues

Each year, budget makers must predict the revenues which the state will collect during the following fiscal year. This process is uncertain, since the tax take depends upon economic conditions— especially in those states that rely heavily upon the income tax, which is very sensitive to economic conditions.

Budget makers have an interest in predicting revenues accurately.

If revenues fall short, they must make painful mid-course hiring and purchasing freezes or rely upon creative accounting techniques to mask the fact that the budget is not in balance. Creative accounting may satisfy constitutional lawyers, but it also may cause bankers to downgrade the state's credit rating, increasing the cost of borrowing money to build highways and schools. Nor should budget makers run a large surplus. The existence of a $7 million surplus in California in 1978 led irate voters to support Proposition 13, a referendum that limited the property tax.

Role of the Governor

State governors are the pivotal figures in setting the budgetary agenda. They set guidelines for agencies to follow in preparing their budget requests. The governor then modifies these budget requests and presents the executive budget to the legislature. As we have seen, the budget-making process is incremental. Agencies tend to request large increases, because they believe their work is important and they need not be sensitive to the political problems of raising taxes. Governors routinely cut agency requests in the process of putting together the executive budget. Legislators tend to go along with the governor's budget requests. In forty-three states, governors can veto individual legislative appropriations. This *item veto* increases the governors' bargaining power with the legislators.[35] Because budgeting is fundamentally an incremental process, interest groups play a limited role.

A Longer Budget Cycle?

In most states, constitutional provision or legislative statute now requires that governors and legislators balance the budget annually. However, some states are considering alternative rules that could force budget makers to tie taxing and spending aggregates to economic indicators and to balance the budget over a three-year cycle.

Moving toward a longer budget cycle has several advantages:

1. Annual budgeting requires much time and energy in budget preparation. Budget decisions are made incrementally in order to keep these preparation costs within reason.

2. A longer budget period would facilitate the process of evaluating program outputs rather than monitoring inputs. As we discussed in Chapter 6, budget makers might well spend more

time on program evaluation and less on the mechanics of budget preparation.

3.   A three-year budget cycle, with disciplined annual taxing and spending targets, permits better response to fluctuations in the economy. The budgetary goal is to build up contingency funds in years of economic prosperity and spread cutbacks over several years in time of fiscal crisis. Deep cuts in funding, demoralizing employee layoffs, and sharp reductions in essential services are avoided.

The danger of a longer budget cycle is that short-term-oriented politicians might tend to overspend in the first year of a three-year budget cycle and worry about the future tomorrow.

Fiscal Crisis in the 1980s

Fiscal crisis occurs when political pressures from public employee unions and advocates of spending exceed available tax revenues. In a city, this imbalance is most likely to occur as factories close and affluent residents move to the suburbs. Then the need for public spending increases just as tax revenues decrease, and public officials are tempted to rely on unsound accounting techniques and budgeting practices. Financial markets ultimately refuse to lend the city enough money to meet its obligations, and nonelected financial experts may be appointed to administer the city's affairs. Thus, the same pressures that generate budget deficits at the federal level generate fiscal crisis at the urban level.[36]

Urban Fiscal Crisis

East St. Louis, Illinois, was a prosperous blue-collar town in 1960, with an economic base of railroads and meat-packing plants. In the 1970s, advances in technology made the old plants obsolete and they were closed down. Other businesses moved away. The population of 82,000 in 1960 declined to 41,000 by 1990. People able to flee the stricken city were mostly white, while those who remained were black and poor. Fully half of city residents were unemployed in 1990.

Since East St. Louis can collect few taxes, the city cannot provide the most basic services. It does not pick up trash, which means residents must pay for private collection, burn the garbage in their backyards, or dump it in vacant lots. The decaying sewer system leaks raw sewage. Police officers patrol in their own cars when the city's police cars are broken down. East St. Louis is a city that has hit rock bottom.[37]

The ingredients of urban fiscal crisis, which have come together in East St. Louis in particularly acute form, are outlined below.

1. Periodic economic recession forces governments to raise taxes or cut services. Either option makes the city a less attractive place to live. During the 1990–1992 recession, state tax revenues grew at about 1 percent per year, while the inflation rate alone was over 5 percent. The quality of public services declined even as tax bills were increasing.

2. The tax base is eroded, as white, middle-class residents flee to the suburbs in growing numbers.

3. Grants-in-aid from federal and state governments decline. In 1976, federal and state governments provided 38 percent of municipal government revenues; by 1988, they provided only 26 percent. At the same time, declining population gives the city less political clout in Washington, D.C., and the state capital. A troubled large city typically contained 30 percent of its state population a generation ago but has only 15 percent today.[38]

4. Demand for Medicaid and social welfare services increases as the percentage of poor residents grows.

The city of Bangor, Maine, is typical of cities and counties having to make painful choices in hard economic times. Bangor had to find $3 million in fiscal year 1992 to maintain current service levels after inflation, and the state had reduced aid to the city by an additional $2.5 million. The city manager proposed two options: (1) raise property taxes by 23 percent (in a recession year) and reduce services by $800,000; or (2) raise property taxes by 14 percent and reduce services by $3 million—which translates into laying off forty police officers and maintenance workers, closing playgrounds and dental clinics, reducing bus service, and halting all purchases of capital equipment.[39]

State Fiscal Crisis

States must confront many of the same budgetary dilemmas as do cities. As recession deepened in 1991, declining revenue and increasing expenses created budget gaps in forty states totaling over $40 billion. About half the deficit will be met through spending cuts, about half through tax increases. To cope with a $14 billion shortfall (30 percent of its $56 billion draft budget), California relied heavily on tax increases. Fees for the University of California system went up by 20 percent; persons earning over $100,000 paid higher income tax rates; the sales tax was extended to various nonessential food items; and the owner of a new car was charged $30 more to register the vehicle.[40]

Coping with Fiscal Crisis

Since state and local governments dislike cutting spending or raising taxes, they seek other ways to ease the pain temporarily without violating constitutional bans on unbalanced budgets.

Among well-known tricks for coping with fiscal crisis are:

1. Making optimistic projections about the costs of social service programs or probable tax receipts.

2. Using accounting gimmicks to balance the budget on paper, if not in reality. For example, a local government can borrow money to pay this year's bills and then pay off the loan with next year's revenue. Or, on the spending side, it can delay recording this year's expenditures until the next fiscal year.

3. Borrowing money to pay operating expenses. All state and local governments have a separate capital budget and are allowed to borrow money to build highways and schools. Since tomorrow's taxpayers will use these projects, they should help to pay off the debt. However, sometimes in times of fiscal crisis money is borrowed to pay ordinary operating expenses, such as employee salaries and office equipment, which really should be funded out of the current year's operating budget. Although this "trick" is sometimes used, it is extremely bad budgeting practice to shift operating expenses to the capital account in order to borrow money to pay for them.

4. Delaying discretionary spending. When the budget is tight, decision makers tend to put off preventive maintenance on vehicles, roads and bridges, and other public works projects. In Chapter 11, we shall estimate to what extent preventive maintenance has been delayed over the last twenty years.

The cost of programs to combat such problems as drugs, AIDS, and homelessness and to provide such services as essential education and health care has been escalating while at the same time federal aid has been sharply curtailed and recession has cut into tax revenues. Cities are worse off than states, since their service-dependent populations are large, their tax bases are shrinking as middle-class taxpayers move to the suburbs, and state aid as well as federal aid has been cut.

Mandates usually accompany the funds that the federal government transfers to the states. For example, mandates require states to broaden health care coverage to poor people and to meet clean air standards. The cost of the mandates generally exceeds the funds provided to pay for them. The same pattern holds at the local level. States impose mandates on community landfill construction or educational staffing without providing local communities adequate funds to pay for the enhanced levels of service.

In the last decade, the federal government has shown less willingness to collect income taxes, redistribute funds to the states, and impose mandates that promote equal service in the fifty states. Therefore, states have greater flexibility to shape their own taxing and spending policies. In the states, some creative experimentation in taxing and spending policies is taking place: for example, relying upon lotteries and user fees to supplement more traditional revenue raising; providing incentives to stimulate economic growth (see Chapter 11); improving school performance (see Chapter 12) and health care delivery (see Chapter 13); and exploring alternative ways to improve environmental quality (see Chapter 14.)

Despite these policy innovations, most governmental activity is the product of day-to-day spending decisions. Continuity is more evident than innovation in state budgetary processes, and incrementalism best explains the evolution of spending patterns over time.

Finally, the public seems to favor a proportional, not a progressive tax system. Since it is built upon the sales and property tax, the state and local tax system tends to be regressive: that is, it tends to transfer income from the poor to the rich. Social welfare spending like Medicaid and food stamps does redistribute income to poor people; however, these redistributive programs arouse more public opposition than do highway and school spending, which benefits the middle-class, taxpaying public.

Recommended Reading

James J. Gosling: *Budgetary Politics in American Governments,* Longman, New York, 1992.

Susan B. Hansen: *The Politics of Taxation: Revenue Without Representation,* Praeger, New York, 1983.

Frank Levy: *Dollars and Dreams: The Changing American Income Distribution,* Russell Sage Foundation, New York, 1987.

Benjamin I. Page: *Who Gets What from Government,* University of California Press, Berkeley, Calif., 1983.

David O. Sears and Jack Citrin: *Tax Revolt: Something for Nothing in California,* Harvard University Press, Cambridge, Mass., 1982.

Martin Shefter: *Fiscal Crisis: The Collapse and Revival of New York City,* Basic Books, Inc., New York, 1985.

CHAPTER 11

Economic Policy

Working adults spend about one-third of their average day at their jobs, earning money to purchase material goods and services. In advanced industrial societies, most goods and services are produced through the interaction of buyers and sellers in the economic marketplace. Markets allocate resources efficiently to the extent that price changes signal the need for adjustments in supply and demand. For example, wages for computer technicians rise when they are in short supply, and then the higher wages encourage more workers to pursue careers as computer technicians.

State and local governments are important participants in the economic process, providing about 11 percent of the total value of goods and services produced. Less directly, state and local governments structure the production of goods and services in four important ways, as this chapter will discuss. First, governments provide infrastructure, which facilitates creation of material wealth. Governments, for example, establish a system of laws, educate young people and build highways. But state and local government spending on infrastructure is not always large enough to promote economic growth.

Second, governments take regulatory action when markets fail. Since the early decades of the industrial revolution, state and local governments have sought to protect citizens from the perverse consequences of markets. For example, they protect workers from being exposed to dangerous conditions in the workplace.

Third, markets tend to create differences in wealth and power. In Chapter 10, we saw that governments redistribute some income to the poor through spending policies. In this chapter, we examine how redistributive policies might affect economic growth.

Fourth, governments seek ways to promote economic growth. In the 1980s state and local governments encouraged private firms to locate within their jurisdictions. Why have state and local governments expanded their efforts to attract private investment? What techniques do they use? Do these techniques work?

Finally, the chapter considers whether size of government affects economic activity. Critics of government argue that government is inefficient and that big government inhibits economic growth. They advocate lower taxes, less regulation of business, and contracting with private firms to provide schooling, garbage collection, and other services that the government itself now provides. Defenders point out that protecting citizens from irresponsible private interests and promoting an equitable distribution of goods and services are important goals that justify government's large role in society.

Providing Infrastructure

State and local governments provide the social and physical infrastructure that makes economic activity possible. For example, a system of law and order guarantees that individuals will be able to work without interference and protect them from criminal attack. In recent years, states have made major investments in prison construction because of higher conviction rates, longer jail sentences, and court decisions to restrict prison overcrowding. State and local governments also set up schools, which teach basic reading, writing, and computational skills essential in the industrial workplace. And governments build and maintain highways, wastewater treatment plants, and solid waste disposal facilities.

Collective Goods

Collective goods (or public goods) are those which, if they are made available to anyone, are made available to everyone. For example, if the government spends money to force industries to stop dumping their waste products into the air, the cleaner air that results is a collective good. Everyone who breathes benefits from it. Similarly, when a community provides for a police force and a judicial system so that citizens may live their lives in peace and safety, everyone benefits.

Collective goods differ from private goods, which are the goods provided to individuals. For example, an article of clothing, a meal at a restaurant, and an automobile are private goods, purchased by an individual who enjoys exclusive access to the good. The economic marketplace specializes in producing private goods, but it cannot produce collective goods very well because a firm cannot force people to pay for their share of the service. Government, on the other hand, can make people pay for services by levying taxes, which all citizens are required to pay.

State and local governments make many collective goods available to their citizens. They provide police and fire protection, maintain roads, and operate schools, services that everyone is free to use and everyone pays for through taxes. The most important economic contribution of our state and local governments is providing these social and physical infrastructure investments. These investments make it possible for private entrepreneurs to build businesses. If individuals were illiterate and unskilled in thinking, a potential employer could not afford to hire them. Public education reduces the training costs of new employees.

Similarly, a good system of highways and bridges is essential to successful economic activity. Businesses must be able to get raw materials to their factories in a timely and inexpensive manner, and finished products must be transported to their purchasers. Yet factory owners could never afford to build and maintain a highway for their own use. Indeed, the initial capital required and the uncertain prospect of collecting tolls would deter entrepreneurs from building roads. Roads would be underprovided, and the economic growth of the community stunted.

The extent to which we treat public services as public rather than private goods is often a matter of policy choice. Historically, Americans have regarded a free public school system and high-quality highways as collective goods which should be made available to everyone regardless of their ability to pay. State and local governments build and maintain the schools and highways, using tax dollars and allowing everyone to use the services free of charge. An alternative approach might require each individual family to pay for its children's schooling, or charge a toll for each highway mile driven, but such an approach is generally not used.

Markets fail to provide public goods when the cost of providing them is great and citizens would be tempted to avoid paying their fair share. Take police protection, for example. If a private firm were to provide police services, the entire community would be safer. But if the firm then sent a bill for its services to each member of the community, a few citizens might calculate that they would receive the benefit of a safer community whether or not they paid their fair share. They would attempt to ride free on the efforts of more fair-minded community residents willing to pay their share.[1] Note that free riding is not possible where private goods are involved. A person who wants a television or a haircut must pay the market price to receive the good or service.

Infrastructure Decay

The condition of physical infrastructure affects state and local economies. Industries that depend heavily upon a well-trained labor force and well-maintained roads and bridges will consider the quality of the social and physical infrastructure before deciding to invest in a state or locality. The quality of local infrastructure is an important factor in business investment decisions.[2] Poor roads and bridges increase transportation costs. Potholes exact a heavy price in vehicle wear and tear. Bottlenecks and traffic delays waste valuable time and fuel.

Experts have raised the alarm that our infrastructure is deteriorating rapidly.[3] The Federal Highway Administration estimates that 30 percent of the bridges on the interstate highways, which carry 82 percent of all traffic, are deficient and in need of major repair. Most were constructed between 1956 and 1960 and are now carrying much larger volumes and heavier loads than their designers planned for.[4] Some 60 percent of the nation's bridges are deficient. While few bridges are in danger of collapse, many have lowered their weight limits, forcing heavier trucks to find more time-consuming and costly alternative routes.

The water and sewer systems of older industrial cities, many constructed over eighty years ago, are simply worn out and must be renewed and upgraded. With each passing year, the probability of disruptive breaks in the main water lines of New York, Chicago, and Philadelphia increases in the absence of adequate preventive maintenance.

In 1989, 44 percent of local government officials surveyed reported that deterioration of physical infrastructure is a serious problem.[5] Yet in the last decade, governments have reduced their spending on construction and maintenance of basic physical infrastructure. In 1960, total spending on physical infrastructure was 3.6 percent of gross national product (GNP); in 1985, spending had declined to 2.6 percent.[6]

Other major infrastructure investments are needed to meet strict wastewater treatment standards mandated by the federal government, to develop recycling programs, to construct less polluting landfills and incinerators, and to upgrade urban mass transit systems and airports. To reach adequate levels, state and local government spending on infrastructure, currently at $80 billion per year, should be increased to about $130 billion per year.[7]

Failure to maintain and expand our physical infrastructure has contributed to low rates of economic growth in the last twenty years. According to a Federal Reserve Bank study, those countries with the most public investment in education and infrastructure have the greatest productivity growth.[8] A centerpiece of President Bill Clinton's program to stimulate economic growth in the 1990s is to increase government spending on productivity-increasing education and infrastructure.

Why is our physical infrastructure wearing out more rapidly than it is being renewed? One reason is that the federal government has cut back on its funding to state and local governments during the 1980s, as was discussed in Chapter 2. In a period of slow economic growth, deep cuts in federal aid to state and local governments, and large budget deficits, elected officials often choose to postpone infrastructure improvements.

Given the deep budget deficits facing many states in the 1990s, finding the money to shrink the infrastructure deficit is difficult. As discussed in Chapter 10, citizens are particularly resistant to tax increases when their personal incomes are not growing. Although high-quality infrastructure contributes to economic growth, taxpayers do not easily see the connection since highways, airports, and water systems are generally adequate to meet personal needs.[9] The average voter, still driving a car and flushing the toilet, is more concerned about taxes. Only when bridges collapse and major urban water mains break do voters and interest groups support infrastructure improvement.

Regulating Economic Activity

Markets have the great virtue of allocating resources efficiently as buyers and sellers respond to changes in prices. But markets do not always work well, and when they fail, state and local governments often take regulatory action. Increased economic growth creates interdependencies, free market imperfections, and expansion of governmental activity.[10] This section examines some common situations that result when freely operating markets impose undesirable consequences on the general public.

Preventing or Regulating Monopoly

Markets work well only when many sellers compete to provide a good or service. In a competitive market, individual sloth or greed is curbed by the knowledge that, if you charge high prices, a competitor will charge less and take away your customer. In the absence of competition, a seller can raise the price and make extraordinary profits at the buyer's expense. Transportation and public utilities are natural monopolies, in that duplicating train tracks or water lines is prohibitively expensive. A private firm that owned the train tracks or water lines could charge monopoly prices; therefore, state and local governments set up regulatory commissions that protect citizens from excessively high prices while allowing the railroad or utility to make a fair profit.

Similarly, state and local governments regulate the prices that telephone, natural gas, or cable companies charge and the services they provide. As an alternative to regulation, many city governments purchase transportation and utility companies and operate them as a public service. In the United States, governments regulate private health care providers, telephone companies, and other public utilities, whereas in Europe, government supplies these services directly. Thus, the government-generated share of gross national product (GNP) in the United States is lower than in other advanced industrial countries (see Table 11.1 on p. 236).

Protecting Consumers

Consumers in a free market economy are warned to "let the buyer beware." The warning underlines the difficulty and high cost to consumers of getting reliable information about the goods and service they purchase. States license dentists, lawyers, real estate agents, and beauticians to ensure that all practitioners are at least minimally competent. Local governments regularly inspect restaurants for cleanliness and monitor the accuracy of scales in grocery stores. Banks and insurance companies are required to provide their customers with detailed, comprehensive information about customer rights and responsibilities.

Alleviating Social Costs

Markets work when all of the costs of providing a good are included in the price of the product. These costs include not only the direct costs of labor, materials, and profit but also indirect costs imposed on third parties, such as the effect of building a factory in a residential neighborhood or exposing workers to hazardous substances.

For example, local governments pass zoning ordinances to locate factories on the outskirts of town. Residents are prevented from starting businesses in their homes. Newcomers are prevented from building houses that are too small, too tall, or too close to the street. These zoning laws restrict individuals from making investments which would detract from the existing character of a neighborhood.

Social costs are also imposed on the public when the price of a product is too low, because not all costs of production are included in the market price. For example, if a fertilizer manufacturer dumps untreated pollutants into the river, that manufacturer can sell fertilizer at a lower cost than can the manufacturer's competitors, who treat water to remove pollutants, before dumping it. The farmer who buys the fertilizer is pleased because the price is low, and the manufacturer is happy with the profit, but health and aesthetic costs are imposed on innocent third parties living downstream. These are real costs which should be counted in the price of the product. So state and local governments, acting under federal mandates, force the companies to clean up their pollution, and the companies pass on the costs to consumers in the form of higher prices.

Some states have passed environmental protection measures that are more stringent than federal rules. A manufacturer of automobiles or fertilizer, for example, must then choose whether to make its product conform to strict state standards or to not operate or sell in that state. When a large state like California or New York imposes strict regulations, a manufacturer is likely to sell, nationwide, products that conform to that large state's standard. Two decades after the federal government introduced environmental policy innovations and then forced states to comply through its control of federal grants-in-aid, states are now taking the policy lead. Manufacturers who in the 1970s thought that federal environmental regulations were too harsh are now urging standardized federal regulation to protect them from having to conform to fifty different sets of state regulations in the 1990s.

The Social Costs of Regulation

State and local governments regulate private economic activity because allowing individuals to pursue their own self-interest in the marketplace creates problems of efficiency and fairness, as described in the previous section. In some cases, the regulated interest may gain control of the regulators who depend upon them for information. The regulated are most likely to capture the regulators when complex technical issues are involved and when the general public is not keenly interested in the outcomes.[11] For example, utility price regulation means a great deal to the utility, but less to its customers, who are not likely to be intensely concerned about an increase of a few dollars in their monthly bills. Customers find it difficult to organize to defend their interests, although in recent decades public interest groups have taken up their case. Those states having competitive party systems and active consumer groups have stronger pro-consumer regulation.[12]

Some critics of regulation argue that government regulation may be an excessively expensive and ultimately unsuccessful effort to solve the deficiencies of markets. In their view, the public interest would be better served if the process were more sensitive to the economic efficiency implications of regulatory decisions. As discussed in Chapter 9, the regulatory process should be more rational-comprehensive. In fact, the process is better described as incremental, in that the regulators make small changes in existing policy as they respond to the latest pressures from either an irate public or a squeezed industry.

Given government regulation, the regulated industry has an incentive to comply to the minimum extent necessary while persuading the regulators that they are complying fully. Since the regulated look for ways to minimize the extent of compliance, state and local governments must pay significant costs for administration and enforcement. In New York City, the process of getting construction permits is so complex that contractors hire specialized "expediters" to negotiate with the regulators on their behalf. City regulators are seeking to license the expediters to ensure that they are suitably knowledgeable about city rules and honest in presenting their client's application for construction permits.

Frequently, negotiations between regulators and the regulated lead to rate structures or other rules that protect existing firms and delay entry of new competitors.[13] For example, the cost of complying with regulations makes setting up a child-care center or entering the construction business very expensive. Sometimes, regulators are inappropriately protective of their clientele. Strong regulation can discourage entrepreneurs from opening up businesses or force them to charge very high rates for their services. In New Jersey, where automobile accident rates are among the highest in the nation, insurance regulators turned down the largest insurance company's request for a substantial rate increase. When the request was denied, the insurance company announced its intention to close down its automobile insurance operations in the state.[14]

Government regulation is excessively expensive when regulators tell the regulated *how* to reduce the external costs they impose upon society. For example, a state environmental agency may fairly tell a large city to reduce its air pollution by 10 percent, but it should not tell the city how to accomplish this objective. The city should be allowed to decide whether placing restrictions on automobile users, or closing down small but dirty industrial polluters, or banning backyard charcoal burning is the most acceptable way to accomplish the goal.

Redistributing Income

A perverse feature of markets is that they are biased in favor of the wealthy, the strong, and the talented. In the United States, the richest 20 percent of households earn 41 percent of incomes; the poorest 20 percent receive less than 5 percent. Poverty is concentrated among the very old and very young, the sick and the disabled, and those who do not enjoy equal opportunity to get education and training. Although able-bodied adults on welfare is a popular image, in fact most poor people are very young, very old, or unskilled.

About 14 percent of state and local government income transfer programs are targeted to benefit society's needy. Community centers and subsidized daily meals, housing, and health care benefit needy senior citizens. The unemployed receive benefits while they are look-ing for a new job. Some female heads of household and their children receive food stamps, subsidized housing, and cash payments. The homeless are offered meals and shelter. In many states, school dis-tricts with large low-income populations receive higher per capita aid than do wealthier districts.

These programs in fact do very little to reduce the gap between the rich and the poor in society. Levy estimates that after subtracting the taxes one pays and the transfer payments one receives, the income of the top 20 percent of households declines from 43 percent of all income to 39 percent; the income of the bottom 20 percent increases from 5 percent to 7 percent. Income redistribution is limited because our largest, politically popular programs like social security and Medicare help mostly middle-income people. Social welfare pro-grams targeted to help the poor, such as food stamps and Aid to Families with Dependent Children (AFDC), are small.[15]

City governments do not redistribute more income to the poor because the poor are not well organized and have low voting turnout rates. Also, in a market economy, cities must compete with each other for capital and skilled labor. Cities cannot stress redistributive policies because they need to keep middle-income residents who contribute to the local revenue base.[16] Private investors tend to pro-mote capital-intensive downtown real estate development rather than job-creating investments in service or manufacturing in depressed inner city neighborhoods.[17]

Promoting Economic Growth

Prior to 1974, the economic policy of state and local governments was largely confined to providing a climate favorable to private investment. Governments maintained adequate physical and social infrastructure while keeping taxes at reasonable rates. Many states spent heavily upon infrastructure without considering whether projects would have a positive impact on economic development. Highway construction or education funds were distributed according to general bureaucratic procedures and well-established political pat-terns.[18] This scattershot approach sought to create a good investment climate that would attract a fair share of business investment to a state or city.

State and local efforts to improve their economies also concen-trated on cultivating close relationships with agencies of the federal government. With federal funds flowing freely to the states, states assigned priority to getting their fair share of these funds through skillful grant writing and political maneuvering.

In the mid-1970s, state and local governments began to take a more direct approach to promoting economic growth in part in response to deteriorating economic conditions. Sharply escalating energy prices in 1974 reduced disposable incomes. National economic policies allowed interest rates to soar and the value of the dollar to climb, which in turn created sharp increases in manufacturing imports. Steel, automobile, textiles, and other heavy industry in what came to be known as the ''rustbelt'' were hard hit by a flood of foreign manufactured imports. In cities like New York, Detroit, and Cleveland, middle-class populations moved to the suburbs in large numbers, and many factories and businesses moved with them. City revenues slumped just as federal revenue sharing funds were cut and the size of the cities' low-income, heavy-service-demanding populations increased.

Changes in technology also increased business mobility. No longer was it essential to center all operations at one facility. With improvements in transportation and telecommunications, firms could locate research and development laboratories in states with excellent universities, and they could place manufacturing in states with low-cost skilled labor forces. In some industries, changes in technology made it possible to develop multiple manufacturing plants close to markets.[19]

Massachusetts was notably successful in attracting high-technology growth industries in the 1970s by providing low-cost capital, lowering business taxes, improving worker skills, and supporting research and development. In 1975, the unemployment rate in Massachusetts was 12 percent, well above the national average. In 1985, the unemployment rate had fallen to 4 percent, far below the national average.

Some Growth-promoting Strategies

One common strategy of states and localities seeking to attract new business investment is to offer various subsidies to firms willing to locate in their jurisdictions. Offering financial incentives to attract business investment is called *smokestack chasing.*

Southern states have enjoyed some success in luring industry away from other states by advertising their low-wage, hard-working, nonunionized labor force; low taxes; and limited regulation. In the 1980s, Tennessee, Kentucky, and Ohio won costly and bitter competitions with other states for Japanese auto plants. Smokestack chasing, however, has limited appeal, since states competing vigorously with each other must offer such attractive packages to industries that the states lose many of the benefits of industrial development. These programs are not worthwhile if one state simply enlarges its economy at the expense of another by providing subsidies rather than creating better products at lower cost.

Financial Incentives

One common financial incentive is to provide loans or grants to defray the costs of starting up a business. For example, state and local governments issue *industrial revenue bonds.* The interest earned on industrial revenue bonds is free of federal taxes, allowing the bonds to carry low interest rates. The money is then loaned directly to investors. This cheap money subsidized potential investors at low cost to state and local taxpayers, with the federal government picking up the bill in foregone taxes. However, since 1990, the federal Internal Revenue Service has restricted the use of industrial revenue bonds.

Another type of financial subsidy is the granting of *tax exemptions* or *tax credits* to a new industry for a period of years. Since taxes are an important cost of doing business, a state offering tax breaks may succeed in luring industry.

Technology transfer programs facilitate contact between researchers in universities and laboratories and businesses seeking to introduce new or improved commercial products. Technology transfer seeks to reduce the time required to translate research discoveries into commercial applications, and to provide research assistance to entrepreneurs with technical problems. In New York State, for example, seven centers for advanced technology specialize in fiber optics, robotics, ceramics, and other high-technology fields.

To help new businesses raise capital, states have set up *venture capital* funds, designed to finance unproven, high-risk business ventures that could not be funded through ordinary commercial sources. Some thirty states have programs to fund fledgling business.

A similar approach is government-sponsored *incubators,* in which a group of fledgling entrepreneurs share inexpensive manufacturing and office space, secretarial services, and technical and business advice. About eighteen states and many cities sponsor incubator programs.[20]

To address the special problems of chronically depressed areas, state and local governments establish *enterprise zones*. Governments provide incentives to businesses willing to set up operations in areas of high unemployment, on the grounds that bringing jobs to the unemployed is easier than moving the unemployed to the jobs. The federal Department of Commerce estimates that enterprise zone activities have attracted $10 billion in new investment in blighted urban areas and created some 120,000 jobs.[21]

Comparative Advantage

Most advocates of state policy to promote economic growth favor a strategy of picking winners: that is, attracting those industries for which the state has a comparative advantage and which are likely to have strong futures.[22] States seek to create new economic wealth rather than competing with other states for existing industries.

Many states identify industrial investment in which they have a comparative advantage over their competitors. Michigan, for example, stresses the good fit of firms developing computerization and robotics with its traditional auto industry. Agricultural states have a comparative advantage in biotechnology and food-processing fields. Tennessee stresses its natural advantages (central geographical location, low-cost labor force, and favorable tax structure) rather than offering large subsidies to relocating firms. Some governments seek to identify a market niche to fill. Indianapolis, for example, built a large sports stadium complex suitable for national and international competitions, and New Jersey has promoted Las Vegas-style casino gambling.[23]

State Development Policies

Promoting economic growth is increasingly big business in state capitals. In two decades, the number of incentive programs per state has doubled, from sixteen per state in 1966 to thirty-two per state in 1985.[24] Two-thirds of the states are now actively involved in export promotion on behalf of their industries. Most states have formal state development agencies, and the average state spent over $850,000 on economic development activities in 1986.[25]

States are most likely to pursue economic development policies in time of economic crisis, when business and labor interests have a shared interest in cooperating. Also, states in which the executive and the legislature have high staffing and spending levels can more easily pursue development policies.

Do Policies Promoting Economic Growth Work?

Weak economic conditions since 1974, including three recessions and the loss of many industrial jobs overseas, gave state and local governments incentives to stimulate economic growth. To what extent have they succeeded? Historically, evidence indicates that state economic development policies drain state resources more than they promote business investment. Purely economic factors, such as labor, raw material and capital costs, and market conditions have largely determined business investment decisions.[26]

Brace's research confirms that states had little discernible impact on economic growth from 1968 to 1979 but had a larger impact in the 1980s. Why? One reason is that states can more easily shape their economies if they are not heavily dependent upon energy prices or federal spending, and states were less dependent in the 1980s. Also, formal economic development policies are more effective in states with strong governors and professionalized legislatures, and previous chapters have shown that state institutional capacity continues to grow.[27]

How Do Economic Development Programs Go Wrong?

Studies indicate that economic development programs have some positive impact, but the studies do not indicate whether these policies to promote economic growth are worth the money spent. Promoting economic growth can be a costly proposition. The larger states employ 500 staff and spend $50 million per year on economic development efforts. As states have competed for new economic development projects, the cost of landing a plant has increased almost fivefold, from $11,000 per job in 1980 to $50,000 in 1986.[28] Some of the more common pitfalls are the following:

1. Paying more to a relocating industry than the value of its contribution to the local economy. For example, in 1978, Pennsylvania spent millions of dollars to win a Volkswagen plant that ended up closing down in 1988. Landing a Toyota plant cost Kentucky $325 million to create 3,000 jobs.[29]

2. Following fads that prompt low-education states to recruit

high-technology firms, visually nondescript states to promote tourism, and too many cities to build convention centers.

3. Letting availability of funding determine strategy. When Congress appropriates funds for urban redevelopment, cities will be inclined to rebuild their downtown areas even if businesses are relocating in suburban shopping malls.

4. Letting assets determine objectives. An incubator set up simply because an old industrial building is available is unlikely to succeed. Strong research and development activity and entrepreneurs seeking commercial applications contribute to a successful incubator project, not availability of a low-cost building.

5. Attributing all business investment decisions to the effects of the economic development program, without asking whether investors would have made the same decisions even without the program. Fewer than 25 percent of local governments conduct formal evaluations of their economic development programs; smaller cities with limited staff are least likely to evaluate their success.[30]

6. Relying heavily upon tax breaks and other subsidies rather than on infrastructure improvements and job training.

Economic Development Programs and Reelection Campaigns

While it is by no means clear to what extent economic development programs stimulate economic growth, their political appeal is undeniable. Campaigning politicians will surely seek to claim credit for business expansion, even if investment decisions are made independently of state efforts. A recent analysis of speeches by thirty governors reveals that jobs and economic development are their number-one subject.[31] An expanding economy has broad electoral appeal; everyone wins and no one loses. Voters seem to respond to the *efforts* of politicians to create jobs rather than their actual success in doing so.[32]

Is Government Too Large?

Americans spend 30 percent of their income on taxes for goods and services produced by federal, state, and local governments. As Table 11.1 shows, government spending in the United States is

Table 11.1   Tax Revenues as a Percentage of GNP: Selected Advanced Industrial Countries

	Year	
Country	1980	1987
Canada	31.6%	34.5%
Denmark	45.5%	52.0%
France	41.7%	44.8%
Italy	30.2%	36.2%
Japan	25.5%	30.2%
Spain	24.1%	33.0%
Sweden	49.4%	56.7%
United Kingdom	35.3%	37.5%the
United States	29.5%	30.0%
West Germany	38.0%	37.6%

Source: *Statistical Abstract of the United States 1990*, p. 845.

among the lowest in the advanced industrial world, primarily because governments in Europe provide health care and operate public utilities, services that are privately owned in the United States. European citizens pay more in taxes but receive more in services.

The government share of gross national product has been increasing in recent decades. Despite the Reagan administration's antigovernment rhetoric, the 1980s were no exception. President Reagan shifted some responsibility from the federal government to state and local governments and shifted spending from social to military programs.

Why Does Government Grow?

Two schools of thought seek to explain government growth in the twentieth century.

Service-Hungry Citizens

One school argues that the increase in government programs is the result of politicians and bureaucrats responding to citizen demands. Public opinion polls, election results, and interest group activities are a constant source of demands upon politicians, who are responsive to the people because they seek reelection.

Anthony Downs has developed a simplified model which assumes that politics takes place within a political marketplace analogous to the economic marketplace. Voters are buyers who express a willingness to pay a price in the form of taxes for a desired package of police protection, highway maintenance, education, and other services. Their elected officials are sellers, offering packages of policies at a price in taxes in competition with other politicians. In casting their ballot, voters choose the most attractive package.[33]

A flaw in this theory is that the political marketplace is even less perfectly competitive than is the economic marketplace. Voter choice is usually limited to two candidates, and voters are less informed about the ''products'' they are choosing (specific policy issues and candidates) than are consumers in the economic marketplace. Downs also ignores the important role of groups representing specialized interests. Doctors may shape health policy and factory owners may shape workplace safety regulations more than ordinary voters do.

However, Downs's model of government that grows because politicians are providing policies which voters demand enjoys some empirical support. As discussed in Chapter 4, elected politicians do enact policies which are consistent with the preferences of citizens as expressed in public opinion polls. Chapter 5 presented evidence that state and local legislators do seek reelection, and being responsive to constituent interests strengthens their reelection prospects.

Expansion-Minded Bureaucrats

A second explanation of government growth argues that expansion-minded bureaucrats, not service-hungry voters, are the principal cause. In his classic study, William Niskanen assumed that government grows because bureaucrats are continuously seeking to enlarge their budgets. Bureaucrats attempt to maximize some combination of salary, reputation, power, and service output, all of which are enhanced when agency budgets are expanding.[34] Bureaucrats get their way, according to Niskanen, because they have a monopoly of information about the true cost of producing a good or service. Legislative committees, under pressure from special interest groups, are inclined to accept agency requests for more funds.

Is Niskanen right? He deserves credit for making the point that bureaucrats are not selfless public servants, implementing the letter of policies articulated by elected legislators and chief executives. Like Anthony Downs, Niskanen believes that bureaucrats are ordinary people with a strong desire to pursue self-interested goals within limits imposed by their organizations. But Niskanen has no doubt overstated the extent to which government is enlarged by budget-maximizing bureaucrats. Whether or not bureaucrats succeed in increasing their budgets depends upon the support of clientele groups, the governor and mayor, and key legislators. Some agencies always do better than others. How government spends depends upon what voters, interest groups, and other political actors see as the pressing issues of the day: for example, building highways, combatting urban blight, fighting drug use, or preventing crime.[35]

A long period of increases in state and local spending on infrastructure and social services has come to a halt in the last decade, with the sharp reductions in federal funding, serious economic problems, and chronic budget deficits. In the 1990s, bureaucrats will struggle to avoid layoffs and cutbacks as elected state and local officials resist spending proposals requiring tax increases. And state and local governments will be under pressure to find more efficient ways to deliver services.

Privatization

State and local governments generally supply services directly through their own agencies. For example, a police department receives tax dollars to hire police officers, operate an academy to train prospective police officers, and service police cars. But today, over half of local government street paving is contracted out, and about 30 percent of local governments hire private firms to collect their citizens' garbage.

Critics of big government have argued that the marketplace can provide services much more efficiently and much more equitably than can government bureaucracies. Private agencies face daily competition, but no forces of competition push government bureaucrats to provide the best possible service at the lowest possible cost. Privatization, by which government agencies contract with private business to provide service, may enable state and local governments to provide better services at a lower cost to taxpayers.

Advantages of Privatization

If government can choose among alternative service providers, competition forces firms to be efficient and low-cost service providers. The owners have an incentive to monitor their employees carefully, since good work means higher profits. The private firm can schedule employees more efficiently. Also, a firm works hard to find the best products and procedures.

In general, services that are easily monitored are the most likely candidates for privatization. For example, a local school district will pay a private firm to provide janitorial services rather than hiring its own janitors and buying their cleaning supplies. Or a state will hire a firm to operate its prison system. Other technical support services, such as school bus operation, food service, legal services, and vehicle fleet maintenance are also frequently contracted out.[36] One study of services in the Los Angeles area showed that municipally provided services were more costly than those provided under contract.[37]

Limits of Privatization

A potential problem with privatization is that a private firm's agenda is to make a profit, not necessarily to provide high-quality service. Therefore, state and local governments need to monitor the performance of contractors carefully, following the principle of "let the buyer beware." It is more feasible to monitor services like cafeteria operation, cleaning, and transportation.

State and local governments may be reaching the limits of privatization. They have contracted out for a range of easily monitored, competitive services, and public employee unions will resist being replaced by low-wage, nonunion labor. Government also provides many public goods for which privatization is not feasible, because either the service is a natural monopoly or all users would not pay their fair share.

Another policy question is whether state and local governments wish to restrict access to public facilities to those who are able to pay. User fees tighten the link between those who use a facility and those who pay for it. Chapter 14 examines the issue of privatizing schools. Parents and students could shop for a public or private school of their liking and pay relatively more or less for the school they choose. While a privatized education system would be more sensitive to individual needs, it would also guarantee that some citizens would have much better access to quality education than others.

The economic policies of state and local governments have broadened beyond providing infrastructure, regulating the market economy, and redistributing income through taxing and spending policies.

Faced by sharp cutbacks in federal aid to states and localities, the energy crisis, disappointing American economic performance since 1974, and heightened global competition, they now provide economic aid directly.

It is not at all clear how successfully governments have promoted economic growth, but the states are serving as policy laboratories, promoting growth in many diverse ways. Although state and local governments probably do not provide services as efficiently as do their private sector counterparts, much government spending does promote economic growth by building infrastructure and correcting market failures. Certainly state and local government continues to grow relative to the private sector of the economy.

Recommended Reading

Pat Choate and S. Walter: *America in Ruins: Beyond the Public Works Pork Barrel,* Council of State Planning Agencies, Washington, D.C., 1981.

Peter K. Eisinger: *The Rise of the Entrepreneurial State,* University of Wisconsin Press, Madison, Wis., 1988.

Susan B. Hansen: *The Political Economy of State Industrial Policy,* University of Pittsburgh Press, Pittsburgh, 1990.

Paul Peterson: *City Limits,* University of Chicago Press, Chicago, 1981.

E. S. Savas: *Privatization: The Key to Better Government,* Chatham House, Chatham, N.J., 1987.

CHAPTER 12

Environmental Policy

Successive generations of immigrants have come to this country in search of economic opportunity. They arrived from Ireland and Germany in 1850, from Italy and Russia in 1920, and from Haiti and Mexico in 1990. Their hard work transformed abundant natural resources into a cornucopia of material wealth, but at the cost of declining environmental quality. We have depleted the fertility of our soils, cut down primeval forests, and used water supplies faster than they can be replenished. Our fields produce meat, milk, and vegetables, but the nation's streams are polluted when fertilizer, pesticide, and animal waste residues run off the land. Factories convert raw materials into appliances, plastic products, and paper, but they also dump waste materials into the air and water.

This chapter discusses how state and local governments balance the competing demands of economic prosperity and environmental quality. Until about 1970, state governments regulated natural resource use and disposal of pollutants into the air, water, and land. Now the federal government sets the broad framework of environmental policy in the areas of air quality, water quality, hazardous waste disposal, and strip-mining reclamation. State and local governments implement these federal environmental laws and regulations in light of their own interests and preferences.

Air pollution control and solid waste management are two important environmental policy areas. Air pollution issues involve how much pollution is acceptable; to what extent automobile or factory emissions should be targets for clean up; and who should pay the cost of cleaning up pollutants that are generated in one state and damage environmental quality in another. Solid waste management has always been a state and local responsibility. Today, most states set solid waste disposal standards for their communities, monitor landfill and incinerator design and operation, and mandate that communities establish recycling programs.

The fifty states are diverse laboratories creating specific environmental policies that reflect differences in population density, wealth, and natural resource base. This chapter discusses how states implement federal environmental policy guidelines; why some states have more energetic environmental policy programs than do others; and how well present environmental policies strike an acceptable balance between economic production and environmental quality for present and future generations.

Balancing Economic Production and Environmental Quality

Choosing a set of policies that permit economic growth and also preserve a high-quality environment involves painful policy choices. Do we wish to maintain wetlands, which are the essential breeding habitat for many diverse animal species, or to build houses with lovely ocean views? Do we require a factory to install pollution control devices on its smokestacks if the price of its product will then increase? Should we use scarce water resources to grow vegetables in California in January for shipment to tables in Ohio? Should we cut down great trees in the Pacific Northwest to build houses in the United States and Japan? Should we close down a dirty factory or a logging operation if such a closing will cost the jobs of several hundred workers? These trade-offs between economic production and environmental quality are not easily resolved.

The Materials Balance Principle

The materials balance principle states that all materials that are withdrawn from the environment (for example, water, plant and animal life, coal and iron ore) must ultimately be returned to the environment, either as solid waste (for example, particulate matter in smoke, household trash) or as waste energy (which warms streams and the atmosphere).[1] This principle is based on the physical law of thermodynamics, which states that matter can be neither created nor destroyed but only altered in form. As population grows and standards of living increase, so too does pressure on the environment.

Individual Preferences

Individuals vary in their preference for greater consumption of economic goods or enjoyment of a cleaner environment. When people have a comfortable and secure standard of living, they may prefer improved environmental quality to more economic growth. Middle-income professionals often choose to live in suburban neighborhoods, in part to avoid crowded, polluted inner city environments. The economically secure are more willing to close down polluting factories. They are more willing to ban logging operations in order to preserve wilderness areas. They are more willing to pay extra for canned goods in order to reduce the cannery's waste emissions into a river.

The poor are left to live in the shadow of factory smokestacks, where rents are cheaper. Their jobs depend on exploiting environmental resources; their first priority is to maintain a healthy growing economy and keep factories operating even if emissions pollute the air. Feeding one's family and paying the rent are of primary importance; an unpleasant smell in the air is of relatively little concern. Smoke means jobs.[2]

Dumping on the Poor

In other ways, the poor are required to pay a disproportionate share of the environmental cost of material prosperity. Facilities to store solid waste are rarely planned for middle-class suburban neighborhoods. Waste dumps, sewage treatment plants, and incinerators are often situated in decaying industrial neighborhoods within inner cities, where residents are less sensitive than suburbanites to pollution issues. In the cities, residents are not particularly sensitive to environmental issues, nor do they have the organizational skills to mount effective political campaigns against undesirable facilities being located near their homes.

Lightly populated rural areas are attractive candidates for locating waste dumps, but typically local residents object strongly to their area's becoming the dumping ground for other people's wastes. "Not in my backyard,'' they protest. They often block or stall projects because their intensity compensates for their small numbers, and the political system provides numerous veto points for intense minorities. The public hearing process is lengthy and expensive; the court system is available to hear claims that project sponsors violate due process rules; local legislators are often attentive to the demands of aroused citizen groups.[3] Hence, the "brown" strategy of placing facilities in already-polluted inner city industrial areas is often favored to the "green" strategy of using rural areas.

Sweetening the Package: Compensation Plans

To make people live near a waste dump because they cannot afford to do anything else is hardly fair. But neighborhoods may agree to provide landfill space if they are offered compensation for their service to the larger community. For example, some communities may be willing to go into the solid waste storage business in exchange for annual fees or royalty payments for each ton of solid waste deposited.

These funds are then used to provide better schools and other public services or to reduce local tax payments. In effect, the local community tolerates some reduction in environmental quality in exchange for a higher material standard of living. This trade-off is hardly unusual in industrial societies; a community usually welcomes a factory that provides jobs, and for the most part its citizens willingly accept the attendant costs of a larger, more impersonal community, traffic jams, and air pollution.[4]

In Texas, for example, a private company is seeking permission from the state to store hazardous wastes in a geologically stable salt dome deep beneath the land surface. The project would create several thousand jobs in an area of high unemployment. Project opponents worry that the site is only ten miles from the lake which supplies water for the city of Houston. They do not want trucks filled with hazardous wastes rolling through neighboring communities, nor the stigma of being a chemical dump site. To win support, the firm has offered to guarantee the value of homes within three miles of the site and to donate $100,000 a year to a college scholarship fund for local high school students.[5] The same debate rages in small communities across the nation over whether or not to accept incinerators and landfills in exchange for economic compensation.

The compensation process has several advantages. First, a site is located amid neighbors who are willing to accept it, in exchange for compensation. Second, since communities bid against each other, competition prevents any community from charging excessively high monopoly prices for their waste disposal services. Third, the higher cost of responsible waste disposal encourages producers to find more environmentally benign production processes and consumers to buy fewer and less environmentally costly goods.

However, communities often reject compensation offers, viewing them as bribe attempts rather than business deals. For example, the fifty states are having little success in finding communities willing to host a storage facility for waste consisting of clothing and tools contaminated with low-level radioactive materials. These facilities must effectively isolate the radioactivity from the environment for hundreds of years. In New York State, only one community has expressed much interest: West Valley, which already stores much highly radioactive material from a nuclear processing plant. The compensation package is huge, including a one-time payment of $4.2 million to fund capital improvements and a $1.5 annual payment, which is what West Valley currently raises in taxes.[6]

Attitudes Toward Risk

Some people are natural gamblers: perhaps they buy lottery tickets, smoke cigarettes, or work as lumberjacks. They estimate that the profit or pleasure they receive is worth the cost of the ticket or the risk of physical injury. Other people avoid flying in airplanes or eating pesticide-sprayed fruit. They always fasten their seat belts and in general do all they can to avoid risk.

People seem to be more willing to accept a risk that is voluntary (hang gliding), rather than involuntary (exposure to a toxic chemical spill); familiar (operating an automobile), rather than dreaded (exposure to radioactivity); and noncatastrophic (200 deaths over several years from a single cause), rather than catastrophic (200 deaths in a single airplane crash).[7] Different types of activities involve different levels of risk. For example, operating a power mower during the summer is a greater health risk than living near a nuclear power plant for a year, yet most people prefer to take their chances with the power mower. Economic compensation packages have been difficult to negotiate because few communities are inclined to take much risk where environmental hazards to health are concerned.

When doubt exists about what level of exposure might be detrimental to human health, standard-setters tend to assume the worst and permit only very low levels of exposure. For example, scientists are uncertain whether exposure to airborne toxics like asbestos causes a handful of deaths or as many as 3,000 deaths per year. The Environmental Protection Agency (EPA) assumes that the higher estimate is the correct one and frames its cleanup requirements accordingly.[8] Environmental policy is based on the premise that damage to human health should be minimized regardless of the cost. In effect, policy makers assume that citizens are much more risk-averse than they may in fact be.

Experts are beginning to question whether the threat to public health justifies large expenditures for pollution cleanup. For example, in 1983, all 2,240 residents of Times Beach, Missouri, were evacuated after dirt roads in the community were contaminated with dioxin. At the time, dioxin was thought to be a lethal chemical, much more hazardous than chain-smoking, but now experts consider exposure to dioxin to be no more risky than sunbathing.[9]

Recently, environmental regulators have been inclined to assume that any risk from exposure to a pollutant below one in a million is "below regulatory concern" and can safely be ignored. Some environmental advocates, however, take strong exception to the principle that any health risk should be below regulatory concern. These staunch environmentalists are probably more risk-averse than the average person.

Discounting the Future

How we trade off material production and environmental quality is also affected by our sense of the future and of intergenerational fairness. The resources we consume and the pollution we produce today have consequences which will show up in future years. We enjoy our air conditioners now; the consequences of depletion of the ozone layer by refrigerants and global warming from the production of carbon dioxide will not be known definitively for decades. Environmental advocates stress the unfairness of using scarce environmental resources today and leaving our descendants a legacy of resource depletion and environmental pollution.[10]

The Politics of Resource Conservation and Pollution Control

The trade-off between environmental quality and material production is worked out in politics through the interaction of organized producer groups and environmental groups, the expressions of citizen opinion in polls and elections, and the judgments of legislators who enact laws and bureaucrats who implement them.

Interest Groups and Public Opinion

Economic interests whose jobs and profits are threatened by environmental protection fight to safeguard those interests. Because electric power utilities in Ohio and Indiana have blocked efforts to clean up emissions at the expense of their electricity buyers, clouds filled with acid rain continue to drift from their tall smokestacks across New York, New England, and Canada. The high-sulfur coal industry in West Virginia and Pennsylvania fought to preserve profits and jobs by demanding that all coal-burning plants be required to install expensive stack-scrubbing equipment, even if they burn low-sulfur coal. This provision removed any incentive for utilities to shift from high-sulfur coal to low-sulfur coal. The cost of electricity to consumers in the west and midwest increased, while air quality improved only marginally.[11] Loggers in Oregon have little sympathy for the spotted owl, whose very existence is threatened by logging's destruction of its habitat.

Over the last three decades, the political forces supporting a high-quality environment have strengthened. Many environmental groups have gained members, enlarged budgets, developed expertise, and expanded their political contacts. The Sierra Club and the Wildlife Federation, for example, publicize the plight of endangered species and the need to protect wilderness areas from encroaching human economic activity. The Environmental Defense Fund and The Natural Resources Defense Council hire lawyers to bring suits against polluting industries or foot-dragging bureaucrats whose rulings do not conform to federal or state law. Greenpeace members take direct action to protest whaling practices or nuclear testing.

Public opinion polls reveal strong symbolic support for a high-quality environment. In 1991, 71 percent of a random national sample agreed that ''protection of the environment should be given priority, even at the risk of curbing economic growth.'' Of those people contacted, 67 percent said they worried a great deal about pollution of drinking water, lakes, and rivers, while 71 percent agreed that the environment should be protected even if it means increased government spending and higher taxes.[12]

Legislators and Bureaucrats

Legislators look for ways to support environmental goals while minimizing negative impact on economic activity. In the 1970s, purportedly strong environmental legislation in effect promised existing polluters that they need not comply fully with the legislation. For example, existing factories did not have to comply with air emissions limits; only new factories were required to install the best pollution-control technology.

Because society values both economic production and environmental protection, regulators must listen to and evaluate competing arguments and evidence. Many environmental regulators are lawyers by training, comfortable with the process of negotiation among adversaries. They also know that interests disappointed by an environmental ruling are likely to seek reversal in the courts.[13]

Although many environmental regulators are personally sympathetic to strong pro environment policies, they are also subject to political pressures from the governor, who appoints top agency officials, and from the legislature, which appropriates their budgets. Elected politicians usually insist that environmental regulators take into account the economic impact of their decisions, and the regulators are likely to heed their advice.[14] In general, environmental regulators tend to be neutral arbiters rather than spirited advocates.

Variations in State Environmental Policy Effort

Not all states equally value material production and environmental quality, and states have very different levels of environmental policy commitment. Some states, like California, New Jersey, Oregon, and Wisconsin, spend more money per capita on environmental programs and sponsor a broader range of programs than do others. Lightly populated southern and border states devote relatively little attention to environmental issues.[15] Why is there a difference in environmental policy effort from state to state?

Intensity of Environmental Concerns

States that have serious environmental pollution problems tend to make the greatest environmental policy effort. The Los Angeles area has the worst air pollution problem in the nation, followed by New Jersey, where eighteen of twenty-one counties fail to meet federal air pollution standards. These densely populated states also have serious water-quality and solid-waste-management problems.

The economies of Oregon and other western states depend upon their natural resources. The conflict between harvesting natural resources to provide a livelihood for loggers and ranchers and protecting a heritage of old growth forest and unspoiled wilderness is the core political issue in Oregon politics. Strong political constituencies call upon the state governments to manage natural resources for economic use and to restrict economic exploitation of land and forest. During economic hard times, Oregon governors pursue policies that promote economic growth; during good times, they tend to protect the environment. On election day, voters tend to support these changes in policy emphasis.[16]

Per Capita Income

States with high per capita incomes are likely to favor environmental quality over economic growth, while those with low per capita incomes tend to support weaker environmental protection policies. California and New Jersey are examples of states with high per capita incomes that devote substantial resources to reducing emissions and protecting environmental quality. High-income residents can provide comfortably for their basic needs, and they are sensitive to the quality of their environment. They join environmental groups and are articulate participants in the political process. Elected politicians respond to their demands by passing pro-environment laws and regulations.

Two decades ago, Arkansas was among the poorest of the states. Trout filled sparkling clear rivers. Land was cheap, wages low, tax breaks to investors generous, and environmental regulations minimal. Chicken and livestock producers flourished, creating thousands of jobs. The Arkansas economy expanded, but then animal waste was allowed to wash into the rivers uncontrolled.

Initially, voters tolerated deteriorating river quality as an acceptable price to pay for economic prosperity. However, in the 1990s, the pendulum began to swing in the opposite direction. Many citizens could now afford pickup trucks, but they drove to troutless streams. Political sentiment demanded that chicken and cattle producers be subjected to much stricter controls on animal waste runoff.[17]

The Environmental Policy Process

The evolution of environmental policy can be divided into stages of agenda setting, policy making, implementation, and evaluation, as described in Chapter 9.

Agenda Setting

Agenda setting is the process by which voters, interest groups, and activist governors and legislators become aware of a problem and call upon government to deal with it. Pollution first became part of the political agenda in major American cities in the late nineteenth century. Ordinary citizens who voted in elections saw and smelled the need to remove garbage from fetid urban streets and to install sewer systems to carry away human waste. Factory owners concluded that environmental pollution was threatening the health of their labor force and their own quality of life.[18]

Not until the late 1940s, however, did environmental issues gain a place on state and local political agenda. Air pollution became a public health issue as well as an aesthetic nuisance in heavy industrial cities like Pittsburgh and Gary, Indiana, where smokestacks belched pollution while factories manufactured the steel needed to fight World War II. The smoke from coal-burning heavy industry cast a lasting haze over the urban landscape.

By the late 1960s, several events had stirred Americans to a new level of environmental consciousness:

1. Rachel Carson's *Silent Spring,* published in 1962, warned that pesticide use threatened the very survival of bird species. The pollution caused by human economic activity was far more than an aesthetic nuisance; many people came to realize that pollution endangered the very ecosystem that supports life itself. This lesson was driven home by the well-publicized 1968 Santa Barbara oil spill in which birds and other wildlife were coated with oil, and by the death of Lake Erie from phosphate pollution.

2. Opposition to the war in Vietnam sparked a reaction against current American values and culture. Many Americans were shocked by the slaughter of innocent Vietnamese and the destruction of fields and forests viewed nightly on the evening news. A new critical spirit challenged the traditional American practice of wanton destruction. Many became aware of the need to respect life and curb our technological power if the fragile, life-sustaining environment were to survive.

3. In 1968, Democratic presidential hopeful Edmund Muskie adopted a strong environmental position, and Republican Richard Nixon followed his lead. Major political figures rec-

ognized broad support among the electorate for bold action to improve environmental quality, and they prepared to enact strong environmental legislation.

Policy Making

Historically, environmental policy making was primarily a state and local responsibility. Farm and factory production had had limited environmental consequences because the atmosphere, rivers, and streams could initially absorb pollution. Noticeable pollution was largely contained with state and often within city boundaries. In accordance with the Tenth Amendment to the Constitution, environmental policy making was reserved to the states. However, states did not take many initiatives to improve environmental quality. They could not afford to develop the technical expertise on pollution issues, they had no jurisdiction over pollution generated in neighboring states upstream or upwind, and polluting industries could threaten to move their operations elsewhere to escape compliance with strict environmental rules.

Air Pollution Control Policy

In the 1940s, heavy industrial cities like Pittsburgh and Gary attempted to regulate emissions from factory smokestacks, but with limited success. They could not prove that pollutants originated in factories rather than in automobiles or home furnaces. Therefore, city ordinances were subject to legal challenge in the courts. And the considerable political influence of the steel companies discouraged city officials from enacting strong regulations.[19]

The state of California passed pioneering legislation in 1948 requiring all automobiles sold in California to have pollution-reducing devices. They did so in response to the plight of Los Angeles, where automotive pollution sometimes concentrated in stagnant air to the point where many inhabitants had difficulty breathing. Automobile makers in Detroit chose to meet the California standards because they had little political influence in California, and they needed to sell cars in the large California market.[20]

In the 1950s and 1960s, state and local governments were slow to react to growing evidence of environmental deterioration. States had little technical capacity to measure pollution and enforce regulations; major industries enjoyed much political influence in state and local government; and, as urban areas sprawled, pollution became a multistate phenomenon requiring coordination among governments. The federal government began to get involved in air pollution control in 1963 with passage of the Clean Air Act. This law provided some federal funds for air pollution research and for support of state pollution control agencies.

In 1970, the federal government took the lead in air pollution control policy. The Clean Air Act Amendments ordered the newly created Environmental Protection Agency (EPA) to establish national air-quality standards, required automobile manufacturers to eliminate 90 percent of automobile pollutants within five years, and authorized heavy fines and jail sentences for polluters who failed to comply with the law. Each state was responsible for creating plans to achieve the air-quality standards set by the EPA.

Solid Waste Disposal Policy

Solid waste disposal has historically been a local responsibility. About 80 percent of solid waste was landfilled, 10 percent incinerated, and 10 percent recycled. In the 1990s, however, state and local governments have been transforming solid waste disposal policy, relying less heavily on landfills and establishing recycling programs.

Because landfills are aesthetic nuisances and pose health threats in heavily populated areas, solid waste disposal has become a very expensive local government problem. Most states now prohibit local governments from simply dumping garbage at some remote location. Today, landfills are required to install clay or plastic liners at their bases, design collection systems to capture water runoff, and cover the garbage daily with a layer of earth. The purpose is to prevent runoff from contaminating local groundwater and surface streams and to control rodents, blowing paper, and odors.

As many states introduced stricter landfill regulations in the 1980s, the charge for dumping wastes increased from about fifteen dollars per ton to approximately fifty dollars per ton. Northeastern cities that have run out of landfill space are now transporting wastes at a total cost of $125 per ton to distant rural landfills in Ohio, Pennsylvania, and Arkansas. New York and New Jersey generate over half of the trash that crosses state lines.

In many cases, these distant landfills are owned by private individuals or corporations that profit from an increased volume of business. But neighbors object to the increased heavy truck traffic and are afraid that groundwater supplies will be contaminated. Several states are placing limits on the amount of solid waste that landfills can receive from other states. The prospect of losing access to reasonably priced, out-of-state landfill space adds urgency to calls for strong recycling programs.[21] Many local governments are setting up recycling programs for newspaper, plastic, glass, and metal because each ton of waste material recycled saves expensive landfill space, as well as natural resources.

Implementation

While the policy-making process establishes an intent to reduce environmental pollution, the details are hammered out in the implementation process.

Implementing Air Pollution Policy

Although the federal government sets the basic outline of air pollution control policy, state and local governments are largely responsible for implementation. While major federal laws and administrative regulations in the 1970s established the broad framework of environmental policy, local interests sought to control the implementation of federal laws and regulations.[22] For this reason, only future investment, not current investment, is required to install pollution control technology. What, if any, requirements should be imposed upon existing plants was left to the states to determine. Also, state and local authorities were given primary responsibility for monitoring and enforcement. In general, however, at a time of spirited competition to attract investment, states have been reluctant to look for violations.

Opposition to Clean Air Proposals.   Specific proposals to clean up the air inevitably arouse opposition. Car owners object to the hassle and expense of emissions inspection; downtown merchants dislike parking taxes which cause their customers to defect to the suburban shopping mall; and taxpayers do not want to fund mass transit improvements. Rather than offend important groups, cities prefer to negotiate with the EPA for easing of standards or extension of deadlines. For its part, the EPA during the Reagan and Bush administrations was sympathetic to appeals for delay. Twenty years after passage of the 1970 Clean Air Act, most American cities have not yet achieved the air-quality standards mandated by the law.

The 1990 Clean Air Act Amendments put pressure directly on industrial firms to curb their emissions. Industries were ordered to install better-performing catalytic converters on automobiles by 1994, to formulate cleaner-burning gasoline for use in urban areas by 1995, and to reduce sulfur dioxide emissions by 50 percent by 2000.

State Implementation Plans.   Because states vary in size, population, industrial base, and climatic conditions, different states employ different strategies to achieve air-quality goals. States are required to establish state implementation plans (SIPS) setting forth how desired air-quality levels will be achieved. For example, a state or city may enact standards that are stricter than federal standards on automotive or industrial emissions, as does California, or restrict the use of wood-burning stoves, as does the city of Denver. To control automobile pollution, a city may introduce taxes on parking or higher bridge tolls; build better mass transit facilities or install bicycle paths; or encourage car pooling to reduce automobile traffic. Similarly, a state can reduce the impact of factory smokestack pollution in several ways. Some states allowed construction of tall smokestacks to disperse pollutants widely and prevent pollutant buildup near the factory, but this practice exports pollution to neighboring states, creating acid rain. Federal rules now forbid new plants from using tall stacks to disperse pollutants.

A utility may be allowed to burn low-sulfur coal, which is less polluting than high-sulfur coal. Or a factory can be required to install a chemical scrubber on its smokestack, which captures pollutants after combustion but before they leave the stack. States have also experimented with emission offset plans, which focus on the level of emissions in a whole city rather than the emissions of individual polluters. A reduction in emissions achieved by closing the old factory offsets the pollution emitted by the new one. A factory may locate in a city that is not in compliance with clean air standards if the city can clean up or close down existing polluting factories. The community gains because the new factory creates more high-paying jobs and more tax revenues while air quality improves.[23]

Implementing Solid Waste Policy

Solid waste planners must make basic policy decisions. Should the state bury household garbage in landfills or burn it in incinerators? How extensively should communities recycle? Should a city seek to buy disposal capacity in other states with more landfill space? What recyclables should be removed from the waste stream? How much should communities spend on recycling education and publicity? Should the recycling program be mandatory or voluntary? Will compliance be encouraged through education, enforcement of fines, or economic incentives such as charging for each bag of garbage collected?

Densely populated New Jersey and lightly populated Wyoming have different solid waste management policies. Since New Jersey cannot find politically acceptable landfill or incinerator sites within the state, they pay landfill operators in other states to accept their solid waste, and they promote recycling programs energetically. In Wyoming, communities continue to dispose of their waste in burn barrels or lightly regulated landfills.

Evaluation

After more than twenty years of designing and implementing policies to improve environmental quality, it is useful to evaluate the programs. How much has environmental quality improved? Have the gains been purchased at an acceptable cost? Are the institutions and procedures working to achieve an appropriate level of environmental quality?

Costs and Benefits of Pollution Control

Air Quality.   After World War II, significant air-quality gains occurred as factories shifted from coal to cleaner-burning natural gas and oil, and state and local laws prohibited burning of leaves. But the Clean Air Act Amendments of 1970 and 1977 have also contributed; nationwide, air pollution concentrations are lower today than they were in 1970, even though a larger population consumes more goods and services. Most important, acute threats to health in major urban areas during high pollution periods are much reduced. Although about 60 percent of counties still do not attain national air-quality standards, many violations are borderline. The standards themselves are very strict, geared to protect people with respiratory problems from discomfort.[24]

The principal benefit of cleaner air is that it enables people to live longer, healthier, and more productive lives. Secondary benefits are higher property values, more productive agriculture, and reduced damage and soiling to clothing, materials, and buildings. The costs to society include capital investment in pollution control equipment, operation and maintenance of that equipment, record keeping, and government regulation. One careful researcher concludes that benefits exceed costs for the stationary-source air pollution control program, but not the automobile emissions or water pollution control programs.[25]

For automobiles, catalytic converters are costly to install, and they rarely work well. Owners have had incentives to disable catalytic converters to improve automobile performance and increase gas mileage. In any case, a catalytic converter often wears out within two or three years, while the car continues to pollute for its remaining ten-year life. Recently, air pollution control officials, in their efforts to control smog, have spent too much to limit gasoline vapors and not enough to curb nitrogen oxides.[26]

Water Quality.   The Federal Water Pollution Control Act of 1972 regulated industrial and municipal point sources of pollution, but these are not the major sources of water pollution. Nonpoint sources—agricultural and urban runoff—are a much larger source of pollutants that flow into lakes and rivers.

While waters are cleaner as a result of investment in factory and municipal wastewater treatment, other methods of water quality improvement would achieve similar results at much lower cost. For example, pumping oxygen into a stream would speed decomposition of organic waste, as would increasing stream flow by releasing more water from upstream dams.[27]

Recycling Programs.   Although the cost of solid waste disposal has skyrocketed in many states, the benefits of saved landfill space and revenues from the sale of recyclables do not yet offset the cost of operating recycling programs. For several reasons, outlined below, they are not likely to break even any time in the near future.

1.   As more communities recycle, the supply of newspaper, office paper, glass, and bimetal cans has increased rapidly, depressing market prices. Buyers of recycled newsprint paid twenty dollars per ton several years ago; in 1992 they charged five dollars per ton to haul the material away. In the future, however, the price may rebound as industries use more low-cost recycled newsprint in their production processes.

2.   Because collecting, sorting, and compacting recyclables are labor-intensive activities, recycling is expensive. At present, the sale of recyclable material and the value of landfill space that is saved do not offset the costs of recycling. However, this gloomy economic picture will improve as recyclable prices recover and landfill or incineration costs continue to escalate.

3.   While 40 percent of the waste stream is recyclable, few re-
     cycling programs approach the 25 percent level. The most
     successful programs are in suburban neighborhoods where
     residents are sensitive to environmental concerns, believe re-
     cycling is important, and have space to separate and store
     recyclables. Given the pressures of crime, poverty, crowding,
     and homelessness, urban residents tend to downplay the im-
     portance of recycling. In many cities, households are recy-
     cling less than 10 percent of their waste stream.

The Standards and Enforcement Approach

The standards and enforcement approach dominates environmental policy. A legislative body or administrative agency establishes a
standard for environmental quality or level of emissions permitted. A
standard may limit discharges per unit of output, which implies that
as production increases, so does the amount of discharge permitted,
or a standard may limit discharge per unit of time, which means that
as production increases, discharges must be reduced per unit of production. A standard may also limit the concentration of pollutants,
which allows dilution rather than reduction. Easy regulations can
encourage industrial expansion; tough regulations can improve environmental quality.[28]

These standards are published and polluters are required by law to
comply with them. Standards require, for example, that rivers and
streams be clean enough for citizens to fish and swim without danger
to their health; that all automobiles be equipped with catalytic converters that reduce emissions by 90 percent of a base level; that
citizens separate recyclables from their household garbage; that landfills have a heavy plastic liner to prevent rain that seeps through the
landfill from contaminating ground water.

Polluters who do not comply with published standards are subject
to fines; in exceptional cases, their officers may be sent to prison. The
American auto industry threatened to close down in 1977 because it
could not meet the emission standards stated in the Clean Air Act;
executives did not wish to risk heavy fines and possible jail sentences.
State governments threaten to withhold state payments from counties
or municipalities that operate substandard landfills. Local governments tell their citizens that if they fail to separate their recyclables,
the garbage hauler will leave their trash at the curb and they may be
fined. This enforcement process requires that government establish a
costly reporting, monitoring, and investigative system.

Criticism of the Standards and Enforcement Approach

The standards and enforcement approach has been severely criticized on the following grounds:

1. Universal environmental quality and emissions standards are insensitive to differences in the urgency of environmental problems. For example, why should automobiles, factories, and landfills in lightly populated rural areas be subject to the same costly pollution control measures as those in densely populated and polluted cities? Also, why should the federal government create a national recycling standard mandating that all states recycle a certain percentage of their waste stream? Setting a national recycling standard ignores important differences between heavily and lightly populated areas. About four-fifths of the states recycle now, including the more-populated states where landfill costs are rising rapidly. In less-populated states where landfill space is abundant and cheap, local citizens are probably better off dumping their trash in a landfill and using the money saved for some other worthy environmental purpose.

2. Environmental protection agencies have tended to regulate environmental pollution control technology rather than environmental quality or emissions levels. It is easy to monitor whether or not pollution control technology has been installed; it is hard to measure emissions levels and even harder to measure environmental quality accurately. Polluters may install the required technology, but they currently have no incentive to make sure that the technology works properly.[29] For example, car owners have no incentive to maintain their catalytic converters in good working order; cities install sewage treatment plants but may not train their employees to use them efficiently.

3. New environmental standards are often applied to new investment but not to existing sources of pollution. This policy wins the support of established industry because existing polluters can keep on polluting, while the added cost of meeting pollution control requirements discourages potential competitors from entering the industry.[30] Requiring that only new investment comply with tough standards encourages existing businesses to continue operating their dirty factories.

4. Industries have no incentive to reduce their pollution by more than the minimum required by the law. A factory might be able to reduce its emissions by 70 percent rather than the required 50 percent at little additional cost, but the factory most likely will not do the additional cleanup—its goal is to minimize the cost of its product, not to provide a cleaner environment for society.

5. When faced with standards, industries often hire lawyers who are adept at negotiating with environmental bureaucrats. They seek to ease the standards, gain more time for compliance, and win favorable rulings about whether or not they are in compliance. Such behavior arouses environmental groups, who argue with environmental bureaucrats for a strict interpretation of the standards. The politics of environmental regulation thus becomes a test of political strength among industrial and environmental groups.[31]

6. The enforcement process relies upon fines and jail terms to penalize noncompliance. However, because enforcement is costly and closing down polluters politically difficult, government inspection and enforcement capability are very limited. Industrial polluters are generally required to monitor their own emissions, and environmental regulators rarely audit their reports. As auditors announce their occasional visits in advance, they are unlikely to find violations. In some states, regulators inspect smoke plumes and water quality from their cars as they drive by—and even if violations are found, penalties are unlikely to be assessed.[32]

Polluters therefore have little incentive to comply with tough regulations. One 1983 sample of 119 firms estimates that only 10 percent had a strong environmental management division supported by top corporate management, monitored emissions carefully, and sought cost-effective ways to achieve better emissions control. Some 30 percent of firms sought to minimize their air and water pollution control expenses, were not in compliance with their state's formal emissions standards, and were making no effort to get into compliance.[33]

Using Economic Incentives

Providing economic incentives for individuals and firms to act in ways that protect the environment is an alternative to the standards and enforcement approach. Economic incentives achieve more emissions control at a lower cost than does the standards and enforcement approach.[34]

Tax on Emissions. One economic approach is to put a tax on emissions. An individual or organization is allowed to dump emissions into the environment, but it must pay for the damage imposed on society. For example, if a car owner were charged for vehicle emissions, the owner would have an incentive to keep the car's catalytic converter in good working order. If factory emissions were taxed, the owners would have an incentive to look for ways to alter their production process, introduce effective pollution control, and develop better monitoring equipment.

A city might collect garbage only if it is packed in official bags sold at a price which covers the cost of garbage disposal. This approach would give householders an incentive to recycle materials and to reduce purchase of unnecessary packaging; the less trash they generated each week, the lower would be their solid waste disposal charge.[35]

The beauty of a tax system is that polluters have an incentive to reduce their pollution; under the present standards and enforcement system, they have an incentive to minimize their pollution control effort.

Emission Permits Trading. Another economic incentive approach establishes a market in emissions permits. After government regulators establish an air-quality goal and determine what levels of emissions are consistent with that goal, they issue permits allowing factories to dump an acceptable quantity of pollutants. For example, if a factory is dumping 100 units of pollution, and the environmental protection agency wants to reduce pollution by 50 percent, the agency will give to that factory emission permits worth 50 units. The factory must then either reduce pollution by 50 units or buy additional permits from another emitter.

Under this system, if a factory's owners can think of cheap and easy ways to reduce the factory's pollution, they will do so. Indeed, if they could reduce the factory's pollution by 75 units, for example, they could sell the unneeded pollution permits to another factory that cannot clean up its pollution easily. Thus, additional revenue from selling pollution permits becomes an incentive for a factory's owners to work hard to reduce its pollution.

In one recent case, the Tennessee Valley Authority bought the right to emit 10,000 tons of sulfur dioxide, the main cause of acid rain, from a Wisconsin utility, which will reduce its emissions by 10,000 tons more than the law requires.[36] The most dramatic example of emissions trading is planned in southern California. The 2,700 largest polluters in the smoggy Los Angeles area face strict emissions quotas, but they may meet their quota either by cleaning up their emissions or by purchasing the right to pollute from another company that has surpassed its cleanup quota.[37]

The beauty of emission permits trading is that the desired level of environmental quality is achieved at lower cost. Polluters actively seek ways to reduce their pollution so they can become sellers rather than buyers of pollution permits. Consumer price rises are slowed, since pollution is reduced by those firms with the lowest pollution removal costs.

Although Americans express a general desire to protect their environment, they are reluctant to sacrifice their standard of living to slow the rate of natural resource use and to reduce pollution. As they implement federal environmental rules, state and local governments have been careful to protect local economic interests from being harmed seriously by environmental regulations.

During the Reagan and Bush administrations, the federal EPA did not pursue an aggressive environmental policy. Some states with strong environmental interests are pressing for state restrictions on pollution that far exceed federal regulation. Ironically, industries that preferred limited, ineffective stage regulation in the 1970s find federal environmental regulation less onerous than the bold environmental policy initiatives being proposed and enacted in California, New Jersey, and other states in the 1990s.

Recommended Reading

Louis Blumberg and Robert Gottlieb: *War on Waste: Can America Win Its Battle with Garbage?*, Island Press, Washington, D.C., 1989.

James P. Lester, ed.: *Environmental Politics and Policy: Theories and Evidence,* Duke University Press, Durham, N.C., 1989.

Paul R. Portney, ed.: *Public Policies for Environmental Protection,* Resources for the Future, Washington, D.C., 1990.

Barry G. Rabe: *Fragmentation and Integration in State Environmental Management,* Conservation Foundation, Washington, D.C., 1986.

Walter A. Rosenbaum: *Environmental Politics and Policy,* Congressional Quarterly Press, Washington, D.C., 1991.

Clifford S. Russell, Winston Harrington, and William J. Vaughn: *Enforcing Pollution Control Laws,* Resources for the Future, Washington, D.C., 1986.

Bruce Yandle: *The Political Limits of Environmental Regulation,* Quorum Books, New York, 1989.

CHAPTER 13

Criminal Justice and State Politics

The criminal justice system is often perceived as a set of connected agencies that work together to process criminals while protecting individual rights. This ideal is not found in the workings of the real world. Federal, state, and local governments have created criminal justice bureaucracies by an incremental policy process. As we saw in Chapter 9, policy does not necessarily proceed in a rational manner but rather evolves as competing interest groups implement programs that produce incremental change. The result in criminal justice is a "system" made up of a series of fragmented and self-interested bureaucracies. Each organization works to accomplish its particular goals, which are often inconsistent with the goals of other criminal justice organizations.

Police departments, court jurisdictions, and correctional enterprises are controlled by different levels of government and have distinct as well as overlapping functions. For example, an automobile accident in a city may be responded to by state police, sheriff deputies, and city police. Most criminal justice functions are the responsibility of state and local governments. The federal government is not a major part of the system and employs only 8 percent of criminal justice personnel.[1] (See Table 13.1 for the percentage of personnel by agency for the three levels of government.)

This chapter outlines the criminal justice system and demonstrates how the policy-making process operates at the state and local level. The chapter begins with a discussion of the agencies that funnel the accused through the system, then considers the role of ideology in criminal justice policy making. The chapter ends with a discussion of the policy-making process with illustrations from the criminal justice system and a case analysis of the difficulties of policy implementation.

The Criminal Justice Funnel

The agencies mandated to control criminal behavior funnel the accused through a series of stages beginning with arrest and ending with punishment or freedom. These agencies operate at the local, state, and federal level, and each level differs in the personnel available to carry out criminal justice goals.

The Police

Public Agencies

The police are usually the first criminal justice agency to become involved in a case. Most police departments are the responsibility of local municipalities and range from small, one-person departments to large departments with over 35,000 employees. Sheriff departments are the responsibility of county governments. States operate state

Table 13.1   Percent of Criminal Justice Personnel Employed in Agencies by the Level of Government Controlling the Agency

Agency	Level of Government		
	Local	State	Federal
Police	77%	15%	8%
Judicial (Courts)	60%	32%	8%
Prosecution and Legal Services	58%	26%	17%
Public Defense	47%	50%	3%
Corrections	35%	61%	4%
Total	62%	31%	8%

Source: *Report to the Nation,* NIJ, 1988, p. 59.

police or highway patrol departments as well as park police and campus security forces at state colleges.

One obvious problem facing this diverse force is the coordination of responsibilities. Consolidation rarely works since the police bureaucracies (as well as politicians) do not want to lose control of police functions. For example, a proposal to combine the personnel in a county-operated sheriff's road patrol and a city-operated police force would result in political battles over who would be responsible for supervising and funding the new department and who would be let go. Another reason for the diversity of forces is that Americans have been cautious about giving the police too much power.[2] Local control ensures police accountability, and each locality has depended upon its own system of control. Any attempt to consolidate the local jurisdictions would decrease the input of each.

As policing agencies evolved, they developed special functions. For example, in many states, sheriff departments are responsible for serving court papers and managing local jails and the state police are responsible for patrolling state highways. In New York State during 1989, of the $3.9 million spent on police functions, 8.6 percent went to sheriff's departments (road patrol). The New York State Police received 5.5 percent, and other authorities (campus police) and special agencies received 15.9 percent. Local agencies received the most funding (70 percent).[3]

Private Forces

Supplementing these public agencies is a growing private funded and controlled police force. The estimated private security force in 1990 was 1.5 million persons, as compared to approximately 600,000 public police officers.[4] This reliance on private police is welcomed by many businesses and citizens who increasingly experience fears about crime affecting their neighborhoods. However, private police may seek private vengeance, protect the public unequally, and undermine the authority of public police agencies. While our fear of crime stimulates a knee-jerk reaction to develop more protection, we must keep in mind that the behavior of public police officers is limited by the rights guaranteed to us by the Constitution. The Constitutional safeguards built into the document by its framers were the result of the eighteenth-century Americans' experience with the tyranny of oppression. Private police forces, such as companies operated for the purpose of selling security to other companies and units operated by large companies to protect assets, do not have the responsibility to the state that the public force does. Unfortunately, as private police forces emerge, the state loses some degree of its responsibility for order maintenance and its monopoly over how order is to be defined. One danger of this circumstance is that the public will be forced to comply with the definition of order determined by private individuals; another is that when accused of a crime a defendant will not have the recourse to constitutional protection accorded people apprehended by the public police force. For example, private police forces are not subject to Fourth Amendment restrictions on searches and seizures as are public agencies. Evidence obtained by a private security force without a warrant would not be excluded from a court case, but such evidence could be excluded when obtained by public officers. Policy makers must be constantly concerned that the private police does not become a vigilante force, serving a few interests at the expense of the rights and safety of the public and to the disadvantage of those who cannot afford the services of a private force.

The Courts

Once a person has been arrested, the judicial system becomes activated. The defendant is arraigned, informed of the reason for arrest, and provided with information pertaining to a citizen's constitutional rights. One of the most important rights guarantees a defendant legal counsel.

Legal Representation

The Sixth Amendment to the United States Constitution guarantees the right to counsel, and lawyers are provided to defendants who do not have the funds to procure their own attorneys. Three types of defender systems operate to serve indigent defendants. *Public defender programs* are provided by public and nonprofit agencies, such as the Legal Aid Society, that are staffed by full-time and part-time lawyers. *Assigned counsel systems* select private attorneys from a list consisting of all eligible attorneys in a court's jurisdiction. *Contract systems* involve the awarding of contracts by counties to private lawyers, law firms, or bar associations that represent indigent clients.[5]

States differ in the extent to which a particular defense system is utilized. Sixty percent of the counties (mostly rural) rely primarily on assigned counsel, while 34 percent are more likely to use public defenders. The rest rely on contracted counsel. Most indigent people are represented by public defenders because most urban counties prefer this type of system and most defendants are found in these counties. Although some state governments (thirteen) operate indigent defense systems themselves, in most states (twenty-five) defense systems for indigent citizens are operated at the county level.[6]

Bail

The criminal justice system decides whether the defendant is to spend time awaiting trial in jail or as a free person. Controversy rages over whether or not to incarcerate people awaiting trial. Studies have found that 10 to 20 percent of defendants awaiting trial are arrested on another charge before the trial.[7] Many have argued that it is important to protect the right of citizens to be free from crime and that more reliance on incarceration before trial is preferable. Critics of this approach counter that our society assumes a person to be innocent until proven guilty and that the incarceration of a defendant before trial punishes the person without such a trial.

A traditional response to this dilemma was for courts to use a monetary commitment in the form of bail or a similar system to ensure a defendant's return to court as an alternative to jail. The unfairness of this system, given its obvious favoritism toward the rich, led to reforms over the last thirty years. One popular procedure has been the use of checklist to determine the likelihood of a defendant's returning to court; those who receive an appropriate score are released from custody. Evaluation of these programs found that only about 4 percent of those released without bail did not return.[8] Recently, the public's fear of crime and the reports of serious crimes being committed by individuals awaiting trial resulted in the passage of legislation in many states that allows the courts to retain some persons until trial without the benefit of bail. The decision to hold a person without the benefit of bail is to be based on the belief that the person is a danger to the community.

Plea Bargaining

Although the administration of a proper punishment to a person judged to be guilty of a crime is a central goal of the criminal justice system, it is, in a sense, its least visible component. This is because 90 percent of all cases adjudicated are the result of guilty pleas arranged as part of a bargain between the state and the defendant. This plea bargain allows the state to punish the defendant without his or her having a trial.[9] States differ in the extent to which this occurs. For example, during 1981, in Indianapolis, Indiana, only 13 percent of criminal cases were reduced to a lesser charge, while in Golden, Colorado, 74 percent of cases resulted in a reduced charge.[10]

Many people who are critical of the plea bargaining system point out that it results in a lessening of the charged offense and therefore fails to accomplish the goal of just punishment. Other critics have argued that the hidden nature of plea bargaining gives the prosecutor too much discretion and may result in some groups such as blacks being given differential treatment.[11] One study found that defendants who accepted a plea bargain received lighter sentences than did defendants who took the option to go to trial.[12] Despite these criticisms, given that plea bargaining has been used since 1881 and is the result of prosecutors' preferences, it is unlikely that the system will change. In two states (Washington and Alaska), experiments to eliminate some or all plea bargaining have met with success, but the fear that courts will be overcrowded has worked against any policy change in the other states.[13]

Jury Trial

Citizens who decide to have a jury trial are taking advantage of a system that evolved from the early British system's rejection of trial by ordeal. In the early thirteenth century the British king's magistrate used citizens as witnesses to determine the facts of a case. By the fourteenth century the jurors were deciding the facts of the case. Today the selection of a jury and the presentation of evidence to a jury has become a science. Lawyers use experts to determine the type of person that would be more likely to accept their account. The attorneys for the subway vigilante Bernard Goetz acquired the services of a psychologist to help select jurors who would be likely to view the subway shooting as a defensive reaction, and the strategy worked. In 1992, critics of the Rodney King police brutality trial argued that the police were acquitted because the jury had little understanding of what it was like to be mistreated by the police. The jury was composed of people not living in Los Angeles and included no African Americans. A consequence of the belief that juries can be manipulated has been a call for reform of the jury system.

Sentencing

Goals of Sentencing.   After a defendant's conviction, a sentence is imposed. Sentencing seeks to accomplish the goals of rehabilitation, deterrence, punishment, incapacitation, and restitution. *Rehabilitation* assumes that to change the person's conduct the individual's self or identity needs to be changed. Such assumptions lead to programs that attempt to change the individual's flaws. These programs range from remedial education programs to psychiatric therapy. *Deterrence* assumes that criminally inclined individuals are motivated by the perceived benefits of criminal activities and that the fear of imprisonment will prevent such activities. *Punishment* is used to invoke costs for committing criminal actions which outweigh the perceived benefits. *Incapacitation* has the goal of keeping criminals out of the population to control them and stop the criminal activity. *Restitution* makes the assumption that a person committing a crime is obligated to attempt to remedy the wrong done. This socialization process can result in the offender's being reintegrated into the community.

Systems of Sentencing.   States differ in the way they prioritize the various goals of sentencing, and their sentencing systems reflect this ranking. Those states emphasizing retribution, deterrence, and incapacitation are more likely to exhibit a *determinate sentencing system*. The determinate sentencing system provides a fixed sentence for any offense without allowing the judge or a parole board to use discretion. The severity of the punishment is determined, and individuals are aware of the penalty to be imposed if they engage in criminal conduct. The consequence is that the criminal is incapacitated for a known period of time. *Indeterminate sentencing systems* allow for discretion but differ by state as to the amount and form that discretion takes. States can set lower and upper limits on the sentence length and allow judges to set limits within the guidelines, or states can set a lower limit of the sentence with the parole board determining when after that the convicted person is to be let out. This system increases discretion. Criminal justice personnel can consider rehabilitation in determining a person's length of stay and can substitute restitution for incarceration.

Probation.   The severity of punishment usually focuses on the extent to which a person is allowed some degree of freedom. Probation allows a person to remain in the community with few limits on mobility. Incarceration in a maximum security facility imposes the most restriction on a person's mobility. Traditional probation may involve checking in with a probation officer periodically, while intensive probation requires daily surveillance.

States differ in the way they control probation departments. Most probation systems are handled by the judiciary or the executive branches of government. States committed to the coordination of the judiciary with probation place the probation department under the supervision of the judiciary. States that are interested in ensuring that budgeting and policy implementation is comprehensive and manpower is effectively utilized place the probation division in the executive branch of government.[14]

States also differ as to which political unit is to be responsible for probation. Statewide systems like the one found in Georgia emphasize the need for consistency in the allocation of services. Other states, such as New York, utilize county-based systems in the belief that county probation departments are more likely to be aware of local resources and attitudes.

Recently technology has increased punishment options. For example, some jurisdictions have begun placing monitoring devices around the ankle to allow the judicial system to monitor an individual constantly. Such monitoring allows for home confinement. Other devices include computerized monitoring systems that allow probationers to record their activities during all hours, and portable alcohol testing kits that monitor the probationer's abstinence.

Some states have begun to take the property of convicted persons through the use of forfeiture statutes. Forfeiture is the process of allowing a state to seize assets. Civil forfeiture does not require a criminal conviction but only a posted notice for the state to confiscate those possessions which a person has used to commit a crime. Criminal forfeiture allows the taking of a person's property after conviction on a charge of racketeering or some drug offenses. Eleven states have statutes that contain criminal forfeiture provisions.[15] The forfeiture statutes are designed to remove the technology needed to commit crimes, such as drug-processing equipment and transportation vehicles. The forfeiture also reduces the profitability of crime.

Since the use of forfeited cars or money received from the sale of forfeited goods may induce overzealousness on the part of the police, the way in which confiscated materials are used has created some controversy. Some states use profits from forfeiture to supplement education revenues, while other states use the money to reinforce the law enforcement community's resources.

Corrections

The State System

The federal government, which operates the Federal Bureau of Prisons, is responsible for but a small proportion of all prisoners.

Handling corrections is primarily the state's responsibility. In fact, more than half of all state justice expenditures go for corrections. Utilizing a diverse set of programs, bureaucracies, and technologies, the correctional enterprise aims to accomplish the goals of rehabilitation, retribution, incapacitation, and just deserts. These goals are often in conflict, and administrators must select which goal will be accomplished. Some groups are not satisfied with the policy decisions made by correctional administrators. For example, a program designed to provide inmates with vocational training such as computer operation may not only cost citizens a large amount of money but may also be perceived as coddling persons deserving of more severe punishment. Given the lack of political support for the correctional enterprise, money is not as readily available for programs benefiting inmates as it is for programs providing services to the disabled or the poor. Consequently, correctional programs find themselves vying with one another for what money does exist.

Another condition that hampers the correctional system in accomplishing its goals is that other parts of the system—the police, courts, and legislatures—determine the number and type of prisoners it is to handle. As the legislature creates laws that require longer sentences and as the courts are less willing to be lenient in sentencing offenders, the inmates in prisons become more numerous. State budgets can rarely provide the money to construct facilities for the influx of prisoners, and the existing facilities become more crowded. Most state systems are operating at between 107 percent and 127 percent capacity.[16] Because overcrowded conditions create a more violent and more stressful environment, courts have ordered states to rectify the conditions or release prisoners before they have completed their sentences. As a consequence, some prisoners have been released. Some states are developing Intensive Probation Supervision programs and placing persons normally sent to prison on probation. Other states have developed alternative punishments such as "shock incarceration," during which prisoners are subjected to a boot camp-type program and released before their sentences are up. Many states fill local jails with prisoners until state prisons have room to accept them. As crime rates increase and people continue to call for harsher sentences, and as state budgets remain strained, the problems will only become worse. One solution tried by some states has been to use private companies as depositories for prisoners.

Private Corrections

Since the middle of the nineteenth century, private facilities have been used to house juvenile offenders. It has only been during the last two decades, however, that the correctional enterprise has expanded to include private facilities for adults. Private companies have argued that they can provide more space for prisoners at a cheaper cost than can state agencies. The private sector is not bound by union agreements which can increase the cost of health benefits and retirement programs. The political problems involved in decisions such as where to place a facility are not as much of a concern for private companies as they are for state agencies. Private facilities can do a better job of budgeting as they can determine the type and number of prisoners that they can handle. The costs of building a private facility would also be lower than for a similar facility built and operated by a state agency. All these factors make for a more efficient, less costly organization.

Critics of the privatization issue are concerned with protecting the rights of prisoners as well as the rights of the public. These critics believe that private facilities will not be supervised with the same dedication as are public facilities. The goal of profit, for example, may supersede the rights of prisoners. In the past, when public institutions have been found to be engaging in cruel treatment of prisoners, the courts have been used to remedy the problem. This recourse to the courts may be harder to achieve in a private setting. The public's right to security may also be compromised as costs are cut. For example, one way to reduce costs would be to decrease the amount of training required of security personnel. The lack of training may result in a greater risk of escape, which would put the public at risk. To compensate for the need to protect the rights of prisoners as well as the public, the state may have to develop mechanisms to control the quality of care and the amount of security. This process would be costly and could make the use of such alternatives less attractive than traditional types of incarceration.

The use of private facilities continues to be experimented with by some states. The extent to which these correctional corporations can demonstrate a lowering of correctional costs and maintain conditions that are constitutional and secure will determine the role that they play in the future.

Juvenile Defendants

Family or Juvenile Courts

Unfortunately, the criminal justice system must deal with people of all ages. In American society, young people are not considered to have the maturity to be responsible for their acts to the same degree as adults. Cases involving minors go to a criminal justice agency known as the family or juvenile court. This separate court was developed at the beginning of the twentieth century with the progressive goal of helping individual children to overcome their problematic behavior through rehabilitation. Most states set the age of adult jurisdiction as eighteen, but others use sixteen or seventeen, and Wyoming uses nineteen.[17]

Two types of cases are petitioned to family court: cases involving juveniles who have committed offenses that would be considered crimes if the individual were an adult, and those involving juveniles who are not complying with social expectations (for example, by disobeying parents or not attending school). Offenders having the latter status are referred to as Persons in Need of Supervision (PINS) or by a similar designation, depending upon the state. The family court has access to public and private agencies that can provide services and out-of-home care, which includes institutions and group homes in the community. The type of agency selected depends upon the needs of the child and the needs of the society. Since the needs of a child may require an unsecured community setting and this may be at odds with society's need for protection from the potential aggression of a youngster in the community, the family court is under constant appraisal.

Prosecution in Adult Court

While age is the determining factor when deciding whether to refer a person to the adult or the juvenile court, the nature of the offense may prompt prosecutors to indict a young person for prosecution in the adult court. During the mid-1970s, crime rates began to increase, and "get tough" policies were instituted in response. One policy was to allow juveniles who had committed serious felonies to be called juvenile offenders but to be prosecuted at the adult level.

All states have provisions to adjudicate youngsters at the adult level, but states differ as to the type of offenses that are prosecuted and the process that determines whether or not the prosecution will occur at the adult level. For example, in 1978, New York passed the Juvenile Offender Law which mandates that fourteen- and fifteen-year-olds who commit serious felonies (such as kidnapping and rape) and thirteen-year-olds accused of murder be handled in the adult court. The adult system has the discretion of transferring the juvenile back to the family court through the use of a waiver by the district attorney, a grand jury, or a judge. In Florida, the prosecutor has concurrent jurisdiction enabling the prosecutor's office to charge the juvenile at the adult or the juvenile court level when the crimes are serious. Most states allow the juvenile court judge to determine that a case be waived to the adult level.

Factors in Criminal Justice Policy Making

The Role of Ideology

Decisions about how to fight crime are rooted in our society's assumptions about the nature of criminals and the impact justice system strategies have on criminal behavior. Many systems of assertions and assumptions, known as ideologies, influence policy through interest groups and politicians. Two ideological positions that have dominated the criminal justice field recently are the social control position advocated by James Q. Wilson and the social reform position advocated by Elliot Currie.

The Social Control Position

Wilson's perspective focuses on how the tools available to the criminal justice system can make the cost of committing crime greater than the benefit.[18] This approach emphasizes deterrence through the control and punishment of criminals rather than the rehabilitation of communities and/or criminals. Wilson argues that as irresponsible people act destructively in a community, citizens living in the vicinity will take less pride in their residences and urban decay will follow. The area becomes blighted and attracts criminals who prey upon residents. Crime rates increase, and a cycle of deterioration and crime continues.[19] The policy that follows Wilson's logic is to strengthen the criminal justice system and work to rid an area of irresponsible activity.

One example of a policy that reflects this ideological position is the police policy of increasing foot patrols in high crime areas in order to apprehend people engaged in crime, and to help communities organize to fight deteriorating conditions. In this way it is hoped that police will get to know residents personally and gather information about people who may be contributing to the crime problem. A primary goal is to rid a crime-ridden neighborhood of persons who are perceived as a threat. The ''street sweep'' program used in the city of Newark reveals how the policy perspective argued by Wilson can be implemented. The police would use loudspeakers to warn people hanging out on corners to leave the area. After a few minutes, vans of police would descend on the area and arrest those who did not heed the warning.[20] These techniques can be controversial, and the program in Newark may not have been legal as it used a vaguely worded statute restricting congregating.

The Social Reform Position

Currie argues in response to Wilson that the way to deal with crime is to eradicate the conditions that create it.[21] He maintains that economic inequality has been associated with crime and that by creating a healthier economy and making jobs available, the pressure to use crime as a way of getting ahead will be reduced. One example of a program that attempted to provide residents in an area with increased resources was the House of Umoja program in Philadelphia. This program gave gang members a place to stay and required them to follow a rigid discipline. The people who ran the sanctuary provided a home and resources but expected residents to work or attend school in return.[22] Currie emphasizes that such programs cannot succeed without monetary and community support, and their inconsistent success is the result of a lack of community support in the form of resources.

Combined Approaches

The ideological positions of social control and social reform used to set the policy agenda focus on different institutions and criminal justice agencies when developing polices to fight crime. For example, Wilson's control perspective relies on the police and the courts to fight criminals, while the social reform approach advocated by Currie focuses on social support agencies such as social services to fight the conditions that foster crime. People who take a position favoring one ideology are not necessarily opposed to the other. Wilson is not opposed, for example, to reducing inequality, nor is Currie opposed to removing from a community people who are a threat. The policy agenda set in any state or locality will reflect the assumptions making up some ideological position but will not do so to the exclusion of policies that reflect other positions.

The Nature of Crime and Social Policy

How we define crime also determines criminal justice policy. For many years policy makers ignored the impact that white-collar crime has on our society. White-collar crime is as threatening to our way of life as is violent predatory crime. There were 19,000 murders and nonnegligent manslaughter incidents and 723,000 reports of aggravated assault in 1985. In the same year, 13,000 deaths and 2.2 million disabling injuries occurred in the workplace.[23] While all of the work-related injuries and deaths are not the result of corporate criminality, many are the result of illegal corporate acts such as the dumping of hazardous wastes.[24] These crimes are punished, but the criminal justice policies designed to curb this white-collar criminal activity are far less severe than those set up for other crimes that result in less or similar harm to the society and to individuals.

How the Policy-Making Process Operates

While both of the ideologies discussed in the section above influence how criminal justice personnel carry out their goals, most recently Wilson's control orientation has dominated the policy arena. Using several of the key stages in the policy-making process outlined in Chapter 9, we will illustrate how policy orientations such as Wilson's are put into practice in the criminal justice field.

Input of Interest Groups

Interest groups and politicians who cater to interest groups are key actors in problem recognition and throughout the policy-making process. An excellent example of this is the impact of groups wishing to eliminate drunk driving. One such group is Mothers Against Drunk Driving (MADD). In 1985, 28 percent of all arrests were for crimes related to drinking, such as driving while intoxicated.[25] Despite these statistics and the knowledge that alcohol and driving do not mix, the DWI (driving while intoxicated) problem was ignored for many years. The joining together of individuals who had an interest in getting drunk drivers off the road put pressure on state governments to change laws and increase the criminal justice system's activities in this area.

In New York State, interest groups with the help of State Senator William Smith, whose daughter was tragically killed by a drunken driver, began lobbying for the creation of agencies at the county level to fund special efforts to increase enforcement of DWI laws. The result was a unique set of agencies known as Stop DWI, which were established at the county level. These agencies distribute money to support special programs such as special DWI patrols, DWI prosecuting attorneys, and educational programs. The agencies receive the fines that are imposed on people convicted of alcohol-related driving infractions. In 1990, the agencies received $22 million to spend on their special programs. Presently, MADD is lobbying states to set the blood alcohol level at which a person can be convicted of DWI at .08 percent. In New York the standard is currently .10 percent.

Implementation

Putting policy into practice is often difficult. Bureaucracies that have emerged to carry out policy are often not committed to changing their priorities (or behavior). For example, a policy known as juvenile decarceration became popular during the early seventies. The intent of the policy was to limit the extent that juveniles were placed in secure facilities. Institutions housing juveniles were criticized for poor living conditions, and new policies had been devised to remove children from these traditional forms of care—which would mean reduction of the bureaucracies that had run traditional programs.

The state of Massachusetts was committed to the policy of juvenile decarceration and maneuvered to remove juveniles from secure facilities (out-of-the-way institutions with barred windows and locked doors) and into less secure community-oriented programs. Massachusetts hired a reform-minded expert, Jerome Miller, to head its juvenile corrections system. Although Miller's reform proposals were supported by many politicians, the people who staffed the institutions were opposed to the suggested changes, and as constituents influenced a number of politicians to remain committed to the traditional system. Any attempt to decrease institutional populations was met with widespread and hostile resistance by staff and their supporters in the legislature. After an alternative system of community-oriented programs was established, Miller used his authority to close the traditional institutions when the legislature was not in session. Inmates in the programs were housed in available institutions such as college dormitories until community placement could be arranged. The bureaucratic resistance had been overcome, but only after a radical move by a committed reformer. Massachusetts developed a continuum of programs that work as well as the former institutions in meeting their criminal justice goals but allow many juvenile delinquents to remain in the community environment.[26]

Evaluation

Most policies are implemented with some controversy and considerable cost. As a result, agencies attempt to assess the impact of the policies they implement. Getting accurate assessment of programs is, however, very problematic. The federal government gathers data on crime and disseminates it to the states. Many programs implemented at the state level receive federal funds with the mandate of a self-evaluation, which requires data beyond that provided by the government. While it is easy to be critical of the data used, these data are all that are available to determine the adequacy of the programs.

The federal government collects criminal justice data in two ways, by the Uniform Crime Reports and the National Crime Survey.

The Uniform Crime Reports

The Uniform Crime Reports (UCR) consist of data furnished by local and state police departments to the FBI. The types of crimes are currently divided into type I and type II offenses. This system is being changed to allow for a more detailed analysis of the crimes described. A serious problem with the data is that many crimes are not reported. It is known, for example, that only about one-third of all crimes are reported to the police and that the type of crime influences whether or not it is reported. For example, only about 55 percent of all completed rapes are reported to the police, but almost 90 percent of motor vehicle thefts involving over $250 are reported. Another statistic is that 47 percent of all violent crimes committed by strangers are reported, but 53 percent of violent crimes committed by relatives are reported. And another: the higher one's income the higher the likelihood that household crime is reported to the police.[27]

The National Crime Survey

A careful reading of the last paragraph will prompt the reader to ask how it can be determined what proportion of crime is reported to the police. The answer: another source of criminal justice data called the National Crime Survey (NCS), gathered by the United States Justice Department's Bureau of Justice Statistics. The bureau collects data for the NCS through sophisticated sampling processes designed to determine the amount of victimization that has occurred throughout the United States. A national sample of 60,000 households and 15,000 businesses as well as a special sample taken in twenty-six cities results in detailed information on the characteristics of victims and the crimes perpetrated against them.[28] The NCS provides invaluable information about criminal conduct: for example, in 1985 about 25 percent of all households were touched by crime, down from 32 percent in 1975.[29]

Other Data

Other data are collected using specially funded surveys—for example, surveys of jail populations and prison populations and studies of police employment. Some studies look for trends and also determine if there are causal relationships between crime and programs implemented to influence crime. These studies are funded by many different agencies at the federal, state, and local levels.

Policy Implementation: A Case Analysis

Changing the criminal justice system to meet the needs of the communities that are experiencing high rates of crime is an arduous task. There is no panacea, and implementation of policy can be discouraging. Many policy makers share the view of Wesley Skogan, who has said: "There are no 'silver bullets' in social policy because . . . the political system deflects them, the social system rejects them, and the legal system protects us against them."[30] What follows is a description of a well-known attempt by the Houston police department to implement a new policy in the department. The policing strategy that the city wanted to put into effect reflected Wilson's position on community policing discussed earlier in the chapter. We will follow Houston's policy implementation strategy using the process outline in Chapter 9: problem recognition, agenda setting, decision making (or policy making), implementation, service delivery, evaluation, and feedback.

James Q. Wilson and George Kelling wrote an article in 1982 that called for the implementation of policies by the police to clean up neighborhoods before attempting to deal with crime.[31] Wilson and Kelling argued that since neighborhood disorder creates fear and attracts criminal elements, the police need to become more involved with community life and to develop programs that meet needs as they are defined by community members. This position was a radical departure from the trend that policing had taken in the early part of the twentieth century. For most of the century the police had increased bureaucratization, formalized relationships with communities, and maintained a distance from citizen encounters.

In Houston, the Wilson and Kelling crime control position was greeted with enthusiasm by many people who influenced the policy-setting agenda. The Police Foundation began funding projects that tested programs such as foot patrol that were developed from the community policing model. Educational institutions began teaching courses and holding seminars that promoted the approach. Local police officials became increasingly aware of the importance of implementing polices that reflected this ideology.

At the same time that the community policing concept was becoming popular, the city of Houston was undergoing changes that resulted in increased activism on the part of citizens and politicians. Citizens were becoming more fearful of crime and also more fearful of the Houston police department.[32] Thirteen people had been killed by the police in a one-month period, and, in a sensational case, a minority suspect was found bound and drowned in a local river. The outrage of minority groups toward the violence that seemed to be directed at them was exacerbated by the outward display of prejudice by police leaders. A coalition of white professionals and leaders from minority communities supported a successful campaign to elect a reform-oriented mayoral candidate. The new mayor, Kathy Whitmire, quickly hired a new police chief who was not identified with the department. This process of selecting an outsider was not accepted by police personnel but gave critics of the police confidence in the new chief as a truly reform-minded leader. Because of earlier police abuses, the community and the politicians were prepared to back the new chief in implementing policies that would reform the police department.

While public support and political backing are important ingredients in the policy-making process, the bureaucrats implementing the programs must also be supportive. As was apparent in the case of deinstitutionalization in Massachusetts discussed in the previous section, strong leaders are essential in a bureaucracy undergoing change. The new leader of the police bureaucracy was Lee Brown. Chief Brown had started his career as a patrolman in San Jose and moved up the ranks to assistant chief when he left to take a county sheriff position in Oregon. He then moved to Atlanta, where as the Atlanta Director of Public Safety he led the investigation of a case of serial murders of children. While gaining experience in these administrative roles he received a Ph.D. in criminal justice and worked as a professor at Portland State and Howard Universities.[33] With the Houston position he became the first black police chief appointed by a white mayor in the United States.[34] He was knowledgeable about the community policing concept and thus was eager to implement policies reflecting this approach.

Lee Brown proceeded to institute a number of reform policies that were widely supported by local elites and the federal government. Four principles that are basic to the community policing concept, as outlined below, guided the reforms.

1. Policing is broadly focused and problem-oriented. This approach avoids the development of policies that may be the concern of politicians or police administrators but not of local communities.

2. Police departments are decentralized, and communication with the public is a reform priority.

3. Police respond to the demands of the public.

4. Police should be a proactive force in the development of community organization and education programs.[35]

The goal of the reforms was to work with communities to solve problems and to develop strong ties between the community and the police, rather than react to crime after it occurred.

Could such policies be implemented? Successful implementation required that police organization, tactics, and subcultural orientation had to be modified. Chief Brown and the Police Foundation selected sites throughout the city of Houston that included a mix of ethnic and racial groups, demonstrating that the program was designed to serve the constituents of all community groups. The districts were surveyed before the programs started in order to collect baseline information from which to compare the changes that were to take place. These target changes included decreases in physical disorder, social disorder, and fear of crime, an increase in area satisfaction, and improved police performance.

Three programs were instituted. The first was the development of storefronts staffed by police officers. It was hoped that community members would frequent these centers. To encourage the public to use them, visitors were welcomed, guest speakers (including a judge and politicians) gave presentations, and responses were made to local complaints.

Community organizing teams (CORTs) were established as a second strategy. These teams met with residents to create organizations that would set goals and solve problems defined by the residents.

The creation of citizen contact patrols (CCPs) was the final program. These patrols were to ignore normal police duties and instead were to concentrate on patrolling particular areas with the intent of meeting residents and talking with them much as did the beat officer of the late nineteenth century. The officers asked questions, gathered information, and gained the trust of informants.

The programs were successfully implemented. This was the result of a number of factors. Interest groups and politicians were supportive. The director of the bureaucracy implementing the policies (Chief Brown) was enthusiastic. The personnel were also supportive as Brown had selected officers from the ranks to help organize and develop the strategies to be used in the program. But, did the programs work?

The assessment and revision stage in policy implementation is just as important as any other stage. The goal of changing departmental procedures through decentralization and the development of community policing strategies had certainly occurred. To determine if there was a reduction in the fear of crime, a decrease in the widespread perception of social and physical disorder, an increase in area satisfaction, and a sense of improved police performance, the selected areas were surveyed before the intervention and again ten or eleven months after the intervention. Each of the programs was found to have been successful in achieving at least two of the five goals.[36]

The assessment, however, also found that all residents were not assisted. Some groups in the communities were not made aware of the programs and were not served by the police.[37] The less fortunate, including minority and lower income groups, were less likely to have been part of the program. What makes this problem more significant is that the goal of the policy change was to increase the police involvement with such excluded groups. The strategy seems to have increased the gap in police involvement with minority groups rather than having reduced it.[38] One goal when revising the programs was to overcome this problem.

We have found that the justice system in the United States operates mostly at the state and local level. Ideologies that are pervasive in state executive, legislative, and judicial systems dictate the programs that make up the criminal justice system. States differ in the way that crimes are defined, crimes are reacted to, lawyers are provided, adjudication proceeds, and criminals are controlled. When policies are created and developed, their implementation becomes a complex political procedure. Although the changes that occur are incremental, the justice system continues to evolve. How it evolves will depend upon the prevailing ideology and the ability of local governments to acquire the necessary resources to make the changes that are perceived as necessary. Support from interest groups, politicians, managers, and the personnel that carry out criminal justice policy must be mobilized toward this end.

Recommended Reading

E. Currie: *Confronting Crime*, Pantheon, New York, 1985.

E. F. McGarrell: *Juvenile Correctional Reform*, State University of New York Press, Albany, N.Y., 1988.

N. Morris and M. Tonry: *Between Prison and Probation*, Oxford University Press, New York, 1990.

W. G. Skogan: *Disorder and Decline*, The Free Press, New York, 1990.

J. H. Skolnick and D. H. Bayley: *The New Blue Line*, The Free Press, New York, 1986.

J. Q. Wilson: *Varieties of Police Behavior: The Management of Law and Order in Eight Communities*, Atheneum, New York, 1973.

J. Q. Wilson: *Thinking About Crime*, Vintage, New York, 1975.

CHAPTER 14

Education

Primary and secondary schools transmit social values and culture. They also teach young people the skills they need to be productive workers. These educational goals endure; whether education is provided in a one-room schoolhouse in an Indiana farming community in 1870, in a three-story brick building in a Chicago neighborhood in 1920 serving children of immigrant parents, or in a sprawling suburban school in 1990.

After an overview of school enrollment and school finances, the chapter looks at the role schools play in transmitting social values and culture and in training a work force. Do the schools serve as an extension of the family, reinforcing family values? Or do schools seek to overcome parochial family values and teach the values of the dominant culture? Are schools molding competent citizens and improving the employability and the productivity of the labor force?

Next we direct our attention to school system politics. Who makes education policy and who allocates education dollars? School systems consist of networks of political actors, which include pupils, parents, taxpayers, local school boards, teachers, and school administrators. These actors struggle to set priorities and distribute resources in light of their own interests and concerns. Parents want services that meet the special interest and needs of their children.

Taxpayers seek to keep the lid on their property tax bills. Teachers prefer larger budgets for instructional materials and, especially, for salaries. School administrators seek the good opinion of their professional colleagues.

The chapter then examines to what extent the educational system is providing adequate schooling. Contemporary schools are challenged to provide equal educational opportunity for all, better math and science training, and a high standard of educational achievement. Yet during recent years, student achievement test scores have declined steadily, and efforts to promote equal opportunity for minorities have aroused controversy.

Finally, we examine two contemporary views of how to reform education. One group of reformers advocates identifying effective schools, analyzing why they are effective, and persuading other schools to follow their examples. A second approach seeks to create competition among schools, rewarding schools that are responsive to the educational demands of parents and students and punishing those that are not responsive.

School Enrollment

Education is a giant industry. In 1990, over 50 million students, about 20 percent of the population, were enrolled in the public schools. The school-age population has remained in the 40 million range since the late 1960s, when the baby boom generation filled the schools.[1] In 1987, about 86 percent of young adults (ages twenty-five to twenty-nine) had completed high school.

Trends in school enrollment among the states reflect larger population movements. In Massachusetts, Michigan, and West Virginia, school systems lost about 17 percent of their student enrollment during the 1980s. During the same period, the student populations in Arizona, Florida, and Nevada increased about 20 percent.[2]

School Finances

Society spends about 7 percent of its annual gross national product (the total value of goods and services produced) on elementary and secondary education. State governments and local school districts provide most of the funds that support elementary and secondary education. But Table 14.1 shows some significant variations in school funding during an eighteen-year period.

**Table 14.1   Elementary and Secondary School Funding
(constant 1988 billion $)**

Source	Year					
	1970		1980		1985	
	$	%	$	%	$	%
Federal	11.4	7.4	15.4	9.1	11.9	5.8
State	53.1	34.6	73.1	43.3	93.3	45.4
Local	72.9	47.5	68.0	40.3	83.2	40.4
Other	16.1	10.5	12.2	7.3	17.3	8.4
Total	153.5	100.0	168.7	100.0	205.7	100.0

Source: Adapted from *Statistical Abstract of the United States 1992*, p. 141.

Notice that federal funding rose sharply in the 1970s, when federal agencies aggressively promoted racial desegregation and mandated more centralized state control of local school districts. But by 1985, the Reagan administration was committed to returning responsibility for education to the states. The Bush administration supported the idea of improving the quality of public schools but did not increase the flow of federal dollars.

The average American school spent about $4,500 per pupil in 1989, but this average masks considerable variation in spending among the states. Connecticut, New Jersey, and New York spent about $7,300 per pupil; Alabama, Arkansas, and Mississippi spent about $2,700 per pupil. These spending differences primarily reflect differences in per capita income and tax base. They cannot be accounted for by differences in cultural attitudes toward education between the northeast and the south. Nor do more competitive political systems within a state generate greater spending on education.[3]

States are currently increasing their support to schools, in part to narrow the gap in per-pupil expenditures between wealthy suburban school districts and inner city and rural school districts that have smaller tax bases. The average state pays 40 percent of education costs, and allocation formulas tend to favor the poorer districts. A number of state courts have decided that highly unequal spending among schools denies children the equal protection of the laws.

Yet complete parity in per-pupil spending is not achievable so long as extreme differences in income are characteristic of American society. Politically, suburban taxpayers insist that their tax dollars support their own schools. And complete parity would reduce local incentives to levy taxes for the support of local schools. Therefore, state policy generally seeks to narrow but not eliminate the gap between the richest and poorest school districts.

As local school districts now rely more heavily upon the states for their education dollars, they are required to follow state mandates that accompany those funds. States impose detailed rules and regulations about curriculum content, teacher certification, and school services. Local school districts become less autonomous and less able to tailor their educational programs to fit local preferences.

The Role of Schools—A Historical Perspective

In colonial times, education had been reserved for the privileged elite. The first public schools were established in New England in the early nineteenth century; these new "common schools" made basic education widely available. By 1820, thirteen of the twenty-three states were providing primary education. During the Jacksonian period, many Americans moved westward to carve farms out of the forests, and individuals were roughly equal in both opportunity and in social and economic circumstance. After the Civil War, schools became a central institution in every community, and by 1900 the public high school was the pinnacle of the education system. In 1910, school attendance rates for six- to fourteen-year-olds were 90 percent in the east and midwest regions and 70 percent in the south. Literacy rates for this age group exceeded 90 percent.[4]

Secular Instruction

Many early American colonists had fled Europe in search of religious freedom. They insisted that individuals should be allowed to worship according to their personal conscience, free of state coercion. Although most schools in colonial America had been sponsored by religious groups, the First Amendment to the Constitution provided for the separation of church and state; thus, the public schools were fundamentally nonsectarian institutions. However, until after World War II, the extent of prayer and other forms of religious observance in the schools was largely a matter of local custom.

Beginning in the 1840s, new waves of European immigrants came to America's shores in search of economic opportunity and religious and political freedom. Early immigrants came from Ireland and Germany, and by the turn of the century floods of Italian, Russian,

Slavic, and Scandinavian peasants had joined the flow. Most of these newcomers did not speak English and had no experience of the principles of political freedom, democratic participation, and individual equality. Schools introduced American values and customs to the children of these immigrant families. The schools were society's instrument for transcending parochial family backgrounds and molding children of diverse backgrounds into Americans with shared values and cultural orientations.[5]

Many American elementary school students learned from William McGuffey's readers, first published in 1836, which taught the values of individualism, thrift, hard work, punctuality, and other moral virtues. By 1920, McGuffey's readers had sold 120 million copies.[6]

In recent decades, the residential neighborhoods, which have historically determined what school a child attends, have become more economically and socially homogeneous. Therefore, a local elementary or secondary school is likely to serve primarily one ethnic or racial group. More students attend segregated schools today than did forty years ago, when school segregation was mandated by law in the southern states. To integrate school populations requires that some students be bused to distant schools, which may improve the quality of a child's education but at the cost of being away from home and neighborhood.

It is estimated that in 1995, about 34 percent of American public high school students will consist of black, Hispanic, Asian, and Native American minorities, up from 29 percent in 1986.[7] Will the schools continue to serve as a melting pot, integrating ethnic minorities into a common white middle-class culture? Or will schools adopt a multicultural curriculum incorporating instruction in the historical traditions and cultural values of minority peoples?

Training a Labor Force

The nation's first public schools were established in the growing factory towns of New England in the early nineteenth century.[8] As workers moved from the farms to the towns, schools were set up to teach the values of punctuality and respect for authority and to prepare children for a life of factory work. After the Civil War, schools taught the same lessons to the children of immigrants in New York, Cleveland, Chicago, and other major industrial cities.

As industrialization expanded, an ever-increasing percentage of jobs required reading and writing skills and problem-solving abilities. In the 1990s, the percentage of jobs in the high-technology sector of the economy is increasing at the expense of traditional manufacturing jobs. The schools will be expected to provide tomorrow's labor force with greater computational and communication skills.

Today, many potential workers do not have the skills to work effectively at available jobs. About 11 percent of high-school-age young people drop out of school before graduation. Also, some graduate from high school without being able to read or write at an eighth-grade level.

School System Politics

School systems are hotbeds of political activity. Parents and taxpayers, school principals and locally elected school boards, teachers and state education officials have different perspectives on how much money should be allocated to the schools and how that money should be spent. Should the school year be lengthened? Should more math and science courses be offered at the expense of courses on sex education, personal ethics, and black history? Should teacher certification requirements be strengthened and teachers' salaries raised? Should special programs for gifted and handicapped children be enhanced or the music and drama offerings strengthened?

In this section, we will examine the influence of various school system participants over how many dollars are raised and how those dollars are spent.

School System Organization

The centerpiece of the school system consists of the 15,000 independent school districts that operate public elementary and secondary schools, each district operating within a locality. A small rural school district may educate 600 students in grades K–12 within one building. A large city school district will operate hundreds of schools and serve several hundred thousand students.

A locally elected school board governs the local school system. The school board is empowered to make policy and to hire and fire the school superintendent, a professional educator who oversees the day-to-day operation of the school system. The local school board sees that the school is responding to local needs and pressures.

The relationship between superintendent and school board is similar to the relationship between a city manager and the elected city council, as described in Chapter 6. The superintendent frames policy discussions, drafts the budget, and supervises the principals of schools within the school district. The superintendent also communicates with the chief state school official (CSSO), whose office distributes funds to the school districts, establishes teacher certification requirements, and mandates curriculum content. The CSSO also defines length of school day, nutritional content of cafeteria meals, and availability of specially trained counselors and health personnel. The CSSO is elected or appointed by the governor of the state.

Power in the Schools

There are two basic models of power in the schools: the democratic model, in which power flows from the bottom up, and the hierarchical model, in which power flows from the top down. The latter is dominant in today's schools.

The Democratic Model

The traditional democratic model of power emphasized local control of the 15,000 independent school districts. Local voters elected school boards, which supervised school officials, framed the budget, and established school policy. In this model, since power theoretically flows from the bottom up, schoolteachers and administrators respond closely to the wishes of local citizens whose children attend the school and whose tax dollars pay for it.

The Dominance of Professional Educators

The democratic model, however, does not accurately describe the realities of power in today's schools. In general, school politics tends to be organized hierarchically, with power flowing from the top down. For several reasons, outlined below, professional educators have a rather free hand to run the schools as they see fit.

Lack of Voter Interest.   One reason for the dominance of professional educators is that only 15 to 30 percent of the eligible electorate bother to vote in a typical local school board election. Attendance is low at school board meetings, and most of those who do attend tend to support school policies and decisions.[9] The electorate are simply not aggressive participants in school politics.

Also, school board members tend to have more education and higher occupational status than does the average member of the community. A school board often pursues its own agenda—whether it be efficient use of tax dollars, building a gymnasium, or stressing basic reading, writing, and arithmetic—rather than being responsive to the voters who elected it. School boards tend to make their own judgments rather than to mirror public opinion, and they much prefer an inactive citizenry, since financial crises, teacher misbehavior, and similar disasters arouse unwanted interest.

Deference to Professional Educators.   Parents and school board members tend to defer to the professional educators. School administrators are the experts, and they control information and set the agenda for school board meetings. Local school boards have a legitimizing role, placing their stamps of approval on policies and decisions made by superintendents or principals. School boards tend to define their role as selling the school program to the community, not channeling popular views to school administrators. The spirit of "leave it to the professionals" dates back to the Progressive era (1890–1920), when reformers sought to empower technically trained experts, to separate policy making from administration, and to weaken urban political machines that used the school district as a source of patronage jobs.[10]

Centralization and Complexity.   Larger school size, greater complexity, and closer state supervision make it more difficult for voters and school board members to control professional educators. The trend has been to consolidate small school districts into larger ones. Children no longer walk to one-room schoolhouses but instead ride buses to large central schools that provide swimming pools, music programs, trained counselors, and other specialized services. Involvement of state governments in education has also increased dramatically. In the 1960s, the federal government mandated that the states enforce civil rights policies and administer various federal programs funded by federal dollars. In the 1970s, court decisions required more equitable financing of schools, and states took greater responsibility for financing education.[11] When the state relieved local taxpayers of 50 percent of their tax burden, the state also assumed substantial control over curriculum content, school calendar, and teacher certification.[12]

Many state governors make education a central focus of their campaigns. Expressing concern about the quality of the schools appeals to parents who are worried about their children's future; to members of the business community, who realize that an educated work force is a key to economic growth; and to teachers, who are numerous and are intensely interested in maintaining high levels of spending on education.[13] Increasingly, important educational decisions are made in the state capital, not at the local school board meeting.

Attempts at Community Control

However, local school boards sometimes do have an impact on the decisions of professional school administrators. Crises may stimulate unusually high levels of community parental and voter participation. In the late 1960s, parents and community activists made a strong effort to gain control of inner city schools in several cities. This effort was largely unsuccessful as teacher unions, school administrators, and central school boards united to resist democratic control of local schools.[14] In some communities, power is divided as school board factions represent different community interests and priorities.[15]

Several studies indicate that minority membership on the school board has a small but measurable effect on improving outcomes for minority students: dropout rates and suspension rates for minorities are reduced, and minority access to gifted and talented programs is improved.[16] But the effects are small for the various reasons mentioned previously. Professional educators have the resources to dominate in the game of school politics.

Assessing School Performance

Over the last three decades, critics have asked whether or not our educational system is providing adequate schooling. Are minority students receiving equal educational opportunities? Are the schools teaching students adequate reading, writing, and computational skills? Does the curriculum teach students what they need to know?

Promoting Equality of Opportunity

During the 1960s and 1970s, school policy was oriented to improving equality of opportunity in education for handicapped, female, and minority students. One major objective was to end racial discrimination in public schools. School busing to promote integration was instituted, and magnet schools with specialized academic programs were established to attract students from many neighborhoods. Other significant initiatives to improve the life chances of the disadvantaged were preschool programs for three- to four-year-olds, mainstreaming of handicapped students, school lunch programs, and bilingual education (primarily for Hispanic students). Federal money for education was concentrated on these projects, which affected virtually all school districts.[17]

Desegregating Schools

Historically, most white and black children attended different schools. In the post-Civil War south, state laws required racial segregation. In the north, schools served local populations, and to the extent that residential neighborhoods were segregated, so too were the schools.

A particularly important issue in education is the effect of racial segregation on the quality of education available to African Americans. Are the schools available to black children inferior to the schools provided for white children? If black and white children attend the same schools, are the educational outcomes (in terms of measurable achievement and less measurable interracial understanding) improved? When segregated neighborhoods create segregated schools, should students be bused within large citywide school districts to create racially balanced schools?

Brown v. Topeka Board of Education.   These highly charged political issues have dominated educational policy discussions in communities throughout the nation since 1954, when the Supreme Court declared in *Brown v. Topeka Board of Education* that segregated schools deprived black children of the equal protection of the laws. This landmark case explicitly overruled *Plessy v. Ferguson*, an 1896 case which held that states could establish by law separate facilities for blacks and whites so long as they provided facilities of equal quality. But per-pupil school expenditures in the south were typically three times larger for white children than for black children. In some cases, the white school was closer to the black student's home than the black school to which he or she was bused. In its 1954 decision, the court ruled that separate facilities were inherently unequal and must be ended with all deliberate speed.

However, white southerners were not inclined to dismantle their segregated school systems at the behest of the Supreme Court, and the ruling met with massive resistance. By 1964, ten years after Brown, 99 percent of black children in the south still attended segregated schools.

The Civil Rights Act of 1964.   After 1964, resistance in the southern states rapidly collapsed. The 1964 Civil Rights Act required federal agencies to cut off federal funds to noncomplying school districts and authorized the U.S. Attorney General to bring suits to force compliance. The black civil rights movement effectively pressed its demand for racial justice in the south, supported actively by liberal business interests.[18] By 1972, 44 percent of black children in the south attended a predominantly white school.

Racial Segregation in the North.   In the last two decades, controversy over racial segregation in the schools has shifted to the cities of the north. In 1970, only 29 percent of black children in northeast and midwest cities attended a predominantly white school,[19] because the majority of blacks live in segregated inner city neighborhoods. The specific legal issue when segregation is the product of neighborhood patterns is whether the equal protection of the laws requires the state to take active measures, such as busing, to create racially integrated schools.

Swann v. Charlotte-Mecklenberg.   In *Swann v. Charlotte-Mecklenberg* (1971), the Supreme Court decided that busing is a legitimate tool to promote school integration. A countywide school district in North Carolina operated 107 schools in a 550-square-mile area. The school system was 71 percent white, and the court ordered that students be distributed within the system so that every school was about 71 percent white. The court thus required the school system to sacrifice the neighborhood school principle to promote integration.

Milliken v. Bradley.   The case of *Milliken v. Bradley* (1974) marked a change in legal direction. The question addressed by the case was this: In order to promote racially balanced schools, could a large metropolitan area, consisting of a heavily black inner city surrounded by a ring of predominantly white suburbs, be treated as a single school district? The Detroit school system was 64 percent black, while the surrounding suburbs, which operated their own school systems, were mostly white. The court decided that the existence of segregated schools owing to residential patterns does not deny the equal protection of the laws. Since the Detroit suburban school districts did not specifically create segregated school systems (as had the earlier southern school districts), they could not be coerced into joining with Detroit in order to achieve racially balanced schools.

Freeman v. Pitts.   The courts continue to debate whether the Constitution simply prohibits school districts from mandating segregation or requires them to promote racial integration. Recently, the Court has indicated its reluctance to require local school boards to promote racial integration. In a 1992 decision, *Freeman v. Pitts*, the Supreme Court ruled that formerly segregated school districts could be returned to local control once they were desegregated. If a school system subsequently became resegregated as a result of demographic shifts, the school system would have no constitutional obligation to remedy the resegregation.

White Flight

In the 1970s and 1980s, white families tended to move from the inner cities to the suburbs. In the nation's 15,000 school districts, minority school enrollment has increased from 21 percent in 1970 to 27 percent in 1982. About half of all black students are concentrated in fewer than 100 districts. School segregation increases as white families move from school districts with a large proportion of blacks to suburban districts having fewer blacks.[20]

It is unlikely that school busing to promote integration in the schools has contributed substantially to white flight. First, most school desegregation was completed by 1972. President Nixon reduced federal pressure on school districts to promote integration, and as a result of conservative appointments the Supreme Court limited busing, affirmed school district autonomy, and allowed segregation if it resulted from segregated neighborhoods.

Second, when whites complain about busing, they often are expressing concerns about broader patterns of black-white relations in society. The controversy over racial desegregation is rooted in the deep-seated racial fears of some whites, who believe that blacks threaten their economic security, their physical safety, and their social status. Opposition to busing often reflects racial attitudes formed early in life.[21]

Third, there appears to be little relationship between the white flight rates of large urban school districts that do desegregate their schools and those that do not, suggesting that other factors, such as street crime, increasing taxes, deteriorating public services, and loss of job opportunities, explain why white families leave the inner cities for the suburbs.[22]

Upgrading Educational Quality

In the 1980s, global economic competition, restructuring of industry, and the Reagan administration's commitment to reducing the presence of the federal government contributed to a shift from promoting equality in education to improving quality. In 1983, *A Nation at Risk*, a report by the National Commission on Excellence in Education, painted a gloomy picture of the quality of education in America. The report expressed the following concerns about the status of education in America:

1. Students in most other leading industrial nations scored better than American students on a variety of standardized tests.

2. American students attend school about 180 days per year, compared to 240 days for German and Japanese students.

3. About 13 percent of the nation's seventeen-year-olds were functionally illiterate.

4. Students spent about four hours per week on homework; they watched television about twenty-four hours per week.

5. SAT scores for high school seniors declined steadily and significantly from 1963 to 1980.

6. Average starting salaries of public schoolteachers in 1988 were $19,400, compared to $23,500 for an average liberal arts graduate.

A 1991 report issued by President George Bush and the fifty state governors concluded that school performance still left much to be desired. The report found that only 13 percent of Americans could summarize the main argument of a long newspaper article and 14 percent could figure out a correct percentage restaurant tip. Quality of learning per se is not the only problem in the schools: 13 percent of high school students reported being threatened by weapons in school during the previous year.[23]

Prospects for Reform

Overhauling a well-established educational system is a daunting task. One problem is lack of money. *A Nation at Risk* estimated that the schools must spend $24 billion per year to make minimally necessary improvements in education. Yet federal funds to state and local governments were reduced in the 1980s (see Table 14.1). And states and cities with the greatest need to improve their schools also have the greatest fiscal woes, as described in Chapter 10.

Another problem is that professional educators are often reluctant to sponsor bold reform. Generally, reforms are modest, reinforcing the educational status quo at higher levels of spending. For example, students need greater scientific and economic knowledge and computer literacy to prepare tomorrow's work force for a technically complex economy. Schools respond by introducing computers into the classrooms rapidly, as Table 14.2 shows. Whether the computers are used to apply knowledge flexibly and to solve problems creatively or to follow mechanical rules mindlessly is difficult to determine.[24]

School Performance and Economic Success

Even if educational reform were easy to accomplish, it is not clear how much of a difference reform would make. The connection between school performance and economic success, on either a national or an individual scale, is not particularly well-established. Society improves the quality of its schools to avoid falling behind in global economic competition. But other factors contribute more directly to competitive weakness. The fact that the national savings rate is much lower for the United States than for its competitors slows development of technology and introduction of consumer products. At the same time, higher U.S. standards of workplace safety and environmental care raise the cost of production.

Equalizing educational opportunities would probably do little to make adult incomes more equal. As was made clear in Chapter 10, Americans live in a society with a highly unequal distribution of income. Some income inequality is needed to encourage individuals to go to school longer and to accept challenging work. But the present disparity in income between the richest 20 percent of the population and the poorest 20 percent is far larger than the need for incentives and differences in ability can justify. Most Americans look to their education system to provide individuals with equal opportunity to climb to the top of the economic ladder, not to shorten the distance between top and bottom rungs of the ladder. Schools reproduce the underlying society more than they redeem the disadvantages of the poor.[25]

Table 14.2   Microcomputers for Student Instruction

Year	% of Public Schools with Microcomputers	Students per Microcomputer
1981	18%	NA
1984	85%	63.5
1988	97%	26.9

Source: *Statistical Abstract of the United States 1990*, p. 145.

Are Integrated Schools Better Schools?

In 1954, Chief Justice Earl Warren asserted that separate but equal facilities were inherently unequal. However, some research indicates that students learn equally well in either segregated or integrated classrooms.[26] When aptitude and family background are held constant, a school's racial composition has no effect upon student aspiration, test scores, or years of school completed.

Some school districts are rethinking the wisdom of mandatory busing programs as a strategy for improving education. Louisville, Kentucky, which has achieved one of the most successful examples of school desegregation, is debating whether to make busing for elementary school children optional. Black parents would decide for themselves whether to send their children to a convenient neighborhood school or have them bused to an integrated school several miles away.[27]

Besides liking the convenience of a neighborhood school, black parents might prefer a black school because it could focus more lessons on black history, address issues of being black in a white-dominated society, and engender a sense of pride in being black. Spanish-speaking parents may prefer to have their children attend a bilingual school where Latino culture is respected and taught.

Per-Pupil Spending and Educational Quality

Money alone does not guarantee strong educational performance. The major empirical research studies find a weak relationship between performance on standardized tests and such factors as per-pupil expenditures, teacher salaries, classroom size, and cost of educational materials. For example, students from similar family backgrounds perform better in Catholic schools, which spend less money than do more affluent public schools.[28] Many expenditures on such amenities as gymnasiums and library books enhance the quality of life in school but have little impact on test scores. Higher teacher salaries are primarily a response to pressures from teachers. Smaller classes are appreciated not because learning outcomes are demonstrably better but because teachers can maintain order more easily.

Of course, this argument does not justify unequal school spending. School resources should be distributed equally, just as are public parks, trash collection, and other valuable government services. Good schools are an end in themselves, like any public service that improves the quality of life. Americans do spend the better part of thirteen years or more in school, and the experience may as well be a positive one.

The learning environment in overcrowded inner city classrooms with broken windows and a shortage of teachers contrasts sharply with conditions in wealthy suburban school districts.[29]

High per-pupil expenditures indicate that middle-class people value school spending and can afford to pay more. To illustrate, about 75 percent of three- to four-year-olds from families with incomes over $75,000 are enrolled in preschool programs. Only 40 percent of families with incomes below $30,000, send their kids to preschool programs. Most of the difference is because wealthier families can afford to provide additional schooling.

Reforming Education

Reformers suggest two ways to improve the performance of our schools: identifying the characteristics of effective schools and create competition among schools.

Identifying the Characteristics of Effective Schools

Some reformers start from the premise that some schools are more effective than others. If educators and reformers can identify what makes the best schools so good, then they can attempt to create the same conditions in other schools. Among the characteristics of effective schools are well-qualified teachers with considerable classroom autonomy; flexible patterns of instruction with regular graded homework on which students can succeed; a strong school administration that supports teachers and monitors teacher performance; and a high percentage of the school day spent on teaching and learning tasks.[30]

Several critics conclude that the most important characteristic of effective schools is that they are free of external bureaucratic influence. Most public schools are managed by large, popularly elected school boards that impose detailed operating guidelines and undermine school autonomy. Dull conformity prevails, teachers are demoralized, and educational performance plummets. If teachers and professional school administrators had more freedom to tailor their educational programs to their unique interests and talents, teachers would be more enthusiastic and schools more diverse as the stultifying conformity imposed by central school bureaucracies was removed.[31]

Creating Competition Among Schools

Traditionally, students attend the school in their residential neighborhood, unless the school district assigns the student to another school. The school system is a monopoly, and monopolies have no incentive to produce services which appeal to the tastes of their customers. If schools were forced to compete for students, they would be more attentive to the needs of their clientele. Their budgets and indeed their very existence would depend upon their providing an attractive education. The educational product would be of higher quality and more varied. Some schools would develop academic specialties, or provide education rooted in religious principles, or celebrate the cultural heritage of minority groups.

Of course, some schools might fail to provide adequate educational services in the absence of formal rules governing curriculum, teacher training, and student achievement. But even now, despite regulation, some of the public schools fail to maintain minimum standards.[32]

Demand for Better Schools

But why should bureaucratic school systems reform themselves? The central school system bureaucrats have no interest in surrendering their power to individual schools and teachers. And professional educators are most sympathetic to an incremental approach to educational reform, which suggests that school districts keep on doing what they are doing, but do it a little bit better.

On the demand side, if students could choose between several public and private schools, they would invest more time and energy in making their choice. Parents would have a stronger incentive to acquire information about their children's options and to take an interest in their schooling. Of course, not all children have parents who are strongly interested in their education. But evidence shows that disadvantaged children are the ones least able to do well under the present assigned school system.

At present, about 95 percent of students attend public schools. Few parents send their children to private schools, primarily because for their children to attend private school, parents must pay twice: in taxes to support the public school and in tuition payments to the private school. If families were given a voucher for each child, which could be used in any public or private school, more would probably choose private school.

The Bush administration favored opening up the public school system to the forces of competition. To promote this concept, the administration offered $230 million in incentives to states that want to develop school-choice plans. But change comes slowly. Buying and selling education in the marketplace is not in the American tradition of equal education for all, and it threatens the autonomy of the professional educators who run the schools.

President Bill Clinton assigned high priority to deficit reduction, health care reform and investment in the nation's infrastructure. His education proposals include more job training for unemployed workers, enrolling of more young children in the successful Head Start program and allowing college students to pay off higher education loans through public service.

School-Choice Plans

At present, eight states and many individual school districts allow some form of school choice among public schools. Massachusetts has combined ten school districts (including the Boston school district), which enroll 18 percent of the public school population. Each school district has magnet schools that offer special programs. The plan has enjoyed some success in attracting white students back to inner city schools.[33]

Milwaukee has the only program that allows students to use state funds to attend private, nonreligious schools. Some large city school districts are experimenting with school-based management, in which the central school board delegates responsibility for operating local schools to local councils consisting of parents, teachers, and school administrators.

In Chicago, the central school board was scaled down in size as it turned over more money and operational control to the local schools. Local school principals were stripped of tenure, received four-year contracts, and were given more authority to select and discipline teachers. Parents and teachers received some input in budget and curriculum matters. After two years (1990 and 1991), the Chicago schools experiment was a qualified success. One reformer judged that most schools are still about the same about 5 percent are worse off, and about 15 percent are working better.[34]

Providing education is the largest single function of state and local government. Many actors struggle to shape educational policy and to control the allocation of education dollars. In recent decades, the power to shape outcomes has passed from parent and school board to professional educators, and from local school districts to state policy makers, who now fund about half of the local school budget.

Since the Supreme Court ruled that segregated schooling denied blacks the equal protection of the laws, racial composition of the schools has been a controversial social and legal issue. It is still not clear whether governments must attempt to correct racial imbalance that results from neighborhood residential patterns rather than from a legal segregation policy.

In the last two decades, economic crisis has coincided with declining student achievement as measured by test scores. Of course, disappointing school performance is not the cause of our economic and social problems. The large gap between the richest 10 percent and the poorest 10 percent of families is created by our market-oriented economic system. Inadequate inner city schools are the product of urban decay. A culture in which people watch television more and read books less—not poor schools—explains declining test scores. Schools don't cause our social problems so much as they reflect them.

Most educational reforms propose building upon the existing locally controlled public school system. Poor schools can be improved by increasing per-pupil spending and by creating in all classrooms the characteristics of effective classrooms. The principal alternative is the expanded choice approach, which proponents claim would encourage experimentation and diversity.

Recommended Reading

John E. Chubb and Terry M. Moe: *Politics, Markets and American Schools*, Brookings, Washington, D.C., 1990.

James S. Coleman and Thomas Hoffer: *Public and Private Schools: The Impact of Communities*, Basic Books, New York, 1987.

Christopher Jencks, et al.: *Inequality: A Reassessment of the Effect of Family and Schooling in America*, Basic Books, New York, 1972.

John D. Pulliam: *History of Education in America*, 4th ed., Merrill Publishing Company, Columbus, Ohio, 1987.

Walter G. Stephen and Joe R. Feagin: *School Desegregation: Past, Present and Future*, Plenum Press, New York, 1980.

Harvey L.Tucker and L. Harmon Zeigler: *Professionals Versus the Public: Attitudes, Communication and Responses in the School District*, Longman, New York, 1980.

Frederick M. Wirt and Michael W. Kirst: *The Political Web of American Schools*, Little, Brown, Boston, 1972.

CHAPTER 15

Welfare and Health Care

All societies devise institutions to provide for some essential needs of the poor, especially for the very old and the very young and for those who are disabled. Families are the oldest and most enduring social institution to provide care for the needy. Churches, community charitable institutions, and private individuals also provide some assistance, but in advanced industrial societies, these traditional institutions fall short of providing adequate care.

Therefore, governments typically establish social welfare programs to provide for the needy. This chapter will first examine the role of state government in financing and administering Aid to Families with Dependent Children (AFDC) and Medicaid. AFDC provides cash payments to households with children headed by a single parent. Medicaid pays for hospital and physician care for poor people experiencing acute illness. The chapter will then discuss various justifications of social welfare programs, compare suggestions for breaking the cycle of poverty, explain why AFDC and Medicaid generate intense political controversy, and outline some state efforts to reform our poverty and health care programs.

Welfare

Some Americans do not have the resources to provide for their fundamental food, clothing, shelter, and health care needs. About 32 million, 13 percent of the U.S. population, are officially classified as poor. The government-defined poverty threshold (income) depends upon where a person lives and how many people live in a household; for example, the poverty level for an urban family of four in 1988 was income at or below $12,000 per year. Half of the poor are over age sixty-five or under age eighteen and are therefore considered too old or too young to work. One-third of all family units in poverty are single-parent households headed by women. Thus, most poor people cannot work themselves out of poverty.

Free market economic institutions allocate resources on the basis of economic productivity, which penalizes the aging, young children, and the disabled, who are unable to work. Furthermore, free market economies are susceptible to periodic recession when many workers are thrown out of work through no fault of their own. Moreover, in recent decades, a number of workers have lost their jobs permanently as altered consumer tastes, technological change, and competitive disadvantage have forced plants to close.

Reasons for Providing Welfare

Advanced industrial societies provide social welfare programs for ethical, economic, and political reasons.

The Greatest Good for the Greatest Number

A basic premise of social welfare programs is that a dollar spent by a poor person provides greater utility than a dollar spent by a rich person. Money that provides basic food, clothing, and shelter for a poor family does more good than the same money spent on caviar, fur coats, and jacuzzis for a rich family. Those who accept this utilitarian premise (and there is no convincing way to demonstrate its validity) generally advocate taxing the economically secure to provide for the poor. As we saw in Chapter 10, the poorest 20 percent of American households receive more dollars through social welfare programs than they pay in taxes. Many taxpayers support the concept of a social safety net simply because they are compassionate and do not want to see the aging and indigent suffer from material want.

Political Considerations

In the last 100 years, periodic depressions in the capitalist economic system have imposed widespread unemployment and suffering on the working class. Many workers in the depression years of the 1890s and the 1930s questioned whether the capitalist system in fact delivered the goods, as its defenders asserted. The rise of socialist political movements in Europe and the 1917 Bolshevik Revolution in Russia presented a strong challenge to democratic capitalism. To beat back the challenge in the United States, President Franklin Roosevelt successfully championed social security and unemployment insurance programs in the 1930s. These social welfare programs persuaded many that the capitalist system did indeed work, and they remain enormously popular today.

Social Welfare Programs

Government-sponsored social welfare programs originated during the Great Depression. The Social Security Act of 1935 set up a trust fund into which workers and their employers would pay. The worker would then collect a monthly pension upon retirement or receive disability payments should he or she be unable to work. In case of early death, the surviving spouse and dependents would receive payments. The Social Security Act also provided for temporary unemployment compensation to workers who lose their jobs.

Many wealthy and politically influential property owners decided not to oppose Roosevelt's social security and unemployment insurance initiatives because the social security system is financed through regressive payroll deductions, which means that average workers pay relatively more than the rich.

Entitlement and Means-Tested Programs

The federal social security program is an *entitlement* program, which means that anyone who meets the eligibility criteria (age, disability) is entitled to receive benefits, regardless of income. Unlike social security, most other social welfare programs are *means-tested*, that is, an applicant is eligible to receive a benefit only if his or her income falls below a minimum standard.

As Table 15.1 shows, many social welfare programs are heavily federally financed. State and local governments usually administer these programs in accordance with detailed federal guidelines. The largest programs that states support are Aid to Families with Depen-

Table 15.1   Social Welfare Programs for Persons of Limited Income (1987)
($ millions)

Program	State and Local	Federal
Medicaid	$32,732	$27,960
AFDC	8,453	9,987
Supplemental Security Income	2,911	10,832
Head Start	276	1,102
Job Training	71	3,782
Food Stamps	0	12,479
Housing Assistance	0	8,125
School Lunch	0	3,281
Public Housing	0	2,161
Women, Infants and Children	0	1,664

Source: *Statistical Abstract of the United States 1990*, p. 353.

dent Children (AFDC) and Medicaid. In 1987, state and local governments spent $32.7 billion for Medicaid and $8.4 billion for AFDC. These programs account for about 70 percent of the $43.8 billion that states spent on cash and in-kind benefits for persons with limited incomes.

The Expansion of Social Welfare Programs

In the 1960s, President Lyndon Johnson pushed for a dramatic expansion in federal social welfare programs to help lift many poor people out of poverty. Most of the programs listed in Table 15.1 were created then. About 22 percent of Americans were poor in 1960. Over the next twenty years the poverty rate fell steadily, reaching 11.7 percent in 1979.[1] During the 1980s, however, the poverty rate averaged 14 percent, as federal and state government funding did not keep up with the rate of inflation.

Most poor people of working age do in fact work, receiving welfare payments only to tide them over during periods of unemployment. One study estimates that 24 percent of Americans were poor in at least one year during the 1970s, but only one out of ten of these Americans was persistently poor. Therefore, most welfare dollars support people who are not capable of working, or who are temporarily unemployed.[2] The able-bodied "welfare bum" is not at all representative of welfare recipients.

Aid to Families with Dependent Children

Of the programs that are partially funded by state and local governments and administered by them, Aid to Families with Dependent Children (AFDC) is the most controversial. AFDC provides cash payments for the most part to poverty-ridden single-parent households, usually headed by women, with children under the age of eighteen. State and local governments provide nearly half of AFDC funds, determine eligibility standards, and administer the program. Benefit levels vary, from a maximum of $663 per month in California to $118 per month in Alabama. Half of AFDC recipients and 60 percent of benefit payments are concentrated in six large industrial states that have relatively generous programs.

AFDC payments increased from 1960 to 1972. After 1972, AFDC payments declined as states failed to adjust payment levels for inflation. Because the poor are politically weak, they have borne more than their share of state budget cuts during recent economic hard times.

Inner City Poverty

Although most of the poor live in rural areas and more welfare recipients are white than black, the problem of poverty among inner city blacks has received close attention because rates of inner city joblessness, teen-age pregnancy, crime, drug use, and welfare dependency have reached alarming proportions over the last twenty years. The total population of the five largest U.S. cities decreased by 9 percent between 1970 and 1980, but the poverty population increased by 22 percent.[3] Why have conditions of life in our inner cities deteriorated since the early 1970s?

Worsening Economy

One important reason for the increase in poverty is that economic conditions have worsened in the inner city. Recession and changes in the American economy have destroyed jobs in the inner city, and declining revenues have weakened the response of state and local governments to the problems of poverty and crime.

Middle-Class Exodus

Another reason for inner city decline is that many middle-class families are fleeing to the suburbs in order to escape high crime rates, deteriorating schools, and the decay of public services. The phenomenon of white flight to the suburbs is well-documented. Less well known is that middle-class black families are also abandoning the inner city. A generation ago, stable black middle-class families were forced to live in segregated inner city communities. They provided positive role models of profamily behavior, respect for the law, and a work ethic. Strong families and neighborhoods and the availability of unskilled jobs made inner city communities more viable than they are today.

Breaking the Cycle of Inner City Poverty

A primarily black poverty class has become a seemingly permanent feature of the American urban landscape. Current thinking about how to break the cycle of poverty falls into two categories: providing economic opportunity and changing a dependency-creating welfare system.

Providing Economic Opportunity

Sociologist William Julius Wilson argues that the fundamental problem in the inner cities is that young black males no longer have access to well-paying jobs.[4] Labor force participation of young black males ages twenty to twenty-four declined from 84 percent in 1960 to 81 percent in 1988. The unemployment rate for black males under age twenty-four was about 20 percent, nearly three times the rate for young white males. Every year, more jobs require skills, education, and experience that many potential workers do not have and cannot get. The factories that formerly provided unskilled work have closed in the face of foreign competition or have moved to the suburbs. In New York City, 492,000 jobs requiring less than a high school education were lost between 1970 and 1984; in Philadelphia during the same period, 172,000 such jobs disappeared.

Lack of jobs leaves many young males with few alternatives to crime, drug use, and welfare dependency. They lack the financial resources to support a family, and out-of-wedlock births and female-headed households are common. In 1980, two-thirds of births to black women ages fifteen to twenty-four were out-of-wedlock. The percentage of female-headed black families increased from 18 percent in 1950 to 42 percent in 1983.

To reverse the deepening cycle of permanent poverty and social disorganization, well-paying jobs must be created for inner city residents. For example, governments might provide transportation for inner city residents to suburban jobs, offer tax breaks to encourage investment in urban enterprise zones within inner cities, and initiate job-training programs in state-of-the-art technology that would make well-paying jobs accessible to inner city residents.

The political obstacles to these job-creating initiatives are considerable. Inner city beneficiaries are less effective politically than are the middle-class taxpayers who would be asked to fund what they see as competition for jobs. Certainly inner city job creation would benefit suburban taxpayers to the extent that access to jobs would strengthen inner city families and social institutions, help to deter crime and drug use, and convert welfare dependents into productive, tax-paying citizens. However, as was discussed in Chapter 14, many whites have objected bitterly to affirmative action programs, which give minorities preferential access to education and job-training slots.

Changing a Dependency-Creating Welfare System

A second approach to breaking the cycle of poverty argues that the problems of the urban underclass are caused by social welfare programs intended to alleviate the condition of the poor. Charles Murray, a widely read and influential social critic, maintains that these programs encourage recipients to live off welfare rather than to seek out low-wage work. Lyndon Johnson's Great Society programs of the 1960s, which were intended to lift recipients out of poverty, in fact mired them more deeply in it. According to Murray, social welfare programs have promoted dependency on the welfare system and lack of personal responsibility to establish families, abide by the laws, and support churches, schools, and other community institutions. Therefore, to reverse the decline of the cities government should cut back on dependency-creating social welfare programs.[5]

While Murray's welfare dependency argument may apply to some of the inner city poor, it does not apply to the broader poverty population. One major study based on a random sample of families who were tracked over a ten-year period shows that most of the poverty population are temporarily poor because of death or divorce within the household or loss of a job. Only about 16 percent are persistently poor. Nor is there any evidence that social welfare programs that help the impoverished reinforce low self-esteem or decrease the motivation to work. Social welfare programs do not foster a culture of poverty, since even in the cities the children of welfare recipients are quite likely to work regularly and to escape from poverty.[6]

Some states with large numbers of welfare recipients and relatively generous provisions are experimenting with ways to break the cycle of welfare dependency for able-bodied adults. California seeks to tighten eligibility requirements and limit payments in order to make working more attractive and to deter poor people from migrating from states with less generous payment schedules. Massachusetts requires that welfare recipients earn their checks by working on state-sponsored public works programs like keeping parks clean and sweeping streets. Wisconsin rewards desirable behavior like being married or staying in school with cash payments and punishes having children out of marriage or dropping out of school with deductions.[7]

Health Care

Most advanced industrial nations pay for health care through government-sponsored national health insurance. But in the United States, with its strong free enterprise tradition, individuals decide when and from whom to seek treatment and how to pay for it. Table 15.2 shows that individuals and private insurance companies pay 58 percent of the national health care bill. Government pays only 42 percent, compared to 73 percent in Japan, 76 percent in Canada, 91 percent in England, and 97 percent in Norway.

Origins of the Health Care System

Availability of physicians and hospitals to provide helpful medical care to the acutely ill is essentially a twentieth-century phenomenon. In 1912, a distinguished medical professor remarked, ''For the

Table 15.2   Who Pays for Health Care in the United States?
(1989)

Source of Payment	Percentage
Private Health Insurance	33%
Individual Payments	21%
Other Private Payments	4%
Medicare	17%
Medicaid	10%
Other Government Programs	15%
Total	100%

Source: Health Care Financing Administration.

first time in human history, a random patient with a random disease consulting a doctor chosen at random stands a better than 50/50 chance of benefitting from the encounter."[8]

Not until the 1930s did private insurance companies begin to sell health insurance, enabling individuals to know that, in exchange for a monthly premium, insurance would pay for their health care needs. Most programs were organized by large employers who would contract with private companies to provide a health care insurance package for their employees. From the beginning, health care was defined as a private good, to be sought out and paid for by the individual who needed care.

Political Dominance of Health Care Providers

Just as professional educators have tended to dominate education policy making, as discussed in Chapter 14, so too have health care providers tended to dominate health care policy. Historically, doctors and hospitals have had a free hand to prescribe treatment and set fees for service. Often, they would provide essential medical care to the poor while charging their more affluent patients enough to cover their expenses and salary. Since their inception in the 1930s, private third-party insurers have allowed doctors and hospitals to set fees for service. Insurers paid these customary and usual charges without question.

When President Franklin Roosevelt sponsored the 1935 Social Security Act, he omitted any provision for national health insurance because doctors adamantly opposed the concept. They feared becoming employees of the national government who would have little control over where they practiced, whom they treated, and how much they charged. When President Harry S Truman, supported by organized labor, first advocated national health insurance in the 1940s, his proposals were also defeated by the opposition of health care providers.[9]

Producer interests often shape public policy at the expense of the general citizenry. In the health care field, providers of medical services can more easily organize than can health care consumers. Doctors, insurance companies, and hospitals are vitally interested in health care policy affecting their incomes and working conditions. They devote their time, money, and knowledge to support interest groups on behalf of this single issue. Interest groups representing health care providers—the American Medical Association (AMA) and the American Hospital Association (AHA)—are powerful because they are unified, well-financed, knowledgeable, and able to disrupt any proposed health care system that is not minimally acceptable.[10]

For consumers in good health and taxpayers generally, health care is not a major issue. They tend to be ineffective players in the game of health politics. Some citizens will cheer the efforts of health care activists but will not join them, preferring to ride free on the efforts of others. They are not motivated to fight for lower cost medicine when medical care represents but a small proportion of the family budget.[11] Health care consumers become more activist and have more influence when health care becomes an issue because of rising costs, fear of financial disaster in case of catastrophic illness, or inadequate insurance coverage for large numbers of people.

Extending Medical Care to the Elderly and the Poor

In 1965, the time was right to extend medical care to the elderly and the poor. The elderly were emerging as a powerful voting and lobbying force in American politics on issues like social security and health care that were of great interest to them. People over age sixty-five now constitute 12 percent of the population, are healthy longer, and participate actively in politics. The American Association of Retired Persons (AARP) increased its membership from 150,000 in 1960 to over 28 million in 1989.

A widely discussed best-selling book revealed that, in 1962, over 40 million people went to bed hungry in the world's richest nation and had little access to health care.[12] Public opinion polls indicated concern about poor health care. When the Democratic party won the presidency in a landslide in 1964 and made large gains in Congress as well, they quickly drafted major legislation to extend health care coverage to retirees and the poor.

Medicare

One group obviously not well served by the private insurance approach was the aging, many of whom lost their health insurance coverage when they retired. Persons over age sixty-five are twice as likely as those under sixty-five to be seriously ill. And in 1965 only 38 percent of retired people had health insurance when their need was greatest.

In 1965, Congress adopted Medicare to meet the health needs of elderly Americans. Part A of Medicare provides hospitalization insurance; Part B permits participants to purchase inexpensive coverage for doctor fees and other medical expenses. Medicare is funded by the federal government. All elderly Americans who have paid into the social security program are eligible for Medicare benefits regardless of income or state of residence.[13]

Medicare won passage in 1965 because the aged were seen as both needy and deserving, and the program was broadly supported by both the aging and their children.[14] Business groups, long supporters of the AMA in opposing socialized medicine, supported Medicare as a way to lessen pressure on corporations to pay retirement medical benefits. Most importantly, the AMA and AHA supported extending care to the aging so long as customary provider-patient relationships were maintained and usual and customary fees were paid.

Medicaid

Medicaid provides health care benefits for the aging poor who did not contribute to social security and are therefore not eligible for Medicare benefits. Also covered by Medicaid are disabled, low-income families with dependent children, and others eligible for social welfare programs. Medicaid is a joint federal-state program financed through national, state, and local taxes, not by the beneficiaries. The federal government pays over half of the Medicaid bill. The state share of Medicaid payments rises with a state's per capita income and ranges from 20 percent in Mississippi to 50 percent in New York and California.

Medicaid has grown at a startling rate over the last twenty years, during a period of slow economic growth and stiff taxpayer resistance to higher taxes. As discussed in Chapter 11, states and localities are spending more on health care as their tax revenues stagnate, voter resistance to tax increases stiffens, and the federal government cuts back on its transfer payments to the states. Neither taxpayers nor Medicaid recipients are well organized politically, but since middle-class taxpayers are more vocal and more likely to vote, politicians are more receptive to their demands.[15]

Differences in State Medicaid Expenditures. Within federal guidelines, states are free to establish eligibility standards and the range of services they pay for. Economic factors explain differences in state Medicaid spending better than do political factors. States with higher per capita incomes spend more on Medicaid.[16] On the other hand, states with more liberal congressional delegations do not have particularly generous Medicaid programs, nor do states with close interparty competition, in which it might seem likely for rival politicians to promise more spending in order to attract votes, spend more on Medicaid.[17]

Criticisms of Medicaid.   Medicaid is a controversial program. States take money from taxpayers and redistribute it to poor people who receive medical care. Redistributive programs like Medicaid are a first target of attack when taxpayers react against their heavy tax burden. Taxpayers are less inclined to grumble about tax dollars spent on education, highway maintenance, or police protection because they benefit from these essential services. In states where Medicaid is a substantial proportion of the budget, recipients of other funds have more incentive to demand efforts to contain Medicaid costs.[18]

Management flaws have also weakened Medicaid. Doctors and hospitals are frustrated by delays in processing claims and paying providers. Some fraudulent providers have billed Medicaid for services never provided. Error rates in determining eligibility exceed federal guidelines.

Cutting Medicaid Costs.   States use several strategies to cut Medicaid costs. Poor people who are employed at low-wage jobs or who have assets like equity in a home may be declared ineligible for Medicaid. Or states may restrict the scope and duration of medical services covered under Medicaid. Many states limit the length of hospital stays, number of physician visits allowed per year, or number of drug prescriptions filled. They also limit payments to medical care providers. They may pay lower "reasonable costs" for physician services or hospital stays rather than the "customary and usual" charges that Medicare and private insurance companies pay.[19]

The quality of health care services financed by Medicaid is often inferior. On average, Medicaid pays doctors about 70 percent of what Medicare and private health insurers pay. Therefore, many doctors simply refuse to treat Medicaid patients. That means overcrowding and more perfunctory care in the offices and emergency rooms that do agree to treat Medicaid patients.

Recently, the cost of medical care has increased far more rapidly than expected, as has the number of Medicaid recipients in many states. To stretch their tight budgets, many states have introduced aggressive cost containment strategies. Practice varies from state to state. Some states like New Jersey and New York are generous in determining eligibility, but they pay doctors only about 50 percent of their usual and customary charges. Arkansas and Indiana pay higher fees to doctors but impose strict eligibility requirements.[20]

Criticisms of the Health Care System

Since passage of Medicare and Medicaid in 1965, criticism of the American health care system has mounted steadily. The two main areas of concern are deficiencies in health care coverage and rapidly increasing costs.

Deficiencies in Health Care Coverage

The American health care effort is the highest in the world, but the United States lags behind many other industrial countries on infant mortality and life-expectancy measures. One reason is that the distribution of doctors denies many Americans adequate access to health care. Physicians tend to be overrepresented in suburban areas, where patients can afford adequate medical care, doctors have access to good hospitals and equipment, and other medical specialists are nearby. Inner cities and lightly populated rural areas tend to be underserved, despite government programs to encourage doctors to practice in these areas.

Most important, some 35 million Americans do not have medical insurance. About three-quarters of those without health insurance are workers and their dependents. They are earners of minimum wage whose employers do not provide health benefits. Most of the remaining uninsured are elderly persons not eligible for Medicare or poor people who do not meet strict Medicaid eligibility standards.

Another social cost of inadequate health insurance is that workers are discouraged from leaving employment that provides secure medical benefits. If a worker has a medical problem, the new employer's insurance company may refuse to pay for treatment of a preexisting condition. Also, since Medicaid benefits are available to the economically destitute, the working poor who do not have medical insurance are encouraged to quit their jobs and become paupers in order to become eligible for Medicaid assistance.

Increasing Health Care Costs

Costs of health care are skyrocketing. Table 15.3 shows how sharply health care expenditures increased since 1970, reaching $500 billion in 1987, about 12 percent of gross national product (GNP).

Table 15.3   National Health Care Expenditures, 1970 to 1987

Year	Total (billion $)	Per Capita ($)	Percent of GNP	Medicare (billion $)	Medicaid (billion $)
1970	$ 75.0	$ 349	7.4%	$ 7.5	$ 6.3
1975	$132.7	$ 591	8.3%	$16.3	$15.1
1980	$248.1	$1055	9.1%	$36.8	$28.1
1985	$419.0	$1696	10.4%	$71.1	$44.5
1987	$500.3	$1987	11.1%	$83.0	$54.2

Source: *Statistical Abstract of the United States 1990*, p. 92.

By 1992, health care spending had escalated to about $800 billion, or 14 percent of GNP.

Why is health care so costly? The basic problem is that neither doctors nor patients have much incentive to hold costs down. On the supply side, American medicine is oriented to developing new medical technology, which tends to benefit the acutely ill at great cost. The United States funds one-half of the world's biomedical research, and pharmaceutical companies are constantly developing a stream of new drugs. Medical research institutes disseminate better methods of saving the lives of the critically ill. The income and status structure of medicine rewards specialists who do expensive organ transplants, not general practitioners who provide basic care. The health care industry has felt little pressure to provide low-cost health care, as insurance companies and Medicare have in the past paid customary and usual charges without complaint.

On the demand side, people expect to have access to the finest medical services available. In one poll, only 25 percent of respondents said they would be willing to have certain expensive treatments like organ transplants not be covered by health insurance. Increased demand for sophisticated medical care has bid up the price. More Americans are living longer; life expectancy has now reached seventy-five years. The percentage of Americans over age sixty-five rose from 9.2 percent in 1960 to about 12.6 percent in 1990, and older people use more health care services than do younger people. Americans who can afford it are willing to pay high prices to enjoy a better quality of life. As per capita incomes rise, people typically choose to spend more money on health care.

Consumers tend to overpurchase medical care because their third-party insurance pays the bills. Once a consumer pays the insurance premium, medical treatment is relatively inexpensive. In 1970, patients paid 41 percent of their health care costs out of their own pockets. By 1989, patients were paying only 25 percent. People have every incentive to become patients when the cost of treatment worth $100 is only $25 because their insurance pays 75 percent of the bill.[21] Since patients do not shop for health care as they do for automobiles and airline tickets, health care providers have no incentive to lower prices in order to win more customers.

Also contributing to rapid cost increases are malpractice suits, which are now a prominent feature of the practice of medicine. In a recent poll, only 39 percent of respondents said they would be willing to give up their right to sue for possible malpractice in order to contain costs.[22] Doctors must increase their charges to pay for expensive malpractice insurance. For protection against suits, they also tend to consult with other doctors and to conduct additional and perhaps unnecessary tests, which add to the costs of treatment.

Also, the paperwork costs of complying with government and insurance company efforts to hold down costs are considerable. One health economist estimates that American doctors spend about half of their average gross income of $260,000 on overhead costs to handle paperwork, pay malpractice insurance, and amortize office medical equipment.[23]

Health Care Reform Proposals

While Americans no doubt benefit from greater spending on health care, the fact remains that the United States spends a larger proportion of its GNP on health care than does any other industrial nation. What society desires and what society can afford are two different things. The challenge is to contain the costs of health care and extend coverage to the uninsured.

Managed Competition

Rapidly increasing health care costs are now generating alternatives to fee-for-service payment. For example, health maintenance organizations (HMOs) charge participants a fixed annual fee for medical services rather than a separate fee for each service. Doctors receive an annual salary from the HMO which employs them. About 15 percent of Americans are enrolled in HMOs. HMOs are an important feature of a cost-containment strategy called managed competition. People choose their health care coverage from among several competing HMOs. Each HMO has an incentive to provide good coverage at the lowest possible cost. Successful HMOs bargain with doctors and hospitals to hold down the cost of service.

In one successful program, 470,000 Seattle residents belong to an HMO that provides high-quality care at lower-than-average cost. The HMO refuses to pay for unnecessary surgery and stresses preventive care, including flu immunization, screening to detect cancer early, and a program for smokers who wish to quit.[24]

Annual Cap on Health Care Spending

Under the present unplanned medical care system, society adds up all of the expenditures at the end of the year and discovers how much they have increased over the previous year. In 1993, the health care bill is 14 percent of GNP and climbing sharply. An alternative approach would be to set an annual health care budget for states and perhaps for individual hospitals. This system would encourage hospitals to offer only cost-effective treatment and to make hard choices concerning how to allocate their health care budgets.

Rationing Care

Investments in costly machines, intensive care units, and elective surgery might also be rationed. In an effort to control Medicaid costs while providing good health care for recipients, Oregon has instituted such a rationing program. Oregon has established a priority rating for 1,600 medical procedures and will not pay for low-priority treatments that are costly and/or provide marginal medical benefit to the patient. For example, acute headaches and bacterial meningitis are at the top of the list; chronic ulcers, sleep disorders, and varicose veins are at the bottom. Insurers then can refuse to pay for low-priority treatments.[25] Officials hope that by eliminating expensive procedures that contribute little to patient quality of life, they may be able to double the number of people receiving some coverage under Medicaid.

Extending Coverage

For those who get into the health care system, available care is the world's finest. But some 35 million Americans, mostly the working poor, have no medical insurance. Low-income families typically spend about 26 percent of their incomes on health care, but when serious illness strikes, the cost of treatment quickly overwhelms their ability to pay. One proposal is for the government to give vouchers to low-income families which they can use to purchase health insurance from private companies. An alternative is to extend present Medicaid program coverage to households with incomes below, say, $15,000.

National Health Insurance

Although health-care-provider interest groups have fought hard against the concept of national health insurance, the idea is gaining support. Germany and Japan offer a model of national health insurance. In these systems, a young adult joins an insurance program and remains enrolled in it for life. The employee and his or her various employers pay 12.8 percent of the worker's pay into the system. The government limits doctor and hospital charges so that total health care expenditures equal about 8 percent of GNP.

Hawaii has already established a near-universal health care plan. About 98 percent of Hawaiians are covered, with employers and employees splitting the costs for most workers and the state paying the bill for the rest. Hawaii's system not only provides coverage for all, but it does so at reasonable cost. Insurance companies bargain aggressively to keep doctor and hospital charges down. Preventive care is emphasized.

Unfortunately, Hawaii's health care plan cannot be easily transferred to other states. Contributing to the success of the system in Hawaii is a low unemployment rate that requires small businesses to compete for good workers. And since the economy is built on tourism, small businesses cannot reduce costs by moving to another state where they could avoid paying expensive health care benefits.[26]

Prospects for Reform

Inadequate health care emerged as a major political issue in the 1992 presidential election campaign. Some 35 million Americans are now uninsured. Workers who are insured express alarm over rapidly rising premiums and the possibility of being wiped out financially by a catastrophic illness. Health care reform now has a firm place on the political agenda. A recent Harris poll finds that 89 percent of Americans believe that fundamental changes in the health care system are needed.

President Bill Clinton has made comprehensive health care reform a top priority. In one of his first actions, he appointed Hillary Rodham Clinton to head a special task force on health care reform. The task force seeks ways to extend basic health care coverage to all and to slow the rate of increase in health care costs. Without reform the cost of Medicare and Medicaid will more than double in six years and make Clinton's deficit reduction goals impossible to achieve.

Clinton has not supported an alternative approach to containing costs, which is to ration medical care. Efforts are now under way to measure the impact of medical treatment on a prospective patient's quality of life. To make these judgments, medical practitioners, health ethicists, and elderly and disabled patients rank the value of medical treatments on quality of life. They take into account how long a patient can expect to live after having a treatment, the quality of those additional years in terms of pain and degree of disability, and the cost of the procedure.[27] If this approach is accepted, the health care system will not make available very expensive drug treatments with disabling side effects for an eighty-year-old patient, nor will the life of a brain-dead accident victim with no hope for recovery be prolonged through artificial feeding and life support.

Specific proposals to extend coverage and control costs will continue to generate intense political controversy. Organized medicine favors employer-financed coverage to the uninsured working poor and opposes efforts to curb doctor and hospital costs. Doctors and hospitals do not favor the annual cap on spending and national health insurance alternatives. Private health insurance providers have signaled their willingness to participate in the reform process; they wish to ensure that reforms do not include national health care insurance or intrusive government control.

Policy makers respect the health care expertise of medical care providers, and the health care industry is very active politically. More than 200 political action committees (PACs) representing the medical, pharmaceutical, and insurance industries have contributed more than $43 million to members of Congress since 1980. Nearly half of the money went to members of congressional committees having jurisdiction over health legislation.

While some health care reforms are inevitable, major change in our health care system is unlikely. The admirable objectives of containing health care costs and extending coverage are not entirely consistent, since extending coverage would inevitably raise costs. The end result of reform will probably resemble our present health care system and be acceptable to organized medicine. The states will continue to experiment with alternative ways to contain costs without compromising quality and extend coverage without raising taxes.

Federal, state, and local governments cooperate in shaping welfare and health care policy. The federal government mandates minimum levels of service and provides some tax dollars. State and local governments decide how to administer welfare and health care programs. Their rules for determining eligibility and payment levels vary with state economic conditions and cultural traditions. The fifty states are important sources of experimentation in ways to build incentives for working-age welfare recipients to find jobs and for hospitals to contain costs.

Most Americans believe that in a wealthy society, all should have access to a basic minimum standard of food, clothing, shelter, and access to health care. Most of the poor are the very old and the very young, who cannot easily provide for their own material needs. In our metropolitan areas, poverty deepens in the inner city as factories close down and middle-class taxpayers move to the suburbs. The challenge is to provide jobs for able-bodied adults, to strengthen families and other social institutions, and to meet the basic needs of the old, the young, and the disabled. In our federal system, the national government sets basic welfare and health care policy. State and local governments adapt that policy to suit their unique circumstances and preferences.

Recommended Reading

Randall R. Bovbjerg and John Holahan: *Medicaid in the Reagan Era: Federal Policy and State Choices*, The Urban Institute Press, Washington, D.C., 1982.

Paul J. Feldstein: *The Politics of Health Legislation: An Economic Perspective*, Health Administration Press, Ann Arbor, Mich., 1988.

Theodor J. Litman and Leonard S. Robins: *Health Politics and Policy*, John Wiley, New York, 1984.

Theodore R. Marmor: *Political Analysis and American Medical Care*, Cambridge University Press, London, 1983.

Charles Murray: *Losing Ground: American Social Policy, 1950–1980*, Basic Books, New York, 1984.

William Julius Wilson: *The Truly Disadvantaged*, University of Chicago Press, Chicago, 1987.

Notes

Chapter 1

1. For an interesting twist on this, see Eileen L. McDonagh, "Representative Democracy and State Building in the Progressive Era," *American Political Science Review,* 86:938–950, 1992.

2. Jack Plano and Milton Greenberg, *The American Political Dictionary,* Harcourt Brace Jovanovich, Forth Worth, Tex., 1993, p. 597.

3. Council of State Governments, *Book of the States, 1989–1990,* Council of State Governments, Lexington, Ky., 1990, p. 40.

4. Richard D. Bingham and David Hedge, *State and Local Government in a Changing Society,* 2d ed., McGraw-Hill, New York, 1991, pp. 32–35.

5. Thomas R. Dye, *Politics in States and Communities,* Prentice-Hall, Englewood Cliffs, N.J., 1991.

6. David Nice, "Interest Groups and State Constitutions: Another Look," *State and Local Government Review,* 20:21–27, 1988.

7. For instance, see Henry J. Raimondo, "State Budgeting in the Nineties," in Carl E. Van Horn, ed., *The State of the States,* Congressional Quarterly Press, Washington, D.C., 1993.

8. Jonathan R. Veum, "Accounting for Income Mobility Changes in the United States," *Social Science Quarterly,* 73:773–785, 1992.

Chapter 2

1. John Dickinson, "Letters from a Pennsylvania Farmer," in A. T. Mason, ed., *Free Government in the Making,* Oxford University Press, New York, 1965.

2. *Ibid.,* p. 104.

C. Calhoun, *A Disquisition on Government,* Bobbs-Merrill, Indi-
_, Ind., 1953.

L. C. Gerckens, "Historical Development of American City Planning,"
 Frank So, I. Stollman, F. Beal, and D. S. Arnold, eds., *The Practice of
Local Government Planning,* International City Management Association,
Washington, D.C., 1979.

5.   For instance, see the argument by Daniel Elazar that there was some
recognizable "cooperative federalism" from the beginning of the republic.
Daniel Elazar, *The American Partnership,* University of Chicago Press, Chicago, Ill., 1962.

6.   *Ibid.* See also Jack C. Plano and Milton Greenberg, *The American
Political Dictionary,* Harcourt Brace Jovanovich, Fort Worth, Tex., 1993;
and George E. Hale and Marian Lief Palley, *The Politics of Federal Grants,*
Congressional Quarterly Press, Washington, D.C., 1981.

7.   For example, Charles Press and Kenneth VerBurg, *State and Community Governments in a Dynamic Federal System,* 3d ed., HarperCollins, New
York, 1991.

8.   For example, see Virginia Gray, Herbert Jacob, and Robert Albritton,
eds., *Politics in the American States,* 5th ed., Scott, Foresman, Glenview, Ill.,
1990.

9.   Morton Grodzins, *The American Political System,* Rand McNally, Chicago, Ill., 1966.

10.   Neil Berch, "Why Do Some States Play the Federal Aid Game Better
Than Others?" *American Politics Quarterly,* 20:366–377, 1992. See also
Hale and Palley, *op. cit.*

11.   J. C. Garand, "Explaining Government Growth in the U.S. States,"
American Political Science Review, 82:837–849, 1988.

12.   Edmund Muskie, quoted in Deil S. Wright, *Understanding Intergovernmental Relations,* Brooks/Cole, Pacific Grove, Calif., 1978.

13.   Press and VerBurg, *op. cit.*

14.   Henry J. Raimondo, "State Budgeting in the Nineties," in Carl E. Van
Horn, ed., *The State of the States,* 2d ed., Congressional Quarterly Press,
Washington, D.C., 1993, p. 47.

15.   Ellen Perlman, "Budget Fisticuffs KO States," *City & State* 7: (November 5–18), 1990, pp. 1, 37.

16.   J. P. Lester, "New Federalism and Environmental Policy," paper presented at the American Political Science Association meeting, New Orleans,
La., 1985.

17.   Jack L. Walker, ''The Diffusion of Innovations among the American States,'' *American Political Science Review,* 63:880–889, 1969; Jack L. Walker, ''Innovation in State Politics,'' in Herbert Jacob and Kenneth N. Vines, eds., *Politics in the American States,* 2d ed., Little, Brown, Boston, Mass., 1971.

18.   Edward C. Banfield and James Q. Wilson, *City Politics,* Vintage Books, New York, 1963.

19.   David C. Nice, *Federalism: The Politics of Intergovernmental Relations,* St. Martin's, New York, 1987.

20.   William Schultze, *State and Local Politics,* West Publishing, St. Paul, Minn., 1988.

21.   *Ibid.*

22.   Molly McCarthy, ''Tax Bills Contain State Mandated Items,'' *The Buffalo News,* December 31, 1992, p. B5.

23.   Richard M. Cion, ''Accommodation Par Excellence: The Lakewood Plan,'' in Michael N. Danielson, ed., *Metropolitical Politics: A Reader,* Little, Brown, Boston, Mass., 1971.

Chapter 3

1.   Daniel Elazar, *American Federalism: A View from the States,* Harper & Row, New York, 1984, p. 110.

2.   Jody L. Fitzpatrick and Rodney E. Hero, ''Political Culture and Political Characteristics of the American States,'' *Western Political Quarterly,* 41:145–154, 1988.

3.   David C. Nice, ''Cooperation & Conformity among the States,'' *Polity,* 16:494–505, 1984.

4.   David Klingman and William W. Lammers, '' 'General Policy Liberalism' Factor in American State Politics,'' *American Journal of Political Science,* 28:598–610, 1984; Charles A. Johnson, ''Political Culture in American States,'' *American Journal of Political Science,* 20:491–510; Fitzpatrick and Hero, *op. cit.*

5.   Johnson, *op. cit.;* Fitzpatrick and Hero, *op. cit.*

6.   *Ibid.*

7.   David Lowery, ''The Distribution of Tax Burdens in the American States,'' *Western Political Quarterly,* 40:137–158, 1987.

8.   James L. Gibson, ''Pluralism, Federalism, and the Protection of Civil Liberties,'' *Western Political Quarterly,* 43:511–534, 1990.

9.   Edward C. Banfield and James Q. Wilson, *City Politics,* Vintage Books, New York, 1963, p. 46.

10.   Richard Hofstadter, *The Age of Reform,* Alfred A. Knopf, New York, 1955, p. 181.

11.   For example, Bryan Jones, *Governing Urban America,* Little, Brown, Boston, Mass., 1983, pp. 242–243.

12.   For instance, see Robert Waste, *The Ecology of City Policy-Making,* Oxford University Press, New York, 1989.

13.   Robert Erikson, "The Relationship Between Public Opinion and State Policy," *American Journal of Political Science,* 20:25–36, 1976.

14.   Anne H. Hopkins, "Opinion Publics and Support for Public Policy in the American States," *American Journal of Political Science,* 18:167–178, 1974. See also Ronald E. Weber and William R. Shaffer, "Public Opinion and State Policy Making," *Midwest Journal of Political Science,* 16:685–699, 1972.

15.   Gerald C. Wright, Jr., Robert Erikson, and John P. McIver, "Public Opinion and Policy Liberalism in the American States," *American Journal of Political Science,* 31:980–1001, 1987.

16.   Benjamin I. Page and Robert Y. Shapiro, "Effects of Public Opinion on Policy," *American Political Science Review,* 77:175–190, 1983. Also see Benjamin I. Page and Robert Y. Shapiro, *The Rational Public,* University of Chicago Press, Chicago, Ill., 1992.

17.   Richard I. Sutton, "The States and the People," *Polity,* 5:451–476, 1973.

18.   David Lowery, Virginia Gray, and Gregory Hager, "Public Opinion and Policy Change in the American States," *American Politics Quarterly,* 17:3–31, 1989.

19.   Sidney Verba and Norman H. Nie, *Participation in America,* Harper & Row, New York, 1972.

20.   *Ibid.,* p. 274.

21.   *Ibid.,* p. 318

22.   Jeffrey M. Berry, Kent E. Portney, and Ken Thomson, "Directions for Democracy," paper presented at the Southern Political Science Association meeting, Atlanta, Georgia, 1988.

23.   John G. Grumm and Russell D. Murphy, *Governing States and Communities,* Prentice-Hall, Englewood Cliffs, N.J., 1991.

24.   Malcolm E. Jewell and David M. Olson, *Political Parties and Elections in American States,* The Dorsey Press, Homewood, Ill., 1989; Jae-On

Kim, John R. Petrocik, and Stephen N. Enokson, "Voter Turnout among the American States," *American Political Science Review,* 69:107–123, 1975; Lee Sigelman, et al., "Voting and Nonvoting: A Multi-Election Perspective," *American Journal of Political Science,* 29:749–765, 1985.

25. Pat Dunham, *Electoral Behavior in the United States,* Prentice-Hall, Englewood Cliffs, N.J., 1991.

26. Joseph LaPalombara and Charles Hagan, quoted in Thomas E. Cronin, *Direct Democracy,* Harvard University Press, Cambridge, Mass., 1989, p. 89.

27. Verba and Nie, *op. cit.;* Howard D. Hamilton, "The Municipal Voter," *American Political Science Review,* 65:1135–1140, 1971; James D. King, "Comparing Local and Presidential Elections," *American Politics Quarterly,* 9:277–290, 1981.

28. Verba and Nie, *op. cit.;* King, *op. cit.;* Lee Sigelman, et al., *op. cit.*

29. Albert K. Karnig and B. Oliver Walter, "Decline in Municipal Voter Turnout," *American Politics Quarterly,* 11:491–506, 1983.

30. Verba and Nie, *op. cit.* The same general pattern holds in other countries, too. See Sidney Verba, Norman H. Nie, and Jae-On Kim, *Participation and Political Equality,* Cambridge University Press, Cambridge, Mass., 1978.

31. Susan B. Hansen, "Participation, Social Structure, and Concurrence," *American Political Science Review,* 69:1198, 1975.

32. David Nachmias and David H. Rosenbloom, *Bureaucratic Government, USA,* St. Martin's Press, New York, 1980.

33. Arnold Vedlitz, James A. Dyer, and Roger Durand, "Citizen Contacts with Local Governments," *American Journal of Political Science,* 24:50–67, 1980. For a more complex discussion of the role of needs, see Michael W. Hirlinger, "Citizen-initiated Contacting of Local Officials," *Journal of Politics,* 54:553–564, 1992. And compare Steven A. Peterson, "Sources of Citizens' Bureaucratic Contacts: A Multivariate Analysis," *Administration & Society,* 20:152–165, 1988; Steven A. Peterson, "Close Encounters of the Bureaucratic Kind: Older Americans and Bureaucracy," *American Journal of Political Science,* 30:347–356, 1986.

34. Daniel Katz, et al., *Bureaucratic Encounters,* Institute for Social Research, Ann Arbor, Mich., 1975; Peterson, "Sources of Citizens' Bureaucratic Contacts . . ."

35. Elaine Sharp, "Citizen-initiated Contacting of Government Officials and Socioeconomic Status," *American Political Science Review,* 76:109–115, 1982; Arnold Vedlitz and Eric Veblen, "Voting and Contacting," *Urban Affairs Quarterly,* 16:31–48, 1980. But compare with Verba and Nie, *op. cit.* And see Peterson, "Sources of Citizens' Bureaucratic Contacts . . ."

36.   Steven D. Brown, "The Explanation of Particularized Contacting," *Urban Affairs Quarterly,* 18:217–234, 1982.

37.   Verba and Nie, *op. cit.* See also Bryan D. Jones, et al., "Bureaucratic Response to Citizen-Initiated Contacts," *American Political Science Review,* 72:148–165, 1977.

38.   *Report of the National Advisory Commission on Civil Disorders,* The New York Times, New York, 1968.

39.   Peter K. Eisinger, "Racial Differences in Protest Participation," *American Political Science Review,* 68:592–606, 1974; Lester W. Milbrath and M. L. Goel, *Political Participation,* 2d ed., Rand McNally, Chicago, Ill., 1977.

40.   Milbrath and Goel, *op. cit.*

41.   Eisinger, *op. cit.*

42.   Joe R. Feagin and Harlan Hahn, *Ghetto Revolts,* MacMillan, New York, 1973.

43.   *Ibid.*

44.   Paul D. Schumaker, "Policy Responsiveness to Protest-Group Demands," *Journal of Politics,* 37:488–521, 1975.

45.   For instance, see Samuel H. Barnes, Max Kaase, et al., *Political Action,* Sage Publications, Beverly Hills, Calif., 1979.

46.   Although it is also clear that the people can be manipulated; see Michael Margolis and Gary A. Mauser, eds., *Manipulating Public Opinion,* Brooks/Cole, Pacific Grove, Calif., 1989; Page and Shapiro, *op. cit.*

Chapter 4

1.   Frank Sorauf and Paul Allen Beck, *Party Politics in America,* 6th ed., Scott, Foresman, New York, 1988, p. 12.

2.   *Ibid.*

3.   Samuel J. Eldersveld, *Political Parties: A Behavioral Analysis,* Rand McNally, Chicago, Ill., 1964.

4.   For useful works on the political machine, see Alexander B. Callow, Jr., ed., *The City Boss in America,* Oxford University Press, New York, 1976; Alexander B. Callow, Jr., *The Tweed Ring,* Oxford University Press, New York, 1966; John M. Allswang, *Bosses, Machines, and Urban Voters,* Kennikat Press, Port Washington, N.Y., 1977; Mike Royko, *Boss,* Signet, New York, 1971; Milton Rakove, *Don't Make No Waves—Don't Back No Losers,* Indiana University Press, Bloomington, Ind., 1975; Lyle W. Dorsett, *The Pendergast Machine,* Oxford University Press, New York, 1968; Alfred Steinberg, *The Bosses,* Signet, New York, 1972.

5.   John F. Bibby, Cornelius P. Cotter, James L. Gibson, and Robert J. Huckshorn, "Parties in State Politics," in Virginia Gray, Herbert Jacob, and Kenneth N. Vines, eds., *Politics in the American States,* 4th ed., Little, Brown, Boston, Mass., 1983; James L. Gibson, John P. Frendreis, and Laura L. Vertz, "Party Dynamics in the 1980s," *American Journal of Political Science,* 33:67–90, 1989.

6.   James L. Gibson, Cornelius P. Cotter, John F. Bibby, and Robert J. Huckshorn, "Whither the Local Parties?" *American Journal of Political Science,* 29:139–160, 1985; Gibson, Frendreis, and Vertz, *op. cit.*

7.   William L. Riordan, *Plunkitt of Tammany Hall,* E. P. Dutton, New York, 1963 edition.

8.   Royko, *op. cit.;* Rakove, *op. cit.*

9.   Phillips Cutright and Peter H. Rossi, "Grass Roots Politicians and the Vote," *American Sociological Review,* 23:171–178, 1958; William J. Crotty, "Party Effort and Its Impact on the Vote," *American Political Science Review,* 65:439–450, 1971; Daniel Katz and Samuel Eldersveld, "The Impact of Local Party Activity upon the Electorate," *Public Opinion Quarterly,* 25:1–24, 1961; Raymond Wolfinger, "The Influence of Precinct Work on Voting Behavior," *Public Opinion Quarterly,* 27:387–398, 1963.

10.   John P. Frendreis, James L. Gibson, and Laura Vertz, "Local Party Organizations in the 1984 Elections," paper presented at the American Political Science Association meeting, New Orleans, La., 1985.

11.   Sorauf and Beck, *op. cit.*

12.   Stuart Nagel, "Political Party Affiliation and Judges' Decisions," *American Political Science Review,* 55:843–850, 1961. More recent studies also demonstrate the effect of party on judges' decisions.

13.   Virginia Gray and Peter Eisinger, *American States & Cities,* Harper-Collins, New York, 1991.

14.   Martin Wattenberg, *The Decline of American Political Parties,* Harvard University Press, Cambridge, Mass., 1984, p. 20.

15.   Michael Gant and Norman Luttbeg, *American Electoral Behavior,* Peacock, Itasca, Ill., 1991.

16.   Robert D. Brown and Gerald C. Wright, "Elections and State Party Polarization," *American Politics Quarterly,* 20:411–426, 1992.

17.   Paul Allen Beck, Lawrence Baum, Aage Clausen, and Charles E. Smith, Jr., "Patterns and Sources of Ticket Splitting in Subpresidential Races," *American Political Science Review,* 86:916–928, 1992.

18.   Malcolm E. Jewell and David M. Olson, *Political Parties and Elections in American States,* 3d ed., The Dorsey Press, Chicago, Ill., 1988, pp. 183–184.

19. Susan E. Howell and James M. Vanderleeuw, "Economic Effects on State Governors," *American Politics Quarterly,* 18:158–168, 1990.

20. Dennis M. Simon, Charles W. Ostrom, Jr., and Robin F. Marra, "The President, Referendum Voting, and Subnational Elections in the United States," *American Political Science Review,* 85:1177–1192, 1991.

21. Gerald Pomper, *Elections in America,* Dodd, Mead, New York, 1968; Jewell and Olson, *op. cit.*

22. James Piereson, "Presidential Popularity and Midterm Voting at Different Electoral Levels," *American Journal of Political Science,* 19:683–694, 1975; Simon, Ostrom, and Marra, *op. cit.*

23. John F. Bibby, *Politics, Parties, and Elections in America,* Nelson-Hall, Chicago, 1987; Stephen Turett, "The Vulnerability of American Governors," *Midwest Journal of Political Science,* 15:108–132, 1971.

24. Gray and Eisinger, *op. cit.;* Malcolm Jewell and Samuel Patterson, *The Legislative Process in the United States,* 4th ed., Random House, New York, 1986, p. 43.

25. Piereson, *op. cit.;* Simon, Ostrom, and Marra, *op. cit.*

26. John E. Chubb, "Institutions, the Economy, and the Dynamics of State Elections," *American Political Science Review,* 82:133–154, 1988; James Campbell, "Presidential Coattails and Midterm Losses in State Legislative Elections," *American Political Science Review,* 80:45–63, 1986.

27. Campbell, *op. cit.*

28. Chubb, *op. cit.*

29. Simon, Ostrom, and Marra, *op. cit.*

30. Gary C. Byrne and J. Kristian Pueschel, "But Who Do I Vote for for County Coroner?" *Journal of Politics,* 36:778–784, 1974.

31. Joel Lieske, "The Political Dynamics of Urban Voting Behavior," *American Journal of Political Science,* 33:150–174, 1989. And see James F. Sheffield, Jr., and Lawrence K. Goering, "Winning and Losing," *American Politics Quarterly,* 6:453–468, 1978.

32. Paul Raymond, "The American Voter in a Nonpartisan, Urban Election," *American Politics Quarterly,* 20:247–260, 1992.

33. V. O. Key, Jr., *Southern Politics,* Vintage Books, New York, 1949, pp. 304 ff.

34. Richard E. Dawson and James A. Robinson, "Interparty Competition, Economic Variables, and Welfare Policies in the American States," *Journal of Politics,* 25:265–289, 1963.

35.   Jack H. Treadway, *Public Policymaking in the American States,* Praeger, New York, 1985, pp. 88–92.

36.   David Lowery, "The Distribution of Tax Burdens in the American States," *Western Political Quarterly,* 40:137–158, 1987.

37.   David C. Nice, "State-Financed Property Tax Relief to Individuals," *Western Political Quarterly,* 140:179–186, 1987.

38.   Richard E. Dawson, "Social Development, Party Competition, and Policy," in William Nisbett Chambers and Walter Dean Burnham, eds., *The American Party Systems,* 2d ed., Oxford University Press, New York, 1975, p. 236.

39.   Paul E. Petersen and Mark Rom, "American Federalism, Welfare Policy, and Residential Choices," *American Political Science Review,* 83:711–728, 1989.

40.   Kenneth J. Meier and Thomas Holbrook, " 'I Seen My Opportunities and I Took 'Em': Political Corruption in the American States," *Journal of Politics,* 54:135–155, 1992.

41.   Steven A. Peterson and James N. Schubert, "Predicting Passage of AIDS Laws in the American States," working paper, Alfred University, 1992.

42.   Ira Sharkansky and Richard Hofferbert, "Dimensions of State Policy," Herbert Jacob and Kenneth N. Vines, eds., *Politics in the American States,* 2d ed., Little, Brown, Boston, Mass., 1971.

43.   Anne Hopkins and Ronald Weber, "Dimensions of Public Policies in the American States,"*Polity,* 8:475–489, 1976.

44.   John F. Bibby, Cornelius P. Cotter, James L. Gibson, and Robert J. Huckshorn, "Parties in State Politics," in Virginia Gray, Herbert Jacob, and Robert Albritton, eds., *Politics in the American States,* 5th ed., Scott, Foresman, Glenview, Ill., 1990, p. 92.

45.   Samuel C. Patterson and Gregory A. Caldeira, "The Etiology of Partisan Competition," *American Political Science Review,* 78:691–707, 1984; Bibby, et al., *op. cit.,* p. 93.

46.   Clive S. Thomas and Ronald J. Hrebenar, "Interest Groups in the States," in Virginia Gray, Herbert Jacob, and Robert Albritton, eds., *Politics in the American States,* 5th ed., Scott, Foresman, Glenview, Ill., 1990, p. 132.

47.   Bryan D. Jones, *Governing Urban America,* Little, Brown, Boston, Mass., 1983, pp. 159–171.

48.   Thomas and Hrebenar, *op. cit.,* p. 144.

49.   Paul D. Schumaker and David Billeaux, "Group Representation in Local Bureaucracies," paper presented at the Southwestern Political Science Association meeting, Dallas, Texas, 1977.

50.   Thomas and Hrebenar, *op. cit.,* p. 147.

51.   Malcolm E. Jewell and Samuel C. Patterson, *The Legislative Process in the United States,* 3d ed., Random House, New York, 1977, pp. 192–196.

52.   Jewell and Patterson, *op. cit.,* p. 291.

53.   Bibby, et al., "Parties in State Politics," p. 113.

54.   Margery Marzahn Ambrosius, "The Role of Occupational Interests in State Economic Development Policy Making," *Western Political Quarterly,* 42:53–68, 1989.

55.   Mancur Olson, *The Rise and Decline of Nations,* Yale University Press, New Haven, Conn., 1982.

56.   Virginia Gray and David Lowery, "Economic Growth in the American States," *American Political Science Review,* 82:109–131, 1988.

57.   Schumaker and Billeaux, *op. cit.*

58.   William H. Dutton and Alana Northrop, "Municipal Reform and the Changing Pattern of Urban Party Politics," *American Politics Quarterly,* 6:429–452, 1978; Alana Northrop and William H. Dutton, "Municipal Reform and Group Influence," *American Journal of Political Science,* 22:691–711, 1978.

Chapter 5

1.   See Bernard Bailyn, *The Origins of American Politics,* Vintage Books, New York, 1968, for a description of the process in more detail.

2.   Bernard Bailyn, *The Ideological Origins of the American Revolution,* Harvard University Press, Cambridge, Mass., 1967.

3.   Alan Rosenthal, *Legislative Life,* Harper & Row, New York, 1981, p. 207.

4.   Joel A. Thompson, "State Legislative Reform: Another Look, One More Time, Again,"*Polity,* 19:27–41, 1986.

5.   Rosenthal, *op. cit.,* pp. 228–230.

6.   Norman R. Luttbeg, *Comparing the States and Communities,* Harper-Collins, New York, 1992, pp. 244–248.

7.   John Grumm, "The Effects of Legislative Structure on Legislative Performance," in Richard I. Hofferbert and Ira Sharkansky, eds., *State and Urban Politics,* Little, Brown, Boston, Mass., 1971.

8.   Sarah McCally Morehouse, "The Governor as Political Leader," in Herbert Jacob and Kenneth N. Vines, *Politics in the American States,* 3d ed., Little, Brown, Boston, Mass., 1976.

9.   Edward G. Carmines, "The Mediating Influence of State Legislatures on the Linkage Between Inter-Party Competition and Welfare Policies," *American Political Science Review,* 68:1118–1124, 1974.

10.   Luttbeg, *op. cit.,* p. 253.

11.   For detail on these, see such standard sources as Charles R. Adrian and Michael R. Fine, *State & Local Politics,* Nelson-Hall, Chicago, Ill., 1991, pp. 178–192.

12.   See, for example, Robert S. Lorch, *State & Local Politics,* Prentice-Hall, Englewood Cliffs, N.J., 1992, pp. 274–278.

13.   Clarence N. Stone, Robert K. Whelan, and William J. Murin, *Urban Policy and Politics in a Bureaucratic Age,* 2d ed., Prentice-Hall, Englewood Cliffs, N.J., 1986, pp. 214–215.

14.   Richard Elling, "The Utility of State Legislative Casework as a Means of Oversight," *Legislative Studies Quarterly,* 4:357, 1979.

15.   Malcolm Jewell and Samuel C. Patterson, *The Legislative Process in the United States,* Random House, New York, 1986, p. 108.

16.   John Wahlke, et al., *The Legislative System,* John Wiley, New York, 1962, pp. 256–258.

17.   Malcolm Jewell, "Legislators and Constituents in the Representative Process," in Gerhard Loewenberg, Samuel C. Patterson, and Malcolm E. Jewell, eds., *Handbook of Legislative Research,* Harvard University Press, Cambridge, Mass., 1985, p. 105. For the classic study, see Heinz Eulau, et al., "The Role of the Representative," *American Political Science Review,* 53:742–756, 1959.

18.   Heinz Eulau and Kenneth Prewitt, *Labyrinths of Democracy,* Bobbs-Merrill, Indianapolis, Ind., 1973, p. 407.

19.   Eulau, et al., *op. cit.*

20.   C. B. McMurray and M. B. Parson, "Public Attitudes toward Representational Roles," *Midwest Journal of Political Science,* 9:167–185, 1965.

21.   Steven A. Peterson and William H. Dutton, "Errand-Boy Behavior and Local Legislatures," paper presented at the Midwest Political Science Association meeting, Cincinnati, Ohio, 1981.

22.   Compare: Joel A. Thompson, "Agency Requests, Gubernatorial Support, and Budget Success in State Legislatures Revisited," *Journal of Politics,* 49:756–779, 1987; Ira Sharkansky, "Agency Requests, Gubernatorial

Support, and Budget Success in State Legislatures," *American Political Science Review,* 62:1220–1231, 1968.

23.   Wahlke, et al., *op. cit.*

24.   Marshall R. Goodman, Debra S. Gross, Thomas A. Boyd, and Herbert F. Weisberg, "State Legislator Goal Orientations: An Examination," *Polity,* 18:707–719, 1986.

25.   Steven A. Peterson and William H. Dutton, "The Responsiveness of Local Legislators: A Case Study," *The Urban Interest,* 4:24, 1982.

26.   Kenneth Prewitt, "Political Ambitions, Volunteerism, and Electoral Accountability," *American Political Science Review,* 64:5–17, 1970.

27.   See Joseph Schlesinger, *Ambition and Politics,* Rand McNally, Chicago, Ill., 1966; William H. Dutton, "The Political Ambitions of Local Legislators: A Comparative Perspective," *Polity,* 7:504–522, 1975.

28.   Elling, *op. cit.*

29.   See, for example, Jewell and Patterson, *op. cit.*

30.   Alan Rosenthal, "The Legislative Institution—In Transition and at Risk," in Carl E. Van Horn, ed., *The State of the States,* 2d ed., Congressional Quarterly Press, Washington, D.C., 1993; Luttbeg, *op. cit.,* 227.

31.   Virginia Gray and Peter Eisinger, *American States & Cities,* HarperCollins, New York, 1991, p. 110.

32.   Wilma Rule, "Why More Women Are State Legislators,"*Western Political Quarterly,* 43:437–448, 1990. For a different conclusion about the south, see Charles S. Bullock III and Susan A. McManus, "Municipal Electoral Structures and the Election of Councilwomen," *Journal of Politics,* 53:65–89, 1991.

33.   See the summary in Thomas C. Dye, *Politics in States and Communities,* Prentice-Hall, Englewood Cliffs, N.J., 1991, pp. 157–161.

34.   Samuel C. Patterson, "State Legislators and the Legislatures," in Virginia Gray, Herbert Jacob, and Robert Albritton, eds., *Politics in the American States,* Scott, Foresman, Glenview, Ill., 1990.

35.   John B. McConaughy, "Some Personality Factors of State Legislators," in Wahlke, et al., *op. cit.;* Ronald Hedlund, "Psychological Predispositions: Political Representatives and the Public," *American Journal of Political Science,* 19:489–505, 1973.

36.   Dye, *op. cit.,* p. 313.

37.   Kenneth Prewitt, *The Recruitment of Political Leaders,* Bobbs-Merrill, Indianapolis, Ind., 1970.

38.   Adrian and Fine, *op. cit.,* pp. 332–333.

39.   Carol S. Weissert, "Determinants and Outcomes of State Legislative Effectiveness," *Social Science Quarterly,* 72:797–806, 1992.

40.   Mark C. Ellickson, "Pathways to Legislative Success: A Path Analytic Study of the Missouri House of Representatives," *Legislative Studies Quarterly,* 17:285–302, 1992.

41.   Gary F. Moncrief, Joel A. Thompson, Michael Haddon, and Robert Hoyer, "For Whom the Bell Tolls: Term Limits and State Legislatures," *Legislative Studies Quarterly,* 17:37–47, 1992; Gerald Benjamin and Michael J. Malbin, eds., *Limiting Legislative Terms,* Congressional Quarterly Press, Washington, D.C., 1992.

42.   See the competing views on this allegation in Benjamin and Malbin, *op. cit.*

43.   For example, see Norman R. Luttbeg, "Legislative Careers in Six States: Are Some Legislatures More Likely to Be Responsive?" *Legislative Studies Quarterly,* 17:49–68, 1992.

44.   John J. Harrigan, *Politics and Policy in States and Communities,* HarperCollins, New York, 1991, p. 226.

45.   Albert K. Karnig, "Black Representation in City Councils," *Urban Affairs Quarterly,* 12:223–243, 1976. See also Richard L. Engstrom and Michael D. McDonald, "The Election of Blacks to City Councils: The Impact of Electoral Arrangements on the Seats/Population Relationship," *American Political Science Review,* 75:344–354, 1981.

46.   Susan Welch, "The Impact of At-Large Elections on the Representation of Blacks and Hispanics," *Journal of Politics,* 52:1050–1076, 1990.

47.   Richard L. Cole and Delbert A. Taebel, "Cumulative Voting in Local Elections: Lessons from the Alamogordo Experience," *Social Science Quarterly,* 73:194–201, 1992.

48.   Jewell and Patterson, *op. cit.*

49.   Diane Kincaid Blair and Ann R. Henry, "The Family Factor in State Legislative Turnover," *Legislative Studies Quarterly,* 6:55–68, 1981.

50.   Prewitt, "Political Ambitions. . . ."

51.   Alvin D. Sokolow, "Legislators Without Ambition: Why Small-Town Citizens Seek Public Office," *State and Local Government Review,* 21:23–30, 1989.

52.   Eric M. Uslaner and Ronald E. Weber, *Patterns of Decision Making in State Legislatures,* Praeger, New York, 1977, p. 34.

53.   Christopher Z. Mooney, "Peddling Information in the State Legislature: Closeness Counts," *Western Political Quarterly,* 4:433–444, 1991.

54.   Eulau, et al., *op. cit.*

55.   James Kuklinski and Richard C. Elling, "Representational Role, Constituency Opinion, and Legislative Roll-Call Behavior," *American Journal of Political Science,* 21:135–147, 1977.

56.   Ronald Hedlund and Paul Friesema, "Representatives' Perceptions of Constituency Opinions," *Journal of Politics,* 34:730–752, 1972; Robert S. Erikson, Norman R. Luttbeg, and William V. Holloway, "Knowing One's District," *American Journal of Political Science,* 19:231–246, 1975. And see Eric M. Uslaner and Ronald E. Weber, "U.S. State Legislators' Opinions and Perceptions of Constituency Attitudes," *Legislative Studies Quarterly,* 4:563–585, 1979.

57.   William H. Dutton and Steven A. Peterson, "Ambitions, Strategies, and Electoral Accountability," paper presented at the Midwest Political Science Association meeting, Chicago, Ill., 1976.

58.   Prewitt, "Political Ambitions. . . ."

59.   Kim Quaile Hill and Kenneth R. Mladenka, *Democratic Governance in American States and Cities,* Brooks/Cole, Pacific Grove, Calif., 1992, p. 194.

60.   Charles W. Wiggins, "Executive Vetoes and Legislative Overrides in the American States," *Journal of Politics,* 42:1110–1117, 1980.

61.   Rosenthal, "The Legislative Institution. . . ."

62.   Adrian and Fine, *op. cit.,* p. 333.

63.   Wahlke, et al., *op. cit.,* Chapter 7.

Chapter 6

1.   *Book of the States 1990–91,* Council of State Governments, Lexington, Ky., 1990, p. 355; *Statistical Abstract of the United States 1990,* Bureau of the Census, Washington, D.C., 1990.

2.   *Book of the States 1988–89,* Council of State Governments, Lexington, Ky., 1988, p. 38; Christine A. Killam, "Salaries of Municipal Officials for 1990," *The Municipal Yearbook 1991,* International City Management Association, Washington, D.C., 1991.

3.   Elder Witt, "Are Our Governments Paying What It Takes To Keep the Best and the Brightest?" *Governing,* December 1988, pp. 30–39.

4.   Dennis R. Judd, *The Politics of American Cities: Private Power and Public Policy,* Little, Brown, Boston, Mass., 1984, pp. 147–149 and 231–238.

5.   *The Book of the States 1990–91, op. cit.*

6.   Herbert Kaufman, *Politics and Policies in State and Local Governments,* Prentice-Hall, Englewood Cliffs, N.J., 1963.

7.   Judd, *op. cit.,* Chapter 2.

8.   Alexander B. Callow, Jr., *The City Boss in America,* Oxford University Press, New York, 1976, p. 91.

9.   Judd, *op. cit.*

10.   *The Book of the States 1990–91, op. cit.*

11.   John M. Orbell and Toru Uno, "A Theory of Neighborhood Problem Solving: Political Action Versus Residential Mobility," *American Political Science Review,* 66: 471–489, 1972.

12.   Peter Eisinger, "Black Employment in Municipal Jobs: The Impact of Black Political Power," *American Political Science Review,* 76: 380–392, 1982.

13.   Richard D. Bingham and David Hedge, *State and Local Government in a Changing Society,* McGraw-Hill, New York, 1991.

14.   Thad L. Beyle, "Governors," in Virginia Gray, Herbert Jacob, and Robert Albritton, eds., *Politics in the American States,* 5th ed., Scott, Foresman, Glenview, Ill., 1991, Chapter 6.

15.   Bingham and Hedge, *op. cit.,* p. 135.

16.   C. S. Weissert, "The National Governor's Association 1908–1983," *State Government,* 1983, 56:3, pp. 44–52.

17.   Beyle, *op. cit.,* p. 229.

18.   Ann O'M. Bowman and Richard C. Kearney, "Dimensions of State Government Capability," *Western Political Quarterly,* 41, June 1988, p. 345.

19.   Thomas R. Dye, *Politics in States and Communities,* Prentice-Hall, Englewood Cliffs, N.J., 1991.

20.   Thad L. Beyle, "The Governor and the Public," *State Government,* 51, Summer 1978, p. 180.

21.   John J. Harrigan, *Politics and Policy in States and Communities,* Little, Brown, Boston, Mass., 1984, p. 269.

22.   Thad L. Beyle, "The Executive Branch: Organization and Issues," in *The Book of the States 1990–91,* Council of State Governments, Lexington, Ky, 1991.

23.   Mark Tompkins, "The Electoral Fortunes of Gubernatorial Incumbents 1947–1981," *Journal of Politics,* 46:2, 1984.

24.   Richard Neustadt, *Presidential Power,* John Wiley, New York, 1960, Chapter 3.

25.   Beyle, "Governors," *op. cit.*

26.   Dye, *op. cit.*

27.   *The Municipal Yearbook 1982, International City Managers Association,* pp. 164–165.

28.   Timothy A. Almy, "Local Cosmopolitanism and U.S. City Managers," *Urban Affairs Quarterly,* 10, March 1975.

Chapter 7

1.   *Statistical Abstract of the United States 1990,* Bureau of the Census, Washington, D.C., p. 303.

2.   Hans Gerth and C. Wright Mills, *From Max Weber,* Oxford University Press, New York, 1946, Chapter 8.

3.   *Statistical Abstract of the United States 1990, op. cit.,* p. 528.

4.   Penelope Lemov, "Purchasing Officials Push New Techniques to Get More for Their Money," *Governing,* August 1988, p. 40.

5.   Frederick Mosher, *Democracy and the Public Service,* Oxford University Press, New York, 1982.

6.   *The Municipal Yearbook 1990,* International City Management Association, Chicago, Ill., Chapter 5.

7.   Committee for Economic Development, *Improving Management of the Public Work Force: The Challenge to State and Local Government,* Committee for Economic Development, New York, 1978, p. 14.

8.   Robert Lineberry, *Equality and Public Policy: The Distribution of Municipal Services,* Russell Sage, Beverly Hills, Calif., pp. 57–66.

9.   Kenneth R. Mladenka, "The Urban Bureaucracy and the Chicago Political Machine: Who Gets What and the Limits to Political Control," *American Political Science Review,* 74:4, 1980.

10.   Judith Gruber, *Controlling Bureaucracy: Dilemmas in Democratic Governance,* University of California Press, Berkeley, Calif., 1987.

11.   *The Book of the States 1992–93,* Council of State Governments, Lexington, Ky., 1992, p. 449.

12.   Richard C. Kearney, *Labor Relations in the Public Sector,* Marcel Dekker, New York, 1984, p. 209.

13.   Kearney, *op. cit.*

14.   William Niskanen, *Bureaucracy and Representative Government,* Aldine Atherton, Chicago, Ill., 1971.

15.   Gary J. Miller and Terry M. Moe, "Bureaucrats, Legislators and the Size of Government," *American Political Science Review,* 77, June 1983.

16.   Andre Blair and Stephanie Dion, ''Are Bureaucrats Budget Maximizers? The Niskanen Model and Its Critics,'' *Polity*, 22:4, Summer 1990.

17.   Terry M. Moe, ''The New Economics of Organization,'' *American Journal of Political Science*, 28:4, 1984.

18.   *Ibid.*

19.   *Ibid.*

20.   Gruber, *op. cit.*, p. 178.

21.   Michael Lipsky, *Street Corner Bureaucrats: Dilemmas of the Individual in Public Services*, New York: Russell Sage Foundation, 1980.

22.   Gruber, *op. cit.*

23.   John M. Greiner, et al., *Productivity and Motivation: A Review of State and Local Government Initiatives*, The Urban Institute Press, Washington, D.C., 1981.

24.   O. G. Stahl, *Public Personnel Administration*, Harper & Row, New York, 1976.

25.   James L. Perry, Beth Ann Petrakis, and Theodore K. Miller, ''Federal Merit Pay Round II: An Analysis of Performance Management and Recognition Systems,'' *Public Administration Review*, 49:1, January/February 1989, pp. 29–37.

26.   Richard C. Elling, ''Bureaucracy,'' in Virginia Gray, Herbert Jacob, and Robert Albritton, eds., *Politics in the American States*, 5th ed., Scott, Foresman, Glenview, Ill., 1990, Chapter 8.

27.   Lipsky, *op. cit.*

28.   Chester Barnard, *The Functions of the Executive*, Harvard University Press, Cambridge, Mass., 1968.

29.   George L. Kelling, et al., *The Kansas City Preventive Patrol Experiment*, The Police Foundation, Washington, D.C., 1974.

30.   S. G. Botner, ''The Use of Budgeting Management Tools by State Governments,'' *Public Administration Review*, 45:5, September/October 1985, pp. 616–620.

31.   Michael Connelly and Gary L. Tompkins, ''Does Performance Matter? A Study of State Budgeting,'' *Political Studies Review*, Winter 1989, pp. 289–299.

32.   Woodrow Wilson, ''The Study of Administration,'' *Political Studies Quarterly*, 22, June 1887, pp. 197–222.

33.   P. Haas and Deil Wright, ''The Changing Profiles of State Administrators,'' *The Journal of State Government*, 60, pp. 270–278.

34.   Elling, *op. cit.*

35.   *Regents of the University of California v. Bakke*, 438 U.S. 265 (1978).

36.   *The Municipal Yearbook 1990, op. cit.*, Chapter 5.

37.   *Fullilove v. Klutznik* (1980).

38.   *Griggs et. al. v. Duke Power Company* (1971).

39.   *Firefighters v. Cleveland*, 478 U.S. 501; *Sheet Metal Workers v. EEOC*, 478 U.S. 421 (1986).

40.   *Firefighters Local Union v. Stotts*, 467 U.S. 561 (1984); *Wygant v. Jackson Board of Education*, 106 S.Ct. 1842 (1986).

41.   Mark Aldrich and Robert Buchele, *The Economics of Comparable Worth*, Ballinger, Cambridge, Mass., 1986, p. 90.

42.   Sara Evans and Barbara Nelson, *Wage Justice: Comparable Worth and the Paradox of Technocratic Reform*, University of Chicago Press, Chicago, Ill., 1989, Chapter 2.

43.   *Ibid.*

44.   *The Municipal Yearbook 1991*, International City Managers Association, Chicago, Ill., p. 11.

45.   Gary Becker, *The Economics of Discrimination*, University of Chicago Press, Chicago, Ill., 1957, pp. 31–37.

Chapter 8

1.   Bernard Bailyn, *The Origins of American Politics*, Vintage Books, New York, 1968.

2.   Alfred H. Kelly and Winfred A. Harbison, *The American Constitution*, 5th ed., W. W. Norton, New York, 1976, pp. 93–94.

3.   On the first two, see Herbert Jacob, *Justice in America*, 4th ed., Little, Brown, Boston, Mass., 1984.

4.   Ann O'M. Bowman and Richard C. Kearney, *State and Local Government*, Houghton Mifflin, Boston, Mass., 1990, p. 286.

5.   Anthony Champagne and Philip S. Berry, "The New Partisanship in Texas Judicial Elections," *Texas Bar Journal*, 50:1102–1107, 1987.

6.   For example, compare Anthony Champagne and Greg Thielemann, "Awareness of Trial Courts," *Judicature*, 74:271–276, 1991, with Nicholas P. Lovrich, John C. Pierce, and Charles H. Sheldon, "Citizen Knowledge and Voting in Judicial Elections," *Judicature*, 73:28–33, 1989.

7.   Lawrence Baum, *American Courts: Process & Policy*, 2d ed., Houghton Mifflin, Boston, Mass., 1990.

8.   John T. Wold and John H. Culver, "The Defeat of the California Justices," *Judicature*, 70:348–355, 1987.

9.   Baum, *op. cit.*

10.   Richard A. Watson and Rondal G. Downing, *The Politics of the Bench and the Bar: Judicial Selection under the Missouri Nonpartisan Court Plan*, John Wiley, New York, 1969, pp. 338–339.

11.   Henry R. Glick and Kenneth N. Vines, *State Court Systems*, Prentice-Hall, Englewood Cliffs, N.J., 1973.

12.   Baum, *op. cit.*

13.   Herbert Jacob, "The Effect of Institutional Differences in the Recruitment Process," *Journal of Public Law*, 33 (1964), 104–119.

14.   Henry R. Glick and Craig F. Emmert, "Selection Systems and Judicial Characteristics," *Judicature*, 70:228–235, 1987.

15.   *Ibid.*

16.   Burton W. Atkins and Henry R. Glick, "Formal Judicial Recruitment and State Supreme Court Decisions," *American Politics Quarterly*, 2:427–449, 1974.

17.   Glick and Vines, *op. cit.*, pp. 47–51; Henry R. Glick and Craig F. Emmert, "Stability and Change," *Judicature*, 70:107–112, 1986.

18.   Harry P. Stumpf, *American Judicial Politics*, Harcourt Brace Jovanovich, San Diego, Calif., 1988, pp. 179–181; Barbara Luck Graham, "Judicial Recruitment and Racial Diversity on State Courts," *Judicature*, 74:28–34, 1990.

19.   Baum, *op. cit.*, p. 180.

20.   For a good sourcebook on Supreme Court opinions that affect the state criminal justice system, see Lloyd L. Weinreb, *Leading Constitutional Cases on Criminal Law*, The Foundation Press, Westbury, N.Y., 1991.

21.   N. Gary Holten and Lawson L. Lamar, *The Criminal Courts*, McGraw-Hill, New York, 1991, Chapter 10.

22.   Harry Kalven, Jr., and Hans Zeisel, *The American Jury*, Little, Brown, Boston, Mass., 1966.

23.   Jonathan D. Casper, "Did You Have a Lawyer When You Went to Court? No, I Had a Public Defender," *Yale Review of Law and Social Action*, 1:4–9, 1971.

24.   James P. LeVine, "The Impact of *Gideon*," *Polity*, 8:215–240, 1975. And see Baum, *op. cit.*

25.   Jacob, *Justice in America*, Chapter 10; Baum, *op. cit.*, Chapter 7.

26.   See the discussion in Virginia Gray and Peter Eisinger, *American States & Cities*, HarperCollins, New York, 1991, p. 172.

27.   Neil Vidmar, "The Unfair Criticism of Medical Malpractice Juries," *Judicature*, 76:118–124, 1992.

28.   Thomas B. Marvell, "Caseload Growth—Past and Future Trends," *Judicature*, 71:154–161, 1987.

29.   Stuart S. Nagel, "Ethnic Affiliations and Judicial Propensities," *Journal of Politics*, 24:92–110, 1962.

30.   Stuart S. Nagel, "Political Party Affiliation and Judges' Decisions," *American Political Science Review*, 54:843–850, 1961.

31.   Glick and Vines, *op. cit.*, p. 62.

32.   John T. Wold, "Political Orientations, Social Backgrounds, and Role Perceptions of State Supreme Court Judges," in S. Sidney Ulmer, ed., *Courts, Law, and Judicial Processes*, The Free Press, New York, 1981.

33.   John M. Scheib II, Terry Bowen, and Gary Anderson, "Ideology, Role Orientations, and Behavior in the State Courts of Last Resort," *American Politics Quarterly*, 19:324–335, 1991.

34.   James Kuklinski and John E. Stanga, "Political Participation and Government Responsiveness: The Behavior of California Superior Courts," *American Political Science Review*, 73:1090–1099, 1979. And see also Melinda Gann Hall, "An Examination of Voting Behavior in the Louisiana Supreme Court," *Judicature*, 71:40–46, 1987; Melinda Gann Hall, "Electoral Politics and Strategic Voting in State Supreme Courts," *Journal of Politics*, 54:427–446, 1992.

35.   Melinda Gann Hall, "Constituent Influence in State Supreme Courts," *Journal of Politics*, 49:1117–1124, 1987.

36.   Owen M. Fiss, "The Bureaucratization of the Judiciary," in Walter F. Murphy and C. Herman Pritchett, eds., *Courts, Judges, & Politics*, 4th ed., Random House, New York, 1986; Richard B. Hoffman, "The Bureaucratic Spectre: Newest Challenge to the Courts," *Judicature*, 66:60–72, 1982.

37.   Thomas B. Marvell, "State Appellate Court Responses to Caseload Growth," *Judicature*, 72:282–291, 1989.

38.   Mary Lou Stow and Harold J. Spaeth, "Centralized Research Staff: Is There a Monster in the Judicial Closet?" *Judicature*, 75:216–221, 1992.

Chapter 9

1.   Thomas Dye, *Understanding Public Policy*, 6th ed., Prentice-Hall, Englewood Cliffs, N.J., 1987.

2.   *Ibid.*, p. 332.

3. John W. Kingdon, *Agendas, Alternatives, and Public Policies*, Little, Brown, Boston, Mass., 1984, p. 106.

4. E. E. Schattschneider, *The Semisovereign People*, reissue ed., The Dryden Press, Hinsdale, Ill., 1975.

5. Charles E. Lindblom, ''The Science of Muddling Through,'' *Public Administration Review*, 14:79–88, 1959.

6. *Ibid.* See also J. G. March and Herbert A. Simon, *Organizations*, John Wiley, New York, 1958.

7. Theodore J. Lowi, *The End of Liberalism*, Norton, New York, 1969.

8. *Ibid.*, p. 200.

9. Eugene Lewis, *The Urban Political System*, The Dryden Press, Hinsdale, Ill., 1973.

10. Kingdon, *op. cit.*, p. 209.

11. Paul Peterson, *City Limits*, University of Chicago Press, Chicago, Ill., 1981.

12. And see Henry J. Raimondo, ''State Budgeting in the Nineties,'' in Carl E. Van Horn, ed., *The State of the States*, Congressional Quarterly Press, Washington, D.C., 1993.

13. Eugene Bardach, *The Implementation Game*, MIT Press, Cambridge, Mass., 1977.

14. Jeffrey L. Pressman and Aaron Wildavsky, *Implementation*, University of California Press, Berkeley, Calif., 1984.

15. Kenneth R. Mladenka, ''The Urban Bureaucracy and the Chicago Political Machine,'' *American Political Science Review*, 74:991–998, 1980.

16. Paul D. Schumaker and D. Billeaux, ''Group Representation in Local Bureaucracies,'' paper presented at the Southwestern Political Science Association meeting, Dallas, Texas, 1977.

17. Bryan D. Jones, et al., ''Bureaucratic Response to Citizen-Initiated Contacts,'' *American Political Science Review*, 72:148–165, 1977.

18. Sidney Verba and Norman H. Nie, *Participation in America*, Harper & Row, New York, 1972.

19. Jack Treadway, *Public Policy-Making in the American States*, Praeger, New York, 1985.

20. Dye, *op. cit.*

21. Ira Sharkansky and Richard Hofferbert, ''Dimensions of State Policy,'' in Herbert Jacob and Kenneth N. Vines, eds., *Politics in the American States*, 2d ed., Little, Brown, Boston, Mass., 1971.

22.   And see also Virginia Gray, "The Socioeconomic and Political Context of States," in Virginia Gray, Herbert Jacob, and Robert B. Albritton, eds., *Politics in the American States*, 5th ed., Scott, Foresman, Glenview, Ill., 1990.

23.   Robert J. Waste, *The Ecology of City Policymaking*, Oxford University Press, New York, 1989.

24.   Peterson, *op. cit.*; Brett W. Hawkins, *Politics and Urban Policies*, Bobbs-Merrill, Indianapolis, Ind., 1971.

25.   Peterson, *op. cit.*

26.   Hawkins, *op. cit.*

27.   *Ibid.*; Floyd Hunter, *Community Power Structure*, University of North Carolina Press, Chapel Hill, N.C., 1954.

28.   P. Simon and J. Zremski, "Monumental Fiscal Crisis Is Beginning to Hit Home for Municipal Governments," *Buffalo News*, January 13:A1, 1991.

Chapter 10

1.   *Economic Report of the President: February 1991*, Government Printing Office, Washington, D.C., 1991.

2.   Frank Levy, *Dollars and Dreams: The Changing American Income Distribution*, Russell Sage Foundation, New York, 1987, p. 63.

3.   David Osborne, *Laboratories of Democracy*, Harvard Business School Press, Boston, Mass., 1988, p. 3.

4.   Stephen Marris, *Deficits and Dollars: The World Economy at Risk*, Institute for International Economics, Washington, D.C., 1985.

5.   Levy, *op. cit.*, p. 93.

6.   Ross Stephens and Karen Tombs Parsons, "Rich States, Poor States," *State and Local Government Review*, Spring 1989, pp. 50–58.

7.   Jacqueline Calmes, "Bricks Without Straw: The Complaints Go On But Congress Keeps Mandating," *Governing*, September 1988.

8.   E. Blaine Liner, "Sorting Out State and Local Relations," *A Decade of Devolution*, Urban Institute Press, Washington, D.C., 1989, p. 6.

9.   Ellen Perlman, "Cities Get Short End," *City and State*, November 5, 1990.

10.   *Statistical Abstract of the United States 1990*, Bureau of the Census, Washington, D.C., pp. 34–36.

11.   Pamela Fessler, "Higher Gas Tax Gives States a Quick Fill-Up," *Governing*, October 1987, p. 66.

12.   Marilyn Marks, "Florida's New Tax Cut: The Budget Cure That May Be Contagious," *Governing*, October 1987, p. 48.

13.   Susan B. Hansen, *The Politics of Taxation: Revenue Without Representation*, Praeger, New York, 1983.

14.   James Barron, "States' Chances for Gold as a Rush Turns into a Stampede," *New York Times*, May 28, 1989, p. A1.

15.   Beth Moncure Winn and Marcia Lynn Whicker, "Indicators of State Lottery Adoptions," *Policy Studies Journal*, 18:2, 1989–90, pp. 293–303.

16.   Robert Guskind, "Casino Round the Bend," *National Journal*, September 14, 1991, p. 2205.

17.   *Municipal Yearbook 1991*, Chapter 3. International City Managers Association, Chicago, Ill.

18.   Penelope Lemov, "User Fees, Once the Answer to City Budget Prayers, May Have Reached Their Peak," *Governing*, March 1989, p. 24.

19.   James J. Gosling, *Budgetary Politics in American Governments*, Longman, New York, 1992, p. 145.

20.   Art Pine, "States Haven't Given Up on Taxing Services," *Governing*, December 1988, p. 59.

21.   Hansen, *op. cit.*

22.   David O. Sears and Jack Citrin, *Tax Revolt: Something for Nothing in California*, Harvard University Press, Cambridge, Mass., 1982, Chapter 11.

23.   Levy, *op. cit.*, p. 14.

24.   Richard C. Michel, "Economic Growth and Income Equality Since the 1982 Recession," *Journal of Policy Analysis and Management*, 10:2, Spring 1991.

25.   *Statistical Abstract of the United States 1990, op. cit.*, p. 298.

26.   Joseph A. Pechner and Benjamin A. Okner, *Who Bears The Tax Burden?*, Brookings, Washington, D.C., 1974, pp. 47–59.

27.   David Berman, "States and Local Governments: Mandates, Finances and Problems," in *Municipal Yearbook 1991, op. cit.*, Chapter 3.

28.   Benjamin Page, *Who Gets What from Government?*, University of California Press, Berkeley, Calif., 1983, p. 97.

29.   Berman, *op. cit.*

30.   Floris Wood, ed., *An American Profile: Opinions and Behavior, 1972–1997*, Gale Research Inc., Detroit, Mich., 1990; David Lowery and Lee Sigelman, "Understanding the Tax Revolt: Eight Explanations," *American Political Science Review*, 75:4, December 1981, pp. 963–974.

31.   David R. Morgan and John Pelisero, "Urban Policy: Does Political Structure Matter?" *American Political Science Review*, 74:4, December 1980, pp. 999–1006.

32.   Jerry Mitchell and Richard Feiock, "A Comparative Analysis of Government Growth in the Fifty American States," *State and Local Government Review*, Spring 1988, pp. 51–56.

33.   David Lowery, Thomas Konda, and James Garand, "Spending in the States: A Test of Six Models," *Western Political Quarterly*, 37:1, March 1984, pp. 48–60.

34.   Lawrence J. Haas, "Spreading the Pain," *National Journal*, June 22, 1991, p. 1547.

35.   Ira Sharkansky, "Agency Requests, Gubernatorial Support and Budget Success in State Legislatures," *American Political Science Review*, 62:4, December 1968, pp. 1220–1231; Joel A. Thompson, "Agency Requests, Gubernatorial Support and Budget Success in State Legislatures Revisited," *Journal of Politics*, 49, 1987, pp. 756–778.

36.   Martin Shefter, *Political Crisis/Fiscal Crisis*, Basic Books, Inc., New York, 1985.

37.   Isabel Wilkerson, "Ravaged City on Mississippi Floundering at Rock Bottom," *New York Times*, April 4, 1991, p. 4.

38.   Robert Pear, "Washington's Plan to Funnel City Aid Through the States Enrages Mayors," *New York Times*, February 10, 1991, p. E2.

39.   "Cities and Counties Facing Bleak Times," *New York Times*, June 3, 1991, p. B6.

40.   Robert Reinhold, "California Stalemate Ends in a Budget," *New York Times*, July 18, 1991.

Chapter 11

1.   Mancur Olson, *The Logic of Collective Action*, Harvard University Press, Cambridge, Mass., 1965.

2.   John Blair and Robert Premus: "Major Factors in Industrial Location," *Economic Development Quarterly*, 1:1, 1987, pp. 72–85.

3.   P. Choate and S. Walter, *America in Ruins: Beyond the Public Works Pork Barrel*, Council of State Planning Agencies, Washington, D.C., 1981; National Council on Public Works Improvement, *Fragile Foundations: A Report on America's Public Works*, Government Printing Office, Washington, D.C., 1988.

4.   Jonathon D. Salant, "U.S. Bridges Keep on Crumbling," *Governance*, May 1989, p. 74.

5.   Joe Morris, "Just Say Yes to Infrastructure," *American City and County*, November 1989, p. 31.

6.   Marshall Kaplan, "Infrastructure Policy: Repetitive Studies, Uneven Response, Next Steps," *Urban Affairs Quarterly*, 25:3, March 1990, pp. 388–409.

7.   John Peterson, "The Future of Infrastructure Needs," *American City and County*, April 1989, p. 10.

8.   Robert J. Genader, "The Municipal Bond Outlook for 1989," *American City and County*, February 1989.

9.   Kaplan, *op. cit.*, p. 379.

10.   Jerry Mitchell and Richard Feiock, "A Comparative Analysis of Government Growth in the 50 American States," *State and Local Government Review*, Spring 1988, p. 52; David Lowery and William D. Berry, "The Growth of Government in the United States: An Empirical Assessment of Competing Explanations, *American Journal of Political Science*, 27, November 1983, pp. 665–694.

11.   Marver H. Bernstein, *Regulating Business by Independent Commission*, Princeton University Press, Princeton, N.J., 1955.

12.   Kenneth Meier, *Regulation*, St. Martin's Press, New York, 1985, pp. 193–194.

13.   Peter VanDoren, "Should Congress Listen to Economists?" *Journal of Politics*, 51:2, May 1989.

14.   *New York Times*, September 17, 1991, p. 1.

15.   Frank Levy, *Dollars and Dreams: The Changing American Income Distribution*, Russell Sage Foundation, New York, 1987, p. 14.

16.   Paul Peterson, *City Limits*, University of Chicago Press, Chicago, Ill., 1981.

17.   Carla Jean Robinson, "Municipal Approaches to Economic Development," *Journal of the American Planning Association,* 55:3, Summer 1989; Richard C. Feiock, "The Effects of Economic Development Policy on Local Economic Growth," *American Journal of Political Science*, 35:3, August 1991, pp. 643–655.

18.   Susan B. Hansen, *The Political Economy of State Industrial Policy*, University of Pittsburgh Press, Pittsburgh, Penn., 1990.

19.   Bruce A. Williams, "Regulation and Economic Development," in Virginia Gray, Herbert Jacob, and Robert A. Albritton, eds., *Politics in the American States*, Scott Foresman, Glenview, Ill., 1990, p. 485.

20.   Virginia Gray and Peter Eisinger, *American States and Cities*, Harper-Collins, New York, Chapter 12.

21. Julian Weiss, "Enterprise Zones Are Just Part of the Answer for Reviving an Urban Economy," *Governing*, August 1988, p. 57.

22. Harvey A. Goldstein, *The State and Local Industrial Policy Question*, American Planning Association Planners Press, Chicago, Ill., Chapter 1.

23. Richard D. Bingham and David Hedge, *State and Local Government in a Changing Society*, McGraw-Hill, New York, 1991, p. 408.

24. Peter K. Eisinger, *The Rise of the Entrepreneurial State*, University of Wisconsin Press, Madison, Wisc., 1988.

25. Marianne C. Clark, *Revitalizing State Economics*, National Governors Association, Washington, D.C., 1986.

26. Michael Kieschnick, "Taxes and Growth: Business Incentives and Economic Development," in Michael Barker, ed., *State Taxation Policy*, Duke University Press, Durham, N.C., 1983; Leonard F. Wheat, "The Determinants of 1963–1977 Regional Manufacturing Growth; Why the South and the West Grow," *Journal of Regional Science*, 26, 1986, pp. 635–659; Margery Marzhan Ambrosius, "The Effectiveness of State Economic Development Policies: A Time Series Analysis," *Western Political Quarterly*, September 1989, pp. 53–68.

27. Paul Brace, "The Changing Context of State Political Economy," *Journal of Politics*, 53:2, May 1991; Paul Brace, "Isolating the Economies of the States," *American Politics Quarterly*, July 1989, pp. 256–276.

28. Williams, *op. cit.*

29. Georgina Fiordalisi, "How to Avoid a Bum Deal When Using Incentives to Win Business, Jobs," *Governing*, August 1988, pp. 11–12.

30. Cheryl Farr, "Encouraging Local Economic Development: The State of the Practice," *The Municipal Yearbook 1990*, International City Management Association, Washington, D.C., Chapter 3.

31. Ellen Schubert, "State By State, 30 Governors Talk Only of Safe Issues," *City and State*, May 7, 1990, pp. 18–19.

32. John E. Chubb, "Institutions, the Economy and the Dynamics of State Elections," *American Political Science Review*, 82:1, March 1988, pp. 133–154.

33. Anthony Downs, *An Economic Theory of Democracy*, Harper & Row, New York, 1957.

34. William Niskanen, *Bureaucracy and Representative Government*, Aldine Atherton, Chicago, 1971.

35. Gary Miller and Terry M. Moe, "Bureaucrats, Legislators and the Size of Government," *American Political Science Review*, 77:2, June 1983.

36.   E. S. Savas, *Privatizing the Public Sector: How to Shrink the Government*, Chatham House, Chatham, N.J., 1982, pp. 89–117.

37.   Eileen Brettler Berenyi and Barbara J. Stevens, "Does Privatization Work? A Study of the Delivery of Eight Local Services," *State and Local Government Review*, 20:1, Winter 1988, p. 11.

Chapter 12

1.   David W. Pearce and R. Kerry Turner, *Economics of Natural Resources and the Environment*, Johns Hopkins University Press, Baltimore, Md., 1990.

2.   Charles O. Jones, *Clean Air: The Policies and Politics of Pollution Control*, University of Pittsburgh Press, Pittsburgh, Penn., 1975.

3.   Daniel Mazmanian and David Morell, "The NIMBY Syndrome: Facility Siting and the Failure of Democratic Discourse," in Norman J. Vig and Michael E. Kraft, *Environmental Policy in the 1990s*, CQ Press, Washington, D.C., 1990.

4.   Thomas H. Rasmussen, "Not in My Backyard: The Politics of Siting Prisons, Landfills and Incinerators," *State and Local Government Review*, Spring 1992.

5.   Steve Lohr, "Site for Toxic Waste Cave Stirs Texas Political Fight," *New York Times*, May 6, 1991, p. B1.

6.   Sam Howe Verhoek, "Town Heatedly Debates Merits of a Nuclear Waste Dump," *New York Times*, June 28, 1991, p. B1.

7.   Nicholas Rescher, *Risk: A Philosophical Introduction to the Theory of Risk Evaluation and Management*, University Press of America, Lanham, Md., 1983, Chapter 10.

8.   George H. Gray and John D. Graham, "Risk Assessment and Clean Air Policy," *Journal of Policy Analysis and Management*, 10:2, 1991.

9.   Keith Schneider, "U.S. Officials Say Dangers of Dioxin Were Exaggerated," *New York Times*, August 14, 1991, p. A1.

10.   Pearce and Turner, *op. cit.*, Chapter 3.

11.   Bruce A. Ackerman and William T. Hassler, *Clean Coal/Dirty Air*, Yale University Press, New Haven, Conn., 1981.

12.   *The Gallup Poll Monthly*, April 1991, The Gallup Poll, Princeton, N.J.

13.   Marc Landy, Marc Roberts, and Stephen Thomas, *The EPA: Asking the Wrong Questions*, Oxford University Press, New York, 1990.

14.   Dan Wood and Richard M. Waterman, "The Dynamics of Political Control of the Bureaucracy," *American Political Science Review*, 85:3, September 1991.

15.   James P. Lester and Emmett N. Lombard, "The Comparative Analysis of State Environmental Policy," *Natural Resources Journal*, 30, Spring 1990.

16.   Jerry F. Medler, "Governors and Environmental Policy," *Policy Studies Journal*, 17:4, Summer 1989.

17.   Keith Schneider, "Pollution in Arkansas Area May Be Key Campaign Issue," *New York Times*, April 20, 1992.

18.   Joel A. Tarr, "The Search for the Ultimate Sink: Urban Air, Land and Water Pollution in Historical America," in Kendall E. Baines, ed., *Environmental History*, University Press of America, Lanham, Md., 1985.

19.   Matthew A. Crenson, *The Un-politics of Air Pollution: A Study of Non-decision Making in the Cities*, Johns Hopkins University Press, Baltimore, Md., 1971.

20.   Henry D. Jacoby and John D. Steinbruner, *Clearing the Air: Federal Policy on Automotive Emissions Control*, Ballinger Press, Cambridge, Mass., 1973.

21.   Margaret E. Kriz, "The Big Stink," *National Journal*, October 19, 1991, p. 2540.

22.   Robert W. Crandall and Paul R. Portney, "Environmental Policy," in Paul R. Portney, ed., *Natural Resources and the Environment: The Reagan Approach*, The Urban Institute, Washington D.C., 1984, pp. 47–81.

23.   Bruce Yandle, *The Political Limits of Environmental Regulation*, Quorum Books, New York, 1989.

24.   Paul R. Portney, ed., *Public Policies for Environmental Protection*, Resources for the Future, Washington, D.C., 1990, Chapter 3.

25.   A. Myrick Freeman III, *Air and Water Pollution Control: A Benefit Cost Assessment*, John Wiley, New York, 1982.

26.   Matthew L. Wald, "U.S. Lag in Controlling Smog Tied To Misplaced Emphasis," *New York Times*, December 14, 1991, p. A1.

27.   Edwin S. Mills and Philip E. Graves, *The Economics of Environmental Quality*, W.W. Norton, New York, 1986, Chapter 6.

28.   Clifford S. Russell, Winston Harrington, and William J. Vaughn, *Enforcing Pollution Control Laws*, Resources for the Future, Washington, D.C., 1986.

29.   *Ibid.*

30.   Robert W. Hahn, "The Political Economy of Environmental Regulation: Towards a Unifying Framework," *Public Choice*, 65, 1990, pp. 21–47.

31.   Landy, Roberts, and Thomas, *op. cit.*

32.   Paul R. Portney, ed., *op. cit.*, Chapter 7.

33.   Joseph M. Petula, *Environmental Protection in the United States*, San Francisco Study Center, San Francisco, 1987, Chapter 3.

34.   Peter Aranson, "Pollution Control: The Case for Competition," in Robert W. Poole, ed., *Instead of Regulation*, Lexington Books, Lexington, Ky., 1982, p. 346.

35.   John Holusha, "Pricing Garbage to Reduce Waste," *New York Times*, May 2, 1991, p. D2.

36.   Matthew L. Wald, "Utility Is Selling the Right to Pollute," *New York Times*, May 12, 1992, p. A1.

37.   Richard W. Stevenson, "Trying a Market Approach to Smog," *New York Times*, March 22, 1992, p. A1.

Chapter 13

1.   *Report to the Nation on Crime and Justice*, U.S. Dept. of Justice, Washington, D.C., 1988, p. 63.

2.   S. Harring, *Policing a Class Society: The Experience of American Cities, 1865–1915*, Rutgers University Press, New Brunswick, N.J., 1983.

3.   M. K. Sparrow, M. H. Moore, and D. M. Kennedy, *Beyond 911: A New Era for Policing*, Basic Books, New York, 1990, p. 48.

4.   W. C. Cunningham, J. J. Strauchs, and C. W. Van Meter, "Private Security and Trends," in *Research in Brief*, National Institute of Justice, Washington, D.C., 1991, p. 1.

5.   *Report to the Nation on Crime and Justice, op. cit.*, p. 74.

6.   R. L. Spangenberg, et al., *National Criminal Defense System Study*, NCJ-94702, Abt Associated, Inc., Cambridge, Mass., 1982.

7.   *Report to the Nation on Crime and Justice, op. cit.*, p. 45.

8.   *Ibid.*, p. 77.

9.   B. Boland and R. Sones, *Prosecution of Felony Arrests 1981*, INSLAW, Inc., Washington, D.C., 1986, p. 20.

10.   *Ibid.*, p. 22.

11.   J. Horney, "Effects of Race on Plea Bargaining Decisions," paper presented at the American Society of Criminology meeting, San Francisco, Calif., 1980.

12. T. M. Uhlman and N. D. Walker, " 'He Takes Some of My Time: I Take Some of His': An Analysis of Sentence Patterns in Jury Cases," *Law and Society Review*, 14:323–341, 1980.

13. L. Friedman, "Plea Bargaining in Historical Perspective," *Law and Society Review*, 13:247, 1979.

14. E. K. Nelson, H. Ohmart, and N. Harlow, *Promising Strategies in Probation and Parole*, U.S. Government Printing Office, Washington, D.C., 1978, p. 92.

15. *Report to the Nation on Crime and Justice, op. cit.*, p. 93.

16. T. R. Clear and G. F. Cole, *American Corrections*, Brooks/Cole, Belmont, Calif., 1990.

17. L. A. Szymanski, *Upper Age of Juvenile Court Jurisdiction Statutes Analysis*, National Center for Juvenile Justice, Pittsburgh, Penn., 1987.

18. J. Q. Wilson, *Thinking About Crime*, Vintage, New York, 1975.

19. J. Q. Wilson and G. L. Kelling, "Police and Neighborhood Safety: Broken Windows," *Atlantic Monthly*, March 1982, pp. 29–38.

20. W. G. Skogan, *Disorder and Decline*, The Free Press, New York, 1990.

21. E. Currie, *Confronting Crime*, Pantheon, New York, 1985.

22. R. L. Woodson, *A Summons to Life: Mediating Structures and the Prevention of Youth Crime*, Ballinger, Cambridge, Mass., 1981.

23. S. L. Hills, ed., *Corporate Violence*, Rowan and Littlefield, Totowa, N.J., 1987, pp. 3–4.

24. A. A. Block and F. R. Scarpitti, *Poisoning for Profit: The Mafia and Toxic Waste in America*, Marrow, New York, 1985.

25. *Report to the Nation on Crime and Justice, op. cit.*, p. 67.

26. R. B. Coates, A. D. Miller, and L. E. Ohlin, *Diversity in a Youth Correctional System: Handling Delinquents in Massachusetts*, Ballinger, Cambridge, Mass., 1978, p. 172.

27. *Report to the Nation on Crime and Justice, op. cit.*, p. 34.

28. *Justice Expenditure and Employment* NCJ-104460, United States Department of Justice, Washington, D.C., 1985.

29. *Report to the Nation on Crime and Justice, op. cit.*, p. 14.

30. Skogan, *op. cit.*, p. 18.

31. Wilson and Kelling, *op. cit.*

32.   J. H. Skolnick and D. H. Bayley, *The New Blue Line*, The Free Press, New York, 1986, p. 90.

33.   Sparrow, Moore, and Kennedy, *op. cit.*, p. 92.

34.   *Ibid.*, p. 92.

35.   *Skogan, op. cit.*, pp. 91–93.

36.   *Ibid.*, p. 105.

37.   *Ibid.*, p. 106.

38.   *Ibid.*, p. 108.

Chapter 14

1.   *Statistical Abstract of the United States 1990*, Bureau of the Census, Washington, D.C., p. 131.

2.   *Ibid.*, p. xiv.

3.   John S. Robey and Hassan Tajalli, "Politics, Economics and Policy Responsiveness in the American States," *State and Local Government Review*, Spring 1988, pp. 59–63.

4.   Patricia Albjerg Graham, *Community and Class in American Education, 1865–1918*, John Wiley, New York, 1974, Chapter 1.

5.   James S. Coleman and Thomas Hoffer, *Public and Private High Schools: The Impact of Communities*, Basic Books, New York, 1987.

6.   John D. Pulliam, *History of Education in America*, 4th ed., Merrill Publishing Company, Columbus, Ohio, 1987.

7.   Karen DeWitt, "Large Increase Is Predicted in Minorities in U.S. Schools," *New York Times*, September 13, 1991, p. A14.

8.   Newton Edwards and Herman G. Richey, *The School in the American Social Order*, Houghton Mifflin, Boston, Mass., 1963, Chapter 3.

9.   Harvey J. Tucker and L. Harmon Zeigler, *Professionals Versus the Public: Attitudes, Communications and Responses in the School District*, Longman, New York, 1980, p. 19.

10.   Harvey J. Tucker and L. Harmon Zeigler, "The Myth of Lay Control," in Mary Frase Williams, ed., *Government in the Classroom*, New York Academy of Political Science, New York, 1978.

11.   Joel Spring, *Conflict of Interests: The Role of American Education*, Longman, White Plains, N.Y., 1988.

12.   National Governors Association, *Time for Results*, 1986. National Governors Association, Washington, D.C.

13.   Frederick Wirt, "School Policy Culture and State Centralization," in Jay D. Scribner, ed., *The Politics of Education*, University of Chicago Press, Chicago, Ill., 1977.

14.   Frederick M. Wirt and Michael W. Kirst, *The Political Web of American Schools*, Little, Brown, Boston, Mass., 1972.

15.   Tucker and Zeigler, Professionals versus the Public: Attitudes, Communications and Responses in the School District, *op. cit.*

16.   J. L. Polinard, Robert D. Wrinkle, and Tomas Longoria, "Education and Governance: Representational Links to Second Generation Discrimination," *Western Political Quarterly*, 1990, pp. 631–643; Kenneth J. Meier and Robert E. England, "Black Representation and Educational Policy: Are They Related?" *American Political Science Review*, 1984, pp. 392–403; Kenneth J. Meier, Joseph Stewart, Jr., and Robert E. England, "The Politics of Bureaucratic Discretion: Educational Access as an Urban Service," *American Journal of Political Science*, 35:1, February 1991, pp. 15–177.

17.   Pulliam, *op. cit.*

18.   Walter G. Stephen and Joe R. Feagin, eds., *School Desegregation: Past, Present and Future*, Plenum, New York, 1980.

19.   Lino A. Graglia, "From Prohibiting Segregation to Requiring Integration," in Stephen and Feagin, *op. cit.*, p. 69.

20.   David R. James, "City Limits and Racial Equality: Effects of City Suburb Boundaries on Public School Desegregation, 1968–1976," *American Sociological Review*, 54:6, December 1989.

21.   David O. Sears, Carl P. Hensler, and Leslie K. Speer, "White Opposition To 'Busing': Self-interest or Symbolic Politics?" *American Political Science Review*, 73:2, June 1979, pp. 369–384.

22.   Christine H. Rossell, "School Desegregation and White Flight," *Political Science Quarterly*, 90:4, Winter 1975, p. 675.

23.   Neal R. Pearce, "We Have Met the Enemy and He Is Us," *National Journal*, October 12, 1991, p. 2503.

24.   David T. Kearns and Dennis P. Doyle, *Winning the Brain Race: A Bold Plan to Make Our Schools Competitive*, Institute for Contemporary Studies Press, San Francisco, 1988.

25.   James S. Coleman and Thomas Hoffer, *Public and Private Schools: The Impact of Communities*, Basic Books, New York, 1987.

26.   Christopher Jencks, *Inequality: A Reassessment of the Effect of Family and Schooling in America*, Basic Books, New York, 1972, Chapter 2.

27.   Michel Marriott, "Louisville Debates Plan to End Forced Busing in Grade School," *New York Times*, December 11, 1991, p. B13.

28.   Coleman and Hoffer, *op. cit.*

29.   Jonathon Kozol, *Savage Inequalities: Children in America's Schools*, Crown Publishing, New York, 1991.

30.   David A. Squires, William G. Huitt, and John K. Segars, *Effective Schools and Classrooms: A Research Based Perspective*, Association for Supervision and Curriculum Development, Alexandria, Va., 1984.

31.   John E. Chubb and Terry M. Moe, *Politics, Markets and America's Schools*, Brookings, Washington, D.C., 1990, Chapter 1; Ernest Boyer, *High School: A Report on Secondary Education in America*, Houghton Mifflin, Boston, 1984.

32.   Chubb and Moe, *ibid.*

33.   Charles L. Gann, "Controlled Choice in Massachusetts Public Schools," *Public Interest*, 103, Spring 1991, pp. 88–105.

34.   Robert Guskind, "Rethinking Reform," *National Journal*, May 25, 1991, p. 1236.

Chapter 15

1.   John E. Schwarz, *America's Hidden Success*, W.W. Norton, New York, 1988.

2.   Mary Corcoran, Greg J. Duncan, Gerald Gurin, and Patricia Gurin, "Myth and Reality: The Causes and Persistence of Poverty," *Journal of Policy Analysis and Management*, 4:4, 1985.

3.   William Julius Wilson, *The Truly Disadvantaged*, University of Chicago Press, Chicago, Ill., 1987, Chapter 1.

4.   *Ibid.*, p. 46.

5.   Charles Murray, *Losing Ground: American Social Policy, 1950–1980*, Basic Books, New York, 1984.

6.   Corcoran, et al., *op. cit.*

7.   Paul Taylor, "An Eat-Your-Vegetables Welfare System," *Washington Post Weekly*, June 17, 1991.

8.   Theodore R. Marmor, *The Politics of Medicare*, Aldine Publishing, Chicago, Ill., 1973, p. 5.

9.   *Ibid.*, Chapter 1.

10.   Theodore R. Marmor, *Political Analysis and American Medical Care*, Cambridge University Press, New York, 1983, p. 15.

11.   *Ibid.*, p. 15.

12.   Michael Harrington, *The Other America: Poverty in the United States*, Macmillan, New York, 1962.

13.   Marmor, *op. cit.*, Chapter 7.

14.   Mark V. Pauly and William L. Kissick, *Lessons From the First Twenty Years of Medicare*, University of Pennsylvania Press, Philadelphia, Penn., 1988.

15.   Philip Fanara, Jr., and Warren Greenburg, "Factors Affecting the Adoption of Prospective Reimbursement Programs by State Governments," in Jack A. Meyer, ed., *Incentives vs. Control in Health Policy*, American Enterprise Institute, Washington, D.C., 1985.

16.   Russell S. Hanson, "The Politics of Medicaid Distribution," *American Journal of Political Science*, 28:2, May 1984, p. 336.

17.   Robert J. Buchanan, Joseph C. Cappelerari, and Robert Ohsfeldt, "The Social Environment and Medicaid Expenditures: Factors Influencing the Level of State Medicaid Spending," *Public Administration Review*, 51:1, January/February 1991, p. 67.

18.   Fanara and Greenburg, *op. cit.*, p. 145.

19.   Randall R. Bovbjerg and John Holahan, *Medicaid in the Reagan Era: Federal Policy and State Choices*, The Urban Institute Press, Washington, D.C., 1982.

20.   John Holahan, *Financing Health Care for the Poor*, The Urban Institute Press, Washington, D.C., 1975, Chapter 2.

21.   Council of Economic Advisers, *Economic Report of the President 1991*, p. 139, Government Printing Office, Washington, D.C.

22.   "Health Costs Found to Slow Job Moves," *New York Times*, September 26, 1991, p. B2.

23.   Milt Freudenheim, "Potential Savings of National Care," *New York Times*, November 12, 1991, p. D2.

24.   Timothy Egan, "Seattle Showpiece of Health Care by Democracy," *New York Times*, May 2, 1991, p. B12.

25.   "Oregon to Use Computer List on Who Will Get Medical Aid," *New York Times*, May 3, 1990 p. A1.

26.   "Hawaii Shows It Can Offer Health Insurance for All," *New York Times*, July 21, 1991, p. A1.

27.   Gina Kolata, "Ethicists Struggle to Judge the 'Value of Life,' " *New York Times*, November 24, 1992, p. C3.

Index

Political participation, 58–69
    influences on, 63–68
    particularistic contacting,
        65–66
    and policy, 58–60, 66, 68–69
    protest, 66–69
    voting, 60–63, 64, 81–84
Political party:
    defined, 72
    effects on policy, 180
    effort, 76–78
    identification, 80–81, 82, 83,
        162
    party-in-electorate, 72, 80–
        84
    party-in-government, 72, 75,
        77, 78–80
    party organization, 72–78, 79,
        80, 87
    reform, 75, 91
Politico, 103
Poverty:
    breaking the cycle of, 309
    reason for, 308
Precinct, 72, 73, 77, 78
Primary election, 75
Privatization, 198, 266, 273
    advantages of, 238
    limits of, 239
Probation, 269
Problem recognition, 181–182
Productivity:
    measurement of, 147, 148
    management by objective,
        147
    program budgeting, 148
    program evaluation, 148
Professionalization, 13, 139
    effects of, 96–98, 104, 105,
        111, 113, 114
    experts as threat to democ-
        racy, 14
    larger staffs, 13
Program evaluation, 186
Progressive reform, 123

Public defenders, 170–171, 266
Public goods, 222–223
Public opinion:
    effect on local policy, 58–
        60
    effect on state policy, 56–58,
        174, 180, 182, 196
    on environmental issues,
        247

Rational-comprehensive
        decision-making, 185–186,
        189
Reapportionment, 109
Recall, 62, 162, 166
Redistributing income, 15, 192,
        197, 229–230
Regulating economic activity:
    costs of, 228–229
    monopoly, 226
    protecting consumers, 226
    social costs, 227
Referendum, 62–63
Revenues:
    federal funding, 120
    revenue pressures, 11
    revenue sharing, 38–39, 46
Reverse discrimination, 153
Reynolds v. Sims, 109
Risk:
    attitudes toward, 245
    Robinson v. Cahill, 160

San Antonio v. Rodriguez, 160
Schattschneider, E. E., 184
School desegregation:
    and educational quality, 298
    *Brown v. Topeka Board of
        Education*, 293
    busing, 295–296
    Civil Rights Act of 1964, 293
    segregation in the north, 294
    white flight, 295

If you liked this book,
you might be interested
in other selections from
**McGRAW-HILL'S
COLLEGE CORE BOOKS SERIES.**
Ask for them at your local bookstore.
If they are not available, check the appropriate
box(es) below and mail with the coupon on the back
to McGraw-Hill, Inc.

☐ **American Government**
ORDER CODE 028207-2 $9.95

☐ **American History Before 1877**
ORDER CODE 057595-9 $9.95

☐ **American History Since 1865**
ORDER CODE 067452-3 $9.95

☐ **English History**
ORDER CODE 067437-x $11.95

☐ **Modern European History**
ORDER CODE 067453-1 $9.95

☐ **Russian History**
ORDER CODE 028649-3 $11.95

☐ **State and Local Politics**
ORDER CODE 049671-4 $12.95

☐ **Western Civilization To 1648**
ORDER CODE 015395-7/015623-9 $9.95

☐ **Western Civilization Since 1600**
ORDER CODE 015396-5/067454-x $9.95

NAME _____
(please print)

ADDRESS _____

CITY _____ STATE _____ ZIP _____

ENCLOSED IS   ☐ A CHECK   ☐ MASTERCARD   ☐ VISA   ☐ AMEX   (✔ ONE)

ACCOUNT # _____ EXP. DATE _____

SIGNATURE _____

PLEASE ADD $1.25 PER BOOK (SHIPPING/HANDLING) AND LOCAL SALES TAX.

MAKE CHECKS PAYABLE TO MCGRAW-HILL., INC.   PRICES SUBJECT TO CHANGE
WITHOUT NOTICE AND MAY VARY OUTSIDE U.S.   FOR THIS INFORMATION, WRITE
TO MCGRAW-HILL OR CALL THE 800 NUMBER.

**PLEASE SEND
COMPLETED FORM TO**

MCGRAW-HILL, INC.
ORDER PROCESSING S-1
PRINCETON ROAD
HIGHTSTOWN, NJ 08520

OR CALL

1-800-338-3987